# Adobe® Creative Cloud®

## ALL-IN-ONE

### 2nd Edition

## by Jennifer Smith and Christopher Smith

for
**dummies®**

A Wiley Brand

## Adobe® Creative Cloud® All-in-One For Dummies®, 2nd Edition

Published by: **John Wiley & Sons, Inc.,** 111 River Street, Hoboken, NJ 07030-5774, www.wiley.com

Copyright © 2018 by John Wiley & Sons, Inc., Hoboken, New Jersey

Published simultaneously in Canada

For general information on our other products and services, please contact our Customer Care Department within the U.S. at 877-762-2974, outside the U.S. at 317-572-3993, or fax 317-572-4002. For technical support, please visit https://hub.wiley.com/community/support/dummies.

Wiley publishes in a variety of print and electronic formats and by print-on-demand. Some material included with standard print versions of this book may not be included in e-books or in print-on-demand. If this book refers to media such as a CD or DVD that is not included in the version you purchased, you may download this material at http://booksupport.wiley.com. For more information about Wiley products, visit www.wiley.com.

Library of Congress Control Number: 2017956631

ISBN 978-1-119-42040-8 (pbk); ISBN 978-1-119-42041-5 (ebk); ISBN 978-1-119-42042-2 (ebk)

Manufactured in the United States of America

10  9  8  7  6  5  4  3  2  1

# Contents at a Glance

# Table of Contents

# Introduction

Adobe software has always been highly respected for creative design and development. Adobe creates tools that allow you to produce amazing designs and creations with ease. The Adobe Creative Cloud is the company's latest release of sophisticated and professional-level software that bundles many separate programs as a suite. Each program in the Creative Cloud works individually, or you can integrate the programs by using *Adobe Bridge*, an independent program that helps you control file management with thumbnails, metadata, and other organizational tools.

With Adobe Creative Cloud, a simple monthly membership gives you the entire collection of Adobe tools and more. Love print? Interested in websites and iPad apps? Ready to edit video? You can do it all. Plus, Creative Cloud members automatically get access to new products and exclusive updates as soon as they're released. And, with cloud storage and the ability to sync to any device, your files are always right where you need them. Creative Cloud is available for individuals or teams.

The first is Creative Services, which are hosted services that you can use in your production work, in the delivery of your content. This includes a font service like Typekit, which enables the use and delivery of a broad foundry of cloud fonts across all of your work. A second area is Digital Publishing, which enables publishing rich media to tablets via the cloud. And the third category is Business Catalyst, which supports designing and operating websites for small businesses, with prebuilt services for things like handling e-commerce, doing customer relationship management, and integrating with social networks.

The second pillar is Creative Community, which is the community of creative people (like you!) around the world and which enables you to connect more easily with other creative people — it's a place to share, to communicate, and to inspire each other with your work. The community is a critical part of our whole ecosystem, and it's a critical part of the cloud. At the center of this is the web presence of the Creative Cloud, which is `creative.adobe.com`. And one of the great things there is it will understand all the formats you're using in your creative work — PSD files, InDesign files, and Illustrator files. Where other cloud services might show you an icon describing the file type, this shows you the actual content, and you can interact with it in a context-sensitive way. It's a much deeper understanding of creative content.

And lastly, the third pillar is Creative Applications — and these are enabling you to create not only on personal computers, but also wherever you are with mobile devices, all connected through the Creative Cloud. This includes a whole new collection of Adobe touch apps to run on tablets and other mobile devices. In addition, membership also includes access to all Adobe creative desktop products you know and love, including Photoshop, Illustrator, Dreamweaver and Premiere and InDesign, Adobe XD, and more. You can download and install any of these applications you choose as part of your membership, and these are all connected to Creative Cloud via desktop sync. They also interact with the touch apps, and you can move files between desktop and touch as you're working.

# Why Is It Important?

You can use the Adobe Creative Cloud programs to create a wide range of products, from illustrations, page layouts, websites, photographic compositions, video, and 3D images. Integrating the CC programs extends the possibilities for you as a designer. Don't worry about the programs being too difficult to figure out — just come up with your ideas and start creating!

# About This Book

*Adobe Creative Cloud All-in-One For Dummies* is written in a thorough and fun way to show you the basic steps of how to use each program included in the Creative Cloud package. You find out how to use each program individually and how to work with the programs together, extending your projects even further. You find out just how easy it is to use the programs by following simple steps so that you can discover the power of the Adobe software. You'll be up and running in no time!

Here are some things you can do with this book:

>> Create page layouts with text, drawings, and images in InDesign.

>> Make illustrations using drawing tools with Illustrator.

>> Manipulate photographs by using filters and drawing or color correction tools with Photoshop.

>> Create PDF (Portable Document Format) documents with Adobe Acrobat or other programs.

>> Create web pages and put them online with Dreamweaver.

>> Create animations and videos with Flash.

>> Create web images, rollovers, image maps, and slices with Fireworks.

You discover the basics of how to create all these different kinds of things through-out the chapters in this book in fun, hands-on examples and clear explanations, getting you up to speed quickly!

Adobe Creative Cloud works for both Windows and the Macintosh. We cover both platforms in this book. When the keys you need to press or the menu choices you need to make differ between Windows and the Mac, we let you know by including instructions for both platforms. For example:

>> Press the Alt (Windows) or Option (Mac) key.

>> Choose Edit⇨Preferences⇨General (Windows) or InDesign⇨Preferences⇨General (Mac).

The programs in Creative Cloud often require you to press and hold down a key (or keys) on the keyboard and then click or drag with the mouse. For brevity's sake, we shorten this action by naming the key you need to hold down and adding a click or drag, like this:

>> Shift-click to select multiple files.

>> Move the object by Ctrl-dragging (Windows) or ⌘-dragging (Mac).

This book is pretty thick; you may wonder whether you have to read it from cover to cover. You don't have to read every page of this book to discover how to use the programs in the Creative Cloud. Luckily, you can choose bits and pieces that mean the most to you and will help you finish a project.

Icons supplement the material in each chapter with additional information that may interest or help you with your work. The Technical Stuff icons are helpful if you want to find out a bit more about technical aspects of using a program or your computer, but don't feel that you need to read these icon paragraphs if technicali-ties don't interest you.

# Foolish Assumptions

You don't need to know much before picking up this book and getting started with Creative Cloud. All you have to know is how to use a computer in a very basic way. If you can turn on the computer and use a mouse, you're ready for this book. A bit of knowledge about basic computer operations and using software helps, but it isn't necessary. We show you how to open, save, create, and manipulate files using the CC programs so that you can start working with the programs quickly. The most important ingredient to have is your imagination and creativity — we show you how to get started with the rest.

# Icons Used in This Book

What's a *For Dummies* book without icons pointing you in the direction of truly helpful information that's sure to speed you along your way? Here we briefly describe each icon we use in this book.

TIP

The Tip icon points out helpful information that's likely to make your job easier.

REMEMBER

This icon marks a generally interesting and useful fact — something you may want to remember for later use.

WARNING

The Warning icon highlights lurking danger. When we use this icon, we're telling you to pay attention and proceed with caution.

TECHNICAL
STUFF

When you see this icon, you know that there's techie-type material nearby. If you're not feeling technical-minded, you can skip this information.

# Beyond the Book

*Adobe Creative Cloud All-in-One For Dummies* is designed so that you can read a chapter or section out of order, depending on what subjects you're most interested in. Where you go from here is entirely up to you!

Book 1 is a great place to start reading if you've never used Adobe products or if you're new to design-based software. Discovering the common terminology, menus, and panels can be quite helpful for later chapters that use the terms and commands regularly!

You can find tips and tricks and more files for you to experiment with and investigate at www.agitraining.com/dummies.

Occasionally, we have updates to our technology books. If this book has any technical updates, they'll be posted at www.dummies.com.

# 1

# Overview of the Creative Cloud Suite

# Contents at a Glance

Chapter **1**

# Getting Started with the Creative Cloud Suite

The Adobe Creative Cloud is a subscription-based service that includes a wide array of applications used in the communication, design, development, and marketing industries.

Over the last several versions, the Creative Cloud has increased in capabilities and application tools. Using the Creative Cloud you can build print, web, video, 3D, and application designs, in addition to building interactive designs that can be used for many purposes. In this book, the focus is mainly on design tools that are used for the creation of printed material, as well as on the designs for websites, mobile apps, and other interactive presentations.

To help you understand the breadth of capabilities, Table 1-1 lists the applications included in your Creative Cloud subscription at the time that this book was written. The bolded applications are covered in detail in this book.

**TABLE 1-1**     ## Creative Cloud Applications

| Application | Description |
| --- | --- |
| **Creative Cloud** | **Quick desktop access to Creative Cloud apps and services** |
| **Photoshop** | **Image editing and compositing** |
| **Illustrator** | **Vector graphics and illustration** |
| **InDesign** | **Page design and layout for print and digital publishing** |
| **Acrobat Pro** | **Create, edit, and sign PDF documents and forms** |
| **Bridge** | **Centralize your creative assets** |
| **Experience Design (Beta)** | **Design and prototype user experiences for web and mobile** |
| Lightroom | Digital photo processing and editing |
| Adobe Premiere Pro | Video production and editing |
| After Effects | Cinematic visual effects and motion graphics |
| Project Felix | Easy 2D and 3D compositing for photo-realistic images |
| Dreamweaver | Design and develop modern, responsive websites |
| Animate | Flash Professional is now Adobe Animate CC. Interactive animations for multiple platforms. |
| Adobe Audition | Audio recording, mixing, and restoration |
| Character Animator | Animate your 2D characters in real time |
| Media Encoder | Quickly output video files for virtually any screen |
| Fuse | Create custom 3D characters for Photoshop projects |
| Flash Builder | IDE for coding Flash apps and mobile device packaging |
| InCopy | Collaborate with copywriters and editors |
| Prelude | Metadata ingest, logging, and rough cuts |
| Spark | Easily create and share impactful visual stories — in minutes |
| Scout | Profile Flash games on web and devices |
| SpeedGrade | Film finishing and color grading |
| Story Plus | Collaborative screenwriting, reporting, and scheduling tools |
| PhoneGap Build | Package mobile apps in the cloud |
| Gaming SDK | Create ActionScript |

# Applications Covered in This Book

If you are a designer of print, web, or mobile content, you will need to know the core applications included in the Creative Cloud. This book is focused on the main design tools, Photoshop, InDesign, Illustrator, Acrobat DC, Adobe Bridge, and Experience Design. You can read on for a brief introduction to each of these applications.

## Crossing the Adobe Bridge

Adobe Bridge is truly an incredible application, especially within the Creative Cloud release, because the processing speed is greatly improved and new features are available.

Even though Adobe Bridge is part of the Creative Cloud, it does not install automatically with your other applications. The first time that you choose File⇨Browse in Bridge from your other Creative Cloud applications, you will be directed to the Creative Cloud app, where you can choose to download it on to your system. You can find out more about Adobe Bridge in Book 2.

## Getting started with Photoshop CC

Photoshop is the industry standard software for web designers, video professionals, and photographers who need to manipulate bitmap images. Using Photoshop, you can manage and edit images by correcting color, editing photos by hand, and even combining several photos to create interesting and unique effects. Alternatively, you can use Photoshop as a painting program, where you can artistically create images and graphics.

Photoshop enables you to create complex text layouts by placing text along a path or within shapes. You can edit the text after it has been placed along a path; you can even edit the text in other programs, such as Illustrator CC, and join text and images into unique designs or page layouts.

Sharing images from Photoshop is easy to do. You can share multiple images in a PDF file, or upload images to an online photo service. You can even set up Photoshop to automatically export multiple assets for interactive apps or websites in one click.

It's hard to believe that Photoshop can be improved on, but Adobe has done it again in Adobe Photoshop CC. Book 3 shows you the diverse capabilities of Photoshop. From drawing and painting to image color correction, Photoshop has many uses for print and interactive design alike.

# Introducing InDesign CC

InDesign is a diverse and feature-rich page layout program. With InDesign, you can create beautifully laid-out page designs. You can also execute complete control over your images and export them to interactive documents, such as Acrobat PDF. You can use InDesign to

>> Use images, text, and even rich media to create unique layouts and designs.

>> Import native files from Photoshop and Illustrator to help build rich layouts in InDesign that take advantage of transparency and blending modes.

>> Export your work as an entire book, including chapters, sections, automatically numbered pages, and more.

>> Create interactive PDF documents that can be used for website or application prototypes or wireframes.

InDesign caters to the layout professional, but it's easy enough for even beginners to use. You can import text from word processing programs (such as Microsoft Word, Notepad, or Adobe InCopy) as well as tables (say, from Microsoft Excel) into your documents and place them alongside existing artwork and images to create a layout. In a nutshell, importing, arranging, and exporting work are common processes when working with InDesign. Throughout the entire process, you have a large amount of control over your work, whether you're working on a simple one-page brochure or an entire book of 800-plus pages. Find out how you can take advantage of this feature-rich application in Book 4.

# Using Illustrator CC

Adobe Illustrator is the industry's leading vector-based graphics software. Aimed at everyone from graphics professionals to interactive designers, Illustrator enables you to design layouts, logos for print, or vector-based images that can be imported into other programs, such as Photoshop, InDesign, or even Experience Design. Adobe also enables you to easily and quickly create files by saving Illustrator documents as templates (so that you can efficiently reuse designs) and using a predefined library and document size.

Illustrator also integrates with the other products in the Adobe Creative Cloud by enabling you to create PDF documents easily within Illustrator. In addition, you can use Illustrator files in Photoshop, InDesign, and the Adobe special effects program, After Effects. Illustrator enables you to beef up your rich interactive documents by introducing Flash features that give you the tools you need to build exciting interactive designs in Animate (formerly Flash).

Here are some of the things you can create and do in Illustrator:

>> Create technical drawings (floor plans or architectural sketches, for example), logos, illustrations, posters, packaging, and web graphics.

>> Create multiple screens for websites or mobile design.

>> Align text along a path so that it bends in an interesting way.

>> Lay out text into multicolumn brochures — text automatically flows from one column to the next.

>> Create charts and graphs using graphing tools.

>> Create gradients that can be imported and edited into other programs, such as Experience Design.

>> Create documents quickly and easily using existing templates and included stock graphics in Illustrator.

>> Save a drawing in almost any graphic format, including the Adobe PDF, PSD, EPS, TIFF, GIF, JPEG, and SVG formats.

>> Save your Illustrator files for the web by using the Asset Export panel, or Export⇨Export As menu item.

Illustrator has new features for you to investigate, many of them integrated in the chapters in Book 5. Find out about new tools, including features to help you use patterns.

## Working with Acrobat DC

Acrobat DC is aimed at both business and creative professionals and provides an incredibly useful way of sharing, securing, and reviewing the documents you create in your Creative Cloud applications.

Portable Document Format (PDF) is the file format used by Adobe Acrobat. It's used primarily as an independent method for sharing files. This format enables users who create files on either Macintosh or PC systems to share files with each other and with users of handheld devices or UNIX computers. PDF files generally start out as other documents — whether from a word processor or a sophisticated page layout and design program.

Although PDF files can be read on many different computer systems using the free Adobe Reader, users with the DC version of Adobe Acrobat can do much more with PDF files. With your version of Acrobat, you can create PDF documents, add security to them, use review and commenting tools, edit documents, and build PDF forms.

Use Acrobat to perform any of the following tasks:

>> Create interactive forms that can be filled out online.

>> Allow users to embed comments within the PDF files to provide feedback. Comments can then be compiled from multiple reviewers and viewed in a single summary.

>> Create PDF files that can include MP3 audio, video, SWF, and even 3D files.

>> Combine multiple files into a single PDF and include headers and footers as well as watermarks.

>> Create secure documents with encryption.

>> Combine multiple files into a searchable, sortable PDF package that maintains the individual security settings and digital signatures of each included PDF document.

>> Use auto-recognize to automatically locate form fields in static PDF documents and convert them to interactive fields that can be filled electronically by anyone using Adobe Reader software.

>> Manage shared reviews — without IT assistance — to allow review participants to see one another's comments and track the status of the review.

>> Enable advanced features in Adobe Reader to enable anyone using free Adobe Reader software to participate in document reviews, fill and save electronic forms offline, and digitally sign documents.

>> Permanently remove metadata, hidden layers, and other concealed information and use redaction tools to permanently delete sensitive text, illustrations, or other content.

>> Save your PDF to Microsoft Word. You can take advantage of improved functionality for saving Adobe PDF files as Microsoft Word documents, retaining the layout, fonts, formatting, and tables.

>> Enjoy improved performance and support for AutoCAD. Using AutoCAD, you can now more rapidly convert AutoCAD drawing files into compact, accurate PDF documents, without the need for the native desktop application.

Want to discover other great Acrobat improvements? Read Book 6 to find out all about Acrobat and PDF creation.

# Prototyping your apps with Experience Design

By designing or importing your art into Adobe XD artboards, you can go from idea to prototype quickly without building an actual app with code. XD lets you do what you do best . . . design! Take your touchable, interactive design and share it with others for feedback or user testing. Find out more about Adobe XD in Book 7.

Some of the things that you can do in Adobe XD include:

>> Build clickable prototypes using multiple artboards as screens.

>> Share your clickable application on mobile devices or on the web.

>> Draw with vector tools.

>> Copy and paste vector images and other assets from other Adobe applications.

>> Import SVG and edit them directly in XD.

>> Build lists of imagery and data quickly.

>> Take advantage of layers and symbols.

# Integrating software

With so many great pieces of software in a single package, it's only natural that you'll want to start using the programs together to build exciting projects. You may want to design a book using InDesign (with photos edited in Photoshop and drawings created in Illustrator) and then design a website or mobile app using Adobe Illustrator and then making an interactive prototype using Adobe XD. Similarly, you may want to take a complex PDF file and make it into something that everyone can view online. All tools in the Adobe Creative Cloud are built to work together, and achieving these tasks suddenly becomes much easier to do because the products are integrated.

Integrating software is typically advantageous to anyone. Integration enables you to streamline the workflow among programs and sometimes team members. Tools exist that let you drop native images into Photoshop, InDesign, Illustrator, and XD. With Adobe Bridge, you can view files and investigate specific information about them, such as color mode and file size, before selecting them for placement.

# Acquiring assets for this book

Many of the files that are referenced in this book are available right in the application sample folders that come with Creative Cloud. The path locations are defined when they are referenced, making it easy to find and use them in the provided step-by-step examples. In addition to these sample files, you can find tips and tricks and more files for you to experiment with and investigate at www. agitraining.com/dummies.

# Chapter **2**

# Creative Cloud Application Management

Before we introduce the Creative Cloud suite, you should understand that the applications in the Creative Cloud do not run "in the cloud." The applications covered in this book are rich desktop applications that reside on your computer but are simply downloaded from the cloud.

## Downloading Your First App

If you are new to the Creative Cloud and are just getting started, you can go to www.adobe.com/creativecloud/catalog/desktop.html and choose the app that you wish to download first. If you do not have an Adobe ID, you will need to set one up at this point.

Click Download to install the app you want. If you are not signed in, you are asked to sign in with your Adobe ID and password. Follow any onscreen instructions that are provided to you. Your app will then begin to download.

At this time the Creative Cloud desktop app appears, as shown in Figure 2-1. The Creative Cloud app manages the rest of the installation process; you can check your download progress in the status bar next to the app's name.

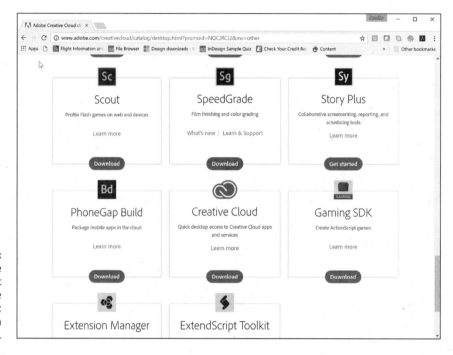

**FIGURE 2-1:**
The Creative Cloud is not just the name of the suite of tools; it's also an application.

The Creative Cloud app is a desktop application that allows you to manage downloads and updates of your Creative Cloud applications. It also lets you take advantage of other cloud-based services, such as storage and stock photos, and allows you to view work by you and others in the design community.

*Note:* If you are downloading a free trial subscription to Creative Cloud, you will be provided a different set of instructions that you should follow.

When you are done, you can launch your app by finding the application's icon in the Apps panel and clicking **Open,** or you can launch your new app the same way you normally launch any app on your computer. Your new app is installed in the same location where your applications are normally installed, such as the Program Files folder (Windows) or the Applications folder (Mac OS).

# Downloading more apps

Now that you downloaded your first app, you can use the Creative Cloud desktop app to easily browse, install, launch, and manage any Creative Cloud app. If you don't see the Creative Cloud icon, you may have quit the application. You can relaunch it by using one of the paths listed below:

» **Windows:** Choose Start⇨Programs⇨Adobe Creative Cloud.

» **Mac OS:** Choose Go⇨Applications⇨Adobe Creative Cloud⇨Adobe Creative Cloud.

# Checking for updates

The Creative Cloud desktop app indicates when updates are available for your installed apps. You can check for updates manually by following these steps:

1. **Open the Creative Cloud desktop app and click the gear icon in the top-right corner.**

2. **Choose Check for App Updates from the drop-down menu. You can also press Ctrl+Alt+R (PC) or Command+Option+R (Mac) to refresh the Creative Cloud desktop app and check for updates.**

   The Apps panel is updated to show all available updates.

Keep in mind that the Creative Cloud applications are updated on a regular basis; to check your account to make sure you are set up to receive regular updates, choose Preferences from the Gear drop-down menu in the Creative Cloud app, as shown in Figure 2-2.

# Getting started

After your applications are installed and up-to-date, you can dive into the next chapter of this book and start bringing your ideas to reality. Remember that you can work anywhere while using your downloaded applications. Once in a while, Adobe checks your license to make sure it is valid and current. Count on this happening about once every 30 days, but don't expect it to cause any problems for you.

**FIGURE 2-2:**
Check your
Creative Cloud
Preferences right
in the application.

IN THIS CHAPTER

» **Other hidden gems in the Creative Cloud**

» **Finding assets such as artwork through the CC Market**

» **Taking advantage of additional fonts and managing them**

» **Sharing and syncing your work using libraries**

» **Promote yourself with Behance and Adobe Portfolio**

Chapter **3**

# Creative Cloud Extras for You

C reative Cloud includes more than just applications. It includes extras that help you keep in touch with changes in your subscription and with recent downloads. It also includes free assets for subscribers such as typefaces, cool images, and illustrations, as well as access to stock photos and prebuilt site management tools to help you connect with the creative community. You can also take advantage of the Creative Cloud to store, sync, and share important files, making collaboration easy.

## Launching the Creative Cloud App

If you launch the Creative Cloud app, an application pane appears that includes a button bar across the top, as shown in Figure 3-1. The choices are Home, Apps, Assets, Stock, and Community. Launching the Creative Cloud app is one way to access many of the additional extras that come with your subscription, but there are other ways discussed in this chapter that you can access these extras right from the applications themselves.

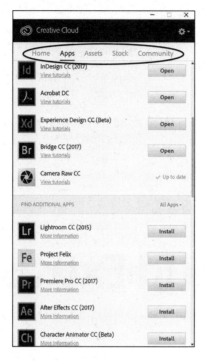

# Home

Click the Home button to see important announcements from Adobe. The Home section also includes new app availability, updates, and installation status.

# Apps

Find the status of the Creative Cloud applications in the Apps tab. Here you see the apps you have presently installed, represented by an Open button to the right. You can also find the apps that are not yet installed, represented by an Install button (or an Update button, if your installed version isn't current). In Figure 3-2, you see that one application, Camera Raw, needs to be updated, and the rest of the listed applications are up to date.

You can also access helpful tutorials right from the Apps section of the Creative Cloud app. Simply click on the View Tutorials text below any of the listed applications.

**FIGURE 3-2:**
Keep track of the
status of your
applications
and updates to
software in the
Apps section.

# Assets

The Creative Cloud Assets tab allows you to access and reuse your desktop-synced files, libraries, projects, and royalty-free assets available from the Creative Cloud Market. When you click Assets, you find three additional tabs, Files, Fonts, and Market, within this section.

## A place to store your stuff

When you select the Files tab, you are provided with the Open Folder option, which opens a Creative Cloud folder in your computer, or the View on Web option, which opens the location in the cloud designated to store your items. The items in the Creative Cloud folder on your computer are synced with the items in the cloud. You can use this available space in many ways: for storage, storing libraries, syncing with other computers, or sharing with other people on your team. See the next section, "Using the Creative Cloud for storage," to learn more about this feature.

*Note:* You can also log in to the Adobe.com website and access your assets from your account.

Keep in mind that you can use the Creative Cloud Files folder not only for storage but also as a key integration tool for you and your team by taking advantage of the CC Libraries integrated into the applications. See more about using libraries in the following section.

## Using the Creative Cloud for storage

If you are looking for space to store files, look no further than your Creative Cloud Files folder. Follow these steps in order to store files in the Creative Cloud:

1. **Open your Creative Cloud Files folder on your computer.**

   If you are not sure where it is located, click the Open Folder button when you launch the Creative Cloud app and then choose Assets➪Files. Click the button that states Open Folder, as shown in Figure 3-3.

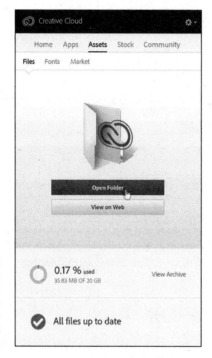

**FIGURE 3-3:**
Locate your Creative Cloud folder by accessing it in the Creative Cloud application.

2. **When the folder appears, drag and drop any files you want to save into the Creative Cloud Files folder.**

   This folder acts like any other folder on your computer. You can open your files, edit them, save them back to the same folder or another, and delete them. The main difference with the contents in this folder is that you can also access the files via the web.

3. **To access your files via the web, launch the Creative Cloud application and click View on Web.**

   You can also point your browser to https://assets.adobe.com. If you logged in using your Adobe ID, the files appear in the browser, as shown in Figure 3-4.

## Sharing your files

Not only can you access your own files anywhere by signing into the Creative Cloud on any computer, you can also share them with others. You can either do this directly in the Creative Cloud Files folder or on the web. The following directions tell you how.

To share from the Creative Cloud Files folder:

1. **Right-click (Ctrl+Click if you do not have a right-clicking mouse) to see the contextual menu.**

2. **Choose the Creative Cloud menu item and Send Link from the sub-menu. On the Mac OS, choose Share Link from the contextual menu.**

3. **If you have not previously shared the selected file, you first need to make it a public link. When the dialog box appears indicating that your link is private, click the Create Public Link button.**

4. **Copy and paste the provided link into your correspondence with the people to whom you want to give access to your file or project.**

To share from the web:

1. **Click the arrow icon in the lower-right corner of a file's thumbnail.**

2. **Choose Send Link from the menu that appears, as shown in Figure 3-4.**

**FIGURE 3-4:** Choose to send a link to your project file right from the web.

3. **If you have not previously shared the selected file, you first need to make it a public link. When the dialog box appears indicating that your link is private, click the Create Public Link button.**

4. **Copy and paste the provided link into your correspondence with the people to whom you want to give access to your file or project.**

## Using libraries

As you start to work on projects, you may want to store or share items that you use on a regular basis. This is where the Creative Cloud libraries come in handy. By using the Creative Cloud Library feature, you can save and share colors, character styles, imagery, and more. You can share them with just yourself, as you move from one computer to another, between applications, or with others on your team. Look for the CC Libraries, and the Libraries panels in your Creative Cloud applications, typically in the Window menu. You can add assets in this panel that you can then open in other applications or computers, as shown in Figure 3-5.

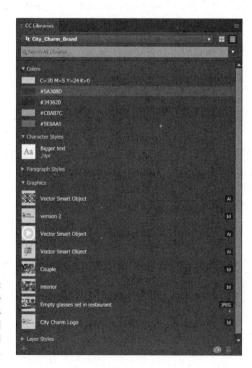

**FIGURE 3-5:**
Look for the Libraries panels in the individual Creative Cloud applications.

Libraries are covered throughout this book as they relate to the application being discussed. However, use the following steps for a quick introduction to how they might work in a typical workflow. You need to have Adobe Photoshop and Adobe InDesign installed and open in order to complete these steps. You also need any image file.

1. **Choose File⇨Open and then open any image file in Adobe Photoshop.**

   If you like, you can access sample images files at www.adobetraining.com/dummies. The one in this example is named Paris_Street.jpg.

   Perhaps this is an image that you want to use on a regular basis in multiple projects, and even share it with others on your team. This can be done easily by using the Libraries panel.

2. **Choose Window⇨Libraries.**

   The Libraries panel appears. If you have not created a custom library, you will do that now.

3. **Select the panel menu in the upper-right corner and select Create New Library. In the example shown in Figure 3-6, the new library is named MyBrand, but you can call your library whatever you like.**

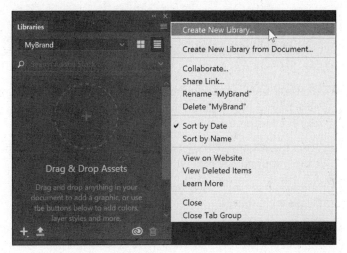

**FIGURE 3-6:**
You can create your own library to store art, styles, colors, and more.

4. **After your library is created, either drag the item or click the Plus (+) sign in the lower-left corner of the Libraries panel, as shown in Figure 3-7. For this example, click the Plus (+) sign. When the dialog box appears, leave the Graphic and Foreground color checked and click Add.**

   Your image has now been added to the library.

   After an item like this photo is added to a library, you can access it on any other computer or you can choose to share it. In this example, you access this library from InDesign and drag the image out to your page layout.

FIGURE 3-7:
Add an item to
your library.

5. **If InDesign is not launched, open it now. Choose File⇨New⇨Document and create a new document. In the New Document window, you can use any size for this example.**

6. **From the Window menu, choose CC Libraries. From the drop-down menu, choose your named library.**

   You should see your saved foreground color and the image that you added in Adobe Photoshop.

7. **Click the image and drag it out to your page, and then click once on your page to release the image and place it. After it is placed, note that the image displays a little cloud icon in the upper-left corner indicating that it is from the cloud, as shown in Figure 3-8.**

8. **Close the InDesign and Photoshop documents without saving.**

FIGURE 3-8:
The cloud icon
indicates that this
item is located in
the cloud.

## Opening up your design opportunities with new fonts

Using fonts in the past was rather cumbersome. You had to purchase a license for a typeface or family, and then make sure that it was loaded correctly. The purchase of these fonts often limited your opportunity to try new typefaces. Then there was the issue with using typefaces for the web. Even though you might have licensed a font, it did not mean that the end user had access to that font. Frequently this led to unexpected display results in various browsers. This is where TypeKit comes to the rescue.

TypeKit allows you to easily access new and interesting fonts created by leading type foundries. By using TypeKit you do not have to worry about licensing, and you can use fonts from TypeKit on the web or in desktop applications. Look for new fonts to use in your web or print design by clicking on the Fonts submenu in the Assets tab of the Creative Cloud App. You can sync your fonts with those available in TypeKit or manage your existing font selections.

In this following steps, you have the opportunity to add a font using TypeKit.

1. **In the Creative Cloud application, click Assets and then Fonts.**

2. **Click the Sync Fonts from TypeKit button.**

3. **A browser window appears displaying font options, as shown in Figure 3-9. In this window, you can filter by serif or sans serif; choose different properties, such as x-height, width, or weight; and even select the language. You can also choose between two recommended categories: headings and paragraphs.**

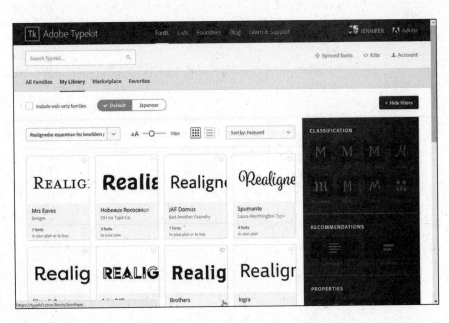

**FIGURE 3-9:** Access a huge trove of fonts by using TypeKit.

4. **After you have decided on a typeface, click on it to enter the details page. On the details page, press the Sync button to the right of the font family to add it to your list of available fonts.**

5. **If you are looking for a font to use on the web, click the Add to Kit button at the top of the details page. As you see in Figure 3-10, you are provided with code that you can copy and insert into your webpage in order to embed the font.**

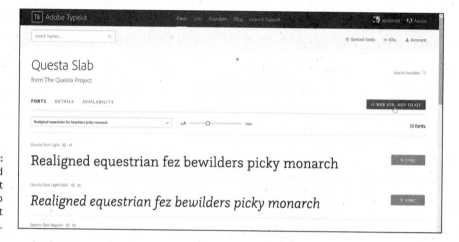

**FIGURE 3-10:**
You can also find the code that enables you to embed your font into a web page.

If you need some great patterns, images, or inspiration, select the Assets tab and then click Market to see featured artwork as well as artwork that can be used specifically for placement, UI, vectors, icons, patterns, and brushes, as shown in Figure 3-11.

To find an item in the market, scroll through one of the categories or press the search icon.

To select an item from the market, you need to have a library created to which the file can be downloaded. You can then access the file using the CC Libraries or the Libraries panels in your individual applications.

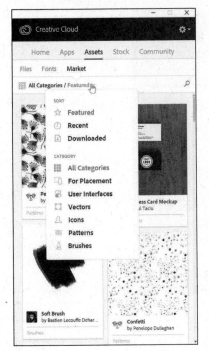

**FIGURE 3-11:**
Access art from
the CC Market.

# Stock

Adobe makes it easy for you to find a varied source of images, graphics, and videos. Simply click on the Stock tab at the top of the Creative Suite application. Keep in mind that even though you can receive an introductory offer of ten images, this is a paid service that is not included with your subscription. Pricing can be considerable for those who have not used a stock service in the past, but there are many benefits to using Adobe Stock:

>> Adobe Stock is easy to locate. It is right there in your Creative Cloud app.

>> You can choose File⇨Search Adobe Stock from almost every application in Creative Cloud.

>> You can search Adobe Stock right in the CC Libraries panel in InDesign, as shown in Figure 3-12. Just drag and drop the image that you want to use as a preview. If you decide to license it, just click the shopping cart icon in the upper-left of the image in the Libraries panel.

**FIGURE 3-12:**
Search and use
Adobe Stock right
in the Libraries
panels.

>> Adobe Stock is searchable right from Adobe Bridge. You can type your search criteria right in the Search box of Adobe Bridge, as shown in Figure 3-13, and generate search results from Adobe Stock.

>> You can easily download previews for your images until you are sure that you want to make a purchase.

**FIGURE 3-13:**
You can search
right in the
Adobe Bridge
application.

# Community

Stay in touch with the creative community by selecting the Community tab in the Creative Cloud application. When you select Community from the Creative Cloud application, you are provided with the option of seeing what others like you are creating, as well as posting and sharing work of your own, as shown in Figure 3-14.

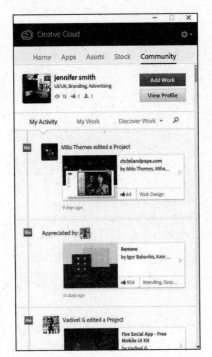

**FIGURE 3-14:**
See work that
others have
posted or work
on your own.

# Adding Work to Behance

If you are promoting yourself, you should consider posting work on Behance. Behance is an online platform that allows users to showcase and discover creative work. Behance is used by creative professionals to find work and by those hiring in the creative field to discover creative professionals that fit their needs.

To create a portfolio, follow these simple steps:

**1.** **First of all, go to www.behance.net and sign up! Look for the Log-in button in the top right and enter your Adobe ID and password.**

This connects your Creative Cloud applications with Behance, as shown in Figure 3-15. By doing this, you can actually choose to save your projects to Behance right from your many, but not all, the Creative Cloud applications. This is usually done by choosing File⇨Share on Behance in your Adobe Creative Cloud applications.

If you have not used Behance before, the first screen that appears asks you to choose two categories of creative work from various options. These are categories that you will follow. Notable artwork within these categories will appear under the Community tab in the Creative Cloud application.

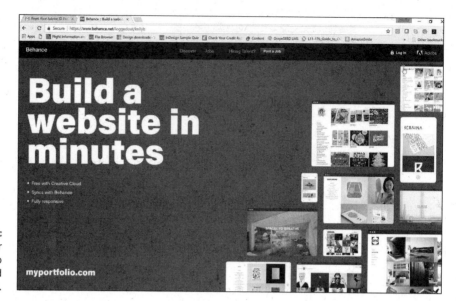

**FIGURE 3-15:**
Start sharing your
work by going to
Behance.net and
logging in.

2. **Click two categories and then press the See My Custom Feed button in the lower right of the screen, as shown in Figure 3-16.**

   Next, you set up to share your work.

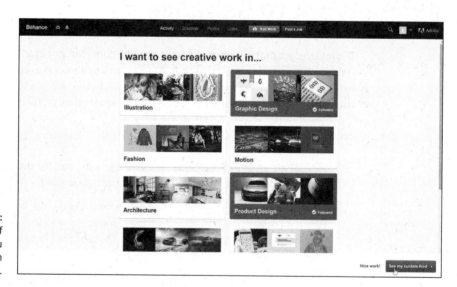

**FIGURE 3-16:**
Select the type of
creative work you
want to see in
your feed.

3. **Select the Add Work Create a Project button at the top of the screen.**

   A project editor loads with buttons in the main screen, as shown in Figure 3-17.

**FIGURE 3-17:**
Start sharing
your artwork by
clicking on the
Files button.

4. You can now follow the buttons in the middle of the screen. Start by clicking Files and then loading any files that you want to share with others. You can load PNG, JPG, or GIF files as content. Keep in mind that your selected content displays at a maximum of 1400 px unless a viewer clicks on it, in which case it will expand.

5. Click the File button in the middle of the screen and select an image using the file browser window that appears.

6. After you select an image, it is added to the screen. You can click the Pencil icon, as seen in Figure 3-18, to edit the image, or click above it to add other elements to the image, such as text or a link.

   *Note:* In order to add an element, such as text, you must click the related icon in the Tools panel that appears above your image.

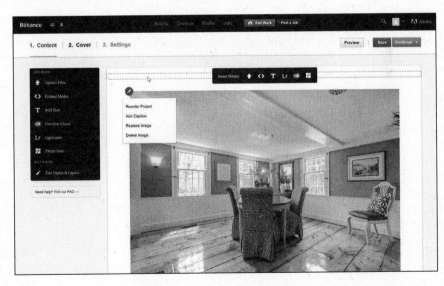

**FIGURE 3-18:**
Add text or edit
your image.

Creative Cloud Extras
for You

7. After you have completed your entry, click Save.

8. You can continue adding more images by selecting Upload Files from the menu on the left, or you can move on to creating a cover for your project by clicking Continue in the upper-right side of the screen.

# Creating a Cover

A cover image is a key part of the Behance browsing experience. By creating a relevant cover, you allow viewers to quickly get an idea of what your project is about. You create a cover by entering a project name and cropping your first image in your project gallery, as shown in Figure 3-19. This will be used as the thumbnail for your project that appears when viewers are browsing in Behance. Keep in mind that the cover image displays at 202 x 158 px, but you must upload an image that is at least 404 x 316 px so that your thumbnail will look great on both regular and high resolution devices.

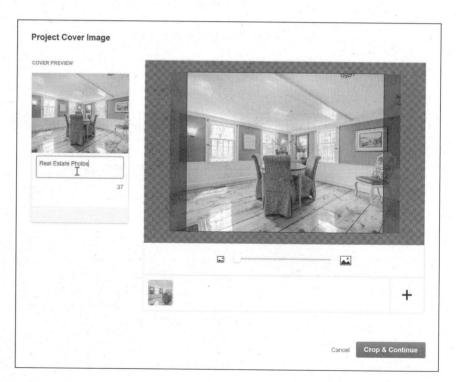

**FIGURE 3-19:**
Create a cover for your image.

If you don't like your first image, simply press the plus sign (+) icon underneath the cover preview and select another.

When you are finished with setting up the cover, you can click the Crop and Continue button to enter the Project Settings dialog box. The information that you enter in this window is what allows you to be found by others. Be careful to select appropriate categories and enter other information about your project accurately. When you are done with this step, click Save to continue working or click Publish to post your project in the Behance website.

# Bonus! Adobe Portfolio

In addition to sharing your work on Behance, you can take advantage of Adobe Portfolio. Adobe Portfolio offers you the opportunity to easily build a beautiful visual resume. You can customize layouts and segment your own categories in extensive galleries of work. One of its greatest features is its compatibility with Behance. Build once in Behance, and your project automatically appears in your portfolio and vice versa.

Follow these steps to open and explore Adobe Portfolio:

1. **In the Creative Cloud application, click Community and then click Profile.**

   This opens a browser window with information about you. This is also the location in which you can launch Adobe Portfolio.

2. **Click View Adobe Portfolio in the upper right of the screen.**

3. **If you have an Adobe ID, you have access to Adobe Portfolio and you can get started by clicking the Layouts button at the top of the screen, as shown in Figure 3-20.**

4. **Click any layout you are interested in. The rest is easy: Simply follow the instructions provided directly to you on the screen.**

5. **As with Behance, you can choose to save your project when you are done or publish to the Adobe Portfolio site.**

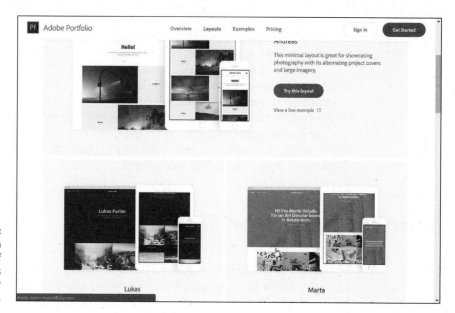

**FIGURE 3-20:**
Choose from
a selection of
different layouts
to start your
portfolio.

# It's Not Just Apps!

Wow . . . and you thought the Creative Cloud was just a collection of applications! As you can see, there is so much more to take advantage of when you have a subscription to the Creative Cloud. You find out how to use the applications that you need to bring your designs to reality in the following minibooks.

IN THIS CHAPTER

» Discovering common menus and dialog boxes

» Addressing Creative Cloud alerts

» Working with common menu options

» Understanding contextual menus

» Speeding up your workflow with shortcuts

» Changing preferences

# Chapter **4**

# Using Common Menus and Commands

**W**hen you work in Adobe CC, you may notice that many menus, commands, and keyboard shortcuts are similar across many of the applications. These similarities can help you migrate more easily from one application to another. This chapter provides an overview of some of the common menus, dialog boxes, options, shortcuts, and preferences that exist in most or all of the applications in Adobe Creative Cloud.

## Discovering Common Menus

When you work with applications in Adobe Creative Cloud, you may notice that many of the menus on the main menu bar are the same. Similar functionality makes finding important features easy, even when you're completely new to the software.

Menu items contain features that control much of the functionality in each application. A menu item may also contain features that are related to a particular task. For example, you might save from the File menu, or change your text in the Type menu. Some of the menu items that commonly appear in the Creative Cloud applications include the following:

>> **File:** Contains many features that control the overall document, such as creating, opening, saving, printing, and setting general properties for the document. The File menu may also include options for importing or exporting data into or from the current document.

>> **Edit:** Contains options and commands for editing the current document. Commands include copying, pasting, and selecting as well as options for opening preferences and setting dialog boxes that are used to control parts of the document. Commands for spell-checking are also common parts of the Edit menu.

>> **Type:** Contains options related to type and typesetting, such as font selection, size, leading, and more.

>> **View:** Contains options for changing the level of magnification of the document. The View menu also sometimes includes options for viewing the workspace in different ways; showing rules, grids, or guides; and turning alignment snapping on and off. *Snapping* helps with precise placement of selection edges, cropping marquees, slices, shapes, and paths.

>> **Window:** Contains options primarily used to open or close whatever panels are available in the application. You can also choose how to view the workspace and save a favorite arrangement of the workspace.

>> **Help:** Contains the option to open the Help documentation that's included with the application. This menu may also include information about updating the software, registration, and tutorials.

Figure 4-1 shows a list of items that appear under the File menu in Photoshop.

Each application has additional application-specific menus determined by the needs of the software. For example, you can use the Photoshop Image menu to resize the image or document, rotate the canvas, and duplicate the image, among other functions. InDesign has a Layout menu you can use to navigate the document, edit page numbering, and access controls for creating and editing the document's table of contents; we discuss these menus where appropriate throughout this book.

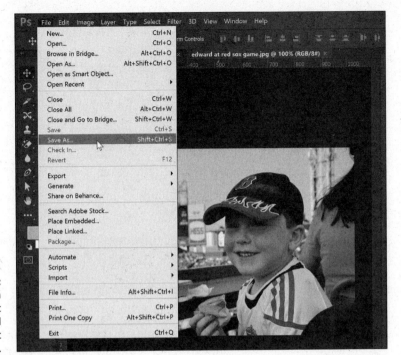

**FIGURE 4-1:**
Menus in
Photoshop let
you choose and
control different
options.

# Using Dialog Boxes

A *dialog box* is a window that appears when certain menu items are selected. It offers additional options in the form of drop-down lists, panes, text fields, option buttons, checkboxes, and buttons that enable you to change settings and enter information or data as necessary. You use dialog boxes to control the software or your document in various ways. For example, when you open a new file, you typically use the Open dialog box to select a file to open. When you save a file, you use the Save As dialog box to select a location for saving the file, to name the file, and to execute the Save command.

Some dialog boxes also include tabs. These dialog boxes may contain many settings of different types that are organized into several sections by using tabs. A dialog box typically has a button that executes the particular command and one that cancels and closes the dialog box without doing anything. Figure 4-2 shows a common dialog box.

FIGURE 4-2:
Using a dialog
box to change
filter settings.

A dialog box in Windows offers the same functionality as a dialog box on the Mac. Dialog boxes perform similar tasks and include the same elements to enter or select information. For example, here are some tasks you perform by using dialog boxes:

>> Save a new version of a file

>> Specify printing or page-setup options

>> Set up preferences for the software you're using

>> Check the spelling of text in a document

>> Open a new document

REMEMBER

You cannot use the application you're working in until the dialog box is closed. Make sure to close the dialog box after you are finished making your changes. Close the dialog box by clicking a button (such as Save or OK) when you're finished or by clicking the Cancel button to close it without making any changes.

# Encountering Alerts

*Alerts*, which are common on any operating system and in most applications, are similar to dialog boxes in that they're small windows that contain information. However, alerts are different from dialog boxes because you can't edit the information in them. Alerts are designed simply to tell you something and give you one or more options that you select by clicking a button. For example, an alert may indicate that you can't select a particular option. Usually you see an OK button to click to acknowledge and close the alert. You may see other buttons on the alert, such as a button to cancel what you were doing or one that opens a dialog box. Figure 4-3 shows a typical alert.

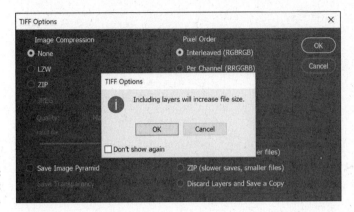

**FIGURE 4-3:**
A simple choice: OK or cancel.

**TIP**

You can sometimes use an alert to confirm an action before executing it. Sometimes an alert window also offers the option (typically in the form of a checkbox) of not showing the alert or warning again. You may want to select this option if you repeatedly perform an action that shows the warning and you don't need to see the warning every time.

# Getting to Know Common Menu Options

Various menu options are typically available in each of the Creative Cloud applications. However, within each of these menus, several other options are available. Some of them open dialog boxes — this type of option is typically indicated by an ellipsis that follows the menu option, as shown in Figure 4-4.

The following menu options are found in several Creative Cloud applications, and these commands either perform similar (or the same) functions or they open similar dialog boxes:

>> **New:** Creates a brand-new document in the native file format. For example, in InDesign, a new *INDD* (the extension for InDesign documents) file is created by choosing File⇨New⇨Document. You can sometimes choose the type of new file you want to create.

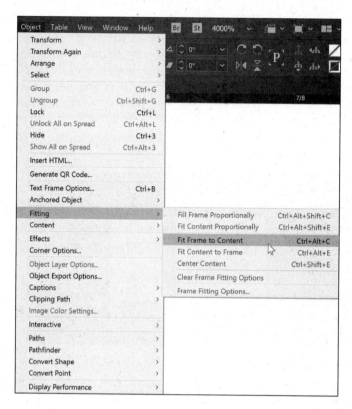

**FIGURE 4-4:**
Choosing a menu
option with an
ellipsis opens a
submenu.

>> **Open:** Opens a dialog box where you can choose a (supported) file to open on your hard drive or a disc.

>> **Close:** Closes the current document. If it has unsaved changes, you're prompted to save those changes first.

>> **Save:** Saves the changes you've made to the current document.

>> **Save As:** Saves a new copy of the current document using a different name.

>> **Import:** Imports a file, such as an image or sound file, into the current document.

>> **Export:** Exports the current data to a specified file format. You can sometimes select several kinds of file formats to save the current data in.

>> **Copy:** Copies the selected data to the computer's Clipboard.

>> **Paste:** Pastes the data from the Clipboard into the current document.

- >> **Undo:** Undoes the most recent task you performed in the application. For example, if you just created a rectangle, the rectangle is removed from the document.

- >> **Redo:** Repeats the steps you applied the Undo command to. For example, if you removed that rectangle you created, the Redo command adds it back to the document.

- >> **Zoom In:** Magnifies the document so that you can view and edit its contents closely.

- >> **Zoom Out:** Scales the view smaller so that you can see more of the document at a time.

- >> **Help:** Opens the Help documentation for the current application.

# About Contextual Menus

A *contextual menu* is similar to the menu types we describe in the previous sections; however, it's context-sensitive and opens when you right-click (Windows) or Control-click (Mac) something in the application. *Contextual* means that which options appear on the menu depend on which object or item you right-click (Windows) or Control-click (Mac).

For example, if you open a contextual menu when the cursor is over an image, commands involving the image are listed on the menu. However, if you right-click (Windows) or Control-click (Mac) the document's background, you typically see options that affect the entire document instead of just a particular element within it. You can therefore select common commands specifically for the item you've selected. Figure 4-5 shows a contextual menu that appears when you right-click (Windows) or Control-click (Mac) an object in Photoshop.

REMEMBER

The tool you select in the Tools panel may affect which contextual menus you can access in a document. You may have to select the Selection tool first to access certain menus. If you want to open a contextual menu for a particular item in the document, make sure that the object is selected before you right-click (Windows) or Control-click (Mac).

TIP

If you're using a Mac, you can right-click to open a contextual menu if you have a two-button mouse hooked up to your Mac. Otherwise, you press Control-click to open a contextual menu.

**FIGURE 4-5:**
Open a contextual menu in Windows by right-clicking an image or object.

# Using Common Keyboard Shortcuts

*Shortcuts* are key combinations that enable you to quickly and efficiently execute commands, such as save or open files or copy and paste objects. Many of these shortcuts are listed on the menus discussed in previous sections. If the menu option has a key combination listed next to it, you can press that combination to access the command rather than use the menu to select it. Figure 4-6 shows shortcuts associated with a menu item in InDesign.

For example, if you open the File menu, next to the Save option is Ctrl+S (Windows) or ⌘+S (Mac). Rather than choose File➪Save, you can press the shortcut keys to save your file. It's a quick way to execute a particular command.

**TIP**

Some commonly used shortcuts in the Adobe Creative Cloud applications are listed in Table 4-1.

Many additional shortcuts are available in each application in the Creative Cloud applications, and not all are listed on menus. You can find these shortcuts throughout the documentation provided with each application. Memorizing the shortcuts can take some time, but the time you save in the long run is worth it.

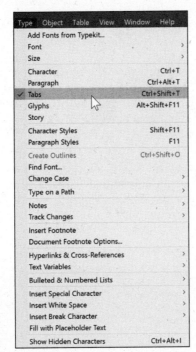

**FIGURE 4-6:**
Shortcuts are
shown next to
their associated
commands.

## TABLE 4-1    Common Keyboard Shortcuts

| Command | Windows Shortcut | Mac Shortcut |
|---|---|---|
| New | Ctrl+N | ⌘+N |
| Open | Ctrl+O | ⌘+O |
| Save | Ctrl+S | ⌘+S |
| Undo | Ctrl+Z | ⌘+Z |
| Redo | Shift+Ctrl+Z | Shift+⌘+Z |
| Copy | Ctrl+C | ⌘+C |
| Paste | Ctrl+V | ⌘+V |
| Print | Ctrl+P | ⌘+P |
| Preferences (General) | Ctrl+K | ⌘+K |
| Help | F1 or sometimes Ctrl+? | F1 or sometimes ⌘+? |

# Changing Your Preferences

Setting your preferences is important when you're working with new software. Understanding what your preferences can do for you gives you a good idea about what the software does. All applications in the Creative Cloud have different preferences; however, the way the Preferences dialog box works in each application is the same.

You can open the Preferences dialog box in each application by choosing Edit ⇨ Preferences (Windows) or *Application Name* ⇨ Preferences ⇨ General (Mac). The Preferences dialog box opens, as shown in Figure 4-7. Click an item in the list on the left side of the dialog box to navigate from one topic to the next.

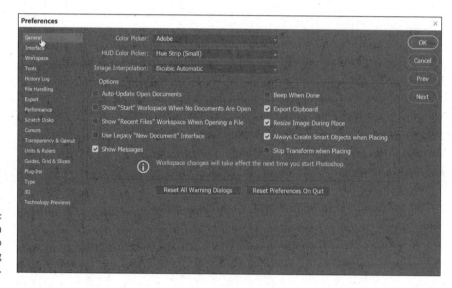

**FIGURE 4-7:** Click an item on the left to navigate among topics.

The Preferences dialog box contains a great number of settings you can control by entering values into text fields using drop-down lists, buttons, checkboxes, sliders, and other, similar controls. Preferences can be quite detailed. However, you don't have to know what each preference does or even change any of them: Most dialog boxes containing preferences are quite detailed in outlining which features the preferences control and are therefore intuitive to use. Adobe also sometimes includes a Description area near the bottom of the dialog box. When you hover the mouse over a particular control, a description of that control appears in the Description area.

In some Preferences dialog boxes, a list box on the left side of the dialog box contains the categories of preferences you can change. When you finish changing the settings in that topic, select a new topic from the list and change the settings for another topic.

In some applications, not all settings you can modify are in the Preferences dialog box. For example, in Illustrator, you can change the color settings by choosing Edit⇨Color Settings to open the Color Settings dialog box. When you hover the mouse pointer over a particular drop-down list or button, a description of that control appears at the bottom of this extremely useful dialog box.

TIP

By launching Adobe Bridge (described in Book 2) and choosing Edit⇨Color Settings, you can change your color preferences across all Creative Cloud applications at one time, as shown in Figure 4-8.

**FIGURE 4-8:**
Change all color settings at one time using Adobe Bridge.

IN THIS CHAPTER

» Exploring the synchronized
workspace

» Manipulating panels in the
workspace

» Discovering different kinds of panels

» Getting to know the common panels
in Adobe Creative Cloud

# Chapter **5**

# Exploring Common Panels

The panel is an integral part of working with most of the programs in Adobe Creative Cloud because they contain many of the important features that you need in order to edit your documents.

The basic functionality of panels is quite similar across the programs in Adobe Creative Cloud, and the purpose of all panels is generally the same. Panels offer a great deal of flexibility in how you organize the workspace and the parts of it you use. The task you use each program for and the level of expertise you have may affect which panels you have open at a given moment. This chapter gives you an overview of how to work with the panels you find in most of the Adobe Creative Cloud applications.

## Understanding the Synchronized Workspace

One thing you immediately notice when opening applications in the Creative Cloud is the synchronized workspace. Most of the applications look similar and have the same set of features to help you organize your workspace.

The tools in InDesign, Illustrator, and Photoshop appear on a space-saving, single-column toolbar, and panels (described in detail in the next section) are arranged in convenient, self-adjusting docks that you can widen to full size or narrow so that the panels are collapsed to icons.

Here are some pointers to help you navigate the workspace in the Creative Cloud applications:

>> **To expand tools to two columns,** click the right-facing double arrows on the gray bar at the top of the Tools panel, as you see in Figure 5-1.

>> **To collapse tools to a single column,** click the left-facing double arrows on the gray bar at the top of the Tools panel.

**FIGURE 5-1:**
Click the arrows at the top of the Tools panel to show tools in two columns or one column.

>> **To expand a docked panel,** simply click the icon in the docking area, as shown in Figure 5-2. The panel you selected expands but goes away when you select a different panel.

**FIGURE 5-2:**
Click an icon to collapse or expand the panel.

If you have difficulty identifying the panel, you can choose the panel you want from the Window menu.

» **To expand all docked panels,** click the left-facing double-arrow icon at the top of the docking area; put away the panels by clicking the right-facing double-arrow icon in the gray bar above them.

» **To undock a panel,** simply click the tab (where the panel name is located) and drag it out of the docking area. You can re-dock the panel by dragging the panel back into the docking area.

# Using Panels in the Workspace

*Panels* are small windows in a program that contain controls, such as sliders, menus, buttons, and text fields, that you can use to change the settings or attributes of a selection or an entire document. Panels may also include information about a section or about the document itself. You can use this information or change the settings in a panel to modify the selected object or the document you're working on.

Whether you're working on a Windows machine or on a Mac, panels are similar in the way they look and work. Here are the basic instructions for working with panels:

» **Open a panel:** Open a panel in a Creative Cloud program by using the Window menu: Choose Window and then select the name of a panel. For example, to open the Swatches panel (which is similar in many programs in the Creative Cloud), choose Window⇨Swatches.

» **Close a panel:** If you need to open or close a panel's tab or panel altogether, just choose Window⇨*Panel's Tab Name*. Sometimes a panel contains a close button (an X button in Windows or the red button on a Mac), which you can click to close the panel.

» **Organize the workspace:** All Creative Cloud programs now offer options for workspace organization. You can return to the default workspace, which restores panels to their original locations, by choosing Window⇨Workspace⇨Default. You can also open frequently used panels, position them where you want, and save a customized workspace by choosing Window⇨Workspace⇨Save (or New) Workspace. Name the workspace and click OK; the saved workspace is now a menu item that you can open by choosing Window⇨Workspace⇨*Your Saved Workspace's Name.*

**TIP**

You can also choose from a wide range of included presets designed for a variety of specialized tasks.

>> **Access the panel menu:** Panels have a panel menu, which opens when you click the arrow in the upper-right corner of the panel, as shown in Figure 5-3. The panel menu contains a bunch of options you can select that relate to the selected tab when you click the panel menu. When you select an option from the panel menu, it may execute an action or open a dialog box. Sometimes a panel menu has just a few options, but particular panels may have a bunch of related functionality and therefore have many options on the panel menu.

>> **Minimize/maximize:** All you need to do to minimize a selected panel is click the Collapse to Icons double-arrow button on the title bar of the panel (if it's available). If the panel is undocked, you can also double-click the tab itself in the panel. This action either partially or fully minimizes the panel. If it only partially minimizes, double-clicking the tab again fully minimizes it. Double-clicking the active tab when it's minimized maximizes the panel again.

Panels that partially minimize give you the opportunity to work with panels that have differing amounts of information, which simplifies the workspace while maximizing your screen real estate.

Most panels contain tabs, which help you organize information and controls in a program into groupings. Panel tabs contain a particular kind of information about a part of the program; a single panel may contain several tabs. The name on the tab usually gives you a hint about the type of function it controls or displays information about, and it's located at the top of the panel. Inactive tabs are dimmed.

# Moving panels

You can move panels all around the workspace, and you can add or remove single tabs from a panel. Each panel snaps to other panels, which makes it easier to arrange panels alongside each other. Panels can overlap each other as well. To snap panels to each other, drag the panel to a new location onscreen, as shown in Figure 5-4; you see the top bar of the panel become shaded, indicating that it's becoming part of another panel's group.

**FIGURE 5-4:**
To move a panel, drag it by its tab.

**TIP**

Group similar tabs by moving them into a single grouped panel. Accessing different functions in your document becomes a lot easier because then you have less searching to do to find related functions for a task. If you want to return to the original workspace, you can choose Reset Workspace from the Window menu in the Workspace category.

**TIP**

You can hide all panels by pressing the Tab key. Press it again to reveal all panels you've hidden.

## Looking at common panels

Many panels are similar across programs in the Creative Cloud. Although not every panel has exactly the same content in every program it's in, many have extremely similar content. You use these panels in similar ways, no matter which program or operating system you're using.

**REMEMBER**

Acrobat doesn't contain numerous panels, like other programs in the Creative Cloud. Instead, Acrobat relies mainly (but not entirely) on a system of menus and toolbars filled with buttons and drop-down lists. In Acrobat, you can open dialog boxes that contain a bunch of settings you can enter for your documents.

The following panels are available in most, but not all, Creative Cloud programs. This list describes what you can do with each one:

>> **Color:** Select or mix colors for use in the document you're working on. You can use different color modes and several ways of mixing or choosing colors in the Colors panel.

>> **Info:** See information about the document itself or a particular selection you've made. The Info panel includes information on the size, positioning, and rotation of selected objects. You can't enter data into the Info panel: It only displays information without accepting it, so you have to use the Transform panel (described in this list) to make these modifications, if necessary.

>> **Swatches:** Create a swatch library, which can be saved and imported into other documents or other programs. You can store on the Swatches panel any colors and gradients you use repeatedly.

>> **Tools:** You use this important panel, sometimes called the *toolbox* (and not available in all Creative Cloud programs), to select tools — such as the Pencil, Brush, or Pen — to use in creating objects in a document.

>> **Layers:** Display and select layers, change the layer order, and select items on a particular layer.

>> **Align:** Align selected objects to each other or align them in relation to the document itself so that you can arrange objects precisely.

>> **Stroke:** Select strokes and change their attributes, such as color, width/weight, style, and cap. The program you're using determines which attributes you can change.

>> **Transform:** Display and change the *shear* (skew), rotation, position, and size of a selected object in the document. You can enter new values for each transformation.

>> **Character:** Select fonts, font size, character spacing, and other settings related to using type in your documents.

# 2

# Adobe Bridge

# Contents at a Glance

Chapter **1**

# Organizing and Managing Your Files with Adobe Bridge

Adobe Bridge is an application included in the Creative Cloud collection of tools. Using Adobe Bridge, you can also organize and manage images, videos, and audio files, as well as preview, search, and sort your files without opening them in their native applications.

With Bridge, you can easily locate files using the Filters panel and import images from your digital camera right into a viewing area that allows you to quickly rename and preview your files. Adobe Bridge will save you time and frustration when looking for files you have worked on in the past; read this chapter to find out how to take advantage of its simple yet useful features.

# Getting to Know the Adobe Bridge Workspace

Before you start, locate and launch Adobe Bridge. In the next few steps you will be taken through the steps to install Adobe Bridge, using the Creative Cloud app, and then shown how to launch the application.

If you open your Programs folder (PC) or Application folder (Mac), you will see a folder named Adobe. If you do not see this folder, you will want to review Book 1, "Overview of the Creative Suite," in order to find out how to download and install your Creative Cloud applications. This folder contains the applications that you downloaded and installed from the Creative Cloud app. If you do not see Adobe Bridge listed, follow these steps:

1. **Locate your Creative Cloud application in either your Programs (PC) or Applications (Mac) folder and double-click it to launch it.**

2. **In the Creative Cloud app, click the Apps tab, scroll down until you see the Adobe Bridge app, and then click the Install button to the right. Follow the directions provided in order to install the application.**

3. **After Bridge is installed, you can press the Open button on the right to launch it, or you can find the application in your Program or Application folder.**

Now that you have launched Adobe Bridge, you might be wondering where to start. In this chapter, we introduce the file management features Adobe Bridge offers in the panels and other menu items shown in Figure 1-1.

Here are some additional details about these components:

» **Application bar:** The Application bar provides buttons for essential tasks, such as navigating the folder hierarchy, switching workspaces, and searching for files. The Application bar is discussed in detail later in this chapter.

» **Path bar:** The Path bar shows the path for the folder you're viewing and allows you to navigate the directory by clicking on the path locations.

» **Favorites panel:** The Favorites bar provides quick access to frequently browsed folders. Essentially these work the same as shortcuts.

» **Folders panel:** The Folders panel shows the folder hierarchy. You can use it to navigate folders.

Path Bar

Application Bar

Favorites Panel    Content Panel

Folders Panel

Preview Panel

Publish Panel

Standard Workspaces

Quick Search Box

**FIGURE 1-1:**
The Adobe Bridge
workspace.

Collections Panel

Filter Panel

Thumbnail Slider

Metadata Panel

View Options

Keywords Panel

>> **Filter panel:** The Filter panel lets you sort and filter files that appear in the Content panel. You can use this panel to easily find files of the same type, files created on the same date, and more.

>> **Collections panel:** The Collections panel offers you the opportunity to use shortcuts to create collections of files that you can easily locate without moving in your directory.

>> **Content panel:** The Content panel displays files specified by the navigational menu buttons, Path bar, Favorites panel, Folders panel, or Collections panel. Basically, these include thumbnails of your files within your selected folder.

>> **Publish panel:** The Publish panel lets you upload photos to Adobe Stock from within the Bridge app. This might be used if you are a photographer who wants to submit images to Adobe Stock.

>> **Preview panel:** The Preview panel displays a preview of the selected file or files. You can reduce or enlarge the preview by resizing the panel.

>> **Metadata panel:** The Metadata panel includes metadata information for the selected file. If multiple files are selected, shared data (such as keywords, date created, and exposure setting) is listed.

>> **Keywords panel:** The Keywords panel helps you organize your images by attaching keywords to them.

## Practice makes perfect

Bridge offers an intuitive approach to using your system file directory. Keep in mind that Adobe Bridge is really just a visual method of accessing your files. It may help to dive right in and try out some of Adobe Bridge's features to understand its benefits. Some step-by-step lessons are included in this minibook; if you would like to follow along with them, you can download work files at www. agitraining.com/dummies.

1. **Go to** https://www.agitraining.com/dummies.

2. **Click the DummiesCCFiles folder to download the compressed folder.**

3. **After the folder is downloaded, either right-click (PC) or Ctrl+Click (Mac) to access the contextual menu. Choose Extract All and locate an easy-to-find location, perhaps the desktop.**

## Finding and using your folders within Adobe Bridge

Let's say that you want to locate a picture in a folder of images that are named using numbers instead of descriptive names. By opening that folder in Adobe Bridge, you can see thumbnails for each image and even locate important information about each file's site, resolution, and more. To do so, follow the steps with your own files or download the DummiesCCfiles folder as instructed earlier:

1. **Select the Essentials workspace in Adobe Bridge.**

2. **Click the Folders tab to make sure it is brought forward.**

   If you have files located on your hard drive, you can navigate to them using the named folders icons in the Folders panel.

3. **Click on Documents in the Folders panel to see saved documents that are stored in that folder. If you saved your DummiesCCFiles on the desktop, click on Desktop to see the files in the center Content pane, which you have sitting on the desktop.**

4. **In the Content pane, double-click the DummiesCCFiles folder to open the contents.**

   You see additional folders that contain files that will be referenced throughout the book.

5. **Double-click the folder named Book02_Bridge to see the images within that folder, as well as a subfolder, as shown in Figure 1-2.**

**FIGURE 1-2:**
You can visually see the contents of a folder using Adobe Bridge.

6. **Now, double-click the Hockey folder. This folder contains images that were named automatically with a digital camera, as shown in Figure 1-3.**

   Finding the right file to open is much easier when you can see thumbnails of the images instead of just the name.

7. **Double-click the image to have it launch Adobe Photoshop.**

   Photoshop is typically the default destination for image files such as the JPGs in this folder, but you can change file associations by choosing Edit➪ Preferences➪File Type Associations (PC) or Adobe Bridge➪Edit➪Preferences➪ File Type Associations (Windows).

   **TIP**

8. **Choose File➪Close in Adobe Photoshop and return to Adobe Bridge.**

   From most Creative Cloud applications, you can choose File➪Browse in Bridge to pop back into the Bridge application.

   **TIP**

**FIGURE 1-3:**
A visual display
of images in a
folder.

# The default workspace

As a default, Bridge is opened in the default Essentials workspace. In this view, you have three columns that you can resize by clicking and dragging the columns. This view also provides you with a Content pane that displays thumbnails of items that are contained in an open folder.

In addition to the Essentials workspace, there are several other preconfigured workspaces that you can access from the Application bar, as shown in Figure 1-4. Depending upon the information you want to showcase, you might want to switch from one workspace to another. Switching workspaces does not change the locations of your files and folders, but it presents information about the items in a different manner.

Experiment with these to see which works best for you.

Here are explanations of the preconfigured workspaces:

>> **Metadata:** Displays the Content panel in List view, along with the Favorites, Metadata, and Filter panels.

>> **Essentials:** Displays the Favorites, Folders, Filter, Collections, Content, Preview, Metadata, and Keywords panels.

>> **Filmstrip:** Displays thumbnails in a scrolling horizontal row along with a preview of the selected item. This workspace also displays the Favorites, Folders, Filter, and Collections panels.

>> **Keywords:** Displays the Content panel in Details view, as well as the Favorites, Keywords, and Filter panels.

**FIGURE 1-4:**
Change your
workspace in the
Application bar.

## Looking for a better view

You may want to resize your thumbnails in the Content pane, especially if you have many files. You can easily do this by using the Thumbnail slider in the lower portion of the Bridge workspace.

You can also change the presentation of the content by using the View options in the lower-right corner, as shown in Figure 1-5. Your choices are

>> Click to lock to thumbnail grid

>> View content as thumbnails

>> View content as details

>> View content as list

## Creating a new folder

Perhaps you want to create a new folder. Whether you create a new folder in your system File directory or in the Finder for the Mac, it will be recognized by Bridge. In this next example, you navigate back using the Path bar, and create a new folder in the Book02_Bridge folder:

**1.** **Make sure that you are still in the Hockey folder and note the information that appears in the Path bar, as shown in Figure 1-6.**

This is the directory path to the folder that you have active and open at this time.

**FIGURE 1-5:**
Change your
view to bring out
additional details.

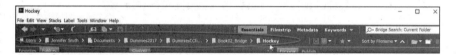

**FIGURE 1-6:**
Use the Path bar
to navigate back
through your
folders.

2. **Click on Book02_Bridge in the Path bar to ensure that you navigate back to that folder.**

3. **To create a new folder inside this folder, click the Create New Folder button in the upper right, as shown in Figure 1-7, or right-click (PC)/ Ctrl+click (Mac) and select New Folder from the contextual menu that appears.**

   A new folder appears, ready to be renamed.

4. **Name the file** Rockets.

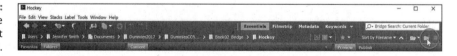

**FIGURE 1-7:**
You can create
new folders right
in Adobe Bridge.

# Moving a file to another folder

Next you select and move some files into your newly created folder:

1. **Click on one of the Rocket images and then, holding down the Ctrl key (PC) or Command key (Mac), click on the other rocket image.**

   Using the Ctrl or Command key allows you to select multiple files.

2. **With both rocket images selected, click and drag them over to your new Rockets folder, as shown in Figure 1-8. Release your mouse when the files are on top of the folder to move them into that folder.**

   **TIP**

   You can also move and copy files using the contextual menu. Right-click (PC) or Ctrl+click (Mac) on any image file to see the contextual menu that appears with options that include moving and copying the selected file.

**FIGURE 1-8:** Move images from one folder to another in Adobe Bridge.

## Making a favorite

When working in the Creative Cloud, you may return to certain folders over and over again. In that situation, it would help to have some Favorite folders established and saved in the Favorites panel. When your most popular folders are saved as favorites, accessing them requires only one click.

Follow these steps in order to save your own favorite. In the following steps, the files from the DummiesCCFile are used. You can follow along with your own files and folders if you like.

1. **Using the Folders panel, navigate your file directory system until you locate the DummiesCCFile folder.**

   In the example shown in Figure 1-9, the folder is located on the desktop.

**FIGURE 1-9:**
Locate the folder that you wish to save as a favorite.

**2.** Make sure that the Favorites panel is forward. Check this by clicking on the tab that says Favorites.

**3.** Click on the DummiesCCFiles folder and drag it to the Favorites panel. Release the mouse when you see a line that indicates where the favorite will appear in the present list, as shown in Figure 1-10.

Now that you have saved the DummiesCCFiles as a favorite, you can access the folder anytime you like simply by clicking on the folder name in the Favorites panel.

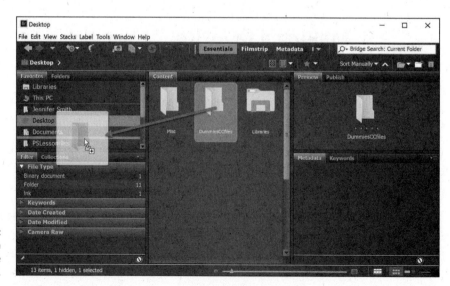

**FIGURE 1-10:**
Click and drag a folder into the Favorites panel.

# Investigating the Application bar

Now that you have spent a little bit of time working in Bridge, the Application bar and its tools will make more sense to you. The Application bar runs along the top of the Bridge workspace. The tools and features are shown in Figure 1-11.

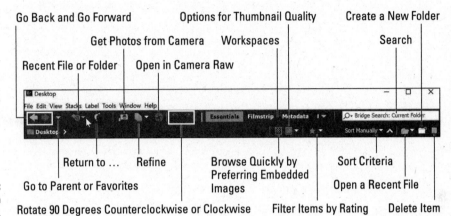

**FIGURE 1-11:**
The Application bar.

There are many features included in the Application bar that help you with navigating, acquiring, and organizing your files. Some important features include Get Photos from Camera, which is covered in Chapter 3 of this minibook, and Sort Criteria, which is covered in Chapter 2.

# Developing a Bridge habit

Now that you have experienced using Adobe Bridge, try making it a habit. Instead of selecting File⇨Open, choose File⇨Browse in Bridge and start recognizing the time savings.

**IN THIS CHAPTER**

» **Creating and locating metadata**

» **Creating a metadata template**

» **Searching for files using Adobe Bridge**

» **Searching by name or keyword**

» **Using the Filter panel**

» **Saving a collection**

Chapter **2**

# Taking Advantage of Metadata in Adobe Bridge

**M**etadata is information that can be stored with images. This information travels with the file and makes it easy to search for and identify the file. Use metadata features and templates to help you save and find your files more easily.

You find out how to attach metadata to your images by following some step-by-step lessons included in this chapter. If you would like to follow along with them, you can download work files at https://www.agitraining.com/dummies.

## Locating Your Files

You can follow these steps with your own files, or you can download the DummiesCCfiles folder, as instructed in Chapter 1 of this minibook.

1. **Select the Essentials workspace in Adobe Bridge.**

2. **Click the Folders tab to make sure it is brought forward.**

   If you have files located on your hard drive, you can navigate to them using the named folders icons in the Folders panel.

3. **Click Documents in the Folders panel to see saved documents that are stored in that folder. If you saved your DummiesCCFiles on the desktop, click Desktop to see in the center Content pane the files you have sitting on the desktop.**

4. **In the Content pane, double-click the DummiesCCFiles folder to open the contents.**

   You see additional folders that contain files that will be referenced throughout the book.

5. **Double-click the folder named Book02_Bridge to see the images within that folder, as well as a subfolder, as shown in Figure 2-1.**

**FIGURE 2-1:**
The contents of the Book02_Bridge folder.

6. **Double-click on the folder named Hockey to see the images displayed.**

7. **Choose Window➪Workspace➪Reset Standard Workspaces. This ensures that you are in the Essentials view and that all the default panels for Adobe Bridge are visible. Alternatively, click Essentials in the Application bar at the top-right of the Bridge workspace. You might need to maximize your Bridge window after you reset the workspace.**

8. **Click once on IMG_4088.JPG, and look for the Metadata and Keywords panels in the lower-right area of the Adobe Bridge workspace.**

**9.** If the Metadata panel is not visible, click the Metadata panel tab. In this panel, as shown in Figure 2-2, you see the image data that is stored with the file. Take a few moments to scroll through the data and view the information that was imported from the digital camera that was used to take the photo.

**FIGURE 2-2:**
Scroll through the Metadata panel on the right side of the Bridge workspace.

**10.** If necessary, click the arrow to the left of IPTC Core to reveal its contents.

IPTC Core is the schema for XMP that provides a smooth and explicit transfer of metadata. Adobe's Extensible Metadata Platform (XMP) is a labeling technology that allows you to embed data about a file, known as metadata, into the file itself. With XMP, desktop applications and back-end publishing systems gain a common method for capturing and sharing valuable metadata.

**11.** On the right side of this list, notice a series of pencil icons. These icons indicate that you can enter information in these fields. Some of the information about the creator has already been included, such as the creator's name and his location. Now you'll add additional information.

*Note:* If you are not able to edit or add metadata information to a file, it could be locked. You can check by right-clicking on the file directly in Bridge and selecting Reveal in Explorer (Windows) or Reveal in Finder (Mac OS). In Windows, right-click the file, choose Properties, and uncheck Read-only; in Mac OS, right-click the file, choose Get Info, then change the Ownership (Sharing) and Permissions to Read and Write.

**12.** **Scroll down until you can see Description Writer and click the pencil next to it. All editable fields are highlighted, and a cursor appears in the Description Writer field.**

**13.** **Type your name, or type** Picture-by-me.

**14.** **Scroll up to locate the Description text field. Click the Pencil icon to the right and type** Goalie in net **to add a description for the image, as shown in Figure 2-3.**

 **15.** **Click the Apply button, located in the bottom-right corner of the Metadata panel, to apply your changes.**

You have now edited metadata that is attached to the image; this information will appear whenever someone opens your image in Bridge or views the image information in Adobe Photoshop using File ⇨ File Info.

# Using Keywords

Using keywords — logical words to help you locate images more quickly — can reduce the amount of time it takes to find an image on a computer. Here's how:

1. **Click the Keywords tab, which appears behind the Metadata panel.**

   A list of commonly used keywords appears.

2. **Click the New Keyword button at the bottom of the Keywords panel, as shown in Figure 2-4. Type** Goalie **into the active text field, and then press Enter (Windows) or Return (Mac).**

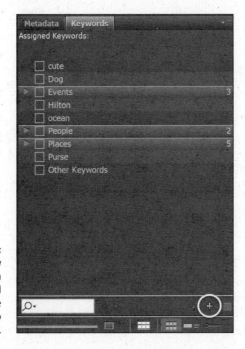

**FIGURE 2-4:**
Click on the New Keyword button (circled) to add your own unique keyword to the file.

3. **Select the empty checkbox to the left of the Goalie keyword. This adds the Goalie keyword to the selected image.**

4. **With the Goalie keyword still selected, click the New Sub Keyword button. Type** Boy **into the active text field, then press Enter (Windows) or Return (Mac).**

5. **Select the empty checkbox to the left of the Boy keyword.**

   You have now assigned a keyword and a sub keyword to the IMG_4088.JPG image. Now you will add a second keyword.

6. **Select the Goalie keyword, and then click the New Keyword button at the bottom of the Keywords panel; a blank text field appears. Type** Peewee **and press Enter (Windows) or Return (Mac). Then, select the checkbox next to Peewee to assign the keyword to this image.**

7. **Right-click (Windows) or Ctrl+click (Mac) on the Peewee keyword, and choose the option Rename. When the text field becomes highlighted, type** Youth, **press Enter (Windows) or Return (Mac). Make sure the Youth checkbox remains selected.**

**TIP**

You can also enter information directly into the image by opening the image in Adobe Photoshop, and then choosing File⇨File Info. The categories that appear on the top include Description, Camera Data, IPTC, and IPTC Extension, among others. After it is entered in the File Info dialog box, the information is visible in Adobe Bridge.

# Creating a Metadata Template

After you have added metadata to an image, you can easily apply it to more images by creating a metadata template. In this exercise, you apply the metadata template from the IMG_4088.JPG image to other images in the same folder:

1. **Make sure that IMG_4088.JPG is selected in Adobe Bridge.**

2. **Choose Tools⇨Create Metadata Template.**

   The Create Metadata Template window appears.

3. **In the Template Name text field (at the top), type** Game Photos.

   In the Create Metadata Template window, you can choose the information that you want to build into a template. In this exercise, we choose information that already exists in the selected file, but if you wanted to, you could add or edit information at this point.

4. **Select the checkboxes to the left of the following categories: Creator, Creator, Description, Keywords, and Date Created, then click Save, as shown in Figure 2-5.**

   You have just saved a template. Next, you apply it to the other two hockey images in this folder.

5. **Select the IMG_4087.JPG image, press and hold the Ctrl (Windows) or Command (Mac) key, and select the IMG_4083.JPG image.**

   Both images are selected.

FIGURE 2-5:
Select a file
and check the
information you
want to save
into a metadata
template.

6. **Choose Tools⇨Append Metadata and select Game Photos, as shown in Figure 2-6. Note that you can also choose Replace Metadata if you want to eliminate existing metadata.**

The same metadata has now been applied to all the images at once.

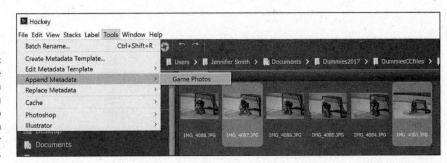

FIGURE 2-6:
Choose the
metadata
template you
want to use to
add metadata
to an image or
images.

Taking Advantage of
Metadata in Adobe Bridge

# Searching for Files Using Adobe Bridge

Find the files that you want quickly and easily by using the Search tools built directly into Adobe Bridge and by taking advantage of the Filter panel.

In this example, you have a limited number of files to search within, but even so, you can still see how helpful these search features can be.

## Searching by name or keyword

The benefit of adding metadata to your images is that you can use it to find your files later. Using the Find dialog box in Adobe Bridge, you can narrow your criteria down to make it easy to find your files when needed. Here's how:

1. **Make sure that you are still viewing the content in the Hockey folder.**

2. **Choose Edit⇨Find, or use the keyboard shortcut Ctrl+F (Windows) or Command+F (Mac OS).**

   The Find dialog box appears.

3. **Select Keywords from the Criteria drop-down menu, and type** Goalie **into the third text field (replacing Enter Text), as shown in Figure 2-7. Then press Enter (Windows) or Return (Mac).**

   Because you are looking within the active folder only, you get a result immediately. The image files that you tagged with the Goalie keyword are visible.

**FIGURE 2-7:**
Search your folders using the tools built right into Adobe Bridge.

4. **Clear the search by clicking the X icon to the right of the New Search icon at the top of the results pane, as shown in Figure 2-8.**

FIGURE 2-8:
Cancel the
search results by
clicking on the
X (circled) in the
Content pane.

# Using the Filter panel

You can use the Filter panel to locate files whose location you can't remember. With the Filter panel, you can look at attributes such as file type, keywords, and date created or modified to narrow down the files that appear in the content window of Adobe Bridge. The following steps show you how:

1. **Make sure that you are still viewing the content of the Hockey folder. Notice that the Filter panel collects the information from the active folder, indicating the keywords that are being used, as well as modification dates and more.**

2. **Click to turn down the arrow next to Keywords in the Filter panel, and select Goalie from the list; notice that only images with the Goalie keyword applied are visible. Click Goalie again to deselect it and view all the images.**

   Find files quickly by selecting different criteria in the Filters panel.

3. **Click the Clear Filter button in the lower right of the Filter panel to turn off any filters.**

4. **Experiment with investigating file types as well. Only file types that exist in the selected folder appear in the list. If you are looking for an Adobe Illustrator file, you might see that there are none located in this folder, but you will see a QuickTime video file that you can select and preview right in Adobe Bridge, as shown in Figure 2-9.**

5. **Again, click the Clear Filter button in the lower-right area of the Filter panel to turn off any filters.**

FIGURE 2-9:
You can select
File Types
from the Filter
panel to locate
them easily.

# Saving a Collection

If you like using favorites, you'll love using collections. A collection allows you to take images from multiple locations and access them in one central location. Understand that when you use a collection, Adobe Bridge essentially creates a shortcut, or alias, to your files and does not physically relocate them or copy them to a different location.

1. **If your Collections tab is not visible, choose Window⇨Collections Panel or click the tab next to Filter.**

   The Collections panel comes forward.

2. **Click the gray area in the Content pane to make sure that nothing is selected, and then click the New Collection button in the lower-right area of the Collections panel. Type** Pictures of hockey **into the new collection text field, as shown in Figure 2-10. Press Return or Enter to confirm your new collection.**

3. **Navigate back to the Bridge02-Folder, and then take two random images and drag them to the Pictures of hockey collection.**

4. **Click the Pictures of hockey collection folder; notice that even though you can easily access the files you added to the collection, the files remain intact in their original location.**

**FIGURE 2-10:**
Create a collection to keep selected Pictures easily accessible.

# Chapter **3**

# Using Automation Tools in Adobe Bridge

You have already discovered how Adobe Bridge can save you time by helping you organize and more easily find your images. In this chapter, you find out how to use automated features that cut out redundant tasks and save even more time.

## Getting Files from Your Camera

 With the Get Photos from Camera feature, you can connect your camera, card reader, or mobile device to the computer using a supported cable. If you want to give this feature a try, follow these steps:

1. **Simply attach your phone via USB, insert a card into your card reader, or connect your camera via cable.**

2. **Launch Bridge.**

3.  **Click the Get Photos from Camera button. The Adobe Bridge CC – Photo Downloader dialog box appears, as shown in Figure 3-1.**

4.  **Click open the Get Photos From drop-down menu and select your device.**

    *Note:* If Bridge does not recognize your device, make sure that you have the latest version installed by launching your Creative Cloud App. Look in the Apps section to see if an update is available. You can also try connecting your device when Bridge is not open and launching it after the device is connected.

    In the Create Subfolders drop-down menu, you can use a standard format for naming your folders or choose Custom to create your own naming convention.

5.  **If you choose to have the Adobe Downloader rename your files, you can choose a standard naming convention using the date, or choose Custom name and create your own custom name.**

6. The options at the bottom offer you the opportunity to see the files in Bridge, convert the files to DNG (Digital Negative Files), delete the files off the device, and save them to another location.

7. Click the triangle to the left of Advanced Options to see a more detailed preview of your files. In this more detailed view, you can individually select and deselect files to be downloaded, as shown in Figure 3-2.

**FIGURE 3-2:**
The Advanced view allows you to select your images.

# Automation Tools in Adobe Bridge

Adobe Bridge provides many tools to help you automate tasks. In this section, you discover how to use a few helpful features that will save you from repeating redundant tasks.

# Batch renaming your files

You might have noticed that in the Book 2–Bridge⇨Hockey folder, many files contain generic filenames. These images were downloaded from *a digital camera*, and instead of changing the names immediately, we opted to change them simultaneously using the batch rename feature in Adobe Bridge. To do so, follow these steps:

1.  **Choose Edit⇨Select All, or press Ctrl+A (Windows) or ⌘+A (Mac OS).**

    All the images are selected. Don't worry if the Graphics folder is selected; the files inside will not be affected.

2.  **Choose Tools⇨Batch Rename.**

    The Batch Rename dialog box appears.

    In this instance, we want a simple, uncomplicated name. If you look in the Preview section at the bottom of the Batch Rename dialog box, you can see that the Current and New filenames are long strings of text and numbers. You can simplify this by eliminating some of text from the filenames.

3.  **In the New File names section, type** Hockey **in the Text field.**

4.  **In the Sequence Number row, verify that it is set to Two Digits.**

5.  **Confirm that the sequence number is starting at 1. You can start it anywhere if you are adding additional images to a folder later.**

6.  **If there is any other criteria, click the Minus sign button (remove this text from the filenames) to remove them. The New filename in the Preview section becomes significantly shorter.**

    If you look in the Preview section at the bottom of the dialog box, you can see that the new filename is a very simple Hockey01 . jpg now.

7.  **Click the Rename button.**

    All the selected filenames are automatically changed. See Figure 3-3.

# Loading files as layers

Adobe Bridge comes with a variety of Photoshop tools that you can use in Bridge as well. In this example, you select three images that you want to incorporate into one composited image. Instead of opening all three images and cutting and pasting or dragging them into one file, you use the Load Files into Photoshop Layers feature.

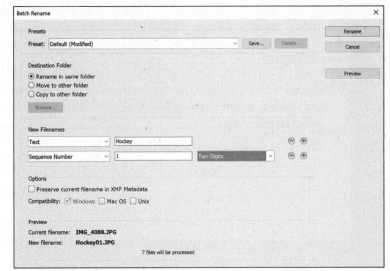

**FIGURE 3-3:**
You can change
multiple
files names
simultaneously in
Adobe Bridge.

Make sure that you are still in the Hockey folder. Hold down your Ctrl (Windows) or ⌘ (Mac) key and Click on any three images. All three images are selected.

Select Tools➪Photoshop. Note that there are many tools that you can use in this menu item; for this example, select the Load Files into Photoshop Layers option. A script immediately launches Photoshop (if it is not already open) and a new layered file is created from the selected images.

You should ensure that your selected images are approximately the same pixel dimensions before running this script; otherwise, you might have to make some transformation adjustments in Photoshop. In this example, the images are approximately the same size.

## Building a contact sheet

If you come from the traditional photography world, you may be familiar with contact sheets. Before digital photography, contact sheets were thumbnail images created from film negatives and were used to help identify which images should be processed. Even though a film negative environment isn't common anymore, contact sheets can be very useful when trying to identify which images you choose to save or edit.

Fortunately there is a contact feature built right into the Adobe Bridge tools. Follow these steps to create your own using your own images, or any of our sample images:

1. **Open a folder of images and either Ctrl/⌘-click on the images you want to include in a contact sheet or press Ctrl+A (Windows)/⌘+A (Mac) to select all the images.**

2. **Choose Tools⇨Photoshop⇨Contact Sheet II.**

    Photoshop is launched and you see the Contact Sheet II dialog box that appears in Figure 3-4.

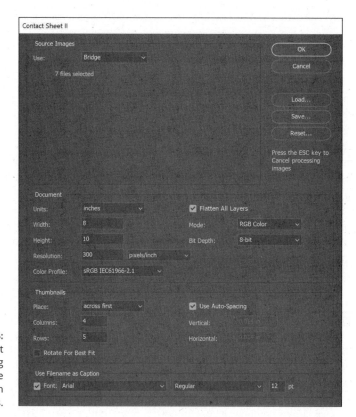

**FIGURE 3-4:**
The Contact
Sheet II dialog
box offers size
and resolution
options.

**3.** Choose your paper size and resolution. The default is 8 inches x 10 inches and 300 dpi, which works fine for reliable results.

Choose how many thumbnails you want across and down using the rows and columns. The fewer rows and columns, the larger the thumbnail images will be.

Check Use Filename as Caption if you want to see the filename listed underneath the thumbnail.

**4.** Press OK to see the final Contact Sheet created, as shown in Figure 3-5.

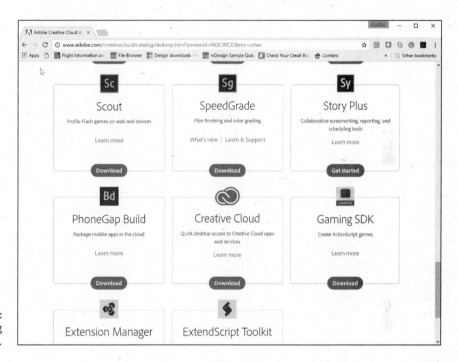

**FIGURE 3-5:**
The resulting contact sheet.

# 3

# Photoshop CC

# Contents at a Glance

Chapter **1**

# Getting into Photoshop CC Basics

n this chapter, you are introduced to the Photoshop CC work area and tools. You'll also find out how to neatly organize and hide panels. In this chapter, you will also find out how to do basic tasks, such as open an image, crop it to a different size, and then resave it.

## The Start Screen

When Photoshop is first launched, or until you change your preferences, you will see a start screen, as shown in Figure 1-1. This start screen can making it easier for you to find files that you have recently worked on or jump right into a new document.

If you would rather not have this screen every time you launch Photoshop, you can choose Edit⇨Preferences⇨General and uncheck Show Start Workspace When No Documents Are Open. On the Mac you would choose Photoshop⇨Preferences⇨ General and uncheck Show Start Workspace When No Documents Are Open.

**FIGURE 1-1:**
The Start
screen in Adobe
Photoshop
appears as a
default.

# The New Document Window

If you are still using Photoshop at its default settings, you can click on the New button in the start screen, or choose File➪New. The initial New Document dialog window appears. Just like the start screen, the default New Document window may be more than you have asked for, but it is meant to offer you more control and options when creating new files. Note in Figure 1-2 that you can choose the type of document that you are working on, such as Photo, Print, Art & Illustration, Web, Mobile, Film and Video.

Each one of these selections offers standard size and resolution defaults for the medium selected in addition to templates that you are able to open and customize for your own needs.

If this is a little much for you and you want the standard, smaller, more compact New Document dialog box, choose the Close button in this window and then select Edit➪Preferences➪General and check Use Legacy "New Document" Interface. (On the Mac, choose Photoshop➪Preferences➪ General and check Use Legacy "New Document" Interface.)

FIGURE 1-2:
The updated New
Document dialog
box has many
options from
which to choose.

# Sample Images Can Help You Investigate More Features

Of course it helps to have an image open while exploring Adobe Photoshop. You are free to use your own or use the samples image files located here: https://www.agitraining.com/dummies. This downloadable file includes files that can be used throughout the entire *Adobe Creative Cloud All-in-One For Dummies* book.

1. **Go to** https://www.agitraining.com/dummies.

2. **Click on the DummiesCCFiles folder to download the compressed folder.**

3. **After the folder is downloaded, right-click (PC) to access the contextual menu and choose Extract All and locate an easy-to-find location or Ctrl+Click (Mac) and choose Open.**

   Inside the DummiesCCFiles folder, you find separate folders for each minibook. Images are available for you to use in the Book03_Photoshop folder.

# Opening an Image

You can open an existing Photoshop image in one of several ways:

>> If you see the start screen, you can click on the Open button and navigate to the folder that contains the image you would like to open.

>> Choose File➪Open, select the file in the Open dialog box and then click the Open button.

>> Choose File➪Browse in Bridge. By selecting Browse in Bridge instead of Open, you launch the Adobe Bridge application. Read more about Adobe Bridge later in this section and also in Book 2.

**REMEMBER**

Photoshop can open a multitude of file formats, even if the image was created in another application, such as Illustrator or another image-editing program. However, you have to open the image in Photoshop by choosing File➪Open or, using Adobe Bridge, by selecting an image and dragging it to the Photoshop icon on the taskbar (Windows) or Dock (Mac). If you double-click an image file (one that wasn't originally created in Photoshop, or from different versions) in a folder, the image may open only in a preview application.

If you're opening a folder of images that you want to investigate first, choose File➪Browse in Bridge to open Adobe Bridge, the control center for Adobe Creative Cloud. You can use Adobe Bridge to organize, browse, and locate the assets you need to create your content. Adobe Bridge keeps available, for easy access, native AI, INDD, PSD, and Adobe PDF files as well as other Adobe and non-Adobe application files. Adobe Bridge does not install by default with Adobe Photoshop. If you do not have it loaded you can read through the directions and highlights of using Adobe Bridge in Book 2, "Adobe Bridge."

# Getting to Know the Tools

You use tools to create, select, and manipulate objects in Photoshop CC. When you have Photoshop open, the Tools panel appears along the left side of the workspace (see Figure 1-3), and panels appear on the right side of the screen. (We discuss panels in the later section "Navigating the Work Area.")

**TIP**

In the Tools panel, look for a tooltip when you hover the cursor over any one of the tools. Following the tool name is a letter in parentheses, which is the keyboard shortcut you can use to access that tool. Simply press the Shift key along with the key command you see to access any hidden tools. In other words, pressing P activates the Pen tool, and pressing Shift+P rotates through the hidden tools under the Pen tool. When you see a small triangle in the lower-right corner of the tool icon, you know that the tool contains hidden tools.

Table 1-1 lists the Photoshop tools, describes what each one is used for, and specifies in which chapter you can find more information about each one.

**FIGURE 1-3:**
The Photoshop CC workspace includes the Tools panel.

**TABLE 1-1**     ## Photoshop CC Tools

| Button | Tool | What You Can Do with It | See This Chapter in Book 3 |
|--------|------|-------------------------|----------------------------|
| | Move (V) | Move selections or layers | 3 |
| | Marquee (M) | Select the image area | 3 |
| | Lasso (L) | Make freehand selections | 3 |
| | Quick Selection (W) | Select similar pixels | 3 |
| | Crop (C) | Crop an image | 1 |
| | Eyedropper (I) | Eyedropper | 7 |

*(continued)*

**TABLE 1-1** *(continued)*

| | | | |
|---|---|---|---|
| | Spot Healing Brush (J) | Retouch flaws | 7 |
| | Brush (B) | Paint the foreground color | 7 |
| | Clone Stamp (S) | Copy pixel data | 7 |
| | History Brush (Y) | Paint from the selected state | 7 |
| | Eraser (E) | Erase pixels | 7 |
| | Gradient (G) | Create a gradient | 7 |
| | Blur | Blur pixels | 7 |
| | Toning (O) | Dodge, burn, saturate | N/A |
| | Pen (P) | Create paths | 4 |
| | Type (T) | Create text | 8 |
| | Path Selection (A) | Select paths | 4 |
| | Hidden Direct Selection (A) | Select individual anchor points on paths | 4 |
| | Vector Shape (U) | Create vector shapes | 8 |
| | Hand (H) | Navigate page | 8 |
| | Zoom (Z) | Increase or decrease the view | 1 |

**TIP**

Looking for the Magic Wand tool, shown in Figure 1-4? Click and hold the Quick Selection tool in the Tools panel to access it.

**FIGURE 1-4:**
Some popular tools may be hidden; click and hold on the arrow in the lower right of the tool to see additional tools.

# Navigating the Work Area

Navigating in Photoshop isn't much different than getting around in other Adobe applications. Most Creative Cloud applications make extensive use of panels. In the following sections, you have an opportunity to experience the Photoshop workspace and configure those panels.

As a default, you are in the Essentials workspace, as shown in Figure 1-5. If you are happy with the panels that appear while in that workspace there is no reason to change your workspace at this time.

## Resetting your workspace

Even though you may be happy with the panels that appear as a default, you might end up moving, closing, or inadvertently collapsing important panels. When working in any workspace, including Essentials, you can easily reset the panel configuration by selecting Windows➪Workspace➪Reset Essentials (or the work-space name). Read the following section to discover how to create and save your own Workspace in Photoshop.

## Docking and saving panels

Panels, panels everywhere — do you really need them all? Maybe not just yet, but as you increase your skill level, you'll start to take advantage of more of those Photoshop panels. Panels give you easy access to important functions. In this chapter we touch on panel organization, but if you want more details about using panels there is a fast read in Book 1, Chapter 5, "Exploring Common Panels."

**REMEMBER**

When you work in Photoshop, keep in mind these two keyboard shortcuts can help temporarily clear up distractive tools and panels while you are working:

» Press Tab to switch between hiding and showing the tools and panels.

» Press Shift+Tab to hide the panels, leaving only the Tools panel visible. Press Shift+Tab to show them again.

If you find that you are frequently using the same panels, close the less used panels that you don't need and arrange the others onscreen where you want them.

Follow one of these three methods to close a panel:

>> **Choose Window⇨*Panel's Tab Name*.** If the panel name is checked, it is open; selecting the panel name in the list closes the panel.

>> **Click on the panel menu in the upper right of the panel and choose Close, as you see in Figure 1-6.**

**FIGURE 1-6:**
Closing a panel
that you do not
use frequently.

>> **Click and drag on a panel name to undock it.** When undocked, the panel displays a close button (an X button in Windows or the red button on a Mac) that you can click to close the panel.

To open and relocate panels that you frequently use, choose Window⇨*Panel's Tab Name.*

## Saving your workspace

After you have displayed and arranged the panels you frequently use, follow these steps to save the configuration:

**1.** **Choose Window⇨Workspace⇨New Workspace.**

The New Workspace dialog box appears.

**2.** **Name your workspace and click Save.**

**3.** **Any time you want the panels to return to your saved locations, choose Window➪Workspace➪*Name of Workspace.***

*Name of Workspace* is the name you supplied in Step 2.

## Taking advantage of workspace features

In addition to the Essentials workspace, Photoshop has workspaces you can take advantage of to open the panels you need for specific tasks. You can use some of these workspaces for photography, painting, or design, for example.

Increase your work area by turning panels into icons, as shown in Figure 1-7. Do so either by right-clicking the tab of a panel and selecting Collapse to Icons or by clicking the double arrows.

**FIGURE 1-7:**
Turn panels into icons.

## Zooming in to get a better look

Images that look fine at one zoom level may look extremely bad at another. You'll zoom in and out quite often while working on images in Photoshop. You can find menu choices for zooming on the View menu, but a quicker way to zoom is to use the keyboard commands listed in Table 1-2.

**TABLE 1-2**  ## Zooming and Navigation Keyboard Shortcuts

| Command | Windows Shortcut | Mac Shortcut |
| --- | --- | --- |
| Actual size | Ctrl+1 | ⌘+1 |
| Fit in window | Ctrl+0 (zero) | ⌘+0 (zero) |
| Zoom in | Ctrl++ (plus sign) or Ctrl+spacebar | ⌘++ (plus sign) or ⌘+spacebar |
| Zoom out | Ctrl+– (minus) or Alt+spacebar | ⌘+– (minus) or Option+spacebar |
| Hand tool | Spacebar | Spacebar |

This list describes a few advantages of working with the Zoom tool to get a better look at your work:

» **100 percent view:** Double-clicking the Zoom tool in the Tools panel gives you a 100 percent view. Do it before using filters to see a more realistic result of making changes.

» **Zoom marquee:** Drag from the upper-left corner to the lower-right corner of the area you want to zoom to. While you drag, a marquee appears; when you release the mouse button, the marqueed area zooms to fill the image window. The Zoom marquee gives you much more control than just clicking the image with the Zoom tool. Zoom out again to see the entire image by pressing Ctrl+0 (Windows) or ⌘+0 (Mac). Doing so fits the entire image in the viewing area.

TIP

» **Keyboard shortcuts:** If a dialog box is open and you need to reposition or zoom to a new location on an image, you can use the keyboard commands without closing the dialog box.

» **A new window for a different look:** Choose Window⇨Arrange⇨New Window to create an additional window for the frontmost image. This technique is helpful when you want to view the entire image (say, at actual size) to see the results as a whole yet zoom in to focus on a small area of the image to do some fine-tuning. The new window is linked dynamically to the original window so that when you make changes, the original and any other new windows created from the original are immediately updated.

» **Cycle through images:** Press Ctrl+Tab (Windows) or ⌘+~ (tilde) (Mac) to cycle through open images.

# Choosing Your Screen Mode

You have a choice of three screen modes in which to work. Most users start and stay in the default (standard screen) mode until they inadvertently end up in another. The following modes are accessible by clicking and holding Screen Mode, located at the bottom of the Tools panel, as shown in Figure 1-8:

**FIGURE 1-8:**
Change your
screen mode.

>> **Standard Screen Mode:** In this typical view, an image window is open, but you can see your desktop and other images open behind it.

>> **Full Screen Mode with Menu Bar:** In this view, the image is surrounded to the edge of the work area with neutral gray. Working in this mode prevents you not only from accidentally clicking out of an image and leaving Photoshop, but also from seeing other images behind the working image.

>> **Full Screen Mode:** A maximized document window fills all available space between docks and resizes when dock widths change.

# Getting Started with Basic Tasks in Photoshop CC

Unless you use Photoshop as a blank canvas for painting, you may rarely create a new file in Photoshop. This is because you typically have a source image you start with that may have been generated by a digital camera, stock image library, or scanner.

The following sections show you how to open an existing image file in Photoshop, create a new image (if you want to use Photoshop to paint, for example), crop an image, and save an edited image.

# DISCOVER CAMERA RAW

If you haven't discovered the Camera Raw capabilities in Adobe Photoshop, you'll want to give them a try. The Camera Raw format is available for image capture in many cameras. Simply choose the format in your camera's settings as Raw instead of JPEG or TIFF. These Raw files are a bit larger than standard JPEG files, but you capture an enormous amount of data with the image that you can retrieve after opening. (See www. adobe.com for a complete list of cameras that support Camera Raw.)

A Camera Raw file contains unprocessed picture data from a digital camera's image sensor, along with information about how the image was captured, such as camera and lens type, exposure settings, and white balance setting. When you open the file in Adobe Photoshop CC, the built-in Camera Raw plug-in interprets the Raw file on your computer, making adjustments for image color and tonal scale.

When you shoot JPEG images with your camera, you're locked into the processing done by your camera, but working with Camera Raw files gives you maximum control over images, such as controlling their white balance, tonal range, contrast, color saturation, and image sharpening. Cameras that can shoot in Raw format have a setting on the camera that changes its capture mode to Raw. Rather than write a final JPEG file, a Raw data file is written, which consists of black-and-white brightness levels from each of the several million pixel sites on the imaging sensor. The actual image hasn't yet been produced, and unless you have specific software, such as the plug-in built in to Adobe Photoshop, opening the file can be difficult, if not impossible.

To open a Camera Raw file, simply choose File➪Browse in Bridge. Adobe Bridge opens, and you see several panels, including the Folders, Content, Preview, and Metadata panels. In the Folders panel, navigate to the location on your computer where you've saved Camera Raw images; thumbnail previews appear in the Content panel. Think of Camera Raw files as photo negatives. You can reprocess them at any time to achieve the results you want.

Right-click (Windows) or Control-click (Mac) a JPEG or TIFF file and choose Open in Camera Raw from the contextual menu. This is a great way to experiment with all the cool features available with this plug-in, but your results aren't as good as if you used an actual Raw file.

If Adobe Photoshop CC doesn't open your Raw file, you may need to update the Raw plug-in. (See www.adobe.com for the latest plug-in.) The plug-in should be downloaded and placed in this location in Windows: `C:\Program Files\Common Files\Adobe\Plug-Ins\CS7\File Formats`. On the Macintosh, place the plug-in here: `Library\Application Support\Adobe\Plug-Ins\CS7\File Formats`.

# Cropping an image

A simple but essential task is to crop an image. *Cropping* means to eliminate all parts of the image that aren't relevant to create a dynamic composition.

Cropping is especially important in Photoshop. Each pixel, no matter what color, takes up the same amount of information, so cropping eliminates unneeded pixels and reduces file size and processing time. For that reason, you should crop images before you start working on them.

You can crop an image in Photoshop CC in two ways:

» Use the Crop tool.

» Select an area with the Marquee tool and choose Image➪Crop.

To crop an image by using the Crop tool, follow these steps:

1. **Press C to access the Crop tool.**

    Make sure that the preset (in the upper-left corner of the control panel) is set to Ratio, or, if you wish, to a specific preset size in the Presets drop-down list, as shown in Figure 1-9.

**FIGURE 1-9**
Select the Crop tool preset before you click and drag.

2. **Click and drag over the area of the image you want to keep.**

3. **If you need to adjust the crop area, drag the handles in the crop-bounding area.**

4. When you're satisfied with the crop-bounding area, double-click in the center of the crop area or press the Return or Enter key to crop the image.

5. If you want to cancel the crop, press the Esc key.

**TIP**

Ever scan in an image that ends up crooked? When using the Crop tool, if you position the cursor outside any handle, a rotate symbol appears. Drag the crop-bounding area to rotate it and line it up the way you want it cropped. When you press Return or Enter, the image straightens out.

## Using grids as you crop

As a default, a three-row and three-column grid appears after you click and drag over an area with your Crop tool. This grid can be used as a guide to help you create more dynamically cropped images. Images whose points of interest appear on the intersections of this grid, or that can be divided into the sections of the grid, are generally considered to be more interesting. (This is the called the *Rule of Thirds*.) See how the image in Figure 1-10 fills the bottom one-third of the image with water, and the upper two-thirds with sky.

**FIGURE 1-10:** Use of the Rule of Thirds overlay in the Crop tool.

If you prefer to change or turn off the overlay, select the Never Show Overlay option from the Set the Overlay Options drop-down list, as shown in Figure 1-11. Keep in mind that you must have already clicked and dragged out your crop area before you can make changes to the overlay.

**FIGURE 1-11:** Select from a multitude of overlays to use as guides, or turn the overlay off.

## Saving images

Save an image file by choosing File➪Save. If you're saving the file for the first time, the Save As dialog box appears. Notice in the Format drop-down list that you have plenty of choices for file formats. (File formats are discussed in more detail in Chapter 9 of this minibook.) You can always play it safe by choosing the native Photoshop (PSD) file format, which supports all Photoshop features, such as channels, layers, text, and other vector objects that are discussed throughout this minibook. Choosing certain other formats may eliminate layers, channels, and other special features.

Many users choose to save a native Photoshop file as a backup to any other file format. Be sure to have a backup or an original file saved as a native Photoshop (PSD) file when you start taking advantage of layers and other outstanding Photoshop elements. As a Creative Cloud user, keep in mind that you can use the native file format for Photoshop in all other Creative Cloud applications.

Chapter **2**

# Messing with Mode Matters

Before taking on working with any imagery in Photoshop, you should understand color modes and the importance of setting up the most optimum color settings. A strong foundation in the use of color plays into the production and editing of all imagery, grayscale, color image, content for websites, movies, and more. Read through this chapter to help you to feel confident in the choices you make.

## Working with Bitmap Images

You may wonder how images in Photoshop show subtle changes in color values. To create those smooth gradations from one color to the next, Photoshop takes advantage of pixels and anti-aliasing. *Bitmap images* (or *raster images*) are based on a grid of pixels, as shown in Figure 2-1. The grid is smaller or larger depending on the resolution of your image. The number of pixels along the height and width of a bitmap image are the pixel dimensions of an image, measured in pixels per inch (ppi). The more pixels per inch, the more detail in the image.

**FIGURE 2-1:**
You can see the grid that makes up the pixel resolution of an image when you zoom in.

Unlike *vector graphics* (mathematically created paths), bitmap images can't be scaled without losing detail. (See Figure 2-2 for an example of a bitmap image and a vector graphic.) Generally, you should use bitmap images at or close to the size you need. If you resize a bitmap image, it can become jagged on the edges of sharp objects. On the other hand, you can scale vector graphics and edit them without degrading sharp edges.

Bitmap          Vector

**FIGURE 2-2:**
Bitmap versus vector.

Photoshop can work on both bitmap and vector art. (In the path line around the vector shape layer, notice that the path isn't pixelated or broken down into a step pattern created by the pixels.) Combining the two technologies gives you, as a designer, incredible opportunities.

**TIP**

For information on changing and adjusting image resolution, see Chapter 6 of this minibook.

# Choosing the Correct Photoshop Mode

Choose Image➪Mode to view the available image mode choices. Selecting the right mode for an image is important because each one offers different capabilities and results. For example, if you choose Bitmap mode, you can work only in black and white. That's it — no shades of color, not even gray. Most features are disabled in Bitmap mode, which is fine if you're working on art for a black-and-white logo, but not for most images. If, instead, you work in RGB (Red, Green, Blue) mode, you have full access to Photoshop's capabilities.

Read on to see which image mode is best for your needs. When you're ready to make your mode selection, open a file and choose Image➪Mode to make a selection. You can read descriptions of each image mode in the following sections.

Keep in mind, if you are not sure which mode will work best, stay in the RGB mode. The RGB mode offers access to most all of Photoshop's features and can easily be changed to a different mode later.

REMEMBER

A *channel* simply contains the color information in an image. The number of default color channels in an image depends on its color mode. For example, a CMYK image has at least four channels — one each for cyan, magenta, yellow, and black information. Grayscale has one channel. If you understand the printing process, think of each channel representing a plate (color) that, when combined, creates the final image.

## Bitmap

Bitmap mode offers little more than the capability to work in black and white. Many tools are unusable, and most menu options are grayed out in this mode. If you're converting an image to bitmap, you must convert it to grayscale first.

## Grayscale

Use Grayscale mode, shown in Figure 2-3, if you're creating black-and-white images with tonal values specifically for printing to one color. Grayscale mode supports 256 shades of gray in 8-bit color mode. Photoshop can work with grayscale in 16-bit mode, which provides more information but may limit your capabilities when working in Photoshop.

When you choose Image➪Mode➪Grayscale to convert to Grayscale mode, a warning message asks you to confirm that you want to discard all color information. If you don't want to see this warning every time you convert an image to grayscale, select the option not to show the dialog box again before you click Discard.

TIP

Using the Black & White adjustment is the best way to create a good grayscale image. Simply click and hold the Create New Fill or Adjustment Layer button at the bottom of the Layers panel and choose Black & White. Set the sliders to achieve the best black-and-white image. After you have adjusted the colors using the Black & White adjustment, choose Image➪Mode➪Grayscale.

**FIGURE 2-3:**
Grayscale
supports 256
shades of gray.

# Duotone

Use Duotone mode when you're creating a one- to four-color image created from spot colors (solid ink, such as Pantone colors). You can also use Duotone mode to create monotones, tritones, and quadtones. If you're producing a two-color job, duotones create a beautiful alternative to full color.

**REMEMBER**

The Pantone Matching System (PMS) helps keep printing inks consistent from one job to the next. By assigning a numbered Pantone color, such as 485 for red, you eliminate the risk of one vendor (printer) using fire engine red and the next using orange-red for your company logo.

To create a duotone, follow these steps:

1. **Choose Image⇨Mode⇨Grayscale.**

2. **Choose Image⇨Mode⇨Duotone.**

3. **In the Duotone dialog box, select Duotone from the Type drop-down list.**

    Your choices range from *monotone* (one-color) up to *quadtone* (four-color). Black is assigned automatically as the first ink, but you can change it, if you like.

4. **To assign a second ink color, click the white swatch immediately under the black swatch.**

    The Color Picker appears, as shown in Figure 2-4.

**FIGURE 2-4:**
Click the white
swatch to open
the Color Picker
dialog box.

5. **Click the Color Libraries button, and then select Pantone Solid Coated as the library.**

6. **Now comes the fun part: Type (quickly!) the Pantone or PMS number you want to access, and then click OK. If you type too slowly, the incorrect number will appear.**

There's no text field for you to enter the number, so don't look for one. Just type the number while the Color Libraries dialog box is open.

Try entering **300** to select PMS 300. You can already see that you've created a tone curve.

7. **Click the Curve button to the left of the ink color to further tweak the colors.**

8. **Click and drag the curve to adjust the black in the shadow areas, perhaps to bring down the color overall. Then experiment with the results.**

9. **(Optional) If you like your duotone settings, store them by clicking the small Preset Options button to the right of the Preset drop-down list, as shown in Figure 2-5. Type a name into the Name text box, browse to a location on your computer, and then click Save.**

**TIP**

You can also use one of the presets that Adobe provides. Do this by selecting an option from the Presets drop-down menu at the top of the Duotone dialog box.

Click the Preset Options button to find your saved presets.

Duotone images must be saved in the Photoshop Encapsulated PostScript (EPS) format in order to support the spot colors. If you choose another format, you risk the possibility of converting colors into a build of CMYK (Cyan, Magenta, Yellow, and Black).

10. **Click OK when you're finished.**

# Index color

Typically you don't edit your images in the Index color mode, but you probably have saved a file in this mode. If you have ever saved a GIF file out of Photoshop, you have experienced working with Indexed color firsthand. Indexed Color mode (see Figure 2-6) uses a color lookup table (CLUT) to create the image from a limited palette of colors.

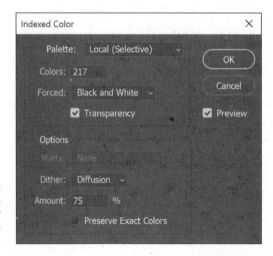

A CLUT contains all colors that make up an image, like a box of crayons used to create artwork. If you have a box of only eight crayons that are used to color an image, you have a CLUT of only eight colors. Of course, your image would look much better if you used the 64-count box of crayons with the sharpener on the back, but those additional colors also increase the size of the CLUT and the file size.

The highest number of colors that can be in Indexed Color mode is 256. When saving web images, you often have to define a color table in order to keep a file size small. We discuss saving files for the web in Chapter 9 of this minibook.

**TIP**

Choose Image⇨Mode⇨Color Table to see the color table making up an image.

# RGB

RGB (Red, Green, Blue) mode, shown in Figure 2-7, is the standard format you work in if you import images from a digital camera or import images from a copier or scanner. For complete access to Photoshop's features, RGB is the best color mode to work in. If you're working on images for use on the web, color copiers, desktop color printers, or onscreen presentations, stay in RGB mode.

**FIGURE 2-7:**
RGB creates the image from red, green, and blue.

**REMEMBER**

If you're having an image printed on a press (for example, if you're having it professionally printed), it must be separated. Don't convert images to CMYK mode until you've finished the color correction and you know that your color settings are accurate. A good print service may want the RGB file so that it can complete an accurate conversion.

# CMYK

CMYK (Cyan, Magenta, Yellow, Black) mode is used for final separations for the press. Use a good magnifying glass to look closely at anything printed in color, and you may see the CMYK colors that created it. A typical four-color printing press has a plate for each color and runs the colors in the order of cyan, magenta, yellow, and then black.

Don't take lightly the task of converting an image into this mode. You need to make decisions when you convert an image to CMYK, such as where to print the file and on which paper stock, so that the resulting image is the best it can be. Talk to your print provider for specifications that are important when converting to CMYK mode.

## LAB color

The LAB (Lightness, A channel, and B channel) color mode is used by many high-end color professionals because of its wide color range. Using LAB, you can make adjustments to *luminosity* (lightness) without affecting color. In this mode, you can select and change an *L* (lightness or luminosity) channel without affecting the *A* channel (green and red) and the *B* channel (blue and yellow).

LAB mode is also good to use if you're in a color-managed environment and want to easily move from one color system to another with no loss of color.

Some professionals prefer to sharpen images in LAB mode because they can select just the Lightness channel and choose Filter⇨Sharpen⇨Unsharp Mask to sharpen only the gray matter of the image, leaving the color noise-free.

## Multichannel

Multichannel is used for many things; you can end up in this mode and not know how you got there. Deleting a channel from an RGB, a CMYK, or a LAB image automatically converts the image to Multichannel mode. This mode supports multiple spot colors.

## Bit depth

You have more functionality in 16-bit and even 32-bit mode. Depending on your needs, however, you may spend most of your time in 8-bit mode, which is more than likely all you need.

*Bit depth,* or *pixel depth* or *color depth,* measures how much color information is available to display or print each pixel in an image. Greater bit depth means more available colors and more accurate color representation in the digital image. In Photoshop, this increase in accuracy also limits some available features, so don't use it unless you have a specific request or need for it.

To use 16-bit or 32-bit color mode, you also must have a source to provide you with that information, such as a scanner or camera that offers a choice to scan in either mode.

IN THIS CHAPTER

» **Discovering the selection tools**

» **Painting selections the easy way**

» **Refining your selections**

» **Keeping selections for later use**

» **Using the Vanishing Point feature**

# Chapter 3

# Making Selective Changes

Photoshop is well known for its capability to create compositions and for its retouching capabilities. What you don't want to see in a finished product is obvious retouching or compositions that look contrived. (The exception is if you intend an image to be humorous, such as putting baby Joey's head on Daddy's body.)

This is when a solid knowledge of the selection tools pays off. In this chapter, you try out several selection methods and see how to use the available tools to make images look as though you *haven't* retouched or edited them. Even if you're an experienced Photoshop user, this chapter provides a plethora of tips and tricks that can save you time and help make your images look absolutely convincing.

## Getting to Know the Selection Tools

You create selections by using selection tools. Think of *selections* as windows in which you can make changes to pixels. Areas not selected are *masked*, which means that they're unaffected by changes, much like when you tape window and door frames before painting the walls. In this section, we briefly describe the selection tools and show you how to use them. You must be familiar with these tools in order to do *anything* in Photoshop.

As with all Photoshop tools, the Options bar (viewed across the top of the Photoshop window) changes when you choose different selection tools. The keyboard commands you read about in this section exist on the tool Options bar and appear as buttons across the top.

If you move a selection with the Move tool, pixels move as you drag, leaving a blank spot in the image. To *clone* a selection (to copy and move the selection at the same time), Alt+drag (Windows) or Option+drag (Mac) the selection with the Move tool.

## The Marquee tool

The Marquee tool is the main selection tool; by that, we mean that you use it most often for creating selections. The exception, of course, is when a special situation calls for a special tool — the Lasso, Magic Wand, Quick Selection, or Refine Radius tool (located in the Refine Edge dialog box). Throughout this section, we describe creating (and then deselecting) an active selection area; we also provide you with tips for working with selections.

The Marquee tool includes the Rectangular Marquee (for creating rectangular selections), Elliptical Marquee (for creating round or elliptical selections), and Single Row Marquee or Single Column Marquee tools (for creating a selection of a single row or column of pixels). You can access these other Marquee tools by holding down the default Rectangle Marquee tool in the Tools panel.

To create a selection, select one of the Marquee tools (remember that you can press M to do this), and then drag anywhere on your image. When you release the mouse button, you create an active selection area. When you're working on an active selection area, whichever effects you choose are applied to the whole selection.

To deselect an area, you have three choices:

>> Choose Select⇨Deselect.

>> Press Ctrl+D (Windows) or ⌘+D (Mac).

>> While using a selection tool, click outside the selection area.

## Creating rectangular and elliptical selections

How you make a selection is important because it determines how realistic your edits appear on the image. You can use the following tips and tricks when creating both rectangular and elliptical selections:

>> Add to a selection by holding down the Shift key; drag to create a second selection that intersects the original selection (see the left image in Figure 3-1). The two selections become one big selection.

**FIGURE 3-1:**
You can add to a selection by holding down the Shift key.

>> Delete from an existing selection by holding down the Alt (Windows) or Option (Mac) key, and then dragging to create a second selection that intersects the original selection where you want to take away from the original selection (shown on the right in Figure 3-1).

>> Constrain a rectangle or an ellipse to a square or circle by Shift+dragging; make sure that you release the mouse button before you release the Shift key. Holding down the Shift key makes a square or circle only when there are no other selections. (Otherwise, it adds to the selection.)

>> Make the selection from the center by Alt+dragging (Windows) or Option+dragging (Mac); make sure that you release the mouse button before releasing the Alt (Windows) or Option (Mac) key.

>> Create a square or circle from the center outward by Alt+Shift+dragging (Windows) or Option+Shift+dragging (Mac). Again, make sure that you always release the mouse button before releasing the modifier keys.

>> When making a selection, hold down the spacebar before releasing the mouse button to drag the selection to another location.

Making Selective Changes

## Setting a fixed size

If you've created an effect that you particularly like — say, changing a block of color in your image — and you want to apply it multiple times throughout, you can do so. To make the same selection multiple times, follow these steps:

1. **With the Marquee tool selected, select Fixed Size from the Style drop-down list on the Options bar.**

   You can also select Fixed Ratio from the Style drop-down list to create a proportionally correct selection not fixed to an exact size.

2. **On the Options bar, type the Width and Height values into the appropriate text fields.**

   You can change ruler increments by choosing Edit➪Preferences➪Units & Rulers (Windows) or Photoshop➪Preferences➪Units & Rulers (Mac).

3. **Click the image.**

   A selection sized to your values appears.

4. **With the selection tool, drag the selection to the location you want selected.**

Shift+drag a selection to keep it aligned to a 45-degree or 90-degree angle.

## Making floating and nonfloating selections

When you're using a selection tool, such as the Marquee tool, your selections are *floating* by default, which means that you can drag them to another location without affecting the underlying pixels. You know that your selection is floating by the little rectangle that appears on the cursor. (See the left image in Figure 3-2.)

**· FIGURE 3-2:**
The Float icon is used on the left, and the Move icon is used on the right.

If you want to, however, you can move the underlying pixels. Using the selection tool of your choice, just hold down the Ctrl (Windows) or ⌘ (Mac) key to temporarily access the Move tool; the cursor changes to a pointer with scissors, denoting that your selection is nonfloating. Now, when you drag, the pixel data comes with the selection (as shown on the right in Figure 3-2).

**TIP**

Hold down Alt+Ctrl (Windows) or Option+⌘ (Mac) while using a selection tool and drag to clone (copy) pixels from one location to another. Add the Shift key, and the cloned copy is constrained to a straight, 45-degree, or 90-degree angle.

## The Lasso tool

Use the Lasso tool for *freeform selections* (selections of an irregular shape). To use the Lasso tool, click and drag to create a path surrounding the area that you want to select. Be careful! If you don't return to the starting point to close the selection before you release the mouse button, Photoshop completes the path by finding the most direct route back to your starting point.

**TIP**

As with the Marquee tool, you can press the Shift key to add to a lasso selection and press the Alt (Windows) or Option (Mac) key to delete from a lasso selection.

Hold down the Lasso tool to show the hidden Lasso tools:

» **Polygonal Lasso tool:** Click a starting point, and then click and release from point to point until you come back to close the selection.

» **Magnetic Lasso tool:** Click to create a starting point, and then hover the cursor near an edge in your image. The Magnetic Lasso tool is magnetically attracted to edges; as you move the cursor near an edge, the Magnetic Lasso tool creates a selection along that edge. Click to manually set points in the selection; when you return to the starting point, click to close the selection.

You may find that the Polygonal Lasso and the Magnetic Lasso tools make less-than-ideal selections. Take a look at the later section "Painting a selection with the Quick Mask tool" for tips on making finer selections.

## The Quick Selection tool

The Quick Selection tool lets you quickly "paint" a selection with a round brush tip of adjustable size. Click and drag, and then watch as the selection expands outward and automatically follows defined edges in the image. A Refine Edge command lets you improve the quality of the selection edges and visualize the selection in different ways for easy editing.

**Making Selective Changes**

Follow these steps to find out how you can take advantage of this tool:

1. **Open a file that requires a selection.**

   If you downloaded the DummiesCCFiles, as noted in Chapter 1 of this mini-book, you can use the file named Model01 in the Book03_Photoshop folder.

2. **Select the Quick Selection tool.**

3. **Position the cursor over the area you want to select. Notice the brush size displayed with the cursor; click and drag to start painting the selection.**

**TIP**

   You can adjust the size of the painting selection by pressing the left bracket key ([) to make the brush size smaller or the right bracket key (]) to make the brush size larger.

   By using the Add to Selection or Subtract from Selection buttons on the Options bar, you can paint more of the selection or deselect active areas. (See Figure 3-3.)

**FIGURE 3-3:**
Use the Quick Selection tool to paint your selection.

If you would rather use keyboard shortcuts to add or delete to the selection, you can hold down the Alt (Windows) or Option (Mac) key to delete from a selection. As a default, you do not have to hold down any key to add to a selection. If adding to the selection is not working, your default Add to Selection tool might have been switched, as pointed out in Figure 3-4. Click on the Center selection button in order to turn Add to Selection back on, or simply hold down the Shift key and paint to add additional content to your selection.

**FIGURE 3-4:**
When the Quick Selection tool is active, you have additional selection options available in the control panel.

The Quick Selection tool does not make a perfect selection, but it provides a great start for even the most difficult selections. Keep reading to see how you can take your selection even further with the Select and Mask feature in Photoshop.

## The Magic Wand tool

The Magic Wand tool is particularly helpful when you're working on an image of high contrast or with a limited number of colors. This tool selects individual pixels of similar shades and colors. Select the Magic Wand tool, click anywhere on an image, and hope for the best — the Magic Wand tool isn't magic. You decide how successful this tool is. What we mean is that *you* control how closely matched each pixel must be in order for the Magic Wand tool to include it in the selection. You do so by setting the tolerance level on the Options bar.

When you select the Magic Wand tool, a Tolerance text field appears on the Options bar. As a default, the tolerance is set to 32. When you click with a setting of 32, the Magic Wand tool selects all pixels within 32 shades (steps) of the color you clicked. If it didn't select as much as you want, increase the value in the Tolerance text field (all the way up to 255). The number you enter varies with each individual selection. If you're selecting white napkins on an off-white tablecloth, for example, you can set the number as low as 5 so that the selection doesn't leak into other areas. For colored fabric with lots of tonal values, on the other hand, you might increase the tolerance to 150.

**TIP**

Don't fret if you miss the entire selection when using the Magic Wand tool. Hold down the Shift key and click in the missed areas. If the tool selects too much, choose Edit➪Undo (step backward) or press Ctrl+Z (Windows) or ⌘+Z (Mac), reduce the value in the Tolerance text field, and try again.

Making Selective Changes

# Painting a selection with the Quick Mask tool

If you have fuzzy selections (fur, hair, or leaves, for example) or you're having difficulty using the selection tools, the Quick Mask tool can be a huge help because it enables you to paint your selection uniformly in one fell swoop. If you want to follow along in this section, you can open the image named duck that is located in the Book03_Photoshop folder in the sample files that have been provided for you.

To enter Quick Mask mode, create a selection, and then press Q. (Pressing Q again exits you from Quick Mask mode.) You can also click the Quick Mask button at the bottom of the Tools panel. If you have a printing background, you'll notice that the Quick Mask mode, set at its default color (red), resembles something that you may want to forget: rubylith and amberlith. (Remember slicing up those lovely films with X-Acto blades before computer masking came along?) In Quick Mask mode, Photoshop shows your image as it appears through the mask. The clear part is selected; what's covered in the mask isn't selected.

**TIP**

Change the default red color of the mask by double-clicking the Edit in Quick Mask Mode button (at the bottom of the Tools panel). The tooltip says Edit in Standard Mode if you're already in Quick Mask mode. This opens the Quick Mask Options dialog box, shown in Figure 3-5.

**FIGURE 3-5:** Change the color of the Quick Mask.

To create and implement a quick mask, follow these steps:

1. **Use the Quick Selection tool or another selection tool to create a selection before you enter the Quick Mask mode. This gives you a kickstart into making a much better mask.**

   In the example of the duck image, the Quick Selection tool was selected and the duck was painted with the tool. The result is shown in Figure 3-6.

2. **Press Q to enter Quick Mask mode.**

3. **Press D to change the foreground and background color boxes to the default colors of black and white.**

4. **Select the Brush tool and start painting with black in the clear area of the image in Quick Mask mode, as shown in Figure 3-6.**

**FIGURE 3-6:**
Start with a selection and then press Q.

It doesn't have to be pretty; just get a stroke or two in there.

5. **Press Q to return to Selection mode.**

You're now out of Quick Mask mode. Notice that where you painted with black (it turned red in Quick Mask mode), the pixels are no longer selected, as shown in Figure 3-7.

**FIGURE 3-7:**
Painting with black in the Quick Mask mode masks out the area and deselects it.

Making Selective Changes

6. **Press Q again to reenter Quick Mask mode, and then press X.**

   Pressing X switches the foreground and background colors, giving you white in the foreground and black in the background.

7. **With the Brush tool, paint several white strokes in the red mask area. If you are working on the duck image, paint over your red lines that you created, and paint over the red eye to make sure that it is selected.**

   The white strokes turn clear in Quick Mask mode.

8. **Press Q to return to Selection mode.**

   The area you painted white in Quick Mask mode is now selected.

When you're in Quick Mask mode, you can paint white over areas you want selected and black over areas you don't want selected. When painting in Quick Mask mode, increase the brush size by pressing the ] key. Decrease the brush size by pressing the [ key.

In Selection mode, your selection seems to have a hard edge; you can soften those hard edges by using a softer brush in Quick Mask mode. To make a brush softer, press Shift+[. To make a brush harder, press Shift+].

Because Quick Mask mode makes selections based on the mask's values, you can create a mask by selecting the Gradient tool and dragging it across the image in Quick Mask mode. When you exit Quick Mask mode, it looks as though there's a straight-line selection, but the selection transitions the same as your gradient did. Choose any filter from the Filters menu and notice how the filter transitions into the untouched part of the image to which you applied the gradient.

If you're working in Quick Mask mode, choose Window➪Channels to see that what you're working on is a temporary alpha channel. See the later section "Saving Selections" for more about alpha channels.

# Manipulating Selections with Refine Selection

After you master creating selections, you'll find that working with the selections — painting, transforming, and feathering them — can be easy and fun.

# Transforming selections

Don't deselect and start over again if you can just nudge or resize a selection. You can scale, rotate, and even distort an existing selection. You can try this feature with the image named flatpanel that is located in the Book03_Photoshop folder.

Follow these steps to transform a selection:

1. **Create a selection, and then choose Select⇨Transform Selection.**

   You can use the bounding box to resize and rotate your selection:

   - Drag the handles to make the selection larger or smaller. Drag a corner handle to adjust width and height simultaneously. Shift+drag a corner handle to size proportionally.

   - Position the cursor outside the bounding box to see the Rotate icon; drag when it appears to rotate the selection. Shift+drag to constrain to straight, 45-degree, or 90-degree angles.

   - Ctrl+drag (Windows) or ⌘+drag (Mac) a corner point to distort the selection, as shown in Figure 3-8.

**FIGURE 3-8:**
Distort, resize, and rotate a selection with the Transform Selection feature.

2. **Press Enter or Return or double-click in the center of the selection area to confirm the transformation; press Esc to release the transformation and return to the original selection.**

# Feathering

Knowing how to retouch an image means little if you don't know how to make the retouching discreet. If you boost the color using curves to the CEO's face, do you want it to look like a pancake has been attached to his cheek? Of course not — that isn't discreet (or wise). If you *feather* a selection (blur its edges) instead, you create a natural-looking transition between the selection and the background of the image, as you see in Figure 3-9.

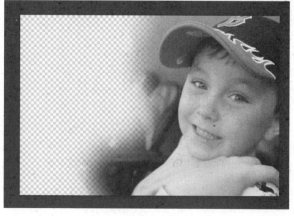

**FIGURE 3-9:**
No feathering applied to the selection (top); feathering applied to the selection (bottom).

To feather a selection, follow these steps:

**1. Create a selection.**

Use any selection technique that you like. You could make a quick selection with the Rectangular or Elliptical Marquee tools, or create a custom selection with the Lasso or Quick Selection tool.

**2. When you have any selection tool active, the Select and Mask button becomes available in the Options across the top of the Photoshop work area. Click the Select and Mask button.**

You are then entered into the Select and Mask workspace. This dialog box on the right provides you with a selection preview option and with many settings that can improve your selection; for right now, however, just focus on feathering.

**3. In the Properties panel, click on the View option and change it to View on Layers, as shown in Figure 3-10.**

This allows you to see the image and any transparency that will be applied when you confirm the mask that you are refining.

**FIGURE 3-10:**
You can change the view of how the image appears in the preview window.

**4. In the Global Refinements section of the Properties panel, click and drag the slider for Feather to the right until you see the right amount of feathering, or *vignetting*, for your image, as in Figure 3-11.**

**FIGURE 3-11:**
Use the Refine Edge feature to preview your feather amount.

**TECHNICAL STUFF**

The results of the feathering depend on the resolution of the image. A feather of 20 pixels in a 72 ppi (pixels per inch) image is a much larger area than a feather of 20 pixels in a 300 ppi image. Typical amounts for a nice vignette on an edge of an image are 20 to 50 pixels. Experiment with images to find what works best for you.

5. **There are actually two directions that you can go after you have determined the right amount of feathering:**

   • *Leave the rest of the settings at their default and click OK.* This enables you to use the feathered selection to apply subtle changes in the image, such as a curve change to lighten or darken an image, as you see in Figure 3-12.

**FIGURE 3-12:**
A curve correction was applied to make this section lighter.

This feathering effect creates a nice, soft edge to your image, but it's also useful when retouching images. If you want to try the change shown in Figure 3-12, follow these steps: a.) Make sure that your feathered selection is still active; if it isn't, try Select⇨Reselect; b.) choose Image⇨Adjustments⇨ Curves; c.) click in the center of the curve to add an anchor point and drag up to lighten the image; this lightens the midtones of the image.

Notice how the lightening fades out so that the correction has no definite edge. You can have more fun like this in Chapter 6 of this minibook, in which we cover color correction.

- *Choose Layer Mask in the Output To drop-down list of the Select and Mask workspace, and then click OK.* This option keeps only the feathered selection, making the area outside your selection transparent, as you see in Figure 3-13.

    When you do this, a layer mask is created, which you can see in Window⇨Layers. Hold the Shift key and click the thumbnail of that mask in the Layers panel to turn it off and on.

**FIGURE 3-13:** The selection used for a mask.

## Tweaking the edges of a selection in the Select and Mask workspace

You can also use the Select and Mask feature to create more difficult selections. In this next section, you review the capabilities of the Select and Mask feature. If you like, you can use the sample image named model for this example.

Follow these steps:

1. **Make a selection.**

    Painting your selection with the Quick Selection tool is an easy way to get started.

2. **With any selection tool active, click the Select and Mask button on the Options bar at the top of the Photoshop window.**

    You are now entered into the Select and Mask workspace.

## Select an appropriate preview method

You can choose a preview method by selecting the View drop-down list at the top of the Properties panel. This preview option helps you to better see the effects of the changes you are making in this dialog box.

This list describes the other selections you can choose from the View drop-down list of the Refine Edge dialog box:

>> **Onion Skin:** Produces a preview similar to what you might see if you were looking through onion skin paper and similar to an animation-style onion skin scheme.

>> **Marching Ants:** Shows the marquee selection with no image masked.

>> **Overlay:** Shows the default, slightly transparent mask. It's typically red unless you have changed the mask color.

>> **On Black:** Reveals black around the masked area.

>> **On White:** Reveals white around the masked area.

>> **Black and White:** Reveals the masked area as black and the nonmasked area as white. This option is helpful if you want to see only the mask and not the image area.

>> **On Layers:** Bound to be the most popular view if you're creating composites. From this view, you can see the layers and how they're affected by your selection.

TIP

You can cycle through views by pressing F or disable the view by pressing X.

For this example, you can choose the On Layers view.

## Making adjustments with Edge Detection

The Edge Detection section of the Properties panel offers you the opportunity to make refinements to the selection edge. To see it in action, follow these steps:

1. **Select the Smart Radius checkbox, as shown in Figure 3-14.**

   The Smart Radius feature automatically adjusts the radius for hard and soft edges found in the border region.

2. **Increase the radius by dragging the slider to the right.**

   The Radius slider lets you precisely adjust the border area in which edge refinement occurs. Depending on the content, you will increase or decrease the radius.

3. **If you're interested in seeing the radius, select the Show Edge checkbox in the upper-right corner of the Select and Mask workspace.**

**FIGURE 3-14:**
Refining the edge
of a selection.

## Using the Refine Radius tool

To further improve the selection, click the Refine Radius tool, shown in Figure 3-15. By pressing either the right (]) or left bracket ([) key, you can increase or decrease the size of the Refine Radius tool and edit your edge selection by painting the edge of it. If your results are a little too drastic, hold down the Alt or Option key while painting over the area with the Refine Radius tool again. This technique is especially helpful for creating selections of hair or fur.

**FIGURE 3-15:**
Use the Refine
Radius tool to
make difficult
selections, like
fur, easier to
create.

**Making Selective Changes**

## Making additional refinements

But wait — there's more! You can find additional refinements in the Adjust Edge section of the Properties panel in the Select and Mask workspace:

>> **Smooth:** Reduces irregular areas in the selection boundary

>> **Feather:** Creates a soft-edged transition between the selection and its surrounding pixels

>> **Contrast:** Sharpens selection edges and removes fuzzy artifacts

>> **Shift Edge:** Contracts or expands to shrink or enlarge the selection boundary

## Selecting color decontamination

Color decontamination can create unwanted artifacts, and when this option is selected, the output option is set to create a new layer, which helps avoid overwriting the original color pixels.

## Choosing output settings

As discussed earlier in this chapter, you can choose how you want selections implemented: only selection edges, a new layer, or a layer mask, for example. If you're like most professionals, you want to make sure not to affect the original imagery unless you're certain that you have the selection nailed down.

Here are your output options on the Output To drop-down list:

>> **Selection:** The typical selection of a dashed selection, referred to as *marching ants*

>> **Layer Mask:** Creates a mask on the active layer

>> **New Layer:** Duplicates the active layer and applies the refined selection to the transparency of the layer

>> **New Layer with Mask:** Duplicates the active layer and uses the refined selection or mask as the layer mask

>> **New Document:** The same as the New Layer option but creates the new layer in a new document

>> **New Document with Layer Mask:** The same as the New Layer with Mask option but creates the new layer in a new document

If you want to play it safe, select Layer Mask from the Output To drop-down list. This option offers you the opportunity to edit the layer mask, using the painting tools just as you did with the Quick Mask tool, or to turn off the mask (by Shift-clicking the mask in the Layers panel). Read more about how to work with layer masks in Chapter 8 of this minibook.

TIP

If you worked hard to make the perfect selection, don't forget to select the Remember Settings checkbox so that your settings apply the next time you open the Refine Edge dialog box.

# Saving Selections

The term *alpha channel* sounds complicated, but it's simply a saved selection. Depending on the mode you're in, you already have several channels to contend with. A selection is just an extra channel that you can call on at any time.

To create an alpha channel, follow these steps:

**1.** **Create a selection that you want to save.**

**2.** **Choose Select⇨Save Selection.**

**3.** **Name the selection and click OK.**

An additional named channel that contains your selection appears in the Channels panel.

To load a saved selection, follow these steps:

**1.** **Choose Select⇨Load Selection.**

The Load Selection dialog box appears.

**2.** **Select a named channel from the Channel drop-down list.**

If you have an active selection and then choose to load a selection, you have additional options. With an active selection, you can select one of the following options:

- *New Selection:* Eliminate the existing selection and create a new selection based on the channel you select.

- *Add to Selection:* Add the channel to the existing selection.

- *Subtract from Selection:* Subtract the channel from the existing selection.

- *Intersect with Selection:* Intersect the channel with the existing selection.

**3.** **Click OK.**

Other Adobe applications, such as InDesign, Illustrator, Premiere, and After Effects, also recognize alpha channels.

# Preserving Corrective Perspective with the Vanishing Point Feature

The incredible Vanishing Point feature lets you preserve correct perspective in edits of images that contain perspective planes, such as the sides of a building. You can do much with this feature, and we provide you with a simple introduction. Try experimenting with multiple planes and copying and pasting items into the Vanishing Point window for even more effects. Follow these steps:

1. **Open a file that you want to apply a perspective filter to.**

   If you don't have an appropriate image handy, you can find one at in the Book03_Photoshop folder. For this example, the vanishing_point_exercise image could work well.

2. **Create a new, blank layer by clicking the Create a New Layer button at the bottom of the Layers panel.**

   If you create a new layer every time you use Vanishing Point, the results appear on a separate layer, preserving your original image, because you can delete the result of the vanishing point filter and still retain the original layer.

3. **Choose Filter⇨Vanishing Point.**

   A separate Vanishing Point window appears. If you see an error message about an existing plane, click OK.

   If you're using a sample file from Photoshop, it will have a perspective plane already created for you. To help you understand this feature better, delete the existing plane by pressing the Delete or Backspace key.

4. **Select the Create Plane tool and define the four corner nodes of the plane surface. In Figure 3-16, the plane is built on the missing stone wall on the left side of the doorway. If necessary, press Ctrl+– (Windows) or ⌘+– (Mac) to zoom back to see the entire image.**

**TIP**

   Try to use objects in the image — for example, parts of the existing wall — to help create the plane.

   After the four corner nodes of the plane are created, the tool automatically is switched to the Edit Plane tool.

**FIGURE 3-16:**
Use objects
in an image
to build a
perspective
plane.

**5.** **Select and drag the corner nodes to make an accurate plane.**

The plane grid should appear blue, not yellow or red, if it's accurate.

After creating the plane, you can move, scale, or reshape the plane. Keep in mind that your results depend on how accurately the plane lines up with the perspective of the image.

**TIP**

You can use your first Vanishing Point session to simply create perspective planes and then click OK. The planes appear in subsequent Vanishing Point sessions when you choose Filter⇨Vanishing Point. Saving perspective planes is especially useful if you plan to copy and paste an image into Vanishing Point and need to have a readymade plane to target.

**6.** **Choose the Stamp tool in the Vanishing Point window and then select On from the Heal drop-down list on the Options bar.**

**7.** **With the Stamp tool still selected, cross over part of the area or part of the image you want to clone and Alt-click (Windows) or Option-click (Mac) to define it as the source to be cloned.**

In the image vanishing_point_exercise, the middle part of the stone wall was Alt/Option+clicked on to set it as the source for the cloning.

**8.** **Without clicking, move toward the back of the perspective plane (you can even clone outside the plane), and then click and drag to reproduce the cloned part of the image.**

Notice in Figure 3-17 that it's cloned as a smaller version, in the correct perspective for its new location.

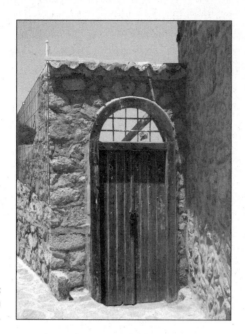

**9.** **Start from Step 7 and clone any region of an image closer to the front of the perspective pane.**

The cloned region is now cloned as a larger version of itself.

You can use the Marquee tool options (Feather, Opacity, Heal, and Move Mode) at any time, either before or after making the selection. When you move the Marquee tool, the Stamp tool, or the Brush tool into a plane, the bounding box is highlighted, indicating that the plane is active.

**10.** **Click OK.**

To preserve the perspective plane information in an image, save your document in JPEG, PSD, or TIFF format.

**IN THIS CHAPTER**

» **Selecting the Pen tool for the task**

» **Using a path as a selection**

» **Creating curved paths**

» **Creating clipping paths**

» **Putting shape layers to work**

Chapter **4**

# Using the Photoshop Pen Tool

The Pen tool is the ultimate method to make precise selections. You can also use it to create vector shapes and clipping paths (silhouettes). In this chapter, you see how to take advantage of this super multitasking tool. This chapter also shows you how to apply paths made with the Pen tool to create selections, shapes, and silhouettes using clipping paths.

**REMEMBER**

If you're interested in fundamental practices when using the Pen tool, check out Book 5, Chapter 4, where we cover the Pen tool in more detail. Using that lesson helps you in Photoshop, too, because the Pen tool works essentially the same way in both Illustrator and Photoshop.

We recommend that you use the Pen tool as much as you can to truly master its capabilities. At first it may seem awkward, but it gets easier! Knowing how to effectively use the Pen tool puts you a grade above the average Photoshop user, and the quality of your selections will show it. Read Book 5 on Adobe Illustrator, Chapter 4 for tips and tricks on how to use the Pen tool. It works very much the same in all the Adobe programs.

# Selecting the Right Pen Tool for the Task

Select the Pen tool from the Tools panel, and note the default mode setting of the Pen tool on the left side of the Options bar. You can select the following options from the Pick Tool Mode drop-down list, as you see in Figure 4-1:

» **Shape:** Creates a new shape layer, a filled layer that contains the vector path.

» **Path:** Creates a path only; no layer is created.

» **Pixels:** Creates pixels directly on the image. No editable path or layer is created. This option may not be useful to new users, but some seasoned users prefer it because it's the only way to access the Line tool from earlier versions.

**FIGURE 4-1:**
Select the mode of the Pen tool from the Options bar.

# Using a Path as a Selection

You can use the Pen tool to create precise selections that would be difficult to create using other selection methods. The Pen tool produces clean edges that print well and can be edited using the Direct Selection tool. Before using the Pen tool, make sure that you select Path from the Pick Tool Mode drop-down list on the Options bar.

To create a path as a selection (which is extremely helpful when you're trying to make a precise selection), follow these steps to create a simple straight line path:

1. **Open any file or create a new, blank file.**

   It is best to practice on an image that has a straight or angular item in it.

2. **Select the Pen tool.**

   Make sure that Path is selected from the Pick Tool Mode drop-down list on the Options bar or else you'll create a shape layer.

REMEMBER

3. **Click to place your first anchor point, and then click another location. Notice that the anchor points are connected with a path.**

### 4. Continue clicking around the object that you are selecting.

When you return to your original starting point, a closed circle appears, indicating that you are closing this path, as you see in Figure 4-2.

**FIGURE 4-2:**
Using the Pen tool, click from one segment to another; close it at the end.

### 5. Choose Window⇨Paths.

In the Paths panel, you can create new paths and activate existing paths, apply a stroke, or turn paths into selections by clicking the icons at the bottom of the panel. (See Figure 4-3.)

### 6. Click and drag the Work Path down to the Create New Path icon at the bottom of the Paths panel.

The path is now named Path 1 and is saved. You can also double-click to rename the path if you like.

Fill Path with Foreground Color

Stroke Path with Brush

Load Path as Selection

Make Work Path from Selection

Delete Current Path

Create New Path

Add a Mask

**FIGURE 4-3:**
The Paths panel and its options.

### 7. Click the Load Path as Selection icon.

The path is converted into a selection.

Using the Photoshop
Pen Tool

Use this quick and easy method for turning an existing path into a selection: Ctrl-click (Windows) or ⌘-click (Mac) the path thumbnail in the Paths panel.

# Creating Curved Paths

To create paths that are on a curve, you first need to understand how the Bézier curve works. A Bézier curve in its most common form is a simple cubic equation that can be used in any number of useful ways, but especially when creating curves in a path. Originally developed by Pierre Bézier in the 1970s for CAD/CAM operations, it became the underpinnings of the entire Adobe PostScript drawing model.

To get a better understanding of Bézier curves, work through this simple exercise:

1. **Open an image.**

    In this example, an image of an apple is used.

2. **Click and drag the edge of the object that you are selecting. A directional line appears. (This is not a path; it is just a directional line determining the curve of your future path.) Drag along the edge of the object and then release, as you see in Figure 4-4.**

3. **Move the cursor along the edge of the object that you want to select and then click and drag again.**

    Pay attention to the directional lines and have them flow, either on the shape or along the side of the shape. The path you want should fall into place with just some minor tweaking.

**FIGURE 4-4:** Click and drag to make curved paths.

4. **Continue clicking and dragging to make the path, and then close the shape.**

Do not worry if the path is not perfect.

5. **Choose the Direct Selection tool by holding down the Path Selection tool, as you see in Figure 4-5.**

Use this tool to adjust your path by clicking anchor points and directional lines and repositioning them to provide you with a more accurate selection, as you see in Figure 4-6.

**FIGURE 4-5:** Select the hidden Direct Selection tool.

**FIGURE 4-6:** Edit your path with the Direct Selection tool.

# Clipping Paths

If you want to create a beautiful silhouette that transfers well to other applications as you see Figure 4-7, create a clipping path. A *clipping path* is essentially a vector path that defines what part of the image is visible and what part is transparent. Typically a path is created around an object that you want to silhouette.

Keep in mind that you do not have to define a clipping path if you are using your image in other Adobe applications, such as InDesign and Illustrator. A clipping path is helpful if you are trying to keep an image transparent in apps such as PowerPoint, Word, or various video-editing applications.

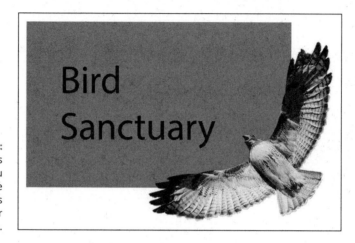

**FIGURE 4-7:**
Clipping paths
enable you
to create
silhouettes
in other
applications.

To create a clipping path, follow these steps:

1. **Use the Pen tool to create a path around the image area that will become the silhouette.**

2. **In the Paths panel, choose Save Path from the panel menu (click the triangle in the upper-right corner of the panel), as shown in Figure 4-8, and then name the path.**

   If Save Path is not visible, your path has already been saved; skip to Step 3.

3. **From the same panel menu, choose Clipping Path.**

4. **In the Clipping Path dialog box, select your path from the drop-down list, if it's not already selected; click OK.**

   Leave the Flatness Device Pixels text field blank unless you need to change it. The flatness value determines how many device pixels are used to create your silhouette. The higher the amount, the fewer points are created, thereby allowing for faster processing time. This speed comes at a cost, though: If you set the flatness value too high, you may see (if you look close) straight edges instead of curved edges.

**FIGURE 4-8:**
Convert your
work path to a
saved path.

**5.** **Choose File➪Save As and, from the Format drop-down list, select Photoshop EPS; in the EPS Options dialog box that appears, accept the defaults and click OK.**

If you see PostScript errors when printing, choose Clipping Path from the panel menu and increase the value to 2 pixels in the Flatness Device Pixels text field. Keep returning to this text field and increasing the value until the file prints, or give up and try printing your document on another printer.

**TIP**

If you're placing this file in other Adobe applications, such as InDesign, you don't need to save the file as EPS; you can leave it as a Photoshop (.psd) file.

Here's an even faster method you can use to create a clipping path that you can use in other Adobe applications, such as InDesign and Illustrator:

**1.** **Create a path around the item you want to keep when you create the clipping path.**

Make sure that you're working on a layer and not on the Background layer. To convert the Background to a layer, hold down the Alt key (Windows) or the Option key (Mac) and double-click the Background layer. The Background layer is now Layer 0.

**2.** **In the Layers panel, click the Add Layer Mask button, and then click the Add Layer Mask button again.**

A layer vector mask is created, and everything outside the path becomes transparent, as shown in Figure 4-9.

You can still edit the path by using the Direct Selection tool.

**Using the Photoshop Pen Tool**

**FIGURE 4-9:**
Creating a
clipping path
the easy way,
with layers.

3. **Save the file in the** `.psd` **format.**

4. **Choose File**➪**Place to put the image, with its clipping path included, into other Adobe applications.**

# Using Shape Layers

When you start creating a path with the Pen tool, Photoshop creates a *path.* You can also choose to make a vector shape or a fill (which essentially creates pixeled, nonvector shapes and paths).

Shape layers can be very useful when the goal of your design is to seamlessly integrate vector shapes and pixel data. A shape layer can contain vector shapes that you can then modify with the same features of any other layer. You can adjust the opacity of the shape layer, change the blending mode, and even apply layer effects to add drop shadows and dimension. Find out how to do this in Chapter 8 of this minibook.

Create a shape layer with any of these methods:

» **Create a shape with the Pen tool.** With the Pen tool, you can create interesting custom shapes and even store them for future use. We show you how in the following section.

» **Use a Vector Shape tool, as shown in Figure 4-10.** *Vector shapes* are premade shapes (you can even create your own) that you can create by dragging the image area with a shape tool.

» **Import a shape from Illustrator.** Choose File➪Place and choose an `.ai` file; when the Options window appears, choose to place the file as a shape layer or a path. This action imports an Illustrator file as a shape layer or path into Photoshop.

**FIGURE 4-10:**
The Vector
Shape tools.

In Photoshop CC, you can access the Vector shape and path tool options directly from the Options bar, as shown in Figure 4-11, when either the Pen tool or a vector shape tool is selected.

**FIGURE 4-11:**
You can switch to
the Vector shape
tool with the
Options bar.

## Creating and using a custom shape

Perhaps you like the wave shape (see Figure 4-12) that's been cropping up in design pieces all over the place.

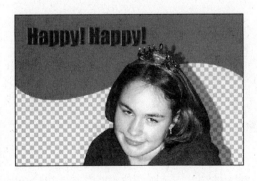

**FIGURE 4-12:**
A custom wave
shape integrated
with an image in
Photoshop.

You can create a wavy shape like that, too. With an image or blank document open, just follow these steps:

1. **Select the Pen tool, and then select Shape from the Pick Tool Mode drop-down list on the Options bar.**

   Refer to Figure 4-11.

2. **Click and drag with the Pen tool to create a wavy shape.**

   Don't worry about the size of the shape. The shape is a vector, so you can scale it up or down to whatever size you need without worrying about making jagged edges. Just make sure to *close* the shape (that is, return to the original point with the end point).

   When you create the shape, it fills in with your foreground color. Try to ignore it if you can; the next section shows you how to change the fill color.

3. **With the shape still selected, choose Edit⇨Define Custom Shape, name the shape wave, and click OK.**

   After you save your custom shape, you can re-create it at any time. If you don't like the shape, choose Window⇨Layers to open the Layers panel, and then drag the shape layer you just created to the Trash Can in the lower-right corner of the panel. If you want to experiment with your custom shape now, continue with these steps.

4. **Click and hold the Rectangle tool to access the other hidden vector tools; select the last tool, the Custom Shape tool.**

   When the Custom Shape tool is selected, a Shape drop-down list appears on the Options bar at the top of the screen, as shown in Figure 4-13.

   You have lots of custom shapes to choose from, including the one you've just created. If you just saved a shape, yours is in the last square; you may have to scroll down to select it.

**FIGURE 4-13:**
A Shape drop-down list appears on the Options bar.

5. **Click to select your custom shape; click and drag in the image area to create your shape.**

   You can make the shape any size you want.

6. **To resize the shape, choose Edit⇨Free Transform Path, press Ctrl+T (Windows) or ⌘+T (Mac), grab a bounding box handle, and drag.**

   Shift+drag a corner handle to keep the shape proportional as you resize it.

**TIP**

Because a shape is created on its own layer, you can experiment with different levels of transparency and blending modes in the Layers panel. Figure 4-14 shows shapes that are partially transparent.

FIGURE 4-14: Experiment with blending modes and opacity changes on shape layers.

## Changing the color of the shape

When you create a shape with a shape tool, the shape takes the color of the current foreground color. To change the color of an existing shape, choose Window⇨Properties. If you have the Shape layer selected, you will see that the Properties panel offers you options for changing the fill and stroke of your shape, as shown in Figure 4-15. The shape layer is considered a live shape because you can make nondestructive changes on this shape, as long as it remains a shape layer and is not flattened into the other parts of the image.

To change the fill, follow these steps:

1. **Create a standard vector shape, such as with the Rectangle tool.**

   *Note:* There is some inconsistency with custom created shapes and the Properties panel at the time of this writing. If you do not see the fill and stroke features in the Properties panel, see the next set of instructions.

2. **Make sure that you have the shape layer selected in the Layers panel.**

3. **Choose Window⇨Properties.**

4. **Click Set Shape Fill Type, as shown in Figure 4-16. A color panel appears from which you can select the type of fill you would like to apply to your selected shape.**

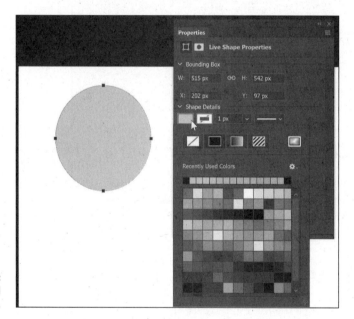

5. **Choose whether you want No fill (clear), a Solid Color fill, a Gradient fill, or a Pattern fill. For this example, use a Solid Color fill.**

6. **From the swatches, choose the color you wish to use. If you prefer to use the Color Picker, click the icon to the right of Pattern fill in the Properties panel.**

# Changing the color fill of a custom shape

If you create a custom shape, you may see only some Mask features in the Properties panel. If that is the case, follow these steps in order to change the color fill:

1. **Select the custom shape layer in the Layers panel.**

2. **Double-click the thumbnail of the shape layer in the Layers panel, as shown in Figure 4-17, or click the Fill color box on the Options bar across the top of the Document window.**

   The Color Picker appears.

3. **To select a new color, drag the Hue slider up or down or click in the large color pane to select a color with the saturation and lightness you want to use. Click OK when you're done.**

**FIGURE 4-17:**
Double-click on the layer thumbnail to choose a fill color from the Picker or from a source outside of the Picker.

**TIP**

With the Color Picker open, you can also move outside the Picker dialog box and sample colors from other open images and objects.

# Changing the stroke on a live vector shape

In addition to changing the fill, you can also change the color, width, and even type of stroke or border on your shape. As with the fill, the Properties panel is used to make these changes, but if you have a custom shape you may not have access to these same controls. The next set of steps take advantage of effects in order to apply a stroke to a custom shape.

To apply a stroke to a live shape, follow these steps:

1. **Select the shape layer to which you want to apply the stroke.**

2. **Choose Window⇨Properties.**

3. **Select Set Shape Stroke Type and choose the type of stroke you wish to apply, as shown in Figure 4-18.**

**FIGURE 4-18:**
Choose the type
of stroke that
you would like
to apply.

4. **Note that you can also change the line width, cap, stroke type, and more. See Figure 4-19 to see some of the other stroke- and shape-related properties you can set in the Properties panel.**

## Creating a stroke on a custom shape

If you want to create a stroke on a custom shape, you may not have the same properties available to you. In order to apply a stroke to a custom shape, follow these steps:

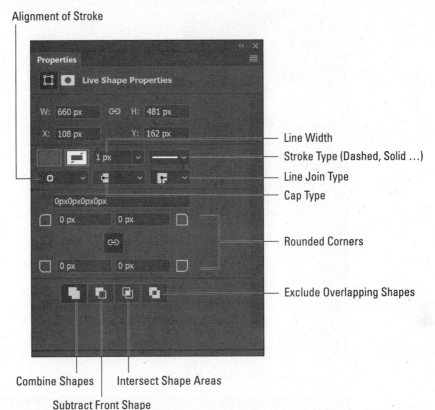

Alignment of Stroke

Line Width

Stroke Type (Dashed, Solid ...)

Line Join Type

Cap Type

Rounded Corners

Exclude Overlapping Shapes

**FIGURE 4-19:**
Stroke- and shape-related properties in the Properties panel.

Combine Shapes

Intersect Shape Areas

Subtract Front Shape

1. Select the custom shape layer in the Layers panel.

2. Choose Stroke from the menu that opens when you click the Add a Layer Style button at the bottom of the Layers panel, as shown in Figure 4-20.

3. When the Layer Style dialog box appears, click the Color swatch to choose a color, as shown in Figure 4-21, and then change any other properties such as Size (width), Position (alignment), Fill Type, and more. Click OK when you are finished making changes.

## Removing a shape layer

Because the Pen tool now has multiple options, you may unexpectedly create a shape layer. You can delete a shape layer by dragging the layer thumbnail to the Trash Can in the lower-right corner of the Layers panel.

If you want to keep your path but throw away the shape layer, choose Window⇨Paths. Then drag the shape vector mask to the Create New Path icon, shown in Figure 4-22, which creates a saved path. Now you can throw away the shape layer.

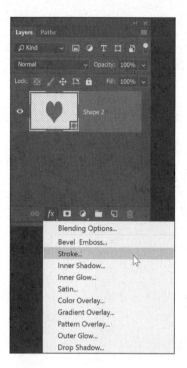

**FIGURE 4-20:**
You can use Layer
styles in order to
add a stroke to a
custom shape.

**FIGURE 4-21:**
Use the Layer
Styles feature in
order to apply
properties for
the Stroke.

**FIGURE 4-22:**
Drag the shape
path to the
Create New
Path icon.

Chapter **5**

# Creating Images in the Right Resolution for Print and the Web

S omething as important as setting the right resolution for your images deserves its own chapter. In this chapter, you discover the recommended resolution for your images, which is dependent upon where the image is to be used. Are you going to use the image in a high-quality annual report or are you going to email it to your family? This is important information to know right from the start. Combine the information about resolution along with the steps to use the color and retouching tools we show you in Chapter 7 of this minibook, and you should be ready to roll with great imagery.

## Creating Images for Print

To begin, you need to know the existing resolution of your image. To see an open image's present size and resolution in Photoshop, choose Image⇨Image Size. The Image Size dialog box appears, as shown in Figure 5-1.

**FIGURE 5-1:**
The Image Size
dialog box.

TIP

At the top of the Image Size dialog box, you see the pixel dimensions noted.

The Width and Height text fields are in inches in the English default; you can change the increments to pixels by selecting Pixels from the measurement unit drop-down menu. The Width and Height text fields can be used for onscreen resizing. By switching the measurement unit back to inches, you can determine the size at which the image will print. The Resolution text field determines the resolution of the printed image; a higher value means a smaller (more pixels crammed in each inch), which typically produces a more finely detailed printed image.

Before you decide on a resolution, you should understand what some of the resolution jargon means:

» **ppi (pixels per inch):** The resolution of an image — how Photoshop measures resolution of images.

» **dpi (dots per inch):** The resolution of an image when printed.

» **lpi (lines per inch):** The varying dot pattern that printers and presses use to create images. (See Figure 5-2.) This dot pattern is referred to as the *lines* per inch, even though it represents rows of dots. The higher the lpi, the finer the detail and the less dot pattern or line screen you see.

» **Dot gain:** The spread of ink as it's applied to paper. Certain types of paper spread a dot of ink farther than others. For example, newsprint has a high dot gain and typically prints at 85 lpi; a coated stock paper has a lower dot gain and can be printed at 133–150 lpi and even higher.

Human eyes typically can't detect a dot pattern in a printed image at 133 dpi or higher.

**FIGURE 5-2:**
The dot pattern used to print images is referred to as lpi (lines per inch).

**TIP**

Deciding the resolution or dpi of an image requires backward planning. If you want to create the best possible image, you should know where it'll print *before* deciding its resolution. Communicate with your printer service if the image is going to press. If you're sending an image to a high-speed copier, you can estimate that it will handle 100 lpi; a desktop printer handles 85 lpi to 100 lpi.

## The resolution formula

When creating an image for print, keep this formula in mind:

$$2 \times lpi = ppi \text{ (pixels per inch)}$$

This formula means that if your image is going to press using 150 lpi, set your image at 300 ppi. To save space, many people in production use $1.5 \times lpi$ because it reduces the file size significantly and you get similar results; you can decide which one works best for you.

## Changing the resolution

Using the Image Size dialog box is only one way that you can control the resolution in Photoshop. Even though you can increase the resolution, do so sparingly and avoid it, if you can. The exception is when you have an image that's large in dimension size but low in resolution, like those you typically get from a digital camera. You may have a top-of-the-line digital camera that produces 72 ppi images, but at that resolution, the pictures are 28 x 21 inches (or larger)!

To increase the resolution of an image without sacrificing quality, follow these steps:

1. **Choose Image ⬄ Image Size.**

   The Image Size dialog box appears, as shown in Figure 5-3.

2. **Deselect the Resample Image checkbox.**

   This way, Photoshop doesn't add any pixels.

3. **Enter a resolution in the Resolution text field.**

   Photoshop keeps the *pixel size* (the size of the image onscreen) the same, but the *document size* (the size of the image when printed) decreases when you enter a higher resolution, as you see in Figure 5-3.

**FIGURE 5-3:** The Image Size dialog box, before and after deselecting Resample and changing the resolution.

4.  **If the image isn't the size you need, select the Resample Image checkbox and type the size in the Width and Height text fields.**

    It's best to reduce the size of a bitmap image, such as a digital photo, rather than increase it.

**REMEMBER**

    You can also deselect the Resample Image checkbox and essentially play a game of give-and-take to see what the resolution will be when you enter the intended size of your printed image in the Width and Height text fields.

    Images can typically be scaled from 50 to 120 percent before looking jagged. (To scale by a percentage, select Percent from the drop-down lists beside the Width and Height text fields.) Keep these numbers in mind when placing and resizing images in a page layout application such as InDesign.

5.  **Click OK when you're finished; double-click the Zoom tool in the Tools panel to see the image at its onscreen size.**

**TIP**

To increase the resolution *without* changing the image size, follow these steps. (This situation isn't perfect because pixels that don't presently exist are created by Photoshop and may not be totally accurate. Photoshop tries to give you the best image, but you may see some loss of detail.)

1.  **Choose Image⇨Image Size.**

2.  **When the Image Size dialog box appears, make sure that the Resample Image checkbox is selected.**

3.  **Enter the resolution you need in the Resolution text field, click OK, and then double-click the Zoom tool to see the image at its actual size.**

**TIP**

Reset your Image Size dialog, or any dialog box in Photoshop by holding down the Alt or Option button. The Cancel button changes to Reset!

# Determining the Resolution for Web Images

Have you ever received an image via email and, after spending ten minutes downloading it, discovered that the image is so huge that all you can see on the monitor is your nephew's left eye? Many people are under the misconception that if an image is 72 dpi, it's ready for onscreen presentation. Actually, pixel dimension is all that matters for viewing images on the web; this section helps you make sense of this concept.

Many people view web pages in their browser windows in an area of about 1024 x 768 pixels. You can use this figure as a basis for any images you create for the web, whether the viewer is using a 14-inch or a 21-inch monitor. (Remember that people who have large monitors set to high screen resolutions don't necessarily want a web page taking up the whole screen.) If you're creating images for a web page or to attach to an email message, you may want to pick a standard size to design by, such as 600 x 400 pixels at 72 ppi.

To use the Image Size dialog box to determine the resolution and size for onscreen images, follow these steps:

1. **Have an image open and choose Image⇨Image Size.**

   The Image Size dialog box appears.

2. **To make the image occupy half the width of a typical browser window, choose Pixels for the unit type in the Width drop-down list and type** 300 **(half of 600) in the Width text field.**

   If a little chain link is visible to the right, the Constrain Proportions checkbox is selected, and Photoshop automatically determines the height from the width you entered.

3. **Click OK and double-click the Zoom tool to see the image at its actual onscreen size.**

   That's it! Whether your image is 3,000 or 30 pixels wide doesn't matter; as long as you enter the correct pixel dimension, the image works beautifully.

# Applying the Unsharp Mask Filter to an Image

When you resample an image in Photoshop, it can become blurry. A good practice is to apply the Unsharp Mask filter. You can see the difference in detail in the images shown in Figure 5-4. This feature sharpens the image based on levels of contrast while keeping smooth the areas that have no contrasting pixels. You have to set up this feature correctly to get good results.

**FIGURE 5-4:**
The image with (left) and without (right) unsharp masking applied.

Here's the down-and-dirty method of using the Unsharp Mask filter:

**1. Choose View⇨100% or double-click the Zoom tool.**

When you're using a filter, view your image at its actual size to best see the effect.

**REMEMBER**

**2. Choose Filter⇨Sharpen⇨Unsharp Mask.**

In the Unsharp Mask dialog box that appears, set these three options:

- *Amount:* The Amount value ranges from 0 to 500. The amount you choose has a lot to do with the subject matter. Sharpening a car or appliance at 300 to 400 is fine, but if you do this to the CEO's 75-year-old wife, you may suffer an untimely death because every wrinkle, mole, or hair will magically become more defined. If you're not sure which amount to use, start with 150 and play around until you find an Amount value that looks good.

- *Radius:* The Unsharp Mask filter creates a halo around the areas that have enough contrast to be considered an edge. Typically, leaving the amount between 1 and 2 is fine for print, but if you're creating a billboard or poster, increase the size.

- *Threshold:* This option is the most important one in the Unsharp Mask dialog box. The Threshold setting determines what should be sharpened. If you leave it at zero, you see noise throughout the image, much like the grain you see in high-speed film. Increase the setting to 10, and it triggers the Unsharp Mask filter to apply the sharpening only when the pixels are ten shades or more away from each other. The amount of tolerance ranges from 1 to 255. Apply too much and no sharpening appears; apply too little and the image becomes grainy. A good number to start with is 10.

To compare the original state of the image with the preview of the Unsharp Mask filter's effect in the Preview pane of the Unsharp Mask dialog box, click and hold the image in the Preview pane; this shows the original state of the image. When you release the mouse button, the Unsharp Mask filter is previewed again.

3. **When you've made your choice, click OK.**

   The image appears to have more detail.

Once in a while, stray colored pixels may appear after you apply the Unsharp Mask filter. If you feel this is a problem with your image, choose Edit⇨Fade Unsharp Mask immediately after applying the Unsharp Mask filter. In the Fade dialog box, select the Luminosity blend mode from the Mode drop-down list and then click OK. This step applies the Unsharp Mask filter to the grays in the image only, thereby eliminating the sharpening of colored pixels.

You can also choose Filter⇨Convert for Smart Filters before you apply the Unsharp Mask filter. Smart filters let you undo all or some of any filter, including sharpening filters you apply to a layer. Find out how by reading Chapter 8 in this minibook.

# Chapter **6**

# Creating a Good Image

When discovering all the incredible things you can do in Photoshop, you can easily forget the basics. Yes, you can create incredible compositions with special effects, but if the people in your image look greenish, their alien skin tone can detract from the final result. Make it part of your image-editing process to create clean images before adding the artsy filters and complex compositions. Color correction isn't complicated, and by following the steps in this chapter you can produce almost magical results. In this chapter, you see how to use the values you read in the Info panel and use the Curves panel to produce quality image corrections.

## Reading a Histogram

Before making adjustments, look at the image's *histogram*, which displays an image's tonal values, to evaluate whether the image has sufficient detail to produce a high-quality image. In Photoshop CC, choose Window➪Histogram to display the Histogram panel.

**REMEMBER**

The greater the range of values in the histogram, the greater the detail. Poor images without much information can be difficult, if not impossible, to correct. The Histogram panel also displays the overall distribution of shadows, midtones, and highlights to help you determine which tonal corrections are needed.

Figure 6-1 shows a good, full histogram that indicates a smooth transition from one shade to another in the image. Figure 6-2 shows that when a histogram is spread out and has gaps in it, the image is jumping too quickly from one shade to another, producing a posterized effect. *Posterization* is an effect that reduces tonal values to a limited amount, creating a more defined range of values from one shade to another. It's great if you want it but yucky if you want a smooth tonal change from one shadow to another.

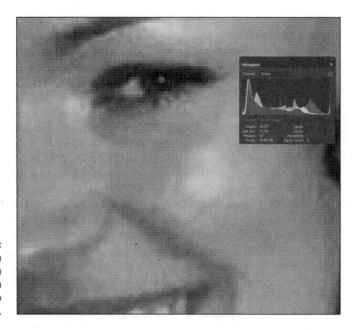

**FIGURE 6-1:**
A histogram showing smooth transitions from one color to another.

So how do you create a good histogram? If you're scanning, make sure that your scanner is set for the maximum number of colors. Scanning at 16 shades of gray gives you 16 lines in your histogram — not good.

**TIP**

If you have a bad histogram, we recommend that you rescan or reshoot the image. If you have a good histogram to start with, keep it that way by not messing around with multiple tone correction tools. Most professionals use the Curves feature — and that's it. Curves (choose Image⇨Adjustments⇨Curves), if used properly, do all the adjusting of levels (brightness and contrast) and color balance, all in one step. You can read more about curves in the section "Creating a Good Tone Curve," later in this chapter.

Figure 6-3 shows what happens to a perfectly good histogram when someone gets too zealous and uses the entire plethora of color correction controls in Photoshop. Just because the controls are there doesn't mean that you have to use them.

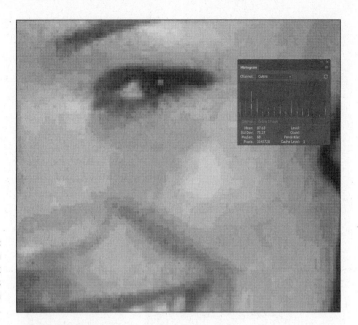

**FIGURE 6-2:**
A histogram
showing a lack
of smoothness
in the gradation
of color.

**FIGURE 6-3:**
Tonal information
is broken up.

**REMEMBER**

If a Warning icon appears while you're making adjustments, double-click anywhere on the histogram to refresh the display.

## Breaking into key types

Don't panic if your histogram is smashed all the way to the left or right. The bars
of the histogram represent tonal values. You can break down the types of images,
based on their values, into three key types that are defined below:

» **High key:** An extremely light-colored image, such as the image shown in
Figure 6-4. Information is pushed toward the right in the histogram. Color
correction has to be handled a little differently for these images to keep the
light appearance to them.

» **Low key:** An extremely dark image, such as the one shown in Figure 6-5.
Information is pushed to the left in the histogram. This type of image is
difficult to scan on low-end scanners because the dark areas tend to blend
together with little definition.

**FIGURE 6-4:**
A high key image
is a light image.

**FIGURE 6-5:**
A low key image
is a dark image.

>> **Mid key:** A typical image with a full range of shades, such as the image shown in Figure 6-6. These images are the most common and easiest to work with. In this chapter, we deal with images that are considered mid key.

## Setting up the correction

To produce the best possible image, avoid correcting in the CMYK (Cyan, Magenta, Yellow, Black) mode. If your images are typically in RGB (Red, Green, Blue) or LAB mode (L for lightness, and A and B for the color-opponent dimensions), keep them in that mode throughout the process. Convert them to CMYK only when you're finished manipulating the image.

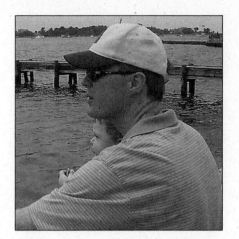

**FIGURE 6-6:**
A typical image
with a full range
of values is a mid
key image.

**REMEMBER**

Don't forget! If your end result will be a printed image, you can press Ctrl+Y (Windows) or ⌘+Y (Mac) to toggle on and off the CMYK preview so that you can see what your image will look like in CMYK mode without converting it.

Set up these items before starting any color correction:

1. **Select the Eyedropper tool (the keyboard shortcut is I); on the Options bar, select the 3 by 3 Average setting from the Sample Size drop-down list.**

   The 3 by 3 Average setting gives you more accurate readings than the Point Sample setting.

2. **If the Histogram panel isn't already visible, choose Window⇨Histogram.**

3. **If the Info panel isn't already visible, choose Window⇨Info to show the Info panel so that you can check values.**

4. **Make sure that your color settings are correct.**

   If you're not sure how to check or set up color settings, see Chapter 2 of this minibook.

# Creating a Good Tone Curve

A *tone curve* represents the density of an image. To produce the best image, you must first find the highlight and shadow points in it. An image created in less-than-perfect lighting conditions may be washed out or have odd color casts. See Figure 6-7 for an example of an image with no set highlight and shadow. Check out Figure 6-8 to see an image that went through the process of setting a highlight and shadow.

Creating a Good Image

**FIGURE 6-7:**
The image is murky before defining a highlight and shadow.

**FIGURE 6-8:**
The tonal values are opened after highlight and shadow have been set.

To make the process of creating a good tone curve more manageable, we've broken the process into four parts:

» Find the highlight and shadow.

» Set the highlight and shadow values.

» Adjust the midtone.

» Find a neutral.

Even though each part has its own set of steps, you must complete all four parts to accomplish the task of creating a good tone curve (unless you're working with grayscale images, in which case you can skip the neutral part). In this example, an adjustment layer is used for the curve adjustments. The benefit is that you can turn off the visibility of the adjustment later or double-click the adjustment layer thumbnail to make ongoing edits without destroying your image.

## Finding the highlight and the shadow

In the noncomputer world, you'd spend a fair amount of time trying to locate the lightest and darkest parts of an image. Fortunately, you can cheat in Photoshop by using some features in the Curves panel. Here's how to access the panel:

1.  **With an image worthy of adjustment — one that isn't perfect already — choose Window➪Layer (if the Layers panel isn't already open).**

2.  **Click and hold the Create New Fill or Adjustment Layer button at the bottom of the Layers panel and select Curves.**

    The Adjustments panel appears with the Curves panel active, as shown in Figure 6-9.

**FIGURE 6-9:**
Access the Curves panel with the Create New Fill or Adjustment Layer button.

Notice the grayed-out histogram behind the image in the Curves panel. The histogram helps you determine where you need to adjust the image's curve.

**TECHNICAL STUFF**

If you're correcting in RGB (as you should be), the tone curve may be the opposite of what you expect. Instead of light to dark displaying as you expect, RGB displays dark to light. Think about it: RGB is generated with light, and no RGB means that there's no light and you therefore have black. If you turn on all RGB full force, you create white. Try pointing three filtered lights — one red, one green, and one blue. The three lights pointed in one direction create white.

If working with RGB confuses you, simply select Curves Display Options from the panel menu in the upper-right corner of the Adjustments panel. When the Curves Display Options dialog box appears, as shown in Figure 6-10, select the Pigment/Ink % radio button and click OK.

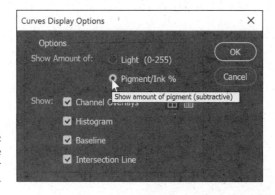

**FIGURE 6-10:**
View the curve using light or pigment.

Note that in the Curves panel, you see a Preset drop-down list that offers quick fixes using standard curves for certain corrections. These settings are great for quick fixes, but for the best image, create a custom curve.

The first thing you need to do in the Curves panel is determine the lightest and darkest parts of the image — referred to as *locating the highlight and shadow*:

1. **Before starting the correction, click the Set Black Point eyedropper once (labeled in Figure 6-11).**

2. **Hold down the Alt (Windows) or Option (Mac) key and click the Shadow input slider (labeled in Figure 6-11).**

   If you did not change your Curve Display Options to display Pigment/Ink %, your highlight and shadow sliders will be opposite of what appears in Figure 6-11.

   When you Alt-click (Windows) or Option-click (Mac), the clipping preview turns on, revealing the darkest area of the image, as shown in Figure 6-12.

   If you don't immediately see a dark area in the clipping preview, you can drag the shadow input slider to the right while holding down the Alt key or Option key. Note where the darkest area of the image appears.

3. **Hold down the Shift key and click directly on the image in that dark region.**

   This step drops a color sampler on the image that helps you reference that point later.

Set White point

Set Gray point

Set Black point

**FIGURE 6-11:**
The critical
tools on the
Curves panel.

Shadow slider        Highlight slider

Calculate a more accurate histogram

**FIGURE 6-12:**
Alt or Option click
on the Shadow
Slider and then
drag slightly to
the right to see
the darkest part
of the image.

4. **Repeat Steps 1 through 3 with the Highlight input slider. Select the Set White Point eyedropper (labeled in Figure 6-11) in the Curves panel.**

5. **Hold down the Alt key or Option key and click the highlight input slider.**

   Again, you can drag the slider toward the left if the lightest point doesn't immediately show up.

   When you locate the lightest point, as indicated by the lightest point in the clipping preview, you can Shift+click to drop a second color sampler, as shown in Figure 6-13.

**FIGURE 6-13:**
You can Shift-click
to drop a color
sampler.

## Setting the highlight and shadow values

After you determine the lightest and darkest points in an image, you can set their values. Follow these steps:

1. **To activate the eyedropper tools, click the Click and Drag button, shown in Figure 6-14.**

**FIGURE 6-14:**
Click the Click and
Drag button.

2. **Double-click the Set White Point eyedropper, the white eyedropper on the left side of the Curves panel.**

   When you double-click the Set White Point eyedropper, the Color Picker dialog box appears.

3. **Enter a generic value for the lightest point in your image: Type 5 in the Cyan text box, type 3 in the Magenta text box, type 3 in the Yellow text box, leave the Black text box at 0 (zero), and then click OK.**

   The Black value helps to correct most images for print and online.

4. **When you receive an alert message asking whether you want to save the new target colors as defaults, click Yes.**

5. **With the Set White Point eyedropper still selected, click the color sampler you dropped on the image, indicating the lightest point in the image.**

   Now, set the shadow point.

6. **Double-click the Set Black Point eyedropper.**

   The Color Picker dialog box appears.

7. **Type 65 in the Cyan text box, type 53 in the Magenta text box, type 51 in the Yellow text box, type 95 into the Black text box, and then click OK.**

   As with the highlight value, the Black value is a generic value that works for most print and online images. Keep in mind that if you set your Color Settings up correctly, you don't have to change the Set Black Point value.

8. **With the Set Black Point eyedropper still selected, click the color sampler you dropped on the image, indicating the darkest point in the image.**

## Adjusting the midtone

You may have heard the phrase, "open up the midtones," which essentially means to lighten the midtonal values of an image. In many cases, opening up the midtones is necessary to add contrast and bring out detail in an image.

To adjust the midtones, follow these steps:

1. **In the Curves panel, click the middle of the curve ramp to create an anchor point; drag up slightly.**

   The image lightens. (If you're in Pigment/Ink % mode, drag down to lighten the image.) Move only a reasonable amount and be careful to observe what's happening in the Histogram panel (which you should always have open when making color corrections).

Because you set highlight and shadow (see the preceding section) and are now making a midtone correction, you see the bars in the histogram spreading out.

2. **To adjust the three-quarter tones (the shades around 75 percent), click halfway between the bottom of the curve ramp and the midpoint to set an anchor point.**

   Use the grid in the Curves panel to find it easily. (In Pigment/Ink %, the three-quarter point is in the upper section of the color ramp.) Adjust the three-quarter area of the tone curve up or down slightly to create contrast in the image. Again, keep an eye on your histogram!

   If you're working on a grayscale image, the tonal correction is done.

   If you're working on a color image, keep the Curves panel open for the final steps, which are outlined in the next section.

## Finding a neutral

The last steps in creating a tone curve apply only if you're working on a color image. The key to understanding color is knowing that equal amounts of color create gray. By positioning the mouse cursor over gray areas in an image and reading the values in the Info panel, you can determine which colors you need to adjust.

1. **With the Curves panel open, position it so that you can see the Info panel.**

   If the Info panel is buried under another panel or a dialog box, choose Window⇨Info to bring it to the front or undock it from its current location.

2. **Position the cursor over an image and, in the Info panel, look for the RGB values in the upper-left section.**

   You see color values and then forward slashes and more color values. The numbers before the slash indicate the values in the image before you opened the Curves panel; the numbers after the slash show the values now that you've made changes in the Curves panel. Pay attention to the values after the slashes.

3. **Position the cursor over something gray in your image.**

   It can be a shadow on a white shirt, a countertop, a road — anything that's a shade of gray. Look at the Info panel. If your image is perfectly color balanced, the RGB values following the forward slashes should all be the same.

4. **If the color isn't balanced, click the Set Gray Point eyedropper in the Curves panel and click the neutral or gray area of the image.**

   The middle eyedropper (Set Gray Point) is a handy way of bringing the location you click closer together in RGB values, thereby balancing the colors.

Curves can be as complex or as simple as you make them. As you gain more confidence in using them, you can check neutrals throughout an image to ensure that all unwanted color casts are eliminated. You can even individually adjust each color's curve by selecting it from the Channel drop-down list in the Curves panel.

When you're finished with color correction, using the Unsharp Mask filter on your image is a good idea. Chapter 5 of this minibook shows you how to use this filter.

# Editing an Adjustment Layer

You may make a curve adjustment only to discover that some areas of the image are still too dark or too light. Because you used an adjustment layer, you can turn off the correction or change it repeatedly with no degradation to the quality of the image.

Here are the steps to take if you still have additional adjustments to make to an image, such as lightening or darkening other parts of the image:

1. **Select the area of the image that needs adjustments.**

   See Chapter 4 of this minibook for a refresher on how to make selections in Photoshop.

2. **Choose Select⇨Modify⇨Feather to soften the selection.**

   The Feather dialog box appears.

3. **Enter a value into the Feather dialog box.**

   If you're not sure what value will work best, enter **15** in the Feather Radius text field and click OK.

   You can also click the Refine Edge button in the Options panel (when you have a selection tool active) to preview the feather amount.

   **TIP**

4. **If the Layers panel isn't visible, choose Windows⇨Layers; click and hold the Create New Fill or Adjustment Layer icon and select Curves.**

5. **In the Curves panel, click the middle of the curve ramp to create an anchor point; drag up or down to lighten or darken the selected area.**

   Notice in the Layers panel (see Figure 6-15) that the adjustment layer, Curves 2 by default, has a mask to the right of it. This mask was automatically created from your selection. The selected area is white; unselected areas are black.

FIGURE 6-15:
Paint on the
adjustment
layer mask.

6. **With the adjustment layer selected in the Layers panel, use the Brush tool to paint white to apply the correction to other areas of the image; paint with black to exclude areas from the correction.**

   You can even change the opacity with the Brush tool in the Options bar at the top to apply only some of the correction!

# Testing a Printer

If you go to all the trouble of making color corrections to images and you still see printed images that look hot pink, it may not be your fault. Test your printer by following these steps:

1. **Create a neutral gray out of equal RGB values. (Double-click the Fill Color swatch in the Tools panel.)**

2. **Create a shape, using neutral gray as the fill color.**

   For example, you can use the Ellipse tool to create a circle or oval.

3. **Choose File⇨Print and click OK to print the image from a color printer.**

If you're seeing heavy color casts, adjust the printer; cleaning or replacing the ink cartridge may fix the problem. Check out Chapter 9 of this minibook for more about printing Photoshop files.

Chapter **7**

# Working with Painting and Retouching Tools

This chapter explains how to use the painting and retouching tools in Photoshop. Have fun and be creative! Because Photoshop is pixel based, you can create incredible imagery with the painting tools. Smooth gradations from one color to the next, integrated with blending modes and transparency, can lead from super-artsy to super-realistic effects. In this chapter, you discover fundamental painting concepts, and also find out how to use tools to eliminate wrinkles, blemishes, and scratches. Don't you wish you could do that in real life?

## Using the Swatches Panel

Use the Swatches panel to store and retrieve frequently used colors. The Swatches panel enables you to quickly select colors and gives you access to many other color options. By using the panel menu, which is shown in Figure 7-1, you can select from a multitude of color schemes, such as Pantone or web-safe color sets. These color systems are converted to the color mode in which you're working.

**FIGURE 7-1:**
Click the panel
menu to access
additional color
options.

To sample and store a color for later use, follow these steps:

1. **To sample a color from an image, select the Eyedropper tool in the Tools panel and click a color in the image.**

   Alternatively, you can use any of the paint tools (the Brush tool, for example) and Alt-click (Windows) or Option-click (Mac).

   The color you click becomes the foreground color.

2. **If the Swatches panel isn't already open, choose Window⇨Swatches.**

3. **Store the color in the Swatches panel by clicking the New Swatch button at the bottom of the Swatches panel.**

Anytime you want to use that color again, simply click it in the Swatches panel to make it the foreground color.

# Choosing Foreground and Background Colors

At the bottom of the Tools panel, you can find the foreground and background color swatches. The *foreground color* is the color you apply when using any of the painting tools. The *background color* is the color you see if you erase or delete pixels from the image.

Choose a foreground or background color by clicking the swatch, which then opens the Color Picker dialog box, shown in Figure 7-2. To use the Color Picker, you can either enter values in the text fields on the right or slide the hue slider.

Foreground and background color swatches

Pick the *hue* (color) you want to start with and then click in the color panel to the left to choose the amount of light and saturation (grayness or brightness) you want in the color. Select the Only Web Colors checkbox to choose one of the 216 colors in the web-safe color palette. The hexadecimal value used in HTML documents appears in the text field in the lower-right corner of the Color Picker.

To quickly save a color, click the Add to Swatches button directly in the Color Picker.

# The Painting and Retouching Tools

Grouped together in the Tools panel are the tools used for painting and retouching. The arrow in the lower-right area of a tool icon indicates that the tool has more related hidden tools; simply click and hold the tool icon to see additional painting and retouching tools, as shown in Figure 7-3. In this chapter, we show you how to use the Brush, Clone Stamp, Eraser, Gradient, Healing Brush, History Brush, Patch, Red Eye, and Spot Healing Brush tools. You also discover ways to fill shapes with colors and patterns.

## Changing the brush

As you click to select different painting tools, you can change the size and diameter of the tool. You can do this by accessing the Brush menu (second from the left) on the Options bar, as shown in Figure 7-4. Click the arrow to open the Brushes Preset picker. You can use the Master Diameter slider to make the brush size larger or smaller and to change the hardness of the brush.

The arrow indicates hidden tools

**FIGURE 7-3:**
The painting and retouching tools have hidden tools available as well.

Click the arrow to open the Brushes Preset picker

**FIGURE 7-4:**
The Brushes Preset picker.

**TIP**

The hardness refers to the fuzziness of the edges; a softer brush is more feathered and soft around the edges, whereas a harder edge is more definite. (See Figure 7-5.)

**TIP**

If you don't feel like accessing the Brushes Preset picker every time you want to make a change, press the right bracket (]) several times to make the brush diameter larger or press the left bracket ([) to make the brush diameter smaller. Press Shift+] to make the brush harder or Shift+[ to make the brush softer.

**FIGURE 7-5:**
The inside border
was created
with a brush set
to a hardness
of 100%. The
outside brush
was set to a
hardness of 0%.

Choose Window➪Brush to see a list of brush presets, plus more brush options you can use to create custom brushes. You can also choose other brush libraries from the panel menu of the Brush Presets panel. When you select an additional library, a dialog box appears, asking whether you want to replace the current brushes with the brushes in the selected library. Click the Append button to keep existing brushes and add the library to the list, or click OK to replace existing brushes.

**TIP**

Access the Brushes Preset picker while you're painting by right-clicking (Windows) or Control-clicking (Mac) anywhere in the image area. Double-click a brush to select it; press Esc to hide the Brushes Preset picker.

## The Spot Healing Brush tool and Content-Aware feature

The Spot Healing Brush tool was a great tool to begin with, but now, with the Content-Aware feature, it's even better. No matter what level of Photoshop user you are, you'll appreciate the magic in this tool option.

In its default settings, the Spot Healing Brush tool quickly removes blemishes and other imperfections in images. Click a blemish and watch it paint matching texture, lighting, transparency, and shading to the pixels being healed. The Spot Healing Brush tool doesn't require you to specify a sample spot — it automatically samples from around the retouched area.

Now take this concept a step further by selecting the Content-Aware option on the Options bar. The concept is the same, but if you look at Figure 7-6, you can see that painting with the Spot Healing Brush sets into action an incredible number of calculations that attempt to render pixels similar in detail to its surroundings.

**FIGURE 7-6:**
Using the Spot Healing Brush tool with the Content-Aware option enabled.

Does this work every time? Of course not. Does it work often enough to save you hours of work? Yes! If you want to follow along, open the image named beach that is located in the Book03-Photoshop folder located in the DummiesCCFiles here: www.agitraining.com/dummies.

You can also take advantage of the Content-Aware feature by using the Fill feature. Simply follow these steps:

**1.** **Select the area to be replaced by the new content.**

It is best to make a tight selection when using this feature.

2. **Choose Edit⇨Fill and, in the Fill dialog box, select Content-Aware from the Use drop-down list, shown in Figure 7-7.**

   The content is replaced.

   Note that if you are working on a Background layer, you can just press Delete and see the same options for replacing with the Content-Aware feature.

## The Healing Brush tool

You can use the Healing Brush tool for repairs, such as eliminating scratches and dust from scanned images. The difference between the Spot Healing Brush tool and the Healing Brush tool is that a sample spot is required before applying the Healing Brush. Follow these steps to use this tool:

1. **Select the Healing Brush tool in the Tools panel.**

   It's a hidden tool of the Spot Healing Brush tool.

2. **Find an area in the image that looks good and then Alt-click (Windows) or Option-click (Mac) to sample that area.**

   For example, if you want to eliminate a tear in an image, such as the one in Figure 7-8, choose a tear-free area of image near the tear.

3. **Position the mouse cursor over the area to be repaired and start painting.**

   The Healing Brush tool goes into action, blending and softening to create a realistic repair of the area.

4. **Repeat Steps 2 and 3 as necessary to repair the additional tears, scratches, blemishes, and wrinkles.**

## The Patch tool

Hidden behind the Healing Brush tool in the Tools panel is the Patch tool. Use it to repair larger areas, such as a big scratch or a large area of skin, by following these steps:

1. **Click and hold the Healing Brush tool to select the Patch tool; on the Options bar, select Normal from the Patch drop down menu and then select the Destination tab.**

   You can patch either the source area or the destination — it's up to you. We recommend dragging a good source over the area that needs to be repaired.

2. **With the Patch tool still selected, drag to create a marquee around the source you want to use as the patch.**

   The source is an unscratched or wrinkle-free area.

3. **After you create the marquee, drag the selected source area to the destination to be repaired.**

   The Patch tool clones the selected source area while you drag it to the destination (the scratched area); when you release the mouse button, the tool blends in the source selection and repairs the scratched area!

**TIP**

Make the patch look better by choosing Edit⇨Fade Patch Selection immediately after you apply the patch. Adjust the opacity until no telltale signs show that you made a change.

## The Red Eye tool

So you finally got the group together and shot the perfect image, but red eye took over! *Red eye* is caused by a reflection of the camera's flash in the retina of your photo's subject or subjects. You see this effect more often when taking pictures in a dark room, because the subject's pupils are wide open. If you can, use your camera's red-eye-reduction feature. Or, use a separate flash unit that you can mount on the camera farther from the camera's lens.

You'll love the fact that red eye is extremely easy to fix in Photoshop. Just follow these steps:

**1.** Select the Red Eye tool (hidden behind the Spot Healing Brush tool).

**2.** Click and drag to surround the red-eye area.

You should see a change immediately, but if you need to make adjustments to the size or the darkness amount, you can change options on the Options bar.

## The Brush tool

Painting with the Brush tool in Photoshop is much like painting in the real world. However, unlike a real brush, the Brush tool offers you nifty keyboard shortcuts that can be much more productive when painting. These shortcuts are truly outstanding, so make sure that you try them while you read about them. By the way, the keyboard commands you see in Table 7-1 work on all the painting tools.

**TABLE 7-1**     **Brush Keyboard Shortcuts**

| Task | Windows | Mac |
|------|---------|-----|
| Choose the Brush tool | B | B |
| Increase the brush size | ] | ] |
| Decrease the brush size | [ | [ |
| Harden the brush | Shift+] | Shift+] |
| Soften the brush | Shift+[ | Shift+[ |

*(continued)*

**TABLE 7-1** *(continued)*

| Task | Windows | Mac |
|------|---------|-----|
| Sample the color | Alt-click | Option-click |
| Switch the foreground and background colors | X | X |
| Change the opacity by a given percentage | Type a number between 1 and 100 | Type a number between 1 and 100 |

If you're really into brushes, don't miss out on the many useful options available in the Brush panel (choose Window⇨Brush to open it), as shown in Figure 7-9.

**FIGURE 7-9:**
Additional options are available for painting in the Brush panel.

You have several attribute choices, most of which have dynamic controls in the menu option. These options enable you to vary brush characteristics by tilting or applying more pressure to a stylus pen (if you're using a pressure-sensitive drawing tablet), among other things.

**REMEMBER**

A warning sign indicates that you don't have the appropriate device attached to use the selected feature, such as a pressure-sensitive drawing tablet.

The following options are available in the Brush panel:

>> **Brush Tip Shape:** Select from these standard controls for determining brush dimensions and spacing.

>> **Shape Dynamics:** Change the size of the brush as you paint.

>> **Scattering:** Scatter the brush strokes and control the brush tip count.

>> **Texture:** Choose from preexisting patterns or your own.

**TIP**

Create a pattern by selecting an image area with the Rectangular Marquee tool. Choose Edit⇨Define Pattern, name the pattern, and then click OK. The pattern is now available in the Brush panel's Texture choices.

>> **Dual Brush:** Use two brushes at the same time.

>> **Color Dynamics:** Change the color as you paint.

>> **Transfer:** Adjusts the dynamics for the build-up of the paint.

>> **Brush Pose:** Adjusts the tilt of the brush. You won't notice a difference when you have a regular rounded brush selected. Activate Pose when you use a beveled brush and change the X and Y tilt using the sliders to see how the angle of the brush is changed.

>> **Noise:** Adds a grainy texture to the brush stroke.

>> **Wet Edges:** Makes the brush stroke appear to be wet by creating a heavier amount of color on the edges of the brush strokes.

>> **Build-up:** Gives airbrush features to the Brush tools and builds up paint based on time instead of movement. Simply hold down the mouse in one area to see the paint expand. You can also enable the effects of an airbrush by selecting the Enable Airbrush-Style Build-Up Effects button in the Options bar.

**TIP**

If you click and hold the Brush tool on the image area, the paint stops spreading. Turn on the Airbrush feature and notice that when you click and hold, the paint keeps spreading, just like using a can of spray paint. You can use the Flow slider on the Options bar to control the pressure.

>> **Smoothing:** Smoothes the path created with the mouse.

>> **Protect Texture:** Preserves the texture pattern when applying brush presets.

After reviewing all the available brush options, you may want to start thinking about how you'll apply the same attributes later. Saving the Brush tool attributes is important as you increase your skill level. See the Saving Presets section later in this chapter to see how.

# The Clone Stamp tool

The Clone Stamp tool is used for pixel-to-pixel cloning. The Clone Stamp tool is different from the Healing Brush tool in that it does no automatic blending into the target area. You can use the Clone Stamp tool for removing a product name from an image, replacing a telephone wire that's crossing in front of a building, or duplicating an item.

Here's how to use the Clone Stamp tool:

1. **With the Clone Stamp tool selected, position the cursor over the area you want to clone and then Alt-click (Windows) or Option-click (Mac) to define the clone source.**

2. **Position the cursor over the area where you want to paint the cloned pixels and then start painting.**

   Note the crosshair at the original sampled area, as shown in Figure 7-10. While you're painting, the crosshair follows the pixels you're cloning.

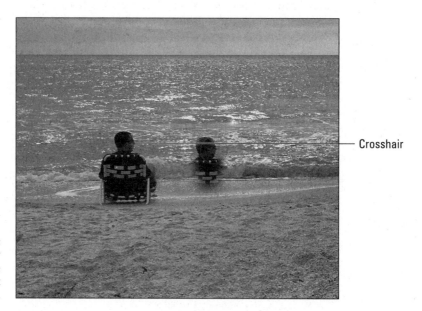

— Crosshair

**FIGURE 7-10:**
A crosshair over the source shows what you're cloning.

TIP

When using the Clone Stamp tool for touching up images, you should resample many times so as to not leave a seam where you replaced pixels. A good clone stamper Alt-clicks (Windows) or Option-clicks (Mac) and paints many times over until the retouching is complete.

Choose Window⇨Clone Source to open the Clone Source panel, shown in Figure 7-11. With this handy little panel, you can save multiple clone sources to refer to while working. Even better, you can scale, preview, and rotate your clone source — before you start cloning.

**FIGURE 7-11:**
Additional options in the Clone Source panel. In this example, the apple rotates 180 degrees while being cloned.

**TIP**

The Clone Source panel can be extremely helpful with difficult retouching projects that involve a little more precision.

Follow these steps to experiment with this fun and interactive panel:

1. **If the Clone Source panel isn't visible, choose Window⇨Clone Source.**

   The Clone Source icons across the top have yet to be defined. The first stamp is selected as a default.

2. **Alt-click (Windows) or Option-click (Mac) in the image area to record the first clone source.**

3. **Click the second Clone Source icon at the top of the Clone Source panel and then Alt-click (Windows) or Option-click (Mac) somewhere else on the page to define a second clone source.**

   Repeat as needed to define more clone sources. You can click the Clone Source icons at any time to retrieve the clone source and start cloning.

4. **Enter any numbers you want in the Offset X and Y, W and H, and Angle text boxes in the center section of the Clone Source panel to set up transformations before you clone.**

5. **Select the Show Overlay checkbox to see a preview of your clone source.**

   Whatever you plan to do, it's much easier to see a preview *before* you start cloning. If you don't use the Clone Source panel for anything else, use it to see a preview of your clone source before you start painting. If it helps to see the clone source better, select the Invert checkbox.

You see an *overlay* (or preview) before cloning begins. This overlay helps you better align your image, which is helpful for precision work. If you want the preview to go away after you start cloning, select the Auto Hide checkbox.

## The History Brush tool

Choose Window⇨History to see the History panel. We could play around for weeks in the History panel, but this section gives you only the basic concepts.

At the top of the History panel is a snapshot of the last-saved version of the image. Beside the snapshot is an icon noting that it's the present History state, as shown in Figure 7-12.

User-saved snapshot

Latest saved version

**FIGURE 7-12:**
The History panel helps you see and select different states in your workflow to revert to.

Sets the source for the History Brush

 When you paint with the History Brush tool, it reverts by default back to the way the image looked in the last saved version. You can click the empty square to the left of any state in the History panel (refer to Figure 7-12) to make it the source for the History Brush tool. Use the History Brush tool to fix errors and add pizzazz to images.

## The Eraser tool

 You may not think of the Eraser tool as a painting tool, but it can be! When you drag the image with the Eraser tool, it rubs out pixels to the background color. (Basically, it paints with the background color.) If you're dragging with the Eraser tool on a layer, it rubs out pixels to reveal the layer's transparent background. (You can also think of using the Eraser tool as painting with transparency.)

The Eraser tool uses all the same commands as the Brush tool. You can make an eraser larger or softer or more or less opaque. Even better, follow these steps to use the Eraser tool creatively:

1. **Open any color image and apply a filter.**

   For example, we chose Filter⇨Blur⇨Gaussian Blur. In the Gaussian Blur dialog box that appears, we changed the blur to 5 and then clicked OK to apply the Gaussian Blur filter.

2. **Select the Eraser tool and press 5 to change it to 50 percent opacity.**

   You can also use the Opacity slider on the Options bar.

3. **Hold down the Alt (Windows) or Option (Mac) key to repaint 50 percent of the original image's state before applying the filter.**

4. **Continue painting in the same area to bring the image back to its original state.**

   The original sharpness of the image returns where you painted.

**REMEMBER**

Holding down the Alt (Windows) or Option (Mac) key is the key to erasing the last saved version (or history state). This tool is incredible for fixing mistakes or removing applied filters.

## The Gradient tool

Choose the Gradient tool and click and drag across an image area to create a gradient in the direction and length of the mouse motion. A short drag creates a short gradient; a long drag produces a smoother, longer gradient.

From the Options bar, you also can choose the type of gradient you want: Linear, Radial, Angle, Reflected, or Diamond.

As a default, gradients are created using the current foreground and background colors. Click the arrow on the Gradient button on the Options bar to assign a different preset gradient.

To create a gradient, follow these steps:

1. **Choose the Gradient tool and click the Gradient Editor button (second from the left) on the Options bar.**

   The Gradient Editor dialog box appears. At the bottom of the gradient preview, you see two or more *stops,* which is where new colors are inserted into the gradient. They look like little house icons. Use the stops on top of the gradient slider to determine the opacity.

2.  **Click a stop and click the color swatch to the right of the word _Color_ to open the Color Picker and assign a different color to the stop.**

3.  **Click anywhere below the gradient preview to add more color stops.**

4.  **Drag a color stop off the Gradient Editor dialog box to delete it.**

5.  **Click the top of the gradient preview to assign different stops with varying opacity, as shown in Figure 7-13.**

A stop on the Gradient slider

Opacity

**FIGURE 7-13:**
Assigning varying amounts of opacity using the stops on top of the gradient slider.

6.  **When you're finished editing the gradient, name it and then click the New button.**

    The new gradient is added to the preset gradient choices.

7.  **To apply your gradient, drag across a selection or image with the Gradient tool.**

# Blending Modes

You can use blending modes to add flair to the traditional opaque paint. Use blending modes to paint highlights or shadows that allow details to show through from the underlying image or to colorize a desaturated image. You access the blending modes for paint tools from the Options bar.

You can't get an accurate idea of how the blending mode works with the paint color and the underlying color until you experiment. (That's what multiple undos are for!) Alternatively, you can copy to a new layer the image you want to experiment with and hide the original layer.

This list describes the available blending modes:

>> **Normal:** Paints normally, with no interaction with underlying colors.

>> **Dissolve:** Gives a random replacement of the pixels, depending on the opacity at any pixel location.

>> **Behind:** Edits or paints only on the transparent part of a layer.

>> **Darken:** Replaces only the areas that are lighter than the blend color. Areas darker than the blend color don't change.

>> **Multiply:** Creates an effect similar to drawing on the page with magic markers. Also looks like colored film that you see on theater lights.

>> **Color Burn:** Darkens the base color to reflect the blend color. If you're using white, no change occurs.

>> **Linear Burn:** Looks at the color information in each channel and darkens the base color to reflect the blending color by decreasing the brightness.

>> **Darker Color:** Compares the total of all channel values for the blend and base color and displays the lower value color.

>> **Lighten:** Replaces only the areas darker than the blend color. Areas lighter than the blend color don't change.

>> **Screen:** Multiplies the inverse of the underlying colors. The resulting color is always a lighter color.

>> **Color Dodge:** Brightens the underlying color to reflect the blend color. If you're using black, there's no change.

>> **Linear Dodge:** Looks at the color information in each channel and brightens the base color to reflect the blending color by increasing the brightness.

>> **Lighter Color:** Compares the total of all channel values for the blend and base color and displays the higher-value color.

>> **Overlay:** Multiplies or screens the colors, depending on the base color.

>> **Soft Light:** Darkens or lightens colors, depending on the blend color. The effect is similar to shining a diffused spotlight on the artwork.

- » **Hard Light:** Multiplies or screens colors, depending on the blend color. The effect is similar to shining a harsh spotlight on the artwork.

- » **Vivid Light:** Burns or dodges colors by increasing or decreasing the contrast.

- » **Linear Light:** Burns or dodges colors by decreasing or increasing the brightness.

- » **Pin Light:** Replaces colors, depending on the blend color.

- » **Hard Mix:** Paints strokes that have no effect with other Hard Mix paint strokes. Use this mode when you want no interaction between the colors.

- » **Difference:** Subtracts either the blend color from the base color or the base color from the blend color, depending on which one has the greater brightness value. The effect is similar to a color negative.

- » **Exclusion:** Creates an effect similar to, but with less contrast than, Difference mode.

- » **Subtract:** Subtracts pixel values of one layer with the other. In case of negative values, black is displayed.

- » **Divide:** Divides pixel values of one layer with the other.

- » **Hue:** Applies the hue (color) of the blend object to underlying objects but keeps the underlying shading or luminosity intact.

- » **Saturation:** Applies the saturation of the blend color but uses the luminance and hue of the base color.

- » **Color:** Applies the blend object's color to underlying objects but preserves the gray levels in the artwork. This mode is helpful for tinting objects or changing their colors.

- » **Luminosity:** Creates a resulting color with the hue and saturation of the base color and the luminance of the blend color. This mode is the opposite of Color mode.

## Painting with color

This section provides an example of using blending modes to change and add color to an image. An example of using a blending mode is tinting a black-and-white (grayscale) image with color. You can't paint color in Grayscale mode, so follow these steps to add color to a black-and-white image:

1. **Open an image in any color mode and choose Image⇨Mode⇨RGB.**

2. **If the image isn't already a grayscale image, choose Image⇨Adjustments⇨ Desaturate.**

   This feature makes it appear as though the image is black and white, but you're still in a color mode and can apply color.

3. **Choose a painting tool (the Brush tool, for example) and, from the Swatches panel, choose the first color you want to paint with.**

4. **On the Options bar, select Color from the Mode drop-down list and then use the Opacity slider to change the opacity to 50 percent.**

   You can also just type **5**.

5. **Start painting!**

   Color Blending mode is used to change the color of pixels while keeping intact the underlying grayscale (shading).

**TIP**

Another way to bring attention to a certain item in an RGB image (such as those cute greeting cards that have the single rose in color and everything else in black and white) is to select the item you want to bring attention to. Choose Select⇨Modify⇨Feather to soften the selection a bit — 5 pixels is a good number to enter in the Feather Radius text field — then click OK. Then choose Select⇨Inverse. With everything else selected, choose Image⇨Adjustments⇨Desaturate. Everything in the image looks black and white, except for the original item you selected.

## Filling selections

If you have a definite shape that doesn't lend itself to being painted, you can fill it with color instead. Make a selection and choose Edit⇨Fill to access the Fill dialog box. From the Use drop-down list, you can select from the following options to fill the selection: Foreground Color, Background Color, Color (to open the Color Picker while in the Fill dialog box), Content-Aware, Pattern, History, Black, 50% Gray, or White.

If you want to use an existing or saved pattern from the Brushes panel, you can retrieve a pattern by selecting Pattern in the Fill dialog box as well. Select History from the Use drop-down list to fill with the last version saved or the history state.

If you'd rather use the Paint Bucket tool, which fills based on the tolerance specified on the Options bar, it's hidden in the Gradient tool. To use the Paint Bucket tool to fill with the foreground color, simply click the item you want to fill.

# Saving Presets

All Photoshop tools enable you to save presets so that you can retrieve them from a list of presets. The following steps show you an example of saving a Tool preset for a brush, but you can use the same method for all other tools as well:

1. **Choose a brush size, color, softness, or any other characteristic.**

2. **Click the Tool Preset Picker button on the left side of the Options bar as shown in Figure 7-14.**

Tool Preset Picker button

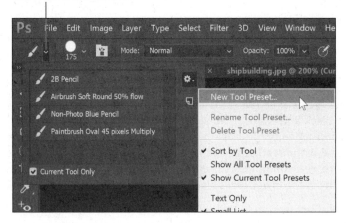

**FIGURE 7-14:**
Choose to save your brush properties as a Tool preset.

3. **Click the Gear icon in the upper-right corner to access the fly-out menu and then choose New Tool Preset.**

The New Tool Preset dialog box appears.

4. **Type a descriptive name in the Name text field (leave the Include Color checkbox selected if you want the preset to also remember the present color) and then click OK.**

5. **Access the preset by clicking the tool's Preset Picker button and selecting it from the tool's Preset Picker list.**

Each preset you create is specific to the tool it was created in, so you can have a crop preset and an eraser preset, for example. After you get in the habit of saving presets, you'll wonder how you ever got along without them.

# Chapter **8**

# Using Layers

B y using layers, you can make realistic additions to an image that can later be removed, edited, and changed with blending modes and transparency settings. This chapter shows you how to create composite images using helpful layer features. Even if you're an experienced Photoshop user, read this chapter to discover all sorts of great keyboard shortcuts that can help improve your workflow.

Add the feature of multiple screens or pages to Photoshop by taking advantage of the Artboard feature. Using the Layers panel, you can divide your Photoshop file into multiple canvases for the purpose of creating screens for interactive applications, or pages for print.

Want to take layers even further? You can convert layers into 3D files. Though many 3D features are beyond the scope of this book, you can still discover enough to be dangerous by reviewing the section "Experimenting with 3D Files," later in this chapter.

# Creating and Working with Layers

Layers make creating *composite images* (images pieced together from other, individual images) easy because you can separate individual elements of the composite onto their own layers. Much like creating collages by cutting pictures from magazines, you can mask out selections on one image and place them on a layer in another image. When pixel information is on its own layer, you can move it, transform it, correct its color, or apply filters only to that layer, without disturbing pixel information on other layers.

The best way to understand how to create and use layers is to, well, create and use layers. The following steps show you how to create a new, layered image:

1. **Choose File⇨New to create a new document.**

   The New dialog box appears.

2. **From the Photo Tab, select the Default Photoshop Size from the Preset list, select the Transparent option from the Background Contents area, and then click OK.**

   Because you selected the Transparent option, the layer appears as a checkerboard pattern, which signifies that it's transparent, versus a white background layer.

   **TIP**

   If you don't like to see the default checkerboard pattern where there's transparency, choose Edit⇨Preferences⇨Transparency and Gamut (Windows) or Photoshop⇨Preferences⇨Transparency and Gamut (Mac). In the Preferences dialog box that appears, you can change the Grid Size drop-down list to None to remove the checkerboard pattern entirely. If you don't want to remove the transparency grid, you can change the size of the checkerboard pattern or change the color of the checkerboard.

   **REMEMBER**

   When you open an existing document (say, a photograph), the image is typically the background layer.

3. **Create a square with the Rectangular Marquee tool on Layer 1.**

   For example, we created a green square by using the Rectangular Marquee tool to create a square selection; we then filled the selection with green by double-clicking the Foreground color swatch, selecting a green shade of color from the Color Picker, and clicking in the selection with the Paint Bucket tool (hidden under the Gradient tool).

   **TIP**

   After you select a color, you can also use the key command Alt+Delete (Windows) or Option+Delete (Mac) to fill the selected area with your foreground color.

4. **To rename the layer, double-click the layer name (Layer 1) in the Layers panel and type a short, descriptive name.**

   A good practice is to name layers based on what they contain; for this example, we named Layer 1 the catchy name green *square*.

5. **Create a new layer by Alt-clicking (Windows) or Option-clicking (Mac) the New Layer button at the bottom of the Layers panel.**

   The New Layer dialog box appears. By holding down Alt (Windows) or Option (Mac), you can name the layer while you create it.

6. **In this example, you add a circle, so name the layer** Red circle. **Click OK.**

7. **Create a circle using the Elliptical Marquee tool on the new layer.**

   In this example, we created a red circle by using the Elliptical Marquee tool and filled it with red.

**TIP**

   The keyboard shortcut for Edit⇔Fill is Shift+F5 (Windows) Shift+Delete (Mac). After the dialog box opens, you can choose Contents⇔Color and select a red color from the Color Picker.

   The new shape can overlap the shape on the other layer, as shown in Figure 8-1.

**FIGURE 8-1:** The circle overlaps the square.

## Duplicating a layer

Perhaps you want to create a duplicate of a layer for your composite. This technique can be helpful for creating do-it-yourself drop shadows and for adding elements to an image, such as more apples in a bowl of fruit.

Press Alt (Windows) or Option (Mac) and drag a layer to the New Layer button at the bottom of the Layers panel to duplicate it. Again, by holding down Alt (Windows) or Option (Mac), you can name the layer while you create it.

## Selecting a layer

When you start working with layers, you may move or adjust pixels only to discover that you accidentally edited pixels on the wrong layer. Select the layer you plan to work on by clicking the layer name in the Layers panel.

**REMEMBER**

Photoshop CC represents a selected layer by simply highlighting the layer in the Layers panel. The indicator paintbrush icon is gone in this version.

Here are some tips to help you select the correct layer:

>> Select the Move tool and then right-click (Windows) or Control-click (Mac) to see a contextual menu listing all layers that have pixel data at the point you clicked and to choose the layer you want to work with.

>> Get in the habit of holding down the Ctrl (Windows) or ⌘ (Mac) key while using the Move tool and when selecting layers. This technique temporarily turns on the Auto Select feature, which automatically selects the topmost visible layer that contains the pixel data you clicked.

>> Press Alt+[ (Windows) or Option+[ (Mac) to select the next layer down from the selected layer in the stacking order.

>> Press Alt+] (Windows) or Option+] (Mac) to select the next layer up from the selected layer in the stacking order.

## Controlling the visibility of a layer

Hide layers that you don't immediately need by clicking the eye icon in the Layers panel. To see only one layer, Alt-click (Windows) or Option-click (Mac) the eye icon of the layer you want to keep visible. Alt-click (Windows) or Option-click (Mac) the eye icon again to show all layers.

## Rearranging the stacking order

Layers are like clear pieces of film lying on top of each other. Change the stacking order of the layers in the Layers panel by dragging a layer until you see a black separator line appear, indicating that you're dragging the layer to that location. You can also use these helpful commands to move a layer:

| Command | Windows Shortcut | Mac Shortcut |
|---|---|---|
| Move selected layer up | Ctrl+] | ⌘+] |
| Move selected layer down | Ctrl+[ | ⌘+[ |

# Creating a Text Layer

When you create text in Photoshop, the text is created on its own layer. By having the text separate from the rest of the image, applying different styles and blending modes to customize the type, as well as repositioning the text, is simplified.

 To create a text layer, choose the Type tool and click the image area. You can also click and drag to create a text area. The Options bar, shown in Figure 8-2, gives you the controls to change the font, size, blending mode, and color of the text.

Toggle Character and Paragraph panels

Font family     Font size     Click for color picker

Font style

Left, center, right align

FIGURE 8-2: The Text tool options.

 When you're finished typing, you must confirm your text entry by selecting the checkbox (on the right of the Options bar) or pressing Ctrl+Enter (Windows) or ⌘+Return (Mac).

REMEMBER

## Warping text

 When you click the Create Warped Text button on the Options bar, the Warp Text dialog box appears. You can use it to apply different types of distortion to your text.

You can still edit text that's been warped. To remove a warp, click the Create Warp Text button again and select None from the Style drop-down list.

Using Layers

## Fine-tuning text

For controls such as leading, baseline shift, and paragraph controls, click the Toggle Character and Paragraph Panels icon near the right end of the Options bar.

Use the keyboard commands in Table 8-1 to fine-tune text in Photoshop. Make sure that you have text selected when you use these shortcuts.

**TABLE 8-1**  ## Helpful Typesetting Key Commands

| Task | Windows | Mac |
| --- | --- | --- |
| Increase the font size | Shift+Ctrl+> | Shift+⌘+> |
| Decrease the font size | Shift+Ctrl+< | Shift+⌘+< |
| Increase the kerning (the cursor must be between two letters) | Alt+→ | Option+→ |
| Decrease the kerning (the cursor must be between two letters) | Alt+← | Option+← |
| Increase the tracking (on several selected letters) | Alt+→ | Option+→ |
| Decrease the tracking (on several selected letters) | Alt+← | Option+← |
| Increase or decrease the leading (on several selected lines) | Alt+↑ or Alt+↓ | Option+↑ or Option+↓ |

TIP

To change the font, drag over the font family name on the Options bar and then press the up-arrow key (↑) to move up in the font list or the down-arrow key (↓) to move down in the font list.

After you're finished editing text, confirm or delete the changes by clicking the buttons on the right end of the Options bar.

TIP

If you'd rather use key commands to confirm or delete changes, press the Esc key to cancel text changes; press Ctrl+Enter (Windows) or ⌘+Return (Mac) to commit text changes (or use the Enter key on the numeric keypad).

# Using Layer Masks

In the following sections, we show you how to create a layer mask from a selection or a pen path. A *layer mask* covers areas of the image that you want to make transparent and exposes pixels that you want visible. Masks can be based on a selection you've created by painting on the mask itself. You can also take advantage of the Pen tool to create a path around the object you want to keep visible.

# Creating a layer mask from a selection

You need to have two images open to follow these steps where we show you how to create layer masks from a selection:

1. **When combining images, choose Image⇨Image Size to make sure that the images are approximately the same resolution and pixel dimensions.**

   Otherwise, you may be astonished by the disproportionate images in your composite.

2. **Choose Window⇨Arrange⇨Tile Vertically or Horizontally to position the images in separate windows.**

3. **Using the Move tool, click one image and drag it to the other image window.**

   A black border appears around the image area when you drop an image into another image window. By dragging and dropping an image, you automatically create a new layer on top of the active layer.

   **TIP**

   Hold down the Shift key when dragging one image to another to perfectly center the new image layer in the document window.

   You can also drag a layer (background or regular layer) to another image file. First make sure that no selection is active. Then use the Move tool to drag the layer from the artboard up to the tab of the image you want it to copy the image to.

4. **Using any selection method, select a part of the image that you want to keep on the newly placed layer, and choose Select⇨Modify⇨Feather to soften the selection.**

   Five pixels should be enough.

5. **Click the Add Layer Mask button at the bottom of the Layers panel.**

   A mask is created to the right of the layer, leaving only your selection visible, as shown in Figure 8-3.

6. **If you click the Layer thumbnail in the Layers panel, the mask thumbnail shows corner edges, indicating that it's activated.**

   While the layer mask is active, you can paint on the mask.

7. **Select the Brush tool and paint black while the mask thumbnail is selected to cover areas of the image that you don't want to see; press X to switch to white and paint to expose areas on the image that you do want to see.**

   You can even change the opacity while you paint to blend images with each other.

Using Layers

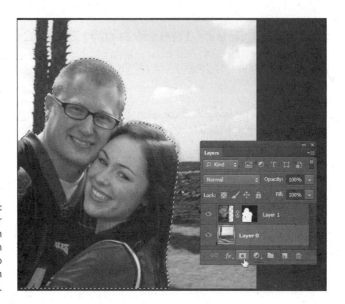

**FIGURE 8-3:**
Click the Layer
Mask button
while you have an
active selection to
create a custom
layer mask.

TIP

To create a smooth transition from one image to another, drag the Gradient tool across the image while the layer mask is selected in the Layers panel.

## Creating a vector mask from a pen path

A *vector mask* masks a selection, but it does so with the precision you can get only from using a path. The following steps show you another, slightly more precise, way to create a layer mask by using a pen path:

1. **Use the Pen tool and click from point to point to make a closed pen path.**

   If you already have a path, choose Window➪Paths and click a path to select it.

   See Chapter 4 of this minibook for more about working with the Pen tool.

2. **On the Layers panel, click the Layer Mask button and then click it again (see Figure 8-4).**

   Wow — a mask from your pen path! Anything not contained within the path is now masked out. You can still adjust your path (and masked selection) by using the Direct Selection tool to click and drag the anchor points and directional lines in your path.

If you no longer want a vector mask, drag the thumbnail to the Trash icon in the Layers panel. An Alert dialog box appears, asking whether you want to discard the mask or apply it. Click the Discard button to revert your image to the way it appeared before applying the mask, or click the Apply button to apply the masked area.

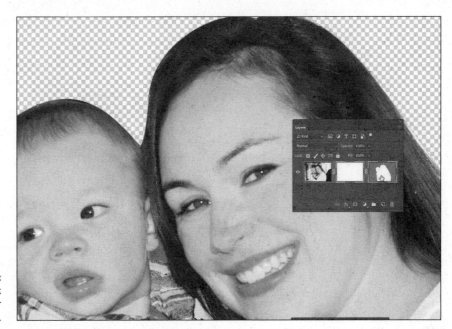

**FIGURE 8-4:**
Create a mask from your pen path.

# Organizing Your Layers

As you advance in layer skills, you'll want to keep layers named, neat, and in order. In this section, we show you some tips to help you organize multiple layers.

## Activating multiple layers simultaneously

Select multiple layers simultaneously by selecting one layer and then Shift-clicking to select additional layers. The selected layers are highlighted. Selected layers move and transform together, making repositioning and resizing easier than activating each layer independently.

Select multiple layers to keep their relative positions to each other and take advantage of alignment features. When you select two or more layers and choose the Move tool, you can take advantage of alignment features on the Options bar (see Figure 8-5). Select three or more layers for distribution options.

## Auto-Align Layers tool

Do you ever have multiple shots of two or more people, say, one with the guy's eyes shut and the girl looking the other way? Or maybe you like the smile in one shot better than in another. With the auto-alignment feature, you can pull the best parts of multiple images into one "best" image.

Distribute Left Edges

Align
Vertical
Centers

Align
Left

Align
Right

Distribute
Vertical
Centers

Distribute
Horizontal
Centers

Align Top

Align Bottom

Align
Horizontal
Centers

Distribute
Top Edges

Distribute
Right Edges

Distribute
Bottom
Edges

**FIGURE 8-5:**
Align multiple
layers
simultaneously
with the
Move tool.

To use this tool, simply have the Move tool active, select multiple layers, and then click the Auto-Align Layers button to the right of the alignment tools. The Auto-Align Layers dialog box appears, as shown in Figure 8-6; make your selection and click OK.

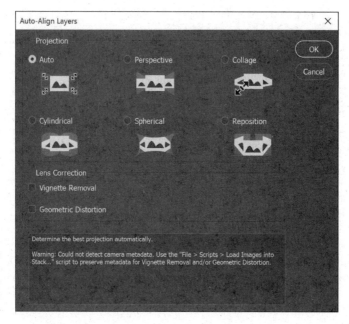

**FIGURE 8-6:**
The Auto-Align
Layers feature
can help create a
better composite.

## Layer groups

After you start using layers, you'll likely use lots of them, and your Layers panel will become huge. If you often scroll to navigate from one layer to another, take advantage of *layer groups*, which essentially act as folders that hold layers you choose, as shown in Figure 8-7. Just as with a folder you use for paper, you can add, remove, and shuffle around the layers within a layer group. Use layer groups to organize layers and make the job of duplicating multiple layers easier.

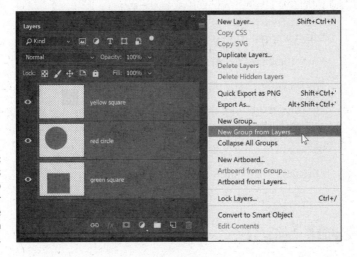

**FIGURE 8-7:**
Select the layers that you want to group together and then choose New Group from Layers.

To create a layer group, follow these steps:

1. **After creating several layers, Shift-click to select the layers you want to group together in a set.**

2. **Choose New Group from Layers from the Layers panel menu, name the group, and then click OK.**

   That's it. You've created a layer group from your selected layers.

**TIP**

With the Blending Mode drop-down list in the Layers panel, you can change all layers within a group to a specific blending mode, or you can use the Opacity slider to change the opacity of all layers in a group at one time. *Pass through* in the blending mode indicates that no individual blending modes are changed.

After you create a layer group, you can still reorganize layers within the group or even drag additional layers in or out. You can open and close a layer group with the arrow to the left of the group name.

## Duplicating a layer group

After you create a layer group, you may want to copy it. For example, you may want to copy an image, such as a button created from several layers topped off with a text layer. The most efficient way to make a copy of that button is to create a layer group and copy the entire group. To copy an image made up of several layers that aren't in a layer group would require you to individually duplicate each layer — how time-consuming!

To duplicate a layer group, follow these steps:

1. **Select a group from the Layers panel.**

2. **From the panel menu, choose Duplicate Group.**

   The Duplicate Group dialog box appears.

3. **For the destination, choose the present document or any open document or create a new document.**

   Be sure to give the duplicated set a distinctive name!

4. **Click OK.**

# Using Layer Styles

Layer styles are wonderful little extra effects that you can apply to layers to create drop shadows and bevel and emboss effects and to apply color overlays, gradients, patterns and strokes, and more.

## Applying a style

To apply a layer style (for example, the drop shadow style, one of the most popular effects) to an image, follow these steps:

1. **Create a layer on any image.**

   For example, you can create a text layer to see the effects of the layer styles.

2. **With the layer selected, click and hold the Add a Layer Style button at the bottom of the Layers panel; from the menu options, choose Drop Shadow.**

   In the Layer Style dialog box that appears, you can choose to change the blending mode, color, distance spread, and size of a drop shadow. You should see that the style has already applied to your text. Position the cursor on the image area and drag to visually adjust the position of the drop shadow.

3. **When you're happy with the drop shadow, click OK to apply it.**

**TIP**

To apply another effect and change its options, click on the Layer Style button in the Layers panel and choose the name of the layer style from the menu that appears — Bevel and Emboss, for example. In the dialog box that appears, change the settings to customize the layer style and click OK to apply it to your image. For example, if you choose Bevel and Emboss from the Layer Styles menu, you can choose from several emboss styles and adjust the depth, size, and softness.

Here are some consistent items you see in the Layer Style dialog box:

>> **Contour:** Use contours to control the shape and appearance of an effect. Click the arrow to open the Contour fly-out menu to choose a contour preset or click the preview of the contour to open the Contour Editor and create your own edge.

>> **Angle:** Drag the crosshair in the angle circle or enter a value in the Angle text field to control where the light source comes from.

>> **Global light:** If you aren't smart about lighting effects on multiple objects, global light makes it seem as though you are. Select the Use Global Light checkbox to keep the angle consistent from one layer style to another.

>> **Color:** Whenever you see a color box, you can click it to select a color. This color can be for the drop shadow, highlight, shadow of an emboss, or for a color overlay.

## Creating and saving a style

If you come up with a combination of attributes you like, click the New Style button in the upper-right area of the Layer Style dialog box. After you name the style, it's stored in the Styles panel. After you click OK, you can retrieve the style at any time by choosing Window ➪ Styles. If it helps, click the panel menu button and choose either Small or Large List to change the Styles panel to show only the name of the styles.

After you apply a layer style to a layer, the style is listed in the Layers panel. You can turn off the visibility of the style by turning off the eye icon or even throw away the layer style by dragging it to the Layers panel's Trash icon.

## Thinking about opacity versus fill

In the Layers panel, you have two transparency options: one for opacity and one for fill. Opacity affects the opacity of the entire layer, including effects. Fill, on the other hand, affects only the layer itself, but not layer styles. Figure 8-8 shows what happens when the Drop Shadow and Inner Glow effects are applied to text

**Using Layers**

and the fill is reduced to 0 percent. This technique gives you the opportunity to make it look like text is chiseled into rock, wood, or even plastic for the look of a personalized credit card.

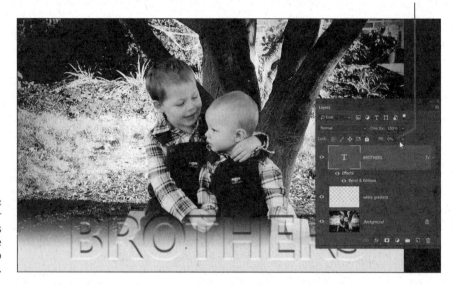

Fill Reduced to 0%

**FIGURE 8-8:**
A text layer with styles applied and the fill reduced to 0 percent.

# Smart, Really Smart! Smart Objects

Choose File➪Place (embedded or linked) and place an image, an illustration, or even a movie into a Photoshop document. A new layer is created and — even better — a Smart Object is created. The double-square icon in the lower-right corner of the layer thumbnail indicates that a layer is a Smart Object. This means that you have much more flexibility in the placement of your images because the original pixel information has essentially been embedded into your image.

Have you ever placed a logo only to find out later that you need it to be three times its size? Resizing is no longer an issue, because the Photoshop Smart Object is linked to an embedded original. If the original is vector, you can freely resize the image repeatedly without worrying about poor resolution. Want to change the spelling of the Illustrator logo you placed? Just double-click the Smart Object, and the embedded original is opened directly in Adobe Illustrator. Make your changes, save the file, and — *voilà* — the file is automatically updated in the Photoshop file.

What could be better? Smart Filters, of course. You can apply Smart Filters to any Smart Object layer, or even convert a layer to use Smart Filters, by selecting Filters➪Convert for Smart Filters. After a layer has been converted to a Smart

Object, you can choose filters, any filters, and apply them to the layer. If you want to paint out the effects of the filter on the layer, simply paint with black on the Filter Effects mask thumbnail. Paint with different opacities of black and white to give an artistic feel to the filter effect, as shown in Figure 8-9. You can even turn off filters by turning off the visibility on the Filter Effects thumbnail by clicking the eye icon to the left of the thumbnail.

**FIGURE 8-9:**
Cover the filter effects by painting on the Filter Effects thumbnail.

# Working with Artboards in Photoshop

Those of you familiar with Adobe Illustrator have been working with artboards for several versions by now. Just like in Adobe Illustrator, Photoshop artboards provide the capability to build separate pages or screens within one document. This can be especially helpful if you are building screens for a mobile application or small brochure.

You can think of an artboard as a special type of layer group created using the Layers panel. Its functionality might not be as intuitive in Photoshop as it is in Adobe Illustrator, but with a little practice you should get the hang of it. Follow these steps to see how you can make artboards on your own:

1. **In this example, a new document is created using the iPhone 6 start document. If you are starting a new document with the legacy New Document window, create a new file with these dimensions: 750 wide x 1334 high. (See Figure 8-10.)**

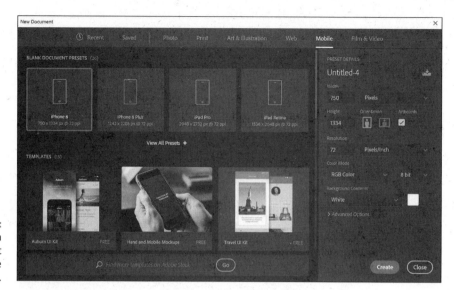

2. **If you created your new document with the iPhone 6 start file, you already see an artboard listed in the Layers panel, as shown in Figure 8-11. If you don't see an artboard, create one now by choosing New Artboard from the Layers panel menu, as shown in Figure 8-12.**

**FIGURE 8-12:**
You can add your
own Artboard
using the Layers
panel menu.

*Note:* While creating artboards, you can choose from a wide variety of preset sizes or define your own custom artboard size.

3. **Choose File⇨Place Embedded and navigate to the Book03-Photoshop folder. Double-click to select the image named water_sky or select the image and press Place.**

4. **When the image appears on the artboard, grab one of the corner handles, hold down the Shift key and click and drag outward in order to scale the image and fill the entire artboard, as shown in Figure 8-13. When the image is sized and positioned, select the Commit checkbox in the Options bar, or press the Enter key to confirm the placement of the image.**

   Next, you add a text layer.

5. **Select the Type tool and click and drag on the artboard in order to create a text area and add a new text layer.**

6. **Type the text, WATER & SKY. Using the controls in the Options bar, set the type to the following properties:**

   - *Font:* Myriad Pro Bold
   - *Size:* 110 pt
   - *Color:* White

7. **Select the Commit button in the Options bar after you have set your type.**

**Using Layers**

**FIGURE 8-13:**
Place an image
and stretch it
to fit the entire
artboard.

**TIP**

You can press Ctrl+Return (Windows) or ⌘+Return (Mac) in order to commit a type layer as well.

The result should be similar to what you see in Figure 8-14.

So as you see, you work with Artboards just like you would work with any other Photoshop document. The difference comes in the next step, where you will find how to add additional artboards to your file.

## Adding additional artboards

In this section, you create additional artboards. Perhaps you want a multi-screen mobile app created in Photoshop, or you just want to create multiple versions of one screen. For this section, you continue with the project started in the previous section.

1.  **Click on the Move tool and select the hidden Artboard tool shown in Figure 8-15.**

    Plus sign icons appear on all sides of the artboard. You can click on these plus sign icons in order to add additional artboards.

2.  **Click the plus sign icon to the right of your existing artboard to see that a new blank artboard is added. (See Figure 8-16.)**

    Take a look in the Layers panel. Ensure that, just like layers, the newest artboard appears above the selected layer.

**FIGURE 8-14:**
· Add a text layer
to your artboard.

**FIGURE 8-15:**
Use the
Artboard tool to
manipulate the
artboards and
create more.

*Note:* You can also use the Artboard tool to create your own custom sized artboard.
Do this by clicking and dragging with the artboard tool on the Photoshop canvas.
From the tool options bar, select a preset size from the Size pop-up menu, or just
leave it in your custom size.

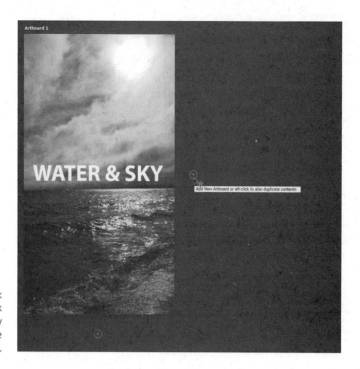

FIGURE 8-16:
Add a blank
artboard by
clicking on the
plus sign icon.

## Naming your artboards

Before this file becomes more complex, it would be wise to name the artboards. This is done in the Layers panel.

1.  Select the initial artboard (Artboard 1) and double-click on the artboard name. When the textbox is active, type the name Home.

2.  Double-click on the name Artboard 2 in the Layers panel and name this layer Beach.

## Adding content to the second artboard

Now, add an image and some text to the second artboard:

1.  Click on the Artboard tool and switch it back to the Move tool.

2.  Make sure that the Beach artboard is selected in the Layers panel and choose File⇨ Place Embedded. Navigate to the Book03_Photoshop folder and select the image named Beach and press Place. The image is added to the second artboard.

3. As with the last image you placed, hold down the Shift key and Shift drag on a corner point in order to proportionally scale the image larger and fill the screen.

4. With the Move tool active, click and drag the image. Note that even though it is in the same document, it does not overlap or interfere with artwork on other artboards.

## Cloning from one artboard to another

Now, clone the text from the Home artboard to the Beach artboard:

1. With the Move tool still selected, Ctrl-click (Windows) or ⌘-click (Mac) on the WATER & SKY text in the Home artboard. This activates that layer.

2. Hold down your Alt (Windows) or Option (Mac) key and click and drag the text from one artboard to the next.

   If you hold down the Shift key while dragging the image will remain aligned.

3. Switch to the artboard and double-click on the newly cloned text to activate the text area and type FUN BEACHES. You should have completed something similar to what you see in Figure 8-17.

FIGURE 8-17:
A Photoshop file with two artboards.

## Moving elements from one artboard to another

To move an element from one artboard to another, simply drag the elements from one artboard to another. When you move an element between artboards,

Photoshop tries to position it in the same location relative to the ruler origins located in the upper-left corners of the artboards.

## Exporting your artboards

You can save your file as a Photoshop file to maintain layers, but in this example you will export the file as a two-page PDF. Or, use the File⇨Export feature in order to export your artboards as PNGs, JPEGs, PDFs, and more.

# Experimenting with 3D Files

As we mention earlier in this chapter, working with 3D files is beyond the scope of this book, but even a 3D novice can experiment with the 3D features in Photoshop CC. Follow these steps to try out some 3D features on your own:

1. **Open an existing Photoshop document.**

   To eliminate any confusion, it's best if this document simply has a Background layer and no additional layers.

2. **If you have an image open with multiple layers, select a layer to which you want to apply 3D perspective.**

3. **Select the Move tool.**

4. **Choose 3D⇨New Mesh from Layer⇨Postcard.**

   If a Warning dialog box appears asking if you want to switch to the 3D workspace, click Yes.

   The image hasn't changed, but you can see that you've entered the 3D workspace that includes a perspective plane. Also, note that the layer now has a 3D icon (looks like a 3D box) on the layer thumbnail in the Layers panel, as shown in Figure 8-18, indicating that it's now a 3D layer.

3D icon

**FIGURE 8-18:**
Creating a
3D layer in
Photoshop CC.

5. **Experiment with angle and positioning by clicking and dragging on the 3D layer, as shown in Figure 8-19.**

**FIGURE 8-19:**
Click and drag with the Rotate the 3D Object tool to reposition the 3D layer.

6. **Use the Object Rotate, Roll, Drag, Slide, and Scale tools located in the Options bar, and shown in Figure 8-20, to change the positioning of the 3D layer.**

Slide the 3D Object

Roll the 3D Object | Scale the 3D Object

**FIGURE 8-20:**
The 3D tools appear when you are in the 3D workspace.

Drag the 3D Object

Rotate the 3D Object

Notice that these tools have additional options available on the Options bar across the top of your Photoshop document.

# Filter Capabilities in the Layers Panel

Now in Photoshop CC, you can filter the display of layers in the Layers Panel, as shown in Figure 8-21. Filter categories include Kind, Name, Effect, Mode, Attribute, and Color.

**FIGURE 8-21:**
Filter layers in the Layers panel to view only the ones you need.

If you would rather not use the filters, you can click the Turn Layer Filtering On/Off toggle switch to the right of the filters.

# Merging and Flattening the Image

*Merging layers* combines several selected layers into one layer. *Flattening* occurs when you reduce all layers to one background layer. Layers can increase file size, thereby also tying up valuable processing resources. To keep down file size, you may choose to merge some layers or even flatten the entire image to one background layer.

## Merging

Merging layers is helpful when you no longer need every layer to be independent, such as when you have a separate shadow layer aligned to another layer and don't plan to move it again or when you combine many layers to create a composite and want to consolidate it to one layer.

To merge layers (in a visual and easy way), follow these steps:

1. **Turn on the visibility of only the layers you want merged.**

2. **Choose Merge Visible from the Layers panel menu.**

   That's it. The entire image isn't flattened, but the visible layers are now reduced to one layer.

To merge visible layers on a *target* (selected) layer that you create while keeping the visible layers independent, create a blank layer and select it. Then hold down Alt (Windows) or Option (Mac) when choosing Merge Visible from the panel menu.

## Flattening

If you don't have to flatten your image, don't! Flattening an image reduces all layers to one background layer, which is necessary for certain file formats. After you flatten an image, you can't take advantage of blending options or reposition layered items. (Read more about saving files in Chapter 9 of this minibook.)

If you absolutely must flatten layers, keep a copy of the original, unflattened document for additional edits later.

To flatten all layers in an image, choose Layer⇨Flatten Image or choose Flatten Image from the panel menu on the Layers panel.

# Chapter 9

# Saving Photoshop Images for Print and the Web

I t may seem like a minor task, saving your image, but you have to make many decisions at this stage. Where will the image be viewed, onscreen or print? Will the image be large, or will it be the size of your thumbnail? Without selecting the correct settings and format, you may not be able to import your file or place it into other applications. If you save the file in the wrong format, you could delete valuable components, such as layers or saved selections. This chapter provides you with the necessary information to save the file correctly for both print and onscreen displays. Here you discover what the file format choices are and then progress into the Export feature (for saving in the GIF, JPEG, PNG, and WBMP file formats).

TIP

Saving files in the correct file format is important not only for file size, but also in support of different Photoshop features. If you're unsure about saving in the right format, save a copy of the file, keeping the original in the PSD format (the native Photoshop format). Photoshop alerts you automatically when you choose a format in the Save As or the Export As dialog box that doesn't support Photoshop features. When you choose a format that doesn't support some of the features you've used, such as channels or layers, a yield sign appears when a copy is being made. With the capability of all Adobe applications (and even non-Adobe applications) to read native Photoshop (.psd) files, be wise and keep files in this native file format unless you have a compelling reason not to.

# Backing Up with a Save

Before covering additional details about saving your files, keep in mind that you can set up Automatic Saving in your Photoshop preferences. This can be helpful if your software crashes or your computer shuts down unexpectedly. You can change these saving options by selecting Edit⇨Preferences⇨File Handling (Windows) Photoshop⇨Preferences⇨File Handling (Mac), as shown in Figure 9-1. Look for the drop-down menu that states Automatically Save Recovery Information Every: and select the length of time you would like to lapse between saving.

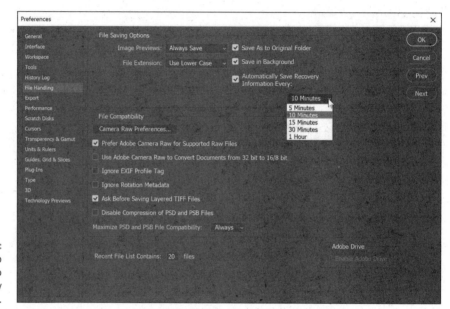

**FIGURE 9-1:**
You can set up Photoshop to automatically save your files.

# Choosing a File Format for Saving

When you choose File⇨Save for the first time (or you choose File⇨Save As to save a different version of a file), you see at least 18 different file formats to choose from in the Save As Type (Windows) or Format (Mac) drop-down list. We don't cover every format in this chapter (some are specific to proprietary workflows), but we show you which formats are best for the typical workflow you may face.

## Wonderful and easy Photoshop PSD

If you're in an Adobe workflow (you're using any Adobe product), you can keep the image in the native Photoshop PSD format. By selecting this format, transparency, layers, channels, and paths are all maintained and left intact when placed in the other applications.

If compatibility with older versions of Photoshop is an issue, choose Edit⇨ Preferences⇨File Handling (Windows) or Photoshop⇨Preferences⇨File Handling (Mac). Select Always from the Maximize PSD and PSB File Compatibility drop-down list. This choice saves a *composite* (flattened) image along with the layers of your document. (The PSB format is used for saving large Photoshop documents — in this case, *large* means they measure more than 30,000 x 30,000 pixels.)

**REMEMBER**

Leaving the Maximize PSD and PSB File Compatibility drop-down list set to Always creates a larger file. If file size is an issue, leave the drop-down list set to Ask and use the feature only when you need to open the Photoshop file in older versions of Photoshop.

## Photoshop EPS

Many applications accept the Encapsulated PostScript (EPS) file format. It's used to transfer PostScript-language artwork between various applications. It supports vector data, duotones, and clipping paths. This means that text layers and other vector-based artwork will remain scalable.

When you choose to save in the EPS format, an EPS Options dialog box appears. Leave the defaults alone and click OK.

**WARNING**

Alter the settings in the EPS Options dialog box *only* if you're familiar with custom printer calibration or if you need to save your image to a specific screen ruling. Screen rulings (*lpi,* or lines per inch) are usually set in a page layout application, such as Adobe InDesign or QuarkXPress.

**TIP**

Even though PowerPoint accepts files saved from Photoshop in the EPS format, it is better to use the PNG format. The PNG format is designed for a better onscreen presentation and produces clearer results. Find out more in the later "PNG" section.

## Photoshop PDF

If compatibility is an issue, save your file in the Photoshop PDF (Portable Document Format) format. PDF files are supported by more than a dozen platforms when viewers use Acrobat or Adobe Reader. (Adobe Reader is available for free at www.adobe.com.) What a perfect way to send pictures to friends and family! Saving a file in the Photoshop PDF format supports the capability to edit the image when you open the file by choosing File⇨Open in Photoshop.

**TIP**

If you're planning to send a layered file by email, choose Layer⇨Flatten Layers before choosing to save the file as a PDF. This command cuts the file size considerably.

## TIFF

The Tagged Image File Format (TIFF) is a flexible bitmap image format that's supported by most image–editing and page-layout applications widely supported by all printers. TIFF supports layers and channels but has a maximum size of 4GB. We hope your files aren't that large!

## DCS

The Photoshop Desktop Color Separation (DCS) 1.0 and 2.0 formats are versions of EPS that enable you to save color separations of CMYK (Cyan, Magenta, Yellow, Black) or multichannel files. Some workflows require this format, but if you've implemented spot color channels in an image, using the DCS file format is required to maintain them.

Choose the DCS 2.0 format unless you receive specific instructions to use the DCS 1.0 format — for example, for reasons of incompatibility in certain workflows.

# Saving Images for the Web

There are many ways that you can save your art for the web or application design but the method that you choose depends upon your content. In this section, you discover the major formats used for website and application design that you can use within Photoshop, PNG, JPG, and GIF.

**TIP**

Ensuring that the image size is correct before you save the file for the web is a good practice. If you need to read up on resizing images, see Chapter 5 of this minibook. Generally speaking, you should resize the image to the right pixel dimensions. Choose Filter⇨Sharpen⇨Unsharp Mask to regain some of the detail that is lost in resizing the image, and then save the image for the web.

## PNG

When you choose to save in the PNG (Portable Network Graphics) format, you have two options from which to choose — PNG-8 and PNG-24.

The PNG-8 format refers to palette variant, which supports only 256 colors, this allows the file format to be smaller in size than some other formats. PNG-8 can be a GIF substitute; see the "Saving a GIF" section, later in this chapter, for more details about that format.

PNG-24 saves 24-bit images that support anti-aliasing (the smooth transition from one color to another). These images work beautifully for continuous-tone images but are much larger than JPEG files. The truly awesome feature of a PNG file is that it supports 256 levels of transparency. In other words, you can apply varying amounts of transparency in an image, as shown in Figure 9-2, where the image shows through to the background.

**FIGURE 9-2:**
A PNG-24 file with varying amounts of transparency.

There are several ways in which you can save a PNG image:

>> **Choose File ↔ Quick Export as PNG:** This does not provide any additional save options other than the ability to change the name. If you want to set up preferences for your Quick Export, you can find settings by going to Edit ↔ Preferences ↔ Export (Windows) or Photoshop ↔ Preferences ↔ Export (Mac), as shown in Figure 9-3. A great format if you have an image set to the right size and don't need any other modifications.

>> **Choose File ↔ Export Save For Web (Legacy).**

>> **In the Preset drop-down menu, in the upper right of the Save for Web dialog box, you can choose PNG-24 or PNG-8 Dithered. Then press Save.**

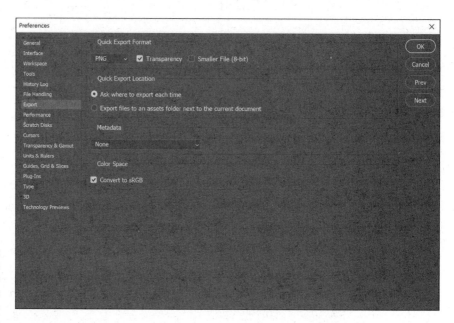

*Note:* Photoshop can use dithering to mix the pixels of available colors to simulate missing colors.

## JPEG

JPEG (Joint Photographic Experts Group) is a good format for continuous-tone images — those with smooth transitions from one color to another, as in photographs — like the image shown in Figure 9-4.

**REMEMBER**

The JPEG format is lossy, so you shouldn't save a JPEG and then open it, edit it, and save it again as a JPEG. Because the JPEG compression causes data to be lost, your image will eventually look like it was printed on the same texture as a paper towel. Save a copy of the file as a JPEG, keeping the original image in PSD format if you need to edit the image later, open the original PSD, make your changes, save the PSD, and then save a copy of the edited file as a JPEG.

The JPEG format does *not* support transparency, but you can cheat the system a bit by using matting.

A good image to save in the JPEG format is a typical photograph or illustration with lots of smooth transitions from one color to the next; this includes graphics that use gradients. To save an image as a JPEG, follow these steps:

**FIGURE 9-4:**
Images with
smooth transi-
tions from one
color to another
are good candi-
dates for the JPEG
file format.

1. **Choose File⇨Export⇨Save for Web (Legacy), and then click the 2-Up tab to view the original image (left) at the same time as the optimized image (right).**

2. **Select one of the JPEG preset settings from the Settings drop-down list.**

   You can choose Low, Medium, or High or customize a level between the presets by using the Quality slider.

3. **Leave the Optimized checkbox selected to build the best JPEG at the smallest size.**

   The only issue with leaving this checkbox selected is that some very old browsers don't read the JPEG correctly (not likely an issue for most viewers).

4. **Leave the Embed Color Profile checkbox deselected unless you're in a color-managed workflow and color accuracy is essential.**

   Selecting this checkbox increases the file size, and most people aren't looking for *exact* color matches from an image on the monitor.

5. **If you have to have the file size even smaller, use the Blur slider to bring down some detail.**

   It's funny, but one JPEG that has exactly the same pixel dimensions as another may vary in file size because the more detailed an image is, the more information is needed. So, an image of lots of apples will be larger than an image of the same size that has one apple in it. The Blur feature blurs the image (surprise!), so you may want to use it for only a low source image in Dreamweaver.

6. **(Optional) Select a matte color from the Matte drop-down list.**

   Because JPEG doesn't support transparency, you can flood the transparent area with a color you select from the Matte drop-down list. Select the color you're using for the background of your web page by selecting Other and entering the hexadecimal color in the lower portion of the Color Picker.

7. **Click Save.**

## GIF

Supposedly, the way you pronounce GIF (Graphics Interchange Format) is based on the brand of peanut butter you eat. Is it pronounced like the peanut butter brand (Jif) or with a hard *g*, as in *gift?* Most people seem to pronounce it as "gift" (minus the T).

Use GIF if you have large areas of solid color, such as a logo like the one shown in Figure 9-5.

**FIGURE 9-5:**
An image with lots of solid color makes a good GIF.

GIF isn't *lossy* (it doesn't lose data when the file is compressed in this format), but it reduces file size by using a limited number of colors in a color table. The lower the number of colors, the smaller the file size. If you've ever worked in Index Color mode, you're familiar with this process.

Transparency is supported by the GIF file format. Generally, GIF files don't do a good job on anything that needs smooth transitions from one color to another because of the format's poor support of *anti-aliasing*, which is the method Photoshop uses to smooth jagged edges. When an image transitions from one color to another, Photoshop produces multiple colors of pixels to create an even blend between the two colors.

Because anti-aliasing needs to create multiple colors for this effect, GIF files generally aren't recommended. In fact, when you reduce the size of a GIF file, you're more apt to see *banding* (an artifact that appears as streaks in the image) because the anti-aliasing can't take place with the limited number of colors available in GIF.

You can, of course, dramatically increase the number of colors to create a smoother transition, but then you risk creating monster files that take forever to download.

## Saving a GIF

When you choose File➪Save for Web, you first see the available GIF options. They may be clearer to you if you have an image open (with lots of solid color in it).

To save a file for the web as a GIF, follow these steps:

1. **Choose File➪Export➪Save for Web (Legacy).**

   The Save for Web dialog box appears.

2. **At the top, click the 2-Up tab.**

   You see the original image on the left and the optimized image on the right (or top and bottom, depending on the image proportions).

   In the lower portion of the display, you see the original file size compared with the optimized file size, as well as the approximate download time. The download time is important. Nobody wants to wait around for a web page to load; most people don't wait more than ten seconds for an entire web page to appear, so try to keep an individual image's download time to a few seconds at the most. Remember that waiting for all images on a page to load can add up to a monstrous wait time for the viewer!

   **TIP**

   Change the estimated download speed by choosing the Select Download Speed drop-down menu to the right of the file size information in the lower-left of the preview window.

3. **Select GIF 32 No Dither from the Preset drop-down list.**

   You may see a change already. As you can see in Figure 9-6, Photoshop supplies you with presets to choose from, or you can customize and save your own.

**FIGURE 9-6:**
Choose from presets, or create your own custom settings.

4. **Choose whether you want dithering applied to the image by selecting an option from the Specify the Dither Algorithm drop-down list.**

   This choice is purely personal. Because you may be limiting colors, Photoshop can use dithering to mix the pixels of available colors to simulate missing colors. Many designers choose the No Dither option because dithering can create unnatural color speckles in an image.

5. **If your image is on a transparent layer and you want to maintain that transparency on a web page, select the Transparency checkbox.**

## Using the color table in the Save for Web dialog box

When you save an image in GIF using the Save for Web feature, you see the color table. This color table displays the limited color palette used in the image and is located on the right side of the Save for Web window. The color table is important because it enables you to see the colors used in the image and to customize the color table by using the options at the bottom.

You may want to customize your color table by selecting some colors to be web safe and locking colors so that they're not bumped off as you reduce the number that's used.

To customize a color table, follow these steps:

1. **If your image has only a few colors that you want to convert to web-safe colors, choose the Eyedropper tool from the left of the Save for Web window and click on the color (right on the image) in the Optimized view.**

   The sampled color is highlighted in the color table.

2. **Click the Web Safe button at the bottom of the color table, as shown in Figure 9-7.**

   When you cross over this button, the tooltip Shifts/Unshifts Selected Colors to Web Palette appears.

   A diamond appears, indicating that the color is now web safe.

3. **Lock colors that you don't want to delete as you reduce the number of colors in the color table.**

   Select a color with the Eyedropper tool, or select it in the color table, and then click the Lock Color button. A white square appears in the lower-right corner, indicating that the color is locked.

   Obviously, if you lock 32 colors and then reduce the color table to 24, some of your locked colors are deleted. If you choose to add colors, those locked colors are the first to return.

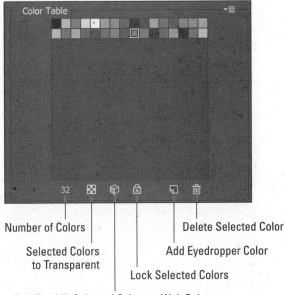

**FIGURE 9-7:** Customize colors by using the color table in the Save for Web window.

Number of Colors

Selected Colors to Transparent

Shift/Unshift Selected Colors to Web Palette

Lock Selected Colors

Add Eyedropper Color

Delete Selected Color

How is the color table created? Based on the color-reduction algorithm method you choose, the Save for Web feature samples the number of colors you indicate. If keeping colors web-safe is important, select the Restrictive (Web) option for the method; if you want your image to look better on most monitors but not necessarily to be web-safe, choose the Adaptive option.

4. **Use the Colors drop-down list or enter a number to add or delete colors from the color table.**

5. **If your image uses transparency, select the Transparency checkbox near the top of the Save for Web dialog box.**

Remember that transparency is counted as one of your colors in the color table.

6. **Select the Interlaced checkbox only if your GIF image is large (25K or larger).**

Selecting this option causes the image to build in several scans on the web page — a low-resolution image that pops up quickly and is then refreshed with the higher-resolution image when the download is complete. Interlacing gives the illusion of the download going faster but makes the file size larger, so use it only if necessary.

7. **Click Save.**

Now the image is ready to be attached to an email message or used in a web page.

## Matte

Matting appears as a choice in the GIF, JPEG, and PNG format options. Matting is useful if you don't want ragged edges appearing around your images. Matting looks for pixels that are 50 percent or more transparent and makes them fully transparent; any pixels that are 49 percent or less transparent become fully opaque.

Even though your image might be on a transparent layer, it will have some "iffy" pixels — the ones that aren't sure what they want to be . . . to be transparent or not to be transparent. Choose a matte color to blend in with the transparent iffy pixels by selecting Eyedropper Color, Foreground Color, Background Color, White, Black, or Other (to open the Color Picker) from the Matte drop-down list in the Save for Web dialog box.

# Saving Settings

Whether you're saving a GIF, JPG, or PNG file, you probably spent some time experimenting with settings to find what works best for your needs. Save selected options to reload later by saving the settings. Do so by clicking the arrow to the right of the Preset drop-down list. Select Save Settings from the list that appears and name your settings. Your named, customized settings then appear in the Preset drop-down list.

## Generating your images assets

If you are busy creating designs for websites and applications, you will appreciate the Generate Image Assets feature. This feature allows you to name layers by adding extensions to layer names that will automatically determine the file format upon saving.

Follow these steps to try out this feature. You can use the image provided named generate-assets in the Book03-Photoshop folder.

1.  **Open the file named Generate-Assets, or any other file that has multiple layers. Note that the Generate-Assets file has three layers.**

2.  **In the Layers panel, add the following extensions to the end of the layer names, as shown in Figure 9-8.**

    - evening-yoga**.gif**
    - sunset**.jpg**
    - gradient**.png**

3.  **Now choose File⇨Generate⇨Image Assets.**

You don't see it happening, but a new folder has been created in the same folder location that is named Generate-Assets-assets. Inside this folder are the named layers, in the format that you indicated by using the extension you added. A great time-saving feature for those creating complex art for applications or the web.

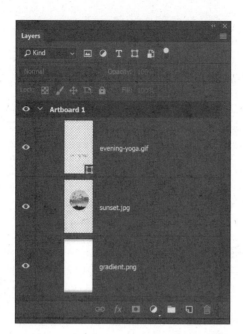

**FIGURE 9-8:**
Add extensions
to the end of the
layers' names.

# InDesign CC

4

# Contents at a Glance

# Chapter 1

# Introducing InDesign CC

nDesign is a sophisticated page-layout program. You can use it to create professional-looking documents, including newsletters, books, and magazines. You can also use it to create documents for distribution on a tablet such as an iPad, and even documents that include interactivity or videos. InDesign has evolved into a tool that lets you publish content to just about any device or in print. For example, using InDesign you can create a document and distribute content in print and then add hyperlinks and video and export it to PDF or EPUB.

As powerful an application as InDesign is, you'd think it would be difficult to use, but you'll find that creating most basic documents is a snap. This minibook shows you how to use InDesign to make creative page layouts. In this chapter, you discover the InDesign interface and start your first publication.

## Getting Started with InDesign CC

InDesign is used for creating page layouts that include type, graphics (such as fills and strokes), and images. The InDesign document you see in Figure 1-1 includes elements from Adobe Illustrator (logos) and Photoshop (images). If this file were to be exported as a PDF or an EPUB file, it could include video or interactive buttons.

**FIGURE 1-1:**
A sample
page layout
created using
InDesign CC.

In the following sections, you get familiar with creating and opening documents in InDesign. In Chapters 2 through 8 in this minibook, you see how to add various elements to your pages.

## Creating a new publication

After you launch InDesign, you can create a new InDesign document. Just follow these steps to create a new publication:

1. **Choose File⇨New⇨Document.**

   The New Document dialog box opens, as shown in Figure 1-2.

2. **Select whether you're designing a print, web, or mobile document from the header Intent menu.**

   **TIP**

   If you want to preview your adjustments in this panel, select the Preview option at the bottom of the New Document window. Your updates in the steps that follow will adjust the appearance of the document in InDesign while you make your settings.

3. **Enter a value in the Number of Pages text field for the number of pages in the document.**

   This value can be between 1 and 9999. If you aren't sure how many pages will be in your document, take a guess. You can easily add or delete pages later using the Pages panel. (See the section, "Pages panel," later in this chapter.)

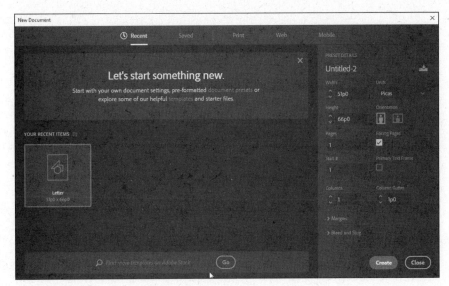

**FIGURE 1-2:**
Setting up a new
document with
InDesign.

4. **For this example, confirm the Facing Pages checkbox has been selected to have the pages arranged as spreads with left and right pages.**

With this option selected, pages in your document are arranged in pairs, so you have *spreads,* which are facing or adjacent pages in a layout. For example, you select this option if you're creating a publication that will be arranged like a book or magazine. If you deselect this option, pages are arranged individually, which is a good choice for a single-page flyer or a document with only a front and back side.

5. **Select a Blank Document Preset.**

The Blank Document Preset should be set to the size of paper you intend to print on or the size at which the content will be displayed. You can also create your own custom sized document by typing values into the Width and Height text boxes.

The Orientation setting changes from Portrait (tall) to Landscape (wide) based on the settings you enter in the Width and Height fields of the Page Size section.

**TIP**

The Intent selection you make determines the choices in the Blank Document Presets list. If you select Web for the Intent, you can choose from various screen resolutions, whereas if you select Mobile, you can select from various popular tablet sizes, such as the iPad, NOOK/Kindle Fire, or Android.

**TIP**

You can enter page sizes using most common forms of measurement or just use the appropriate abbreviation. For example, you enter **8 in** for 8 inches or **15 cm** for 15 centimeters. You can use most forms of measurement in all InDesign dialog boxes and panels; just make sure to specify the form of measurement you want to use. When creating web or mobile documents, these values switch to pixels.

6. **Choose a number for the columns on the page.**

   This step creates guides for columns that do not print or display in the completed project. These guides help you organize your pages as you create them. You can also enter a value in the Gutter field, which specifies the space between each of the columns. For more information about using columns in page layout, see Chapter 3 of this minibook.

7. **Choose values for the page margins.**

   Notice the Make All Settings the Same button, which is a chain icon, to the right of the four text fields where you enter margin values. Toggle this button to set all margins to the same value, or set different values (broken chain icon).

   If you see Top, Bottom, Inside, and Outside, you're specifying margins for a page layout that has facing pages, which you specified earlier. If you see Top, Bottom, Left, and Right, you're creating a page layout without facing pages. The *inside* margins refer to the margins at the middle of the spread, and the *outside* margins refer to the outer left and right margins of a book or magazine. You can set the Inside setting to accommodate the binding of a book, which may need wider margins than the outside.

   **TIP**

   If you use the same settings repeatedly, saving those settings as a preset is a good idea. Get your settings the way you want them, and then click the Save Document Preset button, located to the right of the document title and under the Preset Details header before you click Create. Enter a name for the preset, and then click Save Preset. After you save your preset, select Saved from the header menu (refer to the top of Figure 1-2), and you can select your saved preset whenever you create a new document.

8. **When you're finished, click Create.**

   After you click Create in the New Document dialog box, the new document is created with the settings you just specified.

Margins, columns, orientation, and page size are discussed in more detail in Chapter 3 of this minibook.

## Opening an existing publication

You may have InDesign files on your hard drive that you created or have saved from another source. To open existing InDesign documents (files that end with .indd), follow these steps:

1. **Choose File⇨Open.**

   The Open a File dialog box appears.

2. **Browse your hard drive and select a file to open.**

   Select a file by clicking the document's title. To select more than one document, press Ctrl (⌘ on the Mac) while you click the filenames.

3. **Click the Open button to open the file.**

   The file opens in the workspace.

## Looking at the document setup

If you need to change the size of your pages or the number of pages in a document that's already open in the workspace, you can make those changes in the Document Setup dialog box. To access and modify settings in the Document Setup dialog box, follow these steps:

1. **Choose File⇨Document Setup.**

   The Document Setup dialog box opens.

   *Note:* You can change the value in the Number of Pages text field if you need the number of pages in your document to be greater than or less than the current value.

   The number of pages in your document updates after you close this dialog box. You can also add more pages by choosing Layout⇨Pages⇨Insert Pages to insert several pages, or Layout⇨Pages⇨Add Page to add a single page, or by using the Pages panel.

2. **Select a new option from the Page Size drop-down list or manually enter values into the Width and Height text fields to change the page size.**

   You can also click the up and down arrows in the Width and Height text fields to choose a new value.

3. **Click the Portrait or Landscape button to change the page orientation.**

   The page orientation updates in the workspace after you close this dialog box.

4. **Click OK when you finish changing your document setup.**

   The modifications are applied to the open document.

TIP

If you make changes to the Document Setup dialog box when you have no documents open, the changes become the default settings for all new documents you create.

# Touring the Workspace

Just like the other applications in the Creative Cloud, InDesign has a standardized layout. Using panels that can be docked and a single-row Tools panel, you can keep much more space open in your work area.

The InDesign workspace, or *user interface*, includes a large number of tools and panels — but most users use only a few. You'll likely use several panels over and over again, so you should keep them easily accessible. In the default user workspace, many of these panels are already docked to the right. Figure 1-3 shows how the InDesign workspace layout looks when you open a new document. The Windows workspace is nearly identical to the Macintosh version of InDesign.

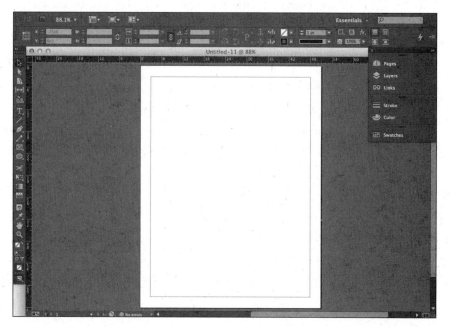

**FIGURE 1-3:**
The InDesign default workspace.

Here are the elements that create the InDesign workspace:

>> **Page:** The main area of the InDesign workspace is a page. It's the area that's printed or exported when you finish making a layout.

>> **Master pages:** You can define how certain text elements and graphics appear in an entire document (or just portions of it) by using a master page. It's much like a template for your document because you can reuse elements through-out the pages. For example, if you have an element you want on each page (such as page numbering), you can create it on the master page. If you need to change an element on the master page, you can change it at any time, and

your changes are reflected on every page that the master page is applied to. You access master pages in the Pages panel. (You find out more about master pages in Chapter 3 of this minibook.)

>> **Spread:** A *spread* refers to a set of two or more pages that will be printed side by side. You usually see spreads in magazines and books when you open them — just like the book you're holding now. If your document has only a single page — front and back, or with only one side — you will not see a spread in the InDesign document window. InDesign will display only the one page, or, for a two-sided page, both pages (if you reduce the magnification).

>> **Pasteboard:** The pasteboard is the area around the edge of a page. You can use the pasteboard to store objects until you're ready to put them into your layout. Pasteboards aren't shared between pages or spreads. For example, if you have certain elements placed on a pasteboard for pages 4 and 5, you can't access these elements when you're working on pages 8 and 9 — so each page or spread has its own pasteboard.

## Tools

The Tools panel (See Figure 1-4) is where you find tools to edit, manipulate, or select elements in your document, as well as tools to make adjustments to pages. Simply use the cursor and click a tool to select it. See Figure 1-4 for the default Tools panel layout.

**FIGURE 1-4:** The Tools panel contains tools for creating, selecting, and editing elements and adjusting pages.

Labels (left side): Selection tool, Page Shift tool, Content Collector tool, Line tool, Pencil tool, Rectangle tool, Free Transform tool, Gradient Feather tool, Eyedropper tool, Zoom tool, Fill, Default Fill and Stroke color, Formatting Affects Container, Normal view

Labels (right side): Direct Selection tool, Gap tool, Type tool, Pen tool, Rectangle Frame tool, Scissors tool, Gradient Swatch tool, Note tool, Hand tool, Stroke, Formatting Affects Text, Apply Color

If you decide that a single row of tools just isn't for you, you can go back to an older version's Tools panel by clicking the two arrows in the gray bar at the top of the Tools panel. If you want to relocate the tools, click the bar at the top of the tools, under the double arrows, and drag the tools panel to a new location.

You find out more about these tools and how to use them in the related chapters of this minibook. For example, we discuss the drawing tools in Chapter 4 of this minibook.

With the tools in the Tools panel, you can do the following:

>> Create stunning new content on a page using drawing, frame, and text tools.

>> Select existing content on a page to move or edit.

>> View the page in different ways by moving (panning) and magnifying the page or spread.

>> Edit existing objects, such as shapes, lines, and text. Use the Selection tool to select existing objects so that you can change them.

When a tool has a small arrow next to the button's icon, more tools are hiding behind it. When you click the tool, and hold down the mouse button, a menu opens that shows you other available tools. While pressing the mouse button, move the cursor to the tool you want and release the mouse button after it's highlighted.

## Menus

The menus on the main menu bar are used to access some of the main commands and control the user interface of InDesign. They also allow you to open and close panels used to edit and make settings for the publication.

InDesign menu commands such as New, Open, and Save are similar to most other applications you're probably familiar with. The InDesign menus also include commands that are especially used for page layout, such as Insert with Placeholder Text. For more information on using menus, see Book 1, Chapter 4. Remember to refer to the common commands and shortcuts that are also detailed in that chapter.

The InDesign main menu has the following options:

>> **File:** This menu includes some of the basic commands to create, open, and save documents. It also includes the Place command to import new content and many options to control document settings, exporting documents, and printing.

» **Edit:** You can access many commands for editing and controlling selections in this menu — such as copying and keyboard shortcuts. The dictionary and spell checker are on this menu, too.

» **Layout:** Use this menu to create guides. These options help you lay elements on the page accurately and properly align them. Use the menu to navigate the document's pages and spreads.

» **Type:** From this menu, you can select fonts and control characters in the layout. You can access the many settings related to text from this menu, which opens the associated panel where you make the changes.

» **Object:** You can modify the look and placement of objects on the page with this menu. Which options are available on this menu depends on which element you've selected in the workspace, such as a text field or an image.

» **Table:** Use this menu to create, set up, modify, and control tables on the page.

» **View:** You can modify the view of the page from this menu, including zooming in and out, as well as work with guides, rulers, or grids to help you lay out elements.

» **Window:** Use this menu to open and close panels or switch between open documents.

» **Help:** This menu is where you can access the Help documents for InDesign and configure any plug-ins you have installed.

# Panels

In the default layout, you see a large area for the document. To the right of the document are several *panels* that snap to the edge of the workspace — panels that are attached to the edge of the workspace are considered *docked.* Panels are used to control the publication and edit elements on pages. Panels can be maximized, minimized, moved around, or closed altogether.

To expand a panel, you can simply click the panel name, and it expands. The panels you expand are automatically collapsed again when a different panel is selected.

If you'd rather work with all panels expanded, simply click the left-facing double arrows on the gray bar above the panels. You can collapse all the panels again by clicking the right-facing double arrows on the gray bar above the expanded panels.

Even though some InDesign panels perform different functions, similar panels are grouped together depending on what they're used for. You can change the groupings by clicking and dragging a panel's tab into another grouping.

Some panels change when you're manipulating specific types of content on an InDesign page. Throughout Chapters 2 through 8 of this minibook, you discover these specific panels as you create layouts. For now, we briefly show you two general InDesign panels: Control and Pages.

## Control panel

The Control panel, located across the top of the document window, is used to edit just about any element you have selected in InDesign, as shown for the Type tool in Figure 1-5. This panel is *context sensitive*, so it changes depending on which element you've selected on a page. For example, if you have selected text within a frame on the page, the Control panel displays options allowing you to edit the text. If you have a shape selected, the panel displays options allowing you to modify the shape.

**FIGURE 1-5:**
The Control panel, when the Type tool is active.

Figure 1-6 shows the Control panel when a frame is selected using the Selection tool. The Control panel menu allows you to select options for the frame.

**FIGURE 1-6:**
The Control panel, when a frame is selected using the Selection tool.

## Pages panel

You can control pages by using the Pages panel, as shown in Figure 1-7. This panel allows you to arrange, add, and delete pages in your document. If you are creating electronic documents, you can also use the Pages panel for creating alternative layouts for vertical and horizontal displays on a tablet. You can also navigate among pages with this panel, which we discuss further in Chapter 3 of this minibook.

You can also add and delete pages by choosing Layout⇨Pages, and even use a keyboard shortcut to add pages, Ctrl+Shift+P (Windows) or ⌘+Shift+P (Mac).

**TIP**

**FIGURE 1-7:**
Use the Pages
panel to add,
delete, and move
pages, as well as
create alternative
layouts for tablet
displays.

**REMEMBER**

You can hide all open panels (including the Control panel) by pressing the Tab key; press Tab for them to return to view. In InDesign CC, you can leave tools and panels hidden and access them when you want by moving the cursor to the left or right side of the work area. Hover your cursor over the thin vertical gray bar on either side, and the tools or panels (depending on which side of the workspace you're in) reappear! By the way, they go away again after you leave the area.

You can navigate the document's pages by using the left- and right-arrow buttons on either side of the page number in the lower-left corner of the document window. You can also move to a specific page by entering a page number into the page field and pressing Enter/Return or by selecting the page from the drop-down list in the lower-left corner of the Document window.

## Contextual menus

*Contextual menus* (or context menus) are menus that pop up when you right-click (Windows) or Control-click (Mac) the mouse. Contextual menus change depending on which element you click and which tool you're using. If you have no elements selected, the contextual menu opens for the overall InDesign document, allowing you to select options such as Zoom, Paste, Rulers, and Guides. If you have an element selected, your options include transforming, modifying, and editing the object.

**REMEMBER**

Contextual menus are context sensitive (hence the name!). Remember to select an element on the page before you right-click (Windows) or Control-click (Mac) to open the contextual menu. If you don't select the object first, the menu that displays is for the document instead of for an object.

You can find out more about editing and transforming elements in Chapters 2 and 3 of this minibook.

# Setting Up the Workspace

Workspace settings are important because they help you quickly create the type of layout you need. Overall document settings control elements such as grids or guides that help you align elements on the page. Neither guides nor grids print when you print or publish your document.

## Showing and hiding grids and guides

Grids and guides are onscreen lines that help you with your layout but, by default, don't appear when printing. A *document grid* is applied across the entire document page area. Use the document grid when you need to divide a document into sections to achieve your intended design. You can have objects on a page align to the document grid, which helps you accurately line up or space objects on your page.

Another type of grid is the *baseline grid,* which runs horizontally across the page. Use the baseline grid to make sure that text in different columns is aligned, thus creating a cleaner page layout.

REMEMBER

The *document grid* is used for aligning elements on the page, and the *baseline grid* is used for aligning the bottom of text across multiple columns.

>> To show or hide the document grid, choose View⇨Grids & Guides⇨Show (or Hide) Document Grid.

>> To show or hide the baseline grid, choose View⇨Grids & Guides⇨Show (or Hide) Baseline Grid. If you don't see the baseline grid, you may be zoomed out below the view threshold of 75%.

You can immediately see the difference between these two kinds of grids.

Guides can be placed anywhere on the page (or pasteboard) and are used to accurately position objects in a layout. Unlike grids, guides are typically created individually. Use them to align specific objects — such as the tops of several images — that appear across a page. Objects can snap to guides just like they can snap to a grid.

To create a guide and show or hide guides, follow these steps:

**1.** **Make sure that rulers are visible by choosing View⇨Show Rulers.**

Rulers appear in the workspace. If you already have rulers visible, the option View⇨Hide Rulers is on the View menu. Don't hide the rulers.

2. **Move the cursor to a horizontal or vertical ruler.**

   Make sure that the cursor is over a ruler.

3. **Click the ruler and drag the mouse toward the page.**

   A *ruler guide* shows on the page as a line.

4. **Release the mouse where you want the guide.**

   You just created a ruler guide!

5. **To hide the guide, choose View⇨Grids & Guides⇨Hide Guides.**

   This step hides the guide you created but doesn't delete it. You can make the guide reappear easily in the next step.

6. **To see the guide again, choose View⇨Grids & Guides⇨Show Guides.**

   The guide you created is shown on the page again.

**TIP**

You can edit the color of the ruler guide you created by positioning the mouse over it, clicking once to select it, and then right-clicking (Windows) or Control-clicking it (Mac) and selecting a new color from the Ruler Guides option.

You can find out more about the different kinds of guides and how to use them in page layout in Chapter 3 of this minibook.

**TIP**

You can also control the color of the guides and grid in your preferences. Access them by choosing Edit⇨Preferences⇨Grids (Windows) or InDesign⇨Preferences⇨Grids (Mac). You may need to scroll down through the Edit drop-down menu to find Preferences. When the Preferences dialog box opens, you can change the color and spacing of the lines. Click Guides & Pasteboards in the list on the left to change the color settings for guides. To change the color of your ruler guides, go to Layout⇨Ruler Guides, and then click on the color drop-down menu to select a different color, or click on the color box and select a custom color from the Color Picker. This changes the color of all future ruler guides.

## Snapping to a grid or a guide

You can have elements on the page snap to a grid or a guide. Grid or guide snapping is useful so that you don't have to eyeball the alignment of several elements to one another, because they're precisely aligned to a grid or guide. To make sure that this setting is enabled, choose View⇨Grids & Guides⇨Snap to Document Grid or View⇨Grids & Guides⇨Snap to Guides. If these options are already selected, clicking them will turn them off.

# Using Smart Guides

Give yourself an added hand when aligning objects on the InDesign page with Smart Guides. Illustrator and Photoshop users may be familiar with these interactive guides, but if you're not, read on to discover how you can take advantage of them.

You can experiment with this capability by creating two objects in an InDesign document. It doesn't matter which object or shape — any will do!

With the Selection tool, click and slowly drag one object in a circular motion around the other. You'll notice guides appear and disappear, indicating when the objects are aligned on the top, center, or bottom of the other object, as shown in Figure 1-8.

**FIGURE 1-8:**
Click and drag one shape around another to see the interaction with Smart Guides.

As a default, pink guides appear when you align an object with the center of the page, as shown in Figure 1-9.

**FIGURE 1-9:**
Know when your object is at the exact center of the page when a guide crosshair appears.

**TIP**

You can see a print preview of your document by clicking the Preview Mode button at the bottom of the Tools panel. Click and hold the Normal button to access the Preview Mode. When you click this button, all object bounding boxes, guides, and the grid disappear.

## Customizing menus

InDesign has many menus and many choices under each menu. It's likely you'll need to use only some of these menu choices. If you discover that you're wading through many menu items to find the items you need, you can customize InDesign to hide menu items you don't use.

To customize your InDesign menus, follow these steps:

**1. Choose Edit⇨Menus.**

The Menu Customization window opens.

**2. In the Application Menu Command column, click the triangle next to the menu(s) you want to customize.**

For example, if you never expect to import XML, which is located under the File menu, click the triangle to the left of the File menu to display this menu item.

**3. Click the eye icon next to the menu item that you want to hide.**

Or if you want to highlight a menu item, click the color column to the right of the eye icon to add a color to the menu choice.

**4. Click the Save As button at the top of the window to save the menu customization set. Enter a name for your customized menu set, click OK to save the name, and then click OK again to close the Menu Customization window.**

The customized menus are saved. To return to the original default menus, or to further customize the menus, choose Edit⇨Menus at any time you're using InDesign.

## Customizing the interface appearance

InDesign lets you adjust the overall appearance of the workspace to customize the color theme. You can set exactly how dark or light you would like the panels and pasteboard to be, or select between several predefined settings.

To customize the InDesign interface appearance, follow these steps:

1. **Choose Edit⇨Preferences⇨Interface (Windows) or InDesign⇨Preferences⇨ Interface (Mac).**

   The Preferences window opens, with the Interface category active. The Appearance section at the top of this window is where you adjust settings that affect the user interface appearance.

2. **In the Appearance section, adjust the color theme for the user interface and pasteboard.**

   The default setting is Medium Dark, and you can switch between each setting and InDesign will preview your selection. Alternatively, you can enter a custom percentage setting to fine-tune the brightness setting.

3. **Select or deselect Match Pasteboard to Theme Color.**

   The option is selected by default, which means the pasteboard (the area around your document) is a darker shade. Deselect this option if you prefer a white pasteboard.

4. **Click OK to apply your changes.**

   The workspace appearance updates.

## Saving a custom workspace

You've seen that InDesign has a number of panels. If you find that you're using some panels more than others, you can have InDesign remember the grouping of panels you use most frequently, including which ones are visible and which ones are hidden. InDesign calls this a *workspace.* The next time you want a certain group of panels open together, you can return to the workspace you previously saved. The workspace isn't attached to a particular document, so you can have one workspace for editing text and another for working with a layout.

To save a custom workspace, follow these steps:

1. **Have the InDesign workspace configured in the way you want to save it — with any panels open that you might want to access together.**

   The open panels will be saved as a custom workspace.

2. **Choose Window⇨Workspace⇨New Workspace.**

   The New Workspace dialog box opens.

3. **Choose whether to save the panel locations or any menus that have been customized. Type a new name for the workspace in the Name text field.**

   Enter a name that reflects the type of work you do in that workspace, such as text editing or layout.

4. **Click OK.**

   The custom workspace is saved. The name you entered for your workspace is displayed on the Workspaces menu.

To access your workspace, choose Window↔Workspace↔*Your Workspace* (where *Your Workspace* is the name you gave the workspace in Step 3).

You can delete the workspace if you no longer want it saved. Simply choose Window↔Workspace↔Delete Workspace.

# Working with Documents

After you're comfortable getting around the InDesign workspace, you're ready to begin working with a new document. After you've started working on a document, you should find out how to import content from other programs and to save that document on your hard drive. A lot of the content you use when creating layouts with InDesign is imported from other programs — both Creative Cloud applications like Photoshop and Illustrator, and non-Creative Cloud applications like Microsoft Word and Excel. You use InDesign to organize, modify, and integrate text and graphics into a layout. To begin, we show you the steps needed to import content and save new files.

We show you how to open new and existing documents earlier in this chapter, in the sections "Creating a new publication" and "Opening an existing publication."

**TECHNICAL STUFF**

You may also be working with a *template,* which is a layout you reuse by applying it to a document that requires a particular predesigned format. For example, a company may use a template for its official letterhead because every new letter requires the same page format and design. InDesign templates use the .indt file extension.

## Importing new content

You can use many different kinds of content in an InDesign document because you can import many supported file types. You can import text, formatted tables, and graphics that help you create an effective layout. This capability makes integration with many different programs easy.

Follow these steps to import an image file into InDesign (in this example, we import a bitmap graphic file):

1. **Choose File⇨New⇨Document.**

   The New Document dialog box appears.

2. **Review the settings, make any changes depending upon the size and type of document you want to create, and then click Create.**

   Feel free to alter the settings to change the number of pages, page size, and intent before clicking Create. Afterwards, a new document opens.

3. **Choose File⇨Place.**

   The Place dialog box opens, enabling you to browse the contents of your hard drive for supported files. If you were to select the Show Import Options checkbox, another dialog box opens before the file imports. Leave this option deselected for now.

4. **Click the file you want to import, and then click Open.**

   Certain files, such as bitmap photo, graphic, and PDF files, show a thumbnail preview at the bottom or to the right of the dialog box.

   When you click Open, the Place dialog box closes, and the cursor becomes an upside-down L.

5. **Click the location on the page where you want the upper-left corner of the imported file (for example, an image) to appear.**

   The imported file is placed on the page.

TIP

Click and drag to place the file into a specific frame size, or if you've created an empty frame on the page, clicking on top of the frame causes the object being imported — whether it's text or an image — to be placed inside the frame.

TIP

You can Ctrl-click (Windows) or ⌘-click (Mac) to place multiple files. After you select the images and click OK, each click places an image on the page, or you can hold down the Shift+Ctrl (Windows) or Shift+⌘ (Mac) while dragging a rectangle to have all selected images placed, spaced evenly, in a grid.

Note that when you're placing multiple images, you can see a thumbnail of each image before it's placed. You can also scroll through the loaded images by pressing the arrow keys on your keyboard.

For general information about importing and exporting using the Adobe Creative Cloud, check out Book 1, Chapter 5. For more information on importing different kinds of file formats, such as text, images, spreadsheets, and PDFs, see Chapters 3 and 6 in this minibook.

## Viewing content

You can view elements in several different ways on your document's pages. For example, sometimes you need to see objects on a page close up so that you can make precise edits. InDesign offers several ways to navigate documents:

» **Scroll bars:** You can use the scroll bars to move pages around. The scroll bars are located below and to the right of the pasteboard. Click a scroll bar handle and drag it left and right or up and down.

» **Zoom:** Zoom in or out from the document to increase or decrease the display of your document. Select the Zoom tool (the magnifying glass icon) from the Tools panel and click anywhere on the page to zoom in. Press the Alt (Windows) or Option (Mac) key and click to zoom out.

» **Hand tool:** Use the Hand tool to move the page around. This tool is perhaps the best and quickest way to move pages around and navigate documents. Select the Hand tool by pressing the spacebar (when using any tool other than the Type tool), and then click and drag to move around the pasteboard.

» **Keyboard:** Press Ctrl++ (plus sign) (Windows) or ⌘++ (plus sign) (Mac) to zoom in using the keyboard; replace the plus sign with the minus sign to zoom out.

## Saving your publication

Even the best computers and applications fail from time to time, so you don't want to lose your hard work unnecessarily. Saving a publication often is important so that you don't lose any work if your computer or software crashes or the power goes out.

To save a file, choose File⇨Save or press Ctrl+S (Windows) or ⌘+S (Mac).

You may also want to save different versions of your files. You may want to do this if you're experimenting with different design options, for example, and you want to retain earlier versions of your files. To do this, use the Save As command, which makes creating different versions of documents easy.

**REMEMBER**

Choose File➪Save before proceeding if you want the current document to save the revisions you've made since you last saved the file. All new additions to the document are made in the new version of the file.

To save a new version of the current document and then continue working on the new document, follow these steps:

1. **Choose File➪Save As.**

   The Save As dialog box opens.

2. **Choose the directory you want to save the file in.**

3. **In the File Name text field, enter a new name for the document.**

   This step saves a new version of the file. Consider a naming scheme at this point. If your file is myLayout.indd, you might call it myLayout02.indd to signify the second version of the file. Future files can then increase the number for each new version.

4. **Click the Save button when you're finished.**

   This step saves the document in the chosen directory with a new name.

The File➪Save As command is also used for other means. You may want to save your design as a template. After you create the template, choose File➪Save As, and then choose InDesign CC Template from the Save As Type (Windows) or Format (Mac) drop-down list.

You can also choose File➪Save a Copy. This command saves with a new name a copy of the current state of the document you're working on, but you then continue working on the original document. Both commands are useful for saving incremental versions of a project you're working on.

To find out more about working with files, go to Chapter 7 of this minibook.

Chapter **2**

# Working with Text and Text Frames

M ost of the documents you create contain text, so it's important to know how to format, style, and control text in your layouts. Text is made up of characters, and the characters are styled in specific fonts. If you want to find out more about fonts and typefaces, check out Book 7, Chapter 6.

This chapter explains how to create, edit, and style text by using InDesign. You get started by editing and manipulating text placed inside *text frames* — containers on the page that hold text content. The most important concepts you can take away from this chapter are how to add text to documents and then change the text so that it looks the way you want on the page. In Chapter 3 of this minibook, find out how to create effective layouts that contain both text and graphics so that your audience is encouraged to read everything you create.

# Understanding Text, Font, and Frames

Text is usually integral to a publication because it contains specific information you want or need to convey to an audience. Understanding the terminology that appears in the following pages is important. *Text* and *font* are quite different from each other:

>> **Text:** The letters, words, sentences, and paragraphs making up content in the text frames in your publication.

>> **Font:** The particular design forming a set of characters used to style text. You can find thousands of styles of fonts from many manufacturers, and many are included in programs you install on your computer. InDesign's Font menu lets you preview font faces and even set favorite fonts.

*Frames* resemble containers that are used to hold content. You can use two kinds of frames in a publication:

>> **Text:** Contains text on the page in your InDesign document. You can link text frames so that text flows from one text frame to another, and you can have text wrap around graphic frames.

>> **Graphic:** Holds an image that you place in your publication.

When you create frames using InDesign, they can contain either text or graphics — so the methods for creating both types of frames are identical. InDesign automatically changes frames to adapt to content, so you can use both the frame and shape tools for designing your layout and creating frames that will contain text or graphics.

# Creating and Using Text Frames

Text frames contain any text you add to a publication. You can create a new text frame in many different ways. In InDesign, you can add text to creative shapes you draw, thereby changing them into text frames. Creating and using text frames in a publication is important because you typically use a lot of text. Throughout the following subsections, we show you how to create text frames in different, but important, ways using three different tools. If you need a guide to the tools, check out Chapter 1 of this minibook.

**TIP**

Text frames are sometimes automatically created when you import text into a publication. You find out how to do this in the "Importing text" section, later in this chapter.

# Creating text frames with the Type tool

You can use the Type tool to create a text frame. If you use the Type tool and click the page, nothing happens unless you've first created a frame to hold the text. Here's how to create a text frame by using the Type tool:

1. **Select the Type tool in the Tools panel and place the tool over the page.**

   The Type tool cursor is an I-bar. Move the cursor to the spot where you want to place the upper-left corner of the text frame.

2. **Drag diagonally to create a text frame.**

   When you click, the mouse has a crosslike appearance. When you drag, an outline of the text frame appears, giving you a reference to its dimensions, as shown in Figure 2-1.

**FIGURE 2-1:**
Using the Type tool, drag to create a text frame.

3. **Release the mouse button when the frame is the correct size.**

   The text frame is created, and an insertion point is placed in the upper-left corner of the frame. You can start typing on the keyboard to enter text or import text from another source. (See the later section, "Importing text.")

# Creating text frames with the Frame tool

You can use the Frame tool to create frames that are rectangular, oval, or polygonal. Then, after you've placed the frame on the page, you can turn it into a text frame or use it as a graphic frame or simply a design object on the page. To create a new text frame with the Frame tool, follow these steps:

1. **Choose the Frame tool from the Tools panel and drag diagonally to create a new frame.**

   A new frame is created on the page.

2. **Select the Type tool and click inside the frame.**

   The X across the frame disappears, and the frame is now a text frame instead of a graphic frame.

3. **Choose the Selection tool and use it to move the text frame.**

   You can move the text frame if you click within the frame using the Selection tool and drag it to a new location.

## Creating text frames from a shape

If you have an interesting shape that you've created with the drawing tools or copied and pasted from Illustrator, you can easily change the shape into a text frame so that it can be filled with text. Just follow these steps:

1. **Use the Pen tool, Pencil tool, or a Shape tool to create a shape with a stroke color and no fill. Or, copy and paste artwork from Illustrator.**

   A shape is created on the page that doesn't have a solid color for the fill.

2. **Select the Type tool from the Tools panel.**

   The Type tool becomes active.

3. **Click inside the shape you created in Step 1 and enter some text or import text. (See the section "Importing text," later in this chapter.)**

   This step changes the shape into a text frame. Notice how the text is confined within the shape as you type.

# Adding Text to Your Publication

In the preceding sections' step lists, you find out how to add text by simply clicking in the text frame and typing new content, but you can also add text to publications in other ways. Doing so is particularly useful when you use other applications to create and edit documents containing text.

# Importing text

You can import text you've created or edited using other software, such as Adobe InCopy or Microsoft Word or Excel. Importing edited text is a typical workflow activity when creating a publication, because dedicated text-editing software is often used to edit manuscripts before layout.

To import text into InDesign, follow these steps:

**1.** **Choose File⇨Place.**

The Place dialog box opens. Choose an importable file (such as a Word document, an InCopy story, or a plain text file) by browsing your hard drive.

**2.** **Select a document to import and click the Open button.**

The Place Text icon, the cursor arrow, and a thumbnail image of the text appear. Move the cursor around the page to the spot where you want the upper-left corner of the text frame to be created when the document is imported.

**3.** **Click to place the imported text.**

This step creates a text frame and imports the text.

**TIP**
If you select a text frame *before* importing text, the text is automatically placed inside the text frame — so, in this case, you wouldn't have to use the cursor to place the text. You can move the text frame anywhere on the page after the text is added or resize the frame, if necessary.

# Controlling text flow

Control the flow of the text by using these simple modifier keys while placing text:

» Choose File⇨Place, select the file you want to import, and click Open. Hold down the Shift key and, when the loaded cursor turns into a curvy arrow, click the document. The text is imported and automatically flows from one column to another or from page to page until it runs out. InDesign even creates pages, if needed.

» Choose File⇨Place, select the file you want to import, and click Open. Hold down the Alt (Windows) or Option (Mac) key. Then click and drag a text area. (Don't release the Alt key or Option key!) As you continue clicking and dragging additional text frames, your text flows from one text frame to another until you run out of copy.

**TIP**
If you select the Show Import Options checkbox in the Place dialog box, a second window appears in which you can choose to remove styles and formatting from text and tables. This action brings in clean, unformatted text to edit. On a Mac, select the Options button to access the Show Import Options checkbox.

# Adding placeholder text

Suppose that you're creating a publication but the text you need to import into it isn't ready to import into InDesign — perhaps the text is still being created or edited. Rather than wait for the final text, you can use placeholder text and continue to create your publication's layout. *Placeholder text* is commonly used to temporarily fill a document with text. The text looks a lot like normal blocks of text, which is more natural than trying to paste the same few words repeatedly to fill up a text frame. However, placeholder text isn't in any particular language, because it's just being used as filler.

InDesign can add placeholder text into a text frame automatically. Here's how:

1. **Create a frame on the page by selecting the Type tool, clicking on the page and dragging diagonally to create a text frame.**

2. **Choose Type⇨Fill with Placeholder Text.**

   The text frame is automatically filled with characters and words, similar to the one shown in Figure 2-2.

**FIGURE 2-2:**
The text frame, filled with placeholder text.

## Copying and pasting text

You can move text from another application into an InDesign publication by copying and pasting the text directly into InDesign. If you select and copy text in another program, you can paste it directly into InDesign from your computer's Clipboard. Here's how:

1. **Highlight the text you want to use in your publication and press Ctrl+C (Windows) or ⌘+C (Mac) to copy the text.**

   When you copy text, it sits on the Clipboard (until it's replaced by something new), and you can transfer this information into InDesign.

2. **Open InDesign and press Ctrl+V (Windows) or ⌘+V (Mac) to create a new text frame and paste the text into it.**

   A new text frame appears centered on the page with your selected text inside it.

**TIP**

You can also click in a text frame and press Ctrl+V (Windows) or ⌘+V (Mac) to paste text from the Clipboard directly into an existing frame. You can do the same thing with an image.

All you need to do is double-click a text frame if you want to access or edit some text or type or paste it into the frame.

**TIP**

You can control what formatting you paste into your file by adjusting InDesign preferences. Select Edit⇨Preferences⇨Clipboard Handling (Windows) or InDesign⇨Preferences⇨Clipboard Handling (Mac), and then choose either All Information (swatches, styles, and so forth) or Text only.

# Looking at Text Frame Options

In the previous sections of this chapter, we show you how to create text frames and enter text into them. In the following sections, we show you how to organize text frames in your publication and achieve the results you need. Controlling text frames so that they do what you need them to do is a matter of knowing how they work after you put text in them.

InDesign gives you a lot of control over the text in your publications. Changing text frame options allows you to change the way text is placed inside a frame. Changing these kinds of settings is sometimes important when you're working with particular kinds of fonts. (To read more about fonts, check out Book 7, Chapter 6.)

The text frame contextual menu contains many options for working with the text frame. You use this menu to perform basic commands, such as copy and paste, fill the text frame with placeholder text, make transformations, add or modify strokes, and change the frame type. Access the text frame contextual menu by right-clicking (Windows) or Control-clicking (Mac) a text frame with the selection tool. You can also find most of these options on the Type and Object menus.

## Changing text frame options

To change text frame options that control the look of the text within the frame, follow these steps:

**1.** **Create a rectangular text frame on the page, select the frame with the Selection tool, and choose Object⇨Text Frame Options.**

You can also press Ctrl+B (Windows) or ⌘+B (Mac) or use the text frame's contextual menu to open the Text Frame Options dialog box.

You can tell that a text frame is selected when it has handles around its bounding box.

The Text Frame Options dialog box appears, showing you the current settings for the selected text frame.

**2.** **Select the Preview checkbox to automatically view updates.**

Now any changes you make in the dialog box are instantly updated on the page, so you can make changes and see how they'll look before you apply them.

**3.** **In the Inset Spacing area of the dialog box, change the Top, Bottom, Left, and Right values.**

These values are used to inset text from the edges of the text frame. The text is pushed inside the frame edge by the value you set. With the Make All Settings Same toggle, the chain symbol, enabled, you only need to enter a value into one of the four text boxes.

You can also indent text, which we discuss in the section "Indenting your text," later in this chapter. You can choose in this dialog box how to align the text vertically (Top, Center, Bottom, or Justify). You can align the text to the top or bottom of the text frame, center it vertically in the frame, or evenly space the lines in the frame from top to bottom (Justify).

**4.** **When you finish making changes in this dialog box, click OK.**

The changes you made are applied to the text frame.

## Using and modifying columns

You can specify that the document contains a certain number of columns on the page when you create a new publication. Using columns allows you to snap new text frames to columns so that they're properly spaced on the page. You can even modify the size of the *gutter*, which is the spacing between columns.

You can also create columns within a single text frame by using the Text Frame Options dialog box. You can add as many as 40 columns in a single text frame. If you already have text in a frame, it's automatically divided among the columns you add. You can choose from three types of columns when creating a layout with text using InDesign:

>> Use **Fixed Number** when you know exactly how many columns you want to appear in a text frame.

>> Use **Fixed Width** when you know the exact width of columns that will appear in a text frame. If the text frame becomes larger or smaller, the number of columns may increase or decrease.

>> Use **Flexible Width** if you want the width of columns to vary depending upon the size of the text frame. With Flexible Width, InDesign adds or reduces the number of columns as needed depending upon the width of the text frame.

The following steps show you how to add columns to a text frame on a page:

**1.** **Create a rectangular text frame on the page.**

Use the Text or Frame tool to create the text frame. You can create columns in text frames that are rectangular, oval, or even freehand shapes drawn on the page.

**2.** **After you create the text frame, the cursor is automatically placed inside of the frame, and you can now enter some text.**

You can type some text, paste text copied from another document, or add placeholder text by choosing Type⇨Fill with Placeholder Text.

**3.** **With the text frame still selected, choose Object⇨Text Frame Options.**

In the Text Frame Options dialog box that opens, you may wish to select the Preview checkbox to immediately view the changes your settings make to the frame on the page.

**4.** **In the Columns section, change the value in the Number text field.**

In this example, we entered **2** in the Number text field. The selected text frame divides the text in the frame into two columns. If you selected the Preview checkbox, when you click in a different text field in the dialog box, the text frame updates on the page to reflect the new value setting.

5. **Change the width of the columns by entering a new value in the Width text field.**

The width of the columns is automatically set, depending on the width of the text frame you created. We entered **10** (picas) in the Width text field for this example. The text frame changes size depending on the width you set in this column.

6. **Change the value in the Gutter text field.**

The gutter value controls the amount of space between columns. If the gutter is too wide, change the value in the Gutter text field to a lower number. We entered **0p5** in the Gutter text field for this example to change the gutter width to half a point.

7. **When you finish, click OK to apply the changes.**

The changes are applied to the text frame you modified.

After you create columns in a text frame, you can resize the frame by using the handles on its bounding box, detailed in the later section, "Resizing and moving the text frame." The columns resize as necessary to divide the text frame into the number of columns you specified in the Text Frame Options dialog box. If you select the Fixed Column Width option from the drop-down menu, your text frames are always the width you specify, no matter how you resize the text frame. When you resize the text frame, the frame snaps to the designated fixed width.

**TIP**

You can also change the number of columns in the Control panel after selecting the text frame with the Selection tool, or by using the paragraph options in the Control panel while using the Type tool. If you are working on a small screen, the control panel may not display these options due to the resolution of your screen. You can still access the Paragraph controls by selecting Window⇨ Type & Tables⇨ Paragraph.

# Modifying and Connecting Text Frames on a Page

Making modifications to text frames and then connecting them to other text frames in a publication so that the story can continue on a separate page is vital in most publications. You typically work with stories of many paragraphs that need to continue on different pages in the document.

When you have a text frame on the page, you need to be able to change the size, position, and linking of the frame. You need to link the frame to other frames on the page so that the text can flow between them — which is important if you're creating a layout that contains a lot of text.

If you paste more text content than is visible in the text frame, the text still exists beyond the boundaries of the text frame — so if you have a text frame that's 20 lines tall but you paste in 50 lines of text, the last 30 lines are cropped off. You need to resize the text frame or have the text flow to another frame in order to see the rest of the text you pasted. You can tell that the frame has more content when you see a small red plus sign (+) in a special handle in the text frame's bounding box.

## Resizing and moving the text frame

When creating layouts, you regularly resize text frames and move them around the document while you figure out how you want the page layout to look. You can resize and move a text frame by following these steps:

**1.** **Use the Selection tool to select a text frame on the page.**

A bounding box with handles appears on the page. If the text frame has more text than it can show at the current size, a small red box with a red plus sign appears in the lower-right corner of the bounding box.

**2.** **Drag one of the handles to resize the text frame.**

The frame updates automatically on the page while you drag the handles, as shown in Figure 2-3. Change the width or height by dragging the handles at the center of each side of the frame, or change the height and the width at the same time by dragging a corner handle.

Shift-drag a corner handle to scale the text frame proportionally.

**FIGURE 2-3:**
Resize a text frame by dragging its handles.

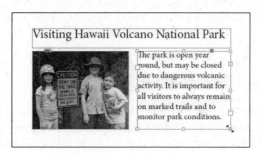

**3.** **When you're finished resizing the text frame, click in the middle of a selected frame and move it around the page.**

If you click within the frame once and drag it, you move the frame around the page. An outline of the frame follows the cursor and represents the spot where the frame is placed if you release the mouse button. Simply release the frame when you finish moving it.

If you're using guides or grids on the page, the text frame snaps to them. Also, if you opened a document with columns, the text frame snaps to the columns when you drag the frame close to the column guidelines.

You can also use the Transform panel to change the location and dimensions of a text frame. If the Transform panel isn't already open, choose Window⇨Object and Layout⇨Transform to open it. Make sure the text frame is selected, then follow these steps:

1. **Change the values in the X and Y text fields.**

   Enter **1** in both the X and Y text fields to move the text frame to the upper-left corner of the page.

   The X and Y coordinates (location) of the text frame update to 1,1. The small square in the middle or along the edge of the text is the *reference point* of the text frame: The X and Y coordinates you set match the position of this point.

   Change the reference point by clicking any square in the reference point indicator in the upper-left corner of the control panel.

2. **Change the values in the W and H text fields.**

   For this example, we entered **35** (picas) in the W and H text fields. The text frame's width and height change to the dimensions you specify. Using the Transform panel to change the width and height is ideal if you need to set an exact measurement for the frame.

You not only can resize and move text frames, but also can change their shapes. Select a text frame and choose the Direct Selection tool from the Tools panel. You can then select the corners on the text frame and move them to reshape the text frame.

## Threading text frames

Understanding how to thread text frames together is important if you plan to build page layouts with a lot of text. *Threading* occurs when text frames are arranged so that the text in one frame continues in a second text frame. Threading is useful for most layouts because you can't always include all text in a single frame.

First, take a look at some of the related terminology because Adobe has given some special names to text frames that are linked. Figure 2-4 shows some of the concepts and icons we refer to in the following list:

>> **Flowing:** Describes text starting in one frame and continuing in a second frame.

An out port with text flowing
into another frame

When space runs
out for text in the
frame on the left
side, it has been
linked so that text
then runs into
the frame located

below it and to
the right. This was
done by linking
the text frames
together by clicking
on the out port on
one frame and then

FIGURE 2-4:
Threaded text
between two
linked text
frames.

An in port with text flowing from
another frame and an overset text indicator

>> **Threading:** Describes two text frames that have text flowing from the first frame to the second.

>> **Story:** The name of a group of sentences and paragraphs in threaded text frames.

>> **In port:** An icon on the upper-left side of a text frame's bounding box indicating that a frame is the first one in a story or has text flowing in from another frame. An In port icon has a story flowing into it if it contains a small arrow; otherwise, the In port icon is empty.

>> **Out port:** An icon on the lower-right side of the text frame's bounding box indicating that a frame has text flowing out of it. The Out port icon contains a small arrow if the frame is threaded to another frame; an empty Out port icon signifies that the frame isn't connected to another text frame.

If a text frame isn't connected to another frame and has *overset text* (more text than can be displayed in a text frame), the Out port shows a small red plus sign (+) icon.

Find a block of text that you want to thread (for best results, use one that has formed sentences as opposed to placeholder text), and then follow these steps:

1. **Copy some text on the Clipboard, such as from the InDesign Help files, a page loaded in a web browser window, or a Word, Notepad, or SimpleText document.**

   The type of content you're pasting doesn't matter. You only need to make sure the text is at least a few paragraphs long so that you have enough text to flow between frames.

In Figure 2-4, you can see the text thread represented by a line connecting one text frame to another. InDesign shows you text threads if you choose View⇨Extras⇨Show Text Threads.

2. **Use the Type tool to create two text frames on a page.**

   The text frames can be above or beside one another, similar to the layout shown in Figure 2-5.

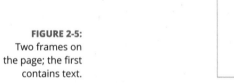

**FIGURE 2-5:**
Two frames on
the page; the first
contains text.

3. **Using the Text tool, click in the first text frame, which is above or to the left of the second text frame.**

   The blinking insertion point that appears in the first text frame lets you know that you can enter or paste text into the frame.

4. **Press Ctrl+V (Windows) or ⌘+V (Mac) to paste the text into the text frame.**

   The text you've copied to the Clipboard enters into the frame. If you've pasted enough text, you see the overset text icon (a red plus sign) on the lower-right side of the text frame. (Refer to Figure 2-5.) If you don't see the overset text icon, use the Paste command a second time so that more text is entered into the frame.

5. **Click the overset text icon with the Selection tool.**

   The cursor changes to the loaded text icon so that you can select or create another text frame to thread the story.

**6.** **Move the cursor over the second text frame and click.**

The cursor changes to the thread text icon when it hovers over the second text frame. When you click the second text frame, the two frames are threaded because the text continues in the second frame.

You can continue creating frames and threading them. You can thread them on the same page or on subsequent pages.

You can *unthread* text as well, which means that you're breaking the link between two text frames. You can rearrange the frames used to thread text, such as changing the page the story continues on when it's threaded to a second text frame. Break the connection by double-clicking the In port icon or the Out port icon of the text frame that you want to unthread. The frame is then unthreaded (but no text is deleted).

TIP

If your document doesn't have multiple pages in it, choose Layout⇨Pages⇨Insert Pages. Indicate the number of pages to add, and then click OK when you're finished. Now you can click through the pages using the Page Field control at the bottom of the workspace and create a new text frame into which you can link your text.

## Adding a page jump number

If your document has multiple pages, you can add a *page jump number* (text that indicates where the story continues if it jumps to a text frame on another page) to an existing file. Before you start, make sure that a story threads between text frames on two different pages, and then follow these steps:

**1.** **Create a new text frame on the first page and type** "continued on page".

**2.** **Use the Selection tool to select the text frame you just created.**

**3.** **Move the text frame so that it slightly overlaps the text frame containing the story (if needed, repeat Steps 1 and 4 from the preceding section, "Threading text threads," and create a new text frame with overset text).**

**4.** **Let InDesign know what text frame it's tracking the story from or to. Overlap the two text frames (and keep them overlapped), as shown in Figure 2-6, so that InDesign knows to associate these text frames (the continued-notice text frame and the story text frame) with each other.**

TIP

You can then *group* these two text frames (so that they move together). To do so, select both frames (Shift-click with the Selection tool to select both text frames), then choose Object⇨Group.

**FIGURE 2-6:**
Slightly overlap the two text frames when creating a page jump, so that the page jump is associated with a specific story.

**5.** **Double-click the new text frame, which contains the text "continued on page." Place the cursor at the spot where you want the page number to be inserted. (This is called the insertion point.)**

The page number is inserted at the insertion point. Make sure that a space appears after the preceding character, so they do not run together. In this example, you would need a space after the word "page."

**6.** **Choose Type⇨Insert Special Character⇨Markers⇨Next Page Number.**

A number is added into the text frame. The number is sensitive to the location of the next threaded text frame, so if you move the second text frame, the page number updates automatically. This example will look like "continued on page 2."

**TIP**

You can repeat these steps at the spot where the story is continued *from* — just choose Type⇨Insert Special Character⇨Markers⇨Previous Page Number in Step 6 instead.

# Understanding Paragraph Settings

You can change the settings for an entire text frame or a single paragraph in a text frame in several ways. You can use the Paragraph panel to make adjustments to a single paragraph or to an entire text frame's indentation, justification, and alignment. Open the Paragraph panel by choosing Window⇨Type & Tables⇨Paragraph.

**TIP**

If you want changes in the Paragraph panel to span across all text frames you create, don't select any paragraph or text frame before making the changes; instead, first select the entire text frame or frames on the page. Then the selections you make in the Paragraph panel affect all paragraphs in the selected text frames, not just one paragraph. If you want the selections you make in the Paragraph panel to affect just one paragraph within a text frame, select that paragraph first by using the Type tool, and then make your changes.

## Indenting your text

You can indent a paragraph in a story by using the Paragraph panel. Indentation moves the paragraph away from the edges of the text frame's bounding box. Here's how to modify indentation:

1. **Create a text frame on the page and fill it with text.**

   You can fill the text frame by typing text, copying and pasting text, or inserting placeholder text by choosing Text⇨Fill with Placeholder Text.

2. **Make sure that the insertion point is blinking in the text frame in the paragraph you want to change or use the Selection tool to select the text frame.**

3. **Choose Window⇨Type & Tables⇨Paragraph to open the Paragraph panel.**

   The Paragraph panel opens, showing the text frame's current settings. See Figure 2-7 to find out the name of each setting control.

**FIGURE 2-7:**
The Paragraph panel.

First line indent

Left indent

Justify with last line left

Align right | Justify with last line center

Center | Justify with last line right

Align left | Justify all lines

Right indent

**4.** **Change the value in the Left Indent text field and press Enter.**

The larger the number, the greater the indent. You can specify the unit of measurement as you enter the text by entering *in* for inches or *pt* for points, using any forms of measurement InDesign supports.

**5.** **Change the value in the First Line Left Indent text field and press Enter.**

To change all paragraphs in a story, click the insertion point in a paragraph and choose Edit➪Select All before changing settings.

## Text alignment and justification

You can use the alignment and justification buttons in the Paragraph panel to format text frames:

>> **Align** helps you left-, center-, or right-align text with the edges of the text frames.

>> **Justification** lets you space text in relation to the edges of the text frame, and it lets you justify the final line of text in the paragraph.

To align or justify a block of text, select the text or the text frame and click one of the Align or Justify buttons. (Refer to Figure 2-7 to see the Align and Justify buttons in the Paragraph panel.)

## Saving a paragraph style

Do you ever go to all the trouble of finding just the right indent, font, or spacing to use in your copy, just to find that you have to apply those attributes a hundred times to complete your project? Or, have you ever decided that the indent is too much? Wouldn't it be nice to change one indent text box and have it update all other occurrences? You can do this using paragraph styles in InDesign.

To create a paragraph style, follow these steps:

**1.** **Create a text frame, add text, and apply a first-line indent of any size you want.**

Select some text — you don't have to select it all.

**2.** **Choose Window➪Styles➪Paragraph Styles.**

The Paragraph Styles panel opens.

3. **From the Paragraph Styles panel menu, choose the new paragraph style icon on the bottom of the panel (piece of paper with folded corner).**

   Single-click the new style, Paragraph Style 1, and note that the Paragraph panel will show that every attribute, font, and size is not in the Paragraph panel and indent is already recorded in this unnamed style.

   Double-click the new style, Paragraph Style 1, and the Paragraph Style Options dialog box opens. You don't have to do anything at this point other than name the style.

4. **Change the name from Paragraph Style 1 to something more appropriate, such as** BodyCopy, **and click OK.**

   Your style is created! After you click OK, the dialog box closes, and the new style is added to the Paragraph Styles panel list. You can modify the settings by double-clicking the style name in the Paragraph Styles panel. You can apply the style to other text frames by selecting the frame and clicking the style in the Paragraph Styles panel.

**TECHNICAL STUFF**

If you want to change an existing style, the Paragraph Style Options dialog box has several different areas in a large list on the left side. Select an item in the list to view and change its associated paragraph properties on the right side of the dialog box to update all instances of that paragraph style.

**TIP**

You can import paragraph styles from other documents or from a file on your hard drive, which is particularly useful when you need to use a particular set of styles for a template. To import paragraph styles, choose Load Paragraph Styles from the Paragraph Styles menu on the right side of the header. A dialog box prompts you to browse your hard drive for a file. Select the file to load, click Open, and then click OK to load the selected styles.

# Editing Stories

Your documents likely contain all sorts of text, and some of that text may need to be edited. InDesign has a built-in story editor for editing text. This feature can be useful when it's inconvenient or impossible to open another text editor to make changes.

**TIP**

InDesign also integrates with another Adobe product: InCopy. It's a text editor that's similar to Microsoft Word but has integration capabilities with InDesign for streamlined page layout. If you work in IT or in editorial management and have some users who only write and others who only handle layout, you might want to have a look at InCopy as a possible text editor.

# Using the story editor

The InDesign story editor lets you view a story outside tiny columns and format the text as necessary. To open the story editor to edit a piece of text, follow these steps:

**1.** **Find a piece of text that you want to edit and select the text frame with the Selection tool.**

A bounding box with handles appears around the text frame.

**2.** **Choose Edit⇨Edit in Story Editor or use the keyboard shortcut Ctrl+Y (Windows) or ⌘+Y (Mac).**

The story editor opens in a new window directly in the InDesign workspace.

**3.** **Edit the story in the window as necessary and click the Close button when you finish.**

Your story appears in one block of text. Any paragraph styles you apply to the text in the story editor are noted in an Information pane on the left side of the workspace.

**TIP**

Notice in Figure 2-8 that you can see tables in the story editor. Click the small table icon to collapse and expand the table in the story editor.

**TIP**

If you want to make text edits but would like to keep the original text unchanged, you can choose Type⇨Track Changes⇨Track Changes in Current Story. The original text remains in the story editor along with your marked changes, but in layout mode only the edited text appears. Later you (or an editor) can use the Track Changes command to accept or reject text edits using the Story Editor.

# Checking for correct spelling

Typos and spelling errors are easy to make. Therefore, you must check for incorrect spelling in a document before you print or export it to a PDF. Here's how to check for spelling in InDesign:

**1.** **Choose Edit⇨Spelling⇨Check Spelling.**

**2.** **In the Check Spelling dialog box that appears, choose a selection to search from the Search drop-down list, and then click the Start button.**

The spell check automatically starts searching the selection, story, or document.

**3.** **Choose from three options:**

**FIGURE 2-8:**
You can see text
and tables in the
story editor.

Table icon

- Click the Skip button to ignore a misspelled word.

- Select a suggested spelling correction from the list in the Suggested Corrections pane and click the Change button.

- Click Ignore All to ignore any more instances of that word.

The spelling is corrected in the text frame and moves to the next spelling error.

4. **Click the Done button to stop the spell check; otherwise, click OK when InDesign alerts you that the spell check is done.**

**TIP**

It is always a good practice to proofread your work manually, even when you use the spell check feature to adjust your writing. The spell checker won't reveal problems such as grammatical errors or word misuse.

## Using custom spelling dictionaries

You can easily add words, such as proper nouns, to your dictionary by clicking the Add button.

You can create a user dictionary or add user dictionaries from previous InDesign versions, from files that other people have sent you, or from a server. The dictionary you add is used for all your InDesign documents.

Follow these steps to create your own, custom dictionary:

1. **Choose Edit⇨Preferences⇨Dictionary (Windows) or InDesign⇨Preferences⇨ Dictionary (Mac).**

   The Preferences dialog box appears with the Dictionary section visible.

2. **From the Language drop-down list, select the language of your dictionary.**

3. **Click the New User Dictionary button below the Language drop-down list.**

4. **Specify the name and location of the user dictionary, and then click Save (Windows) or OK (Mac).**

TIP

If you want to see when a spelling error occurs without opening the Check Spelling dialog box, choose Edit⇨Spelling⇨Dynamic Spelling. Unknown words are then highlighted. To correct the spelling, right-click (Windows) or ⌘-click (Mac) and select the correct spelling from the contextual menu or add the word to your dictionary.

# Using Tables

A *table* is made of columns and rows, which divide a table into cells. You see tables every day on television, in books and magazines, and all over the web. In fact, a calendar is a table: All the days in a month are shown down a column, every week is a row, and each day is a cell. You can use tables for many different tasks, such as listing products, employees, or events.

The following list describes the components of a table and how to modify them in InDesign:

» **Rows:** Extend horizontally across a table. You can modify the height of a row.

» **Columns:** Are vertical in a table. You can modify the width of a column.

» **Cells:** A text frame. You can enter information into this frame and format it like any other text frame in InDesign.

## Creating tables

The easiest way to create a table is to have data ready to go. (Mind you, this isn't the only way.) But flowing in existing data is the most dynamic way of seeing what InDesign can do with tables.

Follow these steps to experiment with the table feature:

**1.** **Create a text area and insert tabbed copy into it.**

The example uses dates for an event:

Summer Events

| June | July | August |
|------|------|--------|
| 1 | 2 | 3 |
| 4 | 5 | 6 |

Notice that the text was simply keyed in by pressing the Tab key between every new entry and pressing the Return or Enter key for each new line. The text doesn't even need to be lined up.

**2.** **Select the text and choose Table⇨Convert Text to Table.**

The Convert Text to Table Options dialog box appears. You can select columns in the window that appears or let the tabs in your text determine columns. You can find out more about table styles in the later section "Creating table styles."

You can assign a table style at the same time you convert text to a table.

**3.** **Click OK to accept the default settings and select the table.**

**4.** **Hold down the Shift key and use your mouse to click and grab the outside right border to stretch the table in or out.**

The cells proportionally accommodate the new table size.

**5.** **Double-click and drag across the top three cells to highlight them, and then choose Table⇨Merge Cells to merge them.**

To create a new table without existing text, follow these steps:

**1.** **Create a new text frame with the Type tool.**

The insertion point should be blinking in the new text frame you create. If it isn't blinking, or if you created a new frame another way, double-click the text frame so that the insertion point (I-bar) is active.

Note that you don't have to have a text frame. You can choose Table⇨Create Table, and a text frame will be automatically created.

**2.** **Choose Table⇨Insert Table.**

**3.** **In the Insert Table dialog box that opens, enter the number of rows and columns you want to add to the table in the Rows and Columns text fields, and then click OK.**

For example, we created a table with four rows and three columns.

# Editing table settings

You can control many settings for tables. InDesign lets you change the text, fill, and stroke properties for each cell or for the table itself. Because of this flexibility, you can create fully customized tables to display information in an intuitive and creative way. In this section, we show you some basic options for editing tables.

To start editing table settings, follow these steps:

1. **Select the table you want to make changes to by clicking in a cell.**

2. **Choose Table⇨Table Options⇨Table Setup.**

   The Table Options dialog box opens with the Table Setup tab selected. The dialog box contains several tabs that contain settings you can change for different parts of the table.

   From the Table Setup tab, you edit the columns and rows, border, and spacing and specify how column or row strokes are rendered in relation to each other. For this example, we changed the number of rows and columns. Now we will change the table border weight to a 3-point stroke.

3. **Select the Preview checkbox at the bottom of the dialog box.**

   The Preview opens so that you can view the changes you make on the page while you're using the dialog box.

4. **Click the Row Strokes tab and change the options.**

   For this example, we selected Every Second Row from the Alternating Pattern drop-down list, changed the Weight option to 2, and changed the Color property for the first row to C=15, M=100, Y=100, K=0 (the CMYK equivalent of red).

   This step causes every second row to have a red, 2-point stroke. You can also click the Column Strokes tab to change the properties for column strokes. The two tabs work the same way.

5. **Click the Fills tab and change the options.**

   For this example, we selected Every Other Row from the Alternating Pattern drop-down list, changed the Color property to the same CMYK equivalent of red, and left the Tint at the default of 20 percent. This step changes the first row and every other row to a red tint.

6. **Click OK.**

   The changes you made in the Table Options dialog box are applied to the table.

7. **Click a table cell so that the insertion point is blinking.**

   The table cell is selected.

8. **Find an image you can copy to the Clipboard, and then press Ctrl+C (Windows) or ⌘+C (Mac) to copy the image.**

9. **Return to InDesign and paste the image into the table cell by pressing Ctrl+V (Windows) or ⌘+V (Mac).**

   The image appears in the table cell, and the height or width (or both) of the cell changes based on the dimensions of the image. Make sure that the insertion point is active in the cell if you have problems pasting the image.

You not only can change the table itself, but also customize the cells within it. Choose Table➪Cell Options➪Text to open the Cell Options dialog box. You can also make changes to each cell by using the Paragraph panel. Similarly, you can change the number of rows and columns and their widths and heights from the Tables panel. Open the Tables panel by choosing Window➪Type & Tables➪Table.

**TECHNICAL STUFF**

InDesign lets you import tables from other programs, such as Excel. If you want to import a spreadsheet, choose File➪Place. The spreadsheet is imported into InDesign as a table that you can further edit as necessary.

## Creating table styles

If you've spent time customizing strokes, fills, and spacing for your table, you certainly want to save it as a style. Creating a table style lets you reuse your table setup for future tables. To create a table style, follow these steps:

1. **Make a table look the way you want.**

   The easiest way to create a table style is to complete the table setup and make a table look the way you want it at completion.

2. **Select the table.**

   Click and drag to select it with the text tool.

3. **Choose Window➪Styles➪Table Styles.**

   The Table Styles panel appears.

4. **Hold down the Alt (Windows) or Option (Mac) key and click the Create New Style button at the bottom of the Table Styles panel.**

   The New Table Style dialog box appears.

5. **Name the style and click OK.**

   Your table attributes are saved as a style.

If you want to edit table style attributes, you can simply double-click the named style in the Table Styles panel. (Make sure nothing is selected.)

# Looking at Text on a Path

You can create some interesting effects with text on a path. Using the Type On a Path tool, you can have text curve along a line or shape. This feature is particularly useful when you want to create interesting titling effects on a page.

To create text on a path, follow these steps:

1. **Use the Pen tool to create a path on the page.**

   Create at least one curve on the path after you create it. (See Chapter 4 of this minibook to find out how to wield the Pen tool with confidence.)

2. **Click and hold the Type tool to select the Type On a Path tool.**

3. **Move the cursor near the path you created.**

   When you move the cursor near a path, a plus sign (+) symbol appears next to the cursor, and you can click and start typing on the path.

4. **Click when you see the + icon and type some text on the path.**

   An insertion point appears at the beginning of the path after you click, and you can then add text along the path. You select type on a path as you would normally select other text — by dragging over the text to highlight it.

To change properties for type on a path, select the text, and use the Type On a Path Options dialog box, which you open by choosing Type⇨Type On a Path⇨Options. In the Type On a Path Options dialog box, you can use effects to modify the way each character is placed on the path. You can also flip the text, change character spacing, and change character alignment to the path in the Align drop-down list or to the stroke of the path in the To Path drop-down list. Play with the settings to see how they affect your type. Click OK to apply changes; to undo anything you don't like, press Ctrl+Z (Windows) or ⌘+Z (Mac).

**TIP**

To hide the path while keeping the text visible, set the stroke weight for the path to 0 pt.

IN THIS CHAPTER

» Working with and importing image files

» Selecting images on the page

» Knowing page layout settings

» Using text and graphics in your layouts

» Working with pages

» Using master pages and spreads

Chapter **3**

# Understanding Page Layout

This chapter shows you how to put graphics and text together so that you can start creating page layouts. Interesting and creative page layouts help draw attention to the pictures and words contained within the publication. An interesting layout motivates more members of the audience to read the text you place on a page.

## Importing Images

You can add many kinds of image files to an InDesign document. Some of the most common are AI, PSD, PDF, JPG, PNG, and TIF. Images are imported into graphic frames. You can create the frames before importing, or if you don't have a frame, InDesign creates one for you instantly when you add the image to the page.

When you import an image into your InDesign layout, the original image is still needed when you print or export the final document. You use special controls to keep track of the linked image and to work on specific settings, such as those that modify the quality and color. You also find additional settings at the time you import an image, which you access using the Image Import Options dialog box. In the "Importing other InDesign documents" section, later in this chapter, you find out how to change various import options.

For now, follow these steps to import an image into your InDesign layout:

1. **Make sure that nothing on the page is selected.**

   If an object on the page is selected, click an empty area so that everything is deselected before you proceed.

2. **Choose File⇨Place.**

   The Place dialog box opens, where you can browse your hard drive for image files to import. You can use this dialog box to import various kinds of files into InDesign, not just images.

3. **Select the image you want to import and click Open.**

   The Place dialog box closes, and the cursor displays a thumbnail of the image you selected.

   You can import multiple images at a time into an InDesign layout. Simply hold down the Ctrl (Windows) or ⌘ (Mac) key and select multiple files in the Place dialog box.

4. **Move the cursor to wherever you want the upper-left corner of the first image to be placed on the page, and then click the mouse.**

   If you've selected multiple images, you can use the left and right arrow keys to navigate the thumbnail images in your loaded cursor before clicking on the page. After you click on the page, the next image is placed, until there are no more images to place.

   Images are imported and placed into the publication inside a graphic frame. You can resize, move, and modify the image by using the Selection or Direct Selection tool or modify the frame and image together by using the Selection tool.

When placing multiple images, you can place all the selected images in one step — space them evenly in a grid by pressing the Shift+Ctrl (Windows) or Shift+⌘ (Mac) keys while dragging a rectangle using your mouse.

Don't worry if the image is imported and is too large for the layout or needs to be cropped. For more information about selecting graphic frames and modifying them, check out Chapter 4 of this minibook. To find out about importing and working with text and stories, see Chapter 2 of this minibook.

**TIP**

It's sometimes easier to create an empty graphic frame and then add an image to it than to import the image and create the frame at the same time. You can create an empty frame and even set fitting properties before you import an image — so that the image fits correctly at the time you import it. To set the fitting properties in a blank frame, choose Object⇨Fitting⇨Frame Fitting Options.

## Importing PDFs

You can import PDF files to place them as images in InDesign layouts. When importing, you can preview and crop the pages by using the Place PDF dialog box. (Choose File⇨Place, select the Show Import Options checkbox, and then click Open. On a Mac, you must click the Options button to be able to see the Show Import Options checkbox.) You import one page at a time, so you need to use the Forward and Back buttons displayed under the preview to select a page to place. Also, you can't import any video, sound, or buttons, and you can't edit the PDF after it's imported into InDesign — so it is more like importing a static image such as a JPEG file.

The Place PDF dialog box offers the following options:

>> **Crop To:** You can crop the page you're importing using this drop-down list. Some options may be unavailable because they depend on what's in the PDF you're importing. The hatched outline in the preview shows you the crop marks.

>> **Transparent Background:** Selecting this checkbox makes the PDF background transparent so that elements on the InDesign page show through. The PDF background is imported as solid white if this option isn't selected.

**TIP**

If your monitor is large enough for you to view your document window and folders on your computer, you can click and drag image files directly into your layout, bypassing the Place command altogether.

## Importing other InDesign documents

You can place one InDesign document inside another. This feature might sound a bit odd, but it has many uses. For example, if you have a page from a book that you want to promote in a catalog, you can import an image of the book page to place into a catalog — all without converting the book page into some type of image format. This strategy not only removes a step, but also creates a higher-quality version of the image being placed into InDesign.

Understanding Page Layout

Here's how to take advantage of this feature:

1. **With a document open, choose File⇨Place or use the keyboard shortcut Ctrl+D (Windows) or ⌘+D (Mac).**

   The Place dialog box appears.

2. **Select the Show Import Options checkbox at the bottom of the Place dialog box.** On a Mac, you must click the Options button to be able to see the Show Import Options checkbox.)

3. **Navigate to an InDesign file and double-click to open it.**

   The Place InDesign Document dialog box appears, as shown in Figure 3-1, offering you the opportunity to choose which page or pages you want to place.

FIGURE 3-1:
Choose pages to import in the Place InDesign Document dialog box.

4. **Click OK.**

5. **Click the page to place the document.**

   If you're placing a document with multiple pages, click again to place each additional page.

# Linking and Embedding Images

You can have images that you import either linked to your document or embedded in your document. Here's the difference between linking and embedding:

>> **Linking:** The image that appears in the InDesign document is a preview of the image stored somewhere else on your computer or network. If the file you linked to your InDesign document is changed, it must be updated.

>> **Embedding:** The image is copied into and saved within the InDesign document itself. It doesn't matter where the original file is located or whether you alter the file, because an embedded image is copied and saved directly within the InDesign document.

When you print or export a document, InDesign uses the linked images to generate the information necessary to create a high-quality printed document, a PDF file, or an image for posting on the web. InDesign keeps track of linked files and alerts you if any of them are moved or changed. You can update links for an image by selecting the image in the Links panel and choosing Update Link or Relink from the Links panel menu. You're prompted to find that file on your hard drive so that the file can be linked to the new location. And, if you send your InDesign file to someone else, make sure to also send its linked files along with the document. You can gain a better understanding of this process in Chapter 7 of this minibook.

**REMEMBER**

If you choose to embed images rather than link to images, your publication's file size increases because of the extra data that's being stored within it.

To find out which files are embedded or linked, look at the Links panel. (See Figure 3-2.) Choose Window➪Links to open the panel and see whether any linked or embedded images are listed in the panel.

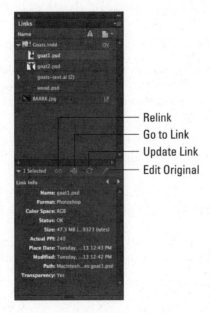

Relink
Go to Link
Update Link
Edit Original

**FIGURE 3-2:**
The Links panel keeps track of all images used in your documents.

Understanding Page Layout

You can embed a file by using the Links panel menu. Select the linked file from the list, then click the drop-down menu in the upper-right corner to access the menu. Select Embed Link if you want a linked file to be embedded within the document. Alternatively, choose Unembed Link from the Link panel menu to link a file rather than have it embedded in the document. We recommend linking to all images so that your files don't become too large and because it provides you with flexibility to manipulate the image files separately.

# Setting Image Quality and Display

You can select quality settings that determine how images are displayed when they're part of an InDesign layout. These settings may help speed up your work if your computer is older or slower, or if you have many images. Displaying images at a higher resolution can give you a better idea of the finished print project and may avoid the need to print the project several times for proofing. These settings are applicable only to how you see the images while using InDesign to create a document — they don't impact the final printed or exported product.

To change the image display quality, choose Edit➪Preferences➪Display Performance (Windows) or InDesign➪Preferences➪Display Performance (Mac). You can then select one of the following settings from the Default View drop-down list:

>> **Fast:** To optimize performance, the entire image or graphic is grayed out.

>> **Typical (default):** This setting tends to make bitmaps look a little blocky, particularly if you zoom in. The speed of zooming in and out is increased if you select this option. InDesign uses a preview that it created (or that was already imported with the file) to display the image on the screen.

>> **High Quality:** The original image is used to display onscreen. You can preview an accurate depiction of the final layout, but you may find that InDesign runs slowly when you use this option.

Notice the difference among these settings in Figure 3-3.

TIP

To change the display for an individual image, select the graphic frame and choose View➪Display Performance. Then choose one of the three options from the submenu.

**FIGURE 3-3:**
From left to right:
Fast Display,
Typical Display,
and High Quality
Display.

# Selecting Images

After you import an image into a document, you can select images in several different ways with the Selection or Direct Selection tools. It's useful to use the different methods depending upon whether you want to select and edit just the graphic frame or just the image inside it.

To select and then edit an image on the page, follow these steps:

1. **Place an image on a page by importing it into InDesign.**

   The image is placed within a graphic frame.

2. **With the Selection tool, drag one of the corner handles on the graphic frame in toward the center of the frame.**

   The graphic frame is resized, but the image isn't. The image appears to be cropped because you resized the graphic frame — though the image remains the same size within the frame, as shown in the center of Figure 3-4.

3. **Choose Edit⇨Undo or press Ctrl+Z (Windows) or ⌘+Z (Mac) to undo changes to the image.**

   The image returns to its original appearance on the page.

4. **Continue to use the Selection tool to click the center of the picture where a circle appears and move the picture within the frame.**

   The frame remains the same size, but its content is relocated. You can also use the Selection tool to move the frame and contents together by clicking anywhere within the frame; however, it is good practice to click on the center section because this works with both the Selection and Direct Selection tools.

5. **Switch to the Direct Selection tool, and then click within the image and drag to move the image within the graphic frame-bounding box.**

   A hand appears when you move the cursor over the graphic; when you move the image just past the edge of the graphic frame boundaries, that part of the image is no longer visible — it doesn't print and doesn't show when exported.

Understanding Page Layout

**FIGURE 3-4:**
The original
image in a
graphic frame
(top); inside a
resized frame
(center); and
repositioning an
image within the
frame (bottom).

**TIP**

You can set the frame or image to resize by choosing Object⇨Fitting and select-ing an option. You can even set this fitting before you place an image, which is especially helpful when creating templates. Resize before an image is placed by choosing Object⇨Fitting⇨Frame Fitting Options.

The Links panel can help you find images within documents, open images so that you can edit them, and view important information about selected images. Figure 3-2 can help you navigate the Links panel and work with your images more effectively.

# Manipulating Text and Graphics in a Layout

InDesign offers many tools that help you work with text and graphics together in a layout. From the tools in the Tools panel, to commands, to panel options, InDe-sign offers you an immense amount of control over the manipulation of graphics and text in a spread.

# Page orientation and size

When you create a new document, you can set its page orientation and size. If you ever need to change your settings after you've created a document, choose File⇨Document Setup and change the following options, which affect all pages in your document:

>> **Page Orientation:** Select either Landscape or Portrait. One of the first things you decide on when you create a new document is how to orient the pages. A *landscape* page is wider than it is tall; a *portrait* orientation is taller than it is wide.

>> **Page Size:** Choose from many standardized preset sizes, such as Letter, Legal, and Tabloid. Alternatively, you can set a custom page size for the document. Make sure to properly set the page size so that it fits the kind of paper you need to print on, or screen size if you're publishing your work digitally.

TIP

You can also use the pages panel to adjust the size of individual pages and make some pages a different size. This topic is covered later in this chapter, in the section "Working with Pages and the Pages Panel."

# Margins, columns, and gutters

Margins, columns, and gutters help divide a page for layout and confine its dimensions:

>> **Margin:** The area between the edge of the page and the main printed area. Together, the four margins (top, bottom, left, and right) look like a rectangle around the page's perimeter. Margins don't print when you print or export the publication.

>> **Column:** Divide a page into sections used for laying out text and graphics on a page. A page has at least one column when you start, which is between the margins. You can add column guides, represented by a pair of lines separated by a gutter area. Column guides aren't printed when you print or export the publication.

>> **Gutter:** The space between two columns on the page. A gutter prevents columns from running together. You can define the gutter's width by choosing Object⇨Text Frame Options; see Chapter 2 of this minibook for more information.

You can set margins and columns when you create a new document, which we discuss in Chapter 1 of this minibook. However, you can also modify margins and columns after the document has been created and specify different values for each page. You can modify the *gutter*, which is the width of the space between each column.

You can change margins and columns by setting new values in the Margins and Columns dialog box. Choose Layout➪Margins and Columns, and then modify each individual page.

**REMEMBER**

Margins and columns are useful for placing and aligning elements on a page. These guides can have objects snap to them, enabling you to accurately align multiple objects on a page.

## Using guides and snapping

Using guides when you're creating page layouts is a good idea because guides help you more precisely align elements on a page and position objects in the layout. Aligning objects by eyeballing them is difficult because you often can't tell whether an object is out of alignment by a small amount unless you zoom in to a large percentage.

**REMEMBER**

Make sure that snapping is enabled by choosing View➪Grids and Guides➪Snap to Guides. *Snapping* makes guides and grids useful. When you drag the object close to the grid, the object attaches to the guideline like it's a magnet. Aligning an object to a guide is easy after you create a guide, and you'll notice that InDesign displays temporary guides when you move an object near another object or near a guide.

Because guides are useful in creating a layout, check out the following kinds, available in InDesign (see Figure 3-5):

>> **Column guides:** Evenly distribute a page into columns and can be used to align text frames in a document. These guides are set when you open a new document in InDesign that contains more than one column. Column guides can also be adjusted after a document is created by choosing Layout➪Margins and Columns.

>> **Margin guides:** Define the area between the edge of the page and the main printable area. (We discuss these guides in the preceding section.)

>> **Ruler guides:** Manually defined and can be used to align graphics, measure objects, or specify the location of a particular asset you want to lay out. See Chapter 1 of this minibook for details about adding ruler guides to the workspace.

Margin guide    Ruler guide    Column guides    Margin guide

**FIGURE 3-5:**
Column guides,
margin guides,
and ruler guides
help create a
layout.

» **Smart guides:** As previously mentioned, smart guides offer the capability to align objects on an InDesign page to other objects or even to the page. Smart Object alignment allows for easy snapping to page item centers or edges or page centers. In addition to snapping, smart guides give feedback to the user indicating the object to which you are snapping.

» **Liquid guides:** Liquid guides are useful when creating layouts that will be displayed on a variety of tablets. They are discussed more in Chapter 8 of this minibook.

To find out how to show and hide grids and guides, see Chapter 1 of this minibook.

TIP

With InDesign CC you can delete all guides at once by right-clicking the ruler (Windows) or Control-clicking the ruler (Mac) and selecting Delete All Guides on Spread from the contextual menu.

## Locking objects and guides

You can lock in place elements such as objects and guides. This feature is particularly useful after you've carefully aligned elements on a page. Locking objects or guides prevents you from accidentally moving them from that position.

To lock an element, follow these steps:

1. **Use a drawing tool to create an object on a page, and then select the object with the Selection tool.**

   A bounding box with handles appears when the object is selected.

2. **Choose Object➪Lock.**

   The object is locked in position. Now when you try to use the Selection or Direct Selection tools to move the object, it doesn't move from its current position.

To lock guides in place, follow these steps:

1. **Drag a couple of ruler guides to the page by clicking within a ruler and dragging toward the page.**

   A line appears on the page. (If rulers aren't visible around the pasteboard, choose View➪Rulers.)

2. **Drag a ruler guide to a new location, if needed; when you're happy with the ruler guides' placements, choose View➪Grids & Guides➪Lock Guides.**

   All guides in the workspace are locked. If you try selecting a guide and moving it, the guide remains in its present position and cannot be moved. If you have any column guides on the page, they're locked as well.

**TIP**

Use layers in your publications for organizing different types of content, including guides. Layers are a lot like transparencies that lie on top of each other, so they can be used for stacking elements on a page. For example, you may want to stack graphics or arrange similar items (such as images or text) on the same layer. Each layer has its own bounding box color, which helps you determine which item is on which corresponding layer. For more information on layers in general, see Book 3, Chapter 8.

# Merging Text and Graphics

When you have text and graphics together on a page, they should flow and work with each other to create an aesthetic layout. Luckily, you can work with text wrap to achieve a visual flow between text and graphics. In this section, you find out how to wrap text around images and graphics in your publications.

# Wrapping objects with text

Images can have text wrapped around them, as shown in Figure 3-6. Wrapping is a typical feature of page layout in print and on the web. You can choose different text wrap options by using the Text Wrap panel, which you open by choosing Window⇨Text Wrap. Use the five buttons at the top of the panel to specify which kind of text wrapping to use for the selected object. Below the buttons are text fields where you can enter offset values for the text wrap. The fields are grayed out if the option isn't available.

(a) No text wrap

(d) Jump object

(b) Wrap around bounding box

(e) Jump to next column

(c) Wrap around object shape

**FIGURE 3-6:** You can wrap text around images in InDesign in several ways.

You use the drop-down list at the bottom of the Text Wrap panel to choose from various contour options. The following list describes what happens when you click one of these buttons to wrap text around an object's shape:

>> **No Text Wrap:** Use the default setting to remove any text wrapping from the selected object.

>> **Wrap around Bounding Box:** Wrap text around all sides of the bounding box of the object.

>> **Wrap around Object Shape:** Wrap text around the edges of an object.

>> **Jump Object:** Make the text wrapping around the image jump from above the image to below it, with no text wrapping to the left or right of the object in the column.

>> **Jump to Next Column:** Make text end above the image and then jump to the next column. No text is wrapped to the left or right of the image.

>> **Offset:** Enter offset values for text wrapping on all sides of the object.

>> **Wrap Options:** Select an option to determine on which sides of the object text will wrap.

>> **Contour Options:** Select a contour from this drop-down list, which tells InDesign how the edges of the image are determined. You can choose from various vector paths or the edges to be detected around an object or image with transparency.

To add text wrapping to an object (a drawing or an image), follow these steps:

1. **Create a text frame on a page with a graphic.**

   Add text to the text frame by typing text, pasting text from elsewhere, or filling the frame with placeholder text. This text wraps around the image, so make sure that the text frame is slightly larger than the graphic frame you'll use.

2. **Use the Selection tool to select a graphic frame on the page and move it over the text frame.**

   Bounding box handles appear around the edges of the image or graphic.

3. **Choose Window⇨Text Wrap to open the Text Wrap panel.**

   The Text Wrap panel opens.

4. **With the graphic frame still selected, click the Wrap around Object Shape button.**

   The text wraps around the image instead of hiding behind it.

5. **If you're working with an image that has a transparent background, select Detect Edges or Alpha Channel from the Contour Options drop-down list.**

   The text wraps around the edges of the image, as in Figure 3-7.

## Modifying a text wrap

If you've applied a text wrap around an object (as we show you how to do in the preceding section), you can then modify that text wrap. If you have an image with a transparent background around which you've wrapped text, InDesign created a path around the edge of the image; if you have a shape you created with the drawing tools, InDesign automatically uses those paths to wrap text around.

**WARNING**

Before proceeding with the following steps, be sure that the object uses the Wrap around Object Shape text wrap. (If not, open the Text Wrap panel and click the Wrap around Object Shape button to apply text wrapping.) Remember to choose Detect Edges if you're using an image with a transparent background.

To modify the path around an image with text wrapping, using the Direct Selection tool, follow these steps:

1. **Select the object by using the Direct Selection tool.**

   The image is selected, and you can see the path around the object.

2. **Click to select one of the anchor points on the text wrap path by using the Direct Selection tool; then click and drag the point to move it.**

   The path is modified according to how you move the point. (For more about manipulating paths, take a look at Chapter 4 of this minibook.) The text wrapping immediately changes, based on the modifications you make to the path around the object.

3. **Select the Delete Anchor Point tool from the Tools panel and delete an anchor point.**

   The path changes again, and the text wrapping modifies around the object accordingly.

**REMEMBER**

You can also use the Offset values in the Text Wrap panel to determine the distance between the wrapping text and the edge of the object. Simply increase the values to move the text farther from the object's edge.

# Working with Pages and the Pages Panel

The *page* is the central part of any publication — it's where the visible part of your publication is created. Navigating and controlling pages are important parts of working in InDesign. The Pages panel allows you to select, adjust, move, and navigate pages in a publication. When you use default settings, pages are created as *facing pages,* which means that they're laid out as two-page pairs, or spreads. Otherwise, pages are laid out individually. Whether a page is part of a spread or a single page is reflected in the Pages panel, the option is specified when you create a new document and can be changed in the Document Setup window.

The Pages panel, which you open by choosing Window➪Pages, also lets you add new pages to the document, duplicate pages, delete a page, or change the size of a page. The pages panel, shown in Figure 3-8, contains two main areas: the master pages (upper) section and the (lower) section containing the document's pages.

To discover more about master pages and how they differ from regular pages in your document, see the "Using Master Spreads in Page Layout" section, later in this chapter.

## Selecting and moving pages

Use the Pages panel to select a page or spread in your publication. Select a page by clicking the page. If you Ctrl-click (Windows) or ⌘-click (Mac) pages, you can select more than one page at a time. The Pages panel also lets you move pages to a new position in the document: Select a page in the document pages area of the panel, and then drag it wherever you want to move the page. A small line and changed cursor indicate where the page will be moved. You can move a page so that it's between two pages in a spread; a hollow line indicates where you're moving the page. If you move a page before or after a spread, a solid line appears. Release the mouse button to move the page to the new location.

Master pages

Document pages

**FIGURE 3-8:**
The Pages
panel with page
previews.

Edit Page Size | Delete Selected Pages

Create New Page

## Adding and deleting pages

You can also add new pages to the publication by using the Pages panel. To add a new page, follow these steps:

**1.** **Choose Window⇨Pages to open the Pages panel.**

The Pages panel opens.

**2.** **Click the Create New Page button.**

A new page is added to the document.

TIP

Alt-click (Windows) or Option-click (Mac OS) the Create New Page button, and you can then specify the exact number of pages to add and the location of these new pages.

**3.** **Select a page in the Pages panel.**

The selected page is highlighted in the Pages panel.

**4.** **Click the Create New Page button again.**

A new page is added following the selected page.

TIP

To delete a page, select it in the Pages panel and click the Delete Selected Pages button. The selected page is removed from the document.

You can also add, delete, and move pages and more without the Pages panel by choosing from the Layout⇨Pages submenu.

## Numbering your pages

When you're working with longer documents, adding page numbers before you print or export the publication is a good idea. You don't have to add them manually: A special InDesign tool lets you number pages automatically. This tool is particularly useful when you move pages around the document. You don't have to keep track of updating the numbering when you make these kinds of edits.

To number pages, follow these steps:

1. **Using the Type tool, create a text frame on the page where you want the page number to be added.**

2. **Choose Type⇨Insert Special Character⇨Markers⇨Current Page Number.**

   The current page number appears in the text frame you selected. If you added the page number to a master page, the master page's letter appears in the field instead.

If you want page numbers to appear on all pages in the document, add the text frame to a master page. Remember that page numbers are added only to the pages in your document that are associated with that master page. If you want to add page numbers to the left and right sides of a book or magazine, you need to repeat this process on the left and right sides of the master pages. Remember that if you add a page number only on a document page — and not on a master — the page number is added to only that single page.

**TIP**

To modify automatic-numbering settings, choose Layout⇨Numbering and Section Options. You can choose to have numbering start from a specific number or use a different style, such as Roman numerals.

# Using Master Spreads in Page Layout

*Master pages* are a lot like templates you use to format page layouts. The settings, such as margins and columns, are applied to each layout that the master page is applied to. If you put a page number on a master page, the number also appears on every page that uses the layout. You can have more than one master page in a single publication, and you can choose which pages use a particular master page.

A master page, or spread, typically contains layout items that are used on many pages, such as page numbering, text frames, background images, or headings that are used on every page. By default, you cannot edit items that have been placed on a master page, on the pages that are using a particular master. You can, however, override or even completely detach these master page elements to modify them directly on a document page by pressing Ctrl+Shift (Windows) or ⌘+Shift (Mac) while clicking on the master page element. This functionality is useful for special cases like changing the background of just one, or removing a page number.

**REMEMBER**

Master pages are lettered. The first master page is the A–Master by default. If you create a second master page, it's the B–Master by default. When you create a new publication, the A–Master is applied to all pages you initially open in the document. You can add pages at the end that don't have a master page applied to them.

Creating master pages and applying them to your publication enables you to create a reusable format for it, which can dramatically speed up your workflow when you put together documents with InDesign.

## Creating a master spread

You may need more than one master page or master spread for a document. You may have another series of pages that need a unique format. In this situation, you need to create a second master page. You can create a master page or a master spread from any other page in the publication, or you can create a new one with the Pages panel.

To create a master page by using a page in the publication, do one of the following:

>> Choose New Master from the Page panel's menu, and then click OK. A blank master page is created.

>> Drag a page from the pages section of the panel into the master page section of the Pages panel. The document page turns into a master page.

**WARNING**

If the page you're trying to drag into the master pages section is part of a spread, select *both pages in the spread* before you drag it into the master pages section. You can drag individual pages into the master page section only if they're *not* part of a spread.

## Applying, removing, and deleting master pages

After you create a master page, you can apply it to a page. You can also remove a page from a master page layout and delete a master page altogether:

>> **To add master page formatting to a page or spread in a publication:** In the Pages panel, drag the master page you want to use from the master page

section on top of the page you want to format in the document pages section. When you drag the master page on top of the page, it has a thick outline around it. Release the mouse button when you see this outline, and the formatting is applied to the page.

» **To remove any master page applied to a document page:** In the Pages panel, drag the None page from the master area in the Pages panel to that document page. You may need to use the scroll bar in the master pages area of the Pages panel to find the None page.

» **To delete a master page:** In the Pages panel, select the unwanted master page, and then choose Delete Master Page from the panel menu.

This action *permanently* deletes the master page — you can't get it back — so think carefully before deleting a master page.

## Changing individual page sizes

Using the Pages panel, you can change the size of individual pages in a document, which is useful if you have one page that folds out and is larger than others. Or, maybe you want to create a single document that includes a business card, an envelope, and a letterhead.

To change the size of individual pages using the Pages panel, follow these steps:

1. **In the Pages panel, click to select the page you want to modify.**

2. **Click the Edit Page Size button at the bottom of the Pages panel and select the new size.**

3. **Repeat the process to adjust the size for any pages you want to modify.**

   When you're done editing the size of the pages, continue to work on their design and layout like you would work on any other pages. The only difference is that some pages in your document may be a different size.

TIP

You can also use the Pages panel to create alternative layouts for display on various tablet devices. These alternative layouts are discussed in Chapter 8 of this minibook.

IN THIS CHAPTER

» Discovering the drawing tools

» Drawing and editing shapes and paths

» Introducing corner effects

» Working with fills and layers

» Creating QR Codes

# Chapter **4**

# Drawing in InDesign

M any of the tools you find in the InDesign Tools panel are used for drawing lines and shapes on a page, so you have several different ways of creating interesting drawings for your publications. You can create anything from basic shapes to intricate drawings inside InDesign, instead of having to use a drawing program such as Illustrator. Even though InDesign doesn't replace Illustrator (see Book 5), which has many more versatile drawing tools and options for creating intricate drawings, InDesign is adequate for many drawing tasks. In this chapter, you discover how to use the most popular InDesign drawing tools and how to add colorful fills to illustrations.

Even if you don't think you'll be drawing using InDesign, you should still take a look at the sections "Modifying Frame Corners" and "Using Fills," later in this chapter, before jumping ahead.

## Getting Started with Drawing

When you're creating a document, you may want drawn shapes and paths to be parts of the layout. For example, you may want to have a star shape for a yearbook page about a talent show or to run text along a path. Whatever it is you need to do, you can draw shapes and paths to get the job done.

# Paths and shapes

Paths can take a few different formats. They can either be open or closed and with or without a stroke:

>> **Path:** The outline of a shape or an object. Paths can be closed and have no gaps, or they can be open like a line on the page. You can draw freeform paths, such as squiggles on a page, freely by hand.

>> **Stroke:** A line style and thickness that you apply to a path. A stroke can look like a line or like an outline of a shape.

Figure 4-1 shows the different kinds of paths and strokes you can create.

**FIGURE 4-1:**
Different kinds of paths and strokes created in InDesign.

Paths contain points where the direction of the path can change. (You can find out more about points in the later section "Points and segments.") You can make paths by using freeform drawing tools, such as the Pen or Pencil tools, or by using the basic shape tools, such as Ellipse, Rectangle, Polygon, or Line.

The shape tools create paths in a predefined way so that you can make basic geometric shapes, such as a star or an ellipse. Just select the shape tool and drag the cursor onto the page, and the shape is automatically drawn. Creating shapes this way is a lot easier than trying to create them manually by using the Pen or Pencil tool. Figure 4-2 shows shapes drawn with the shape tools found in the Tools panel.

You can change shapes into freeform paths, like those drawn with the Pencil or Pen tools. Similarly, you can make freeform paths into basic shapes. Therefore, you don't need to worry about which tool you initially choose.

**FIGURE 4-2:**
You can create
many shapes with
the basic shape
tools.

**TIP**

We created the star and starburst shown in Figure 4-2 by double-clicking the Polygon tool and changing the options. Read more about the Polygon tool in the "Drawing Shapes" section, later in this chapter.

## Points and segments

Paths are made up of points and segments:

>> **Point:** Where the path changes somehow, such as a change in direction. Many points along a path can be joined with segments. Points are sometimes called *anchor points.* You can create two kinds of points:

- *Corner points:* Have a straight line between them. Shapes such as squares and stars have corner points.

- *Curve points:* Occur along a curved path. Circles or snaking paths have lots of curve points.

>> **Segment:** A line or curve connecting two points — similar to connect-the-dots.

Figure 4-3 shows corner points and curve points joined by segments.

**FIGURE 4-3:**
Points are joined by line segments.

# Getting to Know the Tools of the Trade

The following sections introduce you to tools that you'll probably use most often when creating drawings in your publications. When you draw with these tools, you're using strokes and fills to make designs. The following sections show you what these common tools can do to help you create basic or complex illustrations in InDesign.

## The Pencil tool

The Pencil tool is used to draw simple or complex shapes on a page. Because the Pencil tool is a freeform tool, you can freely drag it all over the page and create lines or shapes, instead of having them automatically made for you, such as when you use basic shape tools. The Pencil tool is an intuitive and easy tool to use. You find out how to use it in the later section "Drawing Freeform Paths."

## The Pen tool

You use the Pen tool to create complex shapes on the page. The Pen tool works with other tools, such as the Add, Remove, and Convert Point tools. The Pen tool works by adding and editing points along a path, thereby manipulating the segments that join them.

Drawing with the Pen tool isn't easy at first. In fact, it takes many people a considerable amount of time to use this tool well. Don't become frustrated if you don't get used to it right away — the Pen tool can take some practice to get it to do what you want. You find out how to use the Pen tool in the "Drawing Freeform Paths" section, later in this chapter.

## Basic shapes and frame shapes

*Basic* shapes are preformed shapes that you can add to a document by using tools in the Tools panel. The basic shape tools include the Line, Rectangle, Ellipse, and Polygon tools.

You can also draw these shapes and turn them into *frames* (containers that hold content in a document). You can use a frame as a text frame or as a graphic frame used to hold pictures and text. Draw a basic shape and then convert it to a graphic or text frame by choosing Object➪Content➪Text or Object➪Content➪Graphic. We discuss graphic frames and text frames in more detail in Chapter 2 of this minibook.

**TECHNICAL STUFF**

The frame and shape tools look the same and can even act the same. Both can hold text and images, but look out! By default, shapes created with the shape tools have a 1-point black stroke around them. Many folks don't see these strokes on the screen but later discover them surrounding their text boxes when they print. Stick with the frame tools, and you'll be fine.

# Drawing Shapes

InDesign allows you to create basic shapes in a document. You can easily create a basic shape by following these steps:

1.  **Create a new document by choosing File➪New➪Document.**

2.  **When the New Document dialog box appears, select Print, choose a blank document preset size, and then click Create.**

    A new document opens.

3.  **Select the Rectangle tool in the Tools panel.**

4.  **Click anywhere on the page and drag the mouse diagonally.**

    When the rectangle is the dimension you want, release the mouse button. You've created a rectangle.

That's all you need to do to create a basic shape. You can also use these steps with the other basic shape tools (the Line, Ellipse, and Polygon tools) to create other basic shapes. To access the other basic shapes from the Tools panel, follow these steps:

1.  **Click the Rectangle tool and hold down the mouse button.**

    A menu that contains all the basic shapes opens.

2. **Release the mouse button.**

The menu remains open, and you can mouse over the menu items. Each menu item becomes highlighted when the mouse pointer is placed over it.

3. **Select a basic shape tool by clicking a highlighted menu item.**

The new basic shape tool is now active. Follow the preceding set of steps to create basic shapes by using any of these tools.

**TIP**

To draw a square shape, use the Rectangle tool and press the Shift key while you drag the mouse on the page. The sides of the shape are all drawn at the same length, so you create a perfect square. You can also use the Shift key with the Ellipse tool if you want a perfect circle — just hold down Shift while you're using the Ellipse tool. Release the mouse before the Shift key to ensure that this constrain shape trick works!

## Creating a shape with exact dimensions

Dragging on the page to create a shape is easy, but making a shape with precise dimensions using this method requires a few more steps. If you want to make a shape that's a specific size, follow these steps:

1. **Select the Rectangle tool or the Ellipse tool.**

The tool is highlighted in the Tools panel.

2. **Click anywhere on the page, but don't drag the cursor.**

This point becomes the upper-left corner of the Rectangle or Ellipse *bounding box* (the rectangle that defines the object's vertical and horizontal dimensions). After you click to place a corner, the Rectangle or Ellipse dialog box appears.

3. **In the Width and Height text fields, enter the dimensions for creating the shape.**

4. **Click OK.**

The shape is created on the page, with the upper-left corner at the place where you initially clicked the page.

## Using the Polygon tool

A *polygon* is a shape that has many sides. For example, a square is a polygon with four sides, but the Polygon tool enables you to choose the number of sides you want for the polygon you create. When you're using the Polygon tool, you may not want to create a shape with the default number of sides. You can change these settings before you start drawing the shape.

To customize the shape of a polygon, follow these steps:

1. **Select the Polygon tool in the Tools panel by selecting the Rectangle tool and holding down the mouse button until the menu pops up.**

2. **Double-click the Polygon tool in the Tools panel.**

   The Polygon dialog box opens, as shown at the bottom of Figure 4-4.

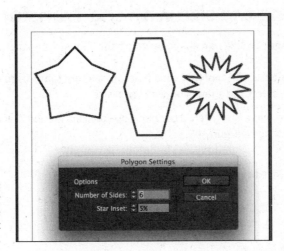

**FIGURE 4-4:**
Change the star inset percentage to create different kinds of shapes.

3. **In the Number of Sides text field, enter the number of sides you want the new polygon to have.**

   To create a star instead of a polygon, enter a number in the Star Inset text field for the percentage of the star inset you want the new shape to have.

   A higher percentage means that the sides are inset farther toward the center of the polygon, creating a star. If you want a regular polygon and not a star, enter **0** in the Star Inset text field. If you want a star, enter **50%**; for a starburst, enter **25%**.

4. **Click OK.**

5. **Move the cursor to the page and click and drag to create a new polygon or star.**

   Your new polygon or star appears on the page.

Figure 4-4 shows what a few different polygons and stars with different settings look like.

# Editing Basic Shapes

You can edit basic shapes InDesign in order to create original shapes and craft exactly the kind of design you want. You aren't stuck with predetermined shapes, such as a square or an oval. You can make these forms take on much more custom shapes.

## Changing the size with the Transform panel

You can change the size of a shape by using the Transform panel. Here's how:

1. **With the Selection tool (the solid black arrow tool that's used to select objects), select the shape you want to resize.**

   When the shape is selected, a bounding box appears around it. You can see a selected shape in Figure 4-5.

Bounding box

Selected object

**FIGURE 4-5:**
A selected shape with the bounding box visible.

2. **Open the Transform panel by choosing Window⇨Object and Layout⇨Transform.**

3. **In the Transform panel that appears, enter different number values in the W and H fields to change the size of the shape.**

   The shape automatically changes size on the page to the new size dimensions you specify in the Transform panel.

# Changing the size with the Free Transform tool

Easily resize objects in InDesign by using the Free Transform tool.

To resize a selected object with the Free Transform tool, follow these steps:

1. **Make sure that *only* the object you want to resize is selected.**

   **TIP**

   Group multiple objects if you want to resize several objects simultaneously. To group objects, select one object and Shift-click to add it to the selection, and then press Ctrl+G (Windows) or ⌘+G (Mac).

2. **Select the Free Transform tool.**

3. **Click any corner point and drag to resize the object.**

   **TIP**

   Hold down the Shift key while dragging to keep the objects constrained proportionally as you resize.

# Changing the stroke of a shape

You can change the stroke of shapes you've created. The *stroke* is the outline that appears around the edge of the shape. The stroke can range from no stroke to a very thick stroke, and it's measured in point sizes. Even if a shape has a stroke set to 0 points, it still has a stroke — you just can't see it.

Follow these steps to edit the stroke of your shapes:

1. **Select a shape on the page.**

   A bounding box appears around the selected shape.

2. **Select a new width for the Stroke by using the Stroke Weight drop-down list in the Control panel.**

   As soon as a value is selected, the stroke automatically changes on the page. This number is measured in points. You use some of the other options in the following step list.

You can click in the Stroke text field and manually enter a numerical value for the stroke width. The higher the number you enter, the thicker the stroke. You can also change the style of the stroke from the Control panel by following these steps:

1. **With a basic shape selected, select the stroke type from the drop-down list in the Control panel and select a new line.**

   As soon as a new line is selected, the stroke automatically changes.

2. **Choose a new line weight from the Stroke Weight drop-down list.**

   For example, we chose 10 points. The shape updates automatically on the page.

**TIP**

If you want to create custom dashes, you can see more options by choosing Window⇨Stroke. Choose the panel menu in the upper-right corner of the panel and select Stroke Styles, and then select New. You can define the dash and gap size. Define custom dashes by clicking in the ruler and dragging to define the dash length. Enter one value for an even dash or several numbers for custom dashes for maps, diagrams, fold marks, and more! Your custom stroke appears in the Stroke panel after you create it.

Add special ends to the lines with the Start and End drop-down lists. For example, you can add an arrowhead or a large circle to the beginning or end of the stroke. The Cap and Join buttons allow you to choose the shape of the line ends and how they join with other paths when you're working with complex paths or shapes.

## Changing the shear value

You can change the shear of a shape by using the Transform panel. *Skew* and *shear* mean the same thing: The shape is slanted, so you create the appearance of some form of perspective for the skewed or sheared element. This transformation is useful if you want to create the illusion of depth on a page.

Follow these simple steps to skew a shape:

1. **With a basic shape selected, choose Window⇨Object & Layout⇨Transform.**

2. **Select a value from the Shear X Angle drop-down list in the lower-right corner of the Transform panel.**

   After you select a new value, the shape skews (or shears), depending on what value you select. Manually entering a numerical value into this field also skews the shape.

## Rotating a shape

You can change the rotation of a shape by using the Transform panel. The process of rotating a shape is similar to skewing a shape (see the preceding section):

1. **With a basic shape selected, choose Window⇨Object & Layout⇨ Transform.**

   The Transform panel opens.

2. **Select a value from the Rotation Angle drop-down list.**

After you select a new value, the shape rotates automatically, based on the rotation angle you specified. You can also manually enter a value into the text field.

# Drawing Freeform Paths

You can use different tools to draw paths. For example, you can use the Pencil tool to draw freeform paths. These kinds of paths typically look like lines, and you can use the Pencil and Pen tools to create simple or complex paths.

## Using the Pencil tool

The Pencil tool is perhaps the easiest tool to use when drawing freeform paths. (See Figure 4-6.)

**FIGURE 4-6:**
This freeform drawing was created with the Pencil tool.

Follow these steps to get started:

1. **To create a new document, choose File⇨New⇨Document⇨Print, and then click Create in the New Document dialog box that appears.**

2. **Select the Pencil tool in the Tools panel. Make sure you have defined a stroke weight and color for your stroke.**

3. **Drag the cursor around the page.**

   You've created a new path by using the Pencil tool.

## Using the Pen tool

Using the Pen tool is different from using the Pencil tool. When you start out, the Pen tool may seem a bit complicated — but after you get the hang of it, using it isn't hard after all. The Pen tool uses points to create a particular path. You can edit these points to change the segments between them. Gaining control of these points can take a bit of practice.

To create points and segments on a page, follow these steps:

1. **Close any existing documents and create a new document by choosing File⇨New⇨Document.**

2. **Select Print, then click Create in the New Document dialog box.**

   A new document opens with the default settings.

3. **Select the Pen tool in the Tools panel. Make sure a stroke weight and color are defined before using this tool.**

4. **Click anywhere on the page, and then click a second location.**

   You've created a new path with two points and one segment joining them.

5. **Ctrl-click (Windows) or ⌘-click (Mac) an empty part of the page to deselect the current path.**

   After you deselect the path, you can create a new path or add new points to the path you just created.

6. **Add a new point to a selected segment by selecting the segment, then hovering the mouse over the line and clicking.**

   A small plus (+) icon appears next to the Pen tool cursor. You can also do the same thing by selecting the Add Anchor Point tool (located on the menu that flies out when you click and hold the Pen icon in the Tools panel).

7. **Repeat Step 6, but this time click a new location on a line segment and drag away from the line.**

This step creates a curved path. The segments change and curve depending on where the points are located along the path. The point you created is a *curve* point.

For more information about working with the Pen tool, check out Book 5, Chapter 4.

# Editing Freeform Paths

Even the best artists sometimes need to make changes or delete parts of their work. If you've made mistakes or change your mind about a drawing, follow the steps in this section to make changes.

To change a path segment, make sure the segment is deselected, then select a point with the Direct Selection tool. When a point is selected, it appears solid; unselected points appear hollow.

**TIP**

You can automatically select the Direct Selection tool by pressing the A key.

All you need to do to select a point is click the point itself. Then you can use the handles that appear when the point is selected to modify the segments. Follow these steps:

1. **Select the Direct Selection tool (or press the A key) from the Tools panel, and then click a point.**

The selected point appears solid. If you select a curve point, handles extend from it.

A curved point and a corner point edit differently when you select and drag them. Curve points have handles that extend from the point, but corner points don't.

2. **Drag the point where you want it; to edit a curve point, click a handle end and drag the handle left or right.**

The path changes, depending on how you drag the handles.

Suppose that you want to make a corner point a curve point. You can do just that with the Convert Direction Point tool. To understand how the Convert Direction Point tool works best, you should have a path that contains both straight and curved segments. Follow these steps to change a corner point into a curved point and vice versa:

1. **Select the Convert Direction Point tool.**

   This tool resides on a menu under the Pen tool in the Tools panel. Hold down the mouse button over the Pen tool icon until a menu appears; select the Convert Direction Point tool from the menu.

2. **Click a curved point with the Convert Direction Point tool.**

   The point you click changes into a corner point, which changes the path's appearance.

3. **Click and drag a corner point with the Convert Direction Point tool.**

   The point is modified as a curved point. This step changes the appearance of the path again.

This tool is handy when you need to alter the way a path changes direction. If you need to manipulate a point in a different way, you may need to change its type by using the Convert Direction Point tool.

# Modifying Frame Corners

You can use corner effects on basic shapes to customize the shape's look. Corner effects are useful for adding an interesting look to borders. You can be quite creative with some of the shapes you apply effects to or by applying more than one effect to a single shape. Here's how to create a corner effect on a rectangle:

1. **Select the Rectangle tool and create a new rectangle anywhere on the page.**

   Hold the Shift key when using the Rectangle tool if you want to create a square.

2. **With the Selection tool, select the shape, and then choose Object➪Corner Options.**

   The Corner Options dialog box opens.

3. **Select the type of corner to apply, then click OK.**

   The corner option is applied to the shape. To apply the corner option to all corners of the shape, make sure the Make All Settings the Same chain icon is selected.

**TIP**

To adjust corner effects visually, use the Selection tool to click and select a frame. With the frame selected, click the yellow box that appears toward the top of the right edge of the frame. After clicking the yellow box, each corner handle becomes yellow and can be dragged horizontally left or right.

# Using Fills

A fill is located inside a path. You can fill paths and shapes with several different kinds of colors, transparent colors, or even gradients. Fills can help you achieve artistic effects and illusions of depth or add interest to a page design.

You may have already created a fill. The Tools panel contains two swatches: one for the stroke (a hollow square) and one for the fill (a solid box). (Refer to Chapter 2 of this minibook to locate the Fill and Stroke boxes.) If the Fill box contains a color, your shape has a fill when it's created. If the Fill box has a red line through it, the shape is created without a fill.

## Creating basic fills

You can create a basic fill in several different ways. One of the most common ways is to specify a color in the Fill swatch before you create a new shape. To create a shape with a fill, follow these steps:

1. **Make sure you don't have anything selected on the page. Make sure that the Fill box is selected so that you aren't adding color to the stroke instead.**

2. **Open the Color panel by choosing Window⇨Color⇨Color.**

3. **Select a color in the Color panel.**

   You can enter values into the CMYK (Cyan, Magenta, Yellow, Black) fields manually or by using the sliders. Alternatively, you can use the Eyedropper tool to select a color from the color ramp at the bottom of the Color panel.

   **TIP**

   Use the Color panel menu to select different color modes if CMYK isn't already selected. Select the Panel menu in the upper right and then select CMYK.

   The Fill box in the Tools panel is updated with the new color you've selected in the Color panel.

4. **Create a new shape on the page.**

   Select a shape tool and drag on the page to create a shape. The shape is filled with the fill color you chose.

**TIP**

As in the other Creative Cloud applications, you can create tints of a color built with CMYK by holding down the Shift key while dragging any color's slider. All color sliders then move proportionally.

You can also choose to use color swatches to select a fill color by using the Swatches panel. (Choose Window➪Color➪Swatches to open the Swatches panel.) Create a new color swatch (of the present color) by clicking the New Swatch button at the bottom of the panel. Double-click the new swatch to add new color properties by using sliders to set CMYK color values or by entering numbers into each text field.

Perhaps you already have a shape without a fill and you want to add a fill to it, or maybe you want to change the color of an existing fill. Select the shape and, with the Fill box in the Tools panel selected, select a color from the Color or Swatches panel. A new fill color is applied to the shape.

**TIP**

You can drag and drop a swatch color to fill a shape on a page, even if that shape isn't selected. Open the Swatches panel by choosing Window➪Color➪Swatches, and then drag the color swatch over to the shape. Release the mouse button, and the fill color is applied automatically to the shape.

## Making transparent fills

Fills that are partially transparent can create some interesting effects for the layout of your document. You can set transparency to more than one element on the page and layer those elements to create the illusion of depth and stacking.

Follow these steps to apply transparency to an element on the page:

1. **Using the Selection tool, select a shape on the page.**

   A bounding box appears around the selected shape.

2. **Open the Effects panel by choosing Window➪Effects.**

3. **Use the Opacity slider to specify how transparent the shape appears.**

   Click the arrow to open the slider or click in the text field to manually enter a value using the keyboard. The effect is immediately applied to the selected shape.

4. **Select Stroke or Fill in the Effects panel to apply a separate opacity to each one.**

# Looking at gradients

A *gradient* is the color transition from one color (or no color) to a different color. Gradients can have two or more colors in the transition.

Gradients can add interesting effects to shapes, including 3D effects. Sometimes you can use a gradient to achieve glowing effects or the effect of light hitting a surface. The two kinds of gradients available in InDesign are radial and linear, as shown in Figure 4-7 and described in this list:

>> **Radial:** A transition of colors in a circular fashion from a center point radiating outward

>> **Linear:** A transition of colors along a straight path

**FIGURE 4-7:**
A linear gradient (left) and radial gradient (right).

You can apply a gradient to a stroke or a fill or even to text. To apply a gradient to a stroke, simply select the stroke instead of the fill.

**WARNING**

Even though you can apply a gradient to the stroke of live text, you'll create a printing nightmare — use these features sparingly!

Here's how to add a gradient fill to a shape:

1. **With the Selection tool, select the object you want to apply a gradient to and then choose Window⇨Color⇨Swatches.**

   The Swatches panel opens.

2. **Choose New Gradient Swatch from the Swatches panel drop-down menu.**

   The New Gradient Swatch dialog box opens. (See Figure 4-8.)

3. **Type a new name for the swatch in the Swatch Name field.**

   Sometimes, giving the swatch a descriptive name, such as one indicating what the swatch is being used for, is helpful.

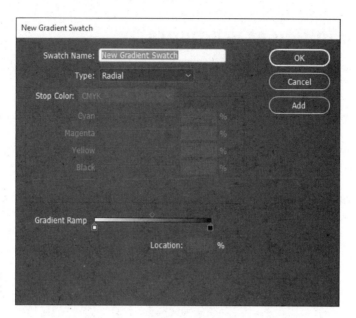

FIGURE 4-8:
The New Gradient
Swatch dialog box.

4. **Select Linear or Radial from the Type drop-down list.**

   This option determines the type of gradient the swatch creates every time you use it. We selected Radial from the drop-down list. (Refer to Figure 4-8.)

5. **Manipulate the gradient stops, below the Gradient Ramp, to position each color in the gradient.**

   *Gradient stops* are the color chips located below the Gradient Ramp. You can move the diamond shape above the Gradient Ramp to determine the center point of the gradient. You can select each gradient stop to change the color and move them around to edit the gradient. When the gradient stops are selected, you can change the color values in the Stop Color area by using sliders or entering values in each CMYK text field. If a list of swatches comes up and you want the CMYK sliders, select CMYK from the Stop Color drop-down menu.

**TIP**

   You can add a new color to the gradient by clicking the area between gradient stops. Then you can edit the new stop, just like you edit the others. To remove the gradient stop, drag the stop away from the Gradient Ramp.

6. **Click OK.**

   The gradient swatch is created and applied to the selected object.

**REMEMBER**

To edit a gradient, double-click the gradient's swatch in the Swatches panel. This step opens the Gradient Options dialog box, where you can modify the settings made in the New Gradient Swatch dialog box.

# Removing fills

Removing fills is even easier than creating them. Follow these steps:

**1.** **Select the shape with the Selection tool.**

A bounding box appears around the shape.

**2.** **Click the Fill box in the Tools panel.**

**3.** **Click the Apply None button, located below the Fill box.**

The button is white with a red line through it. The fill is removed from the selected shape, and the Fill box changes to No Fill. You also see the None fill on the Swatches and Color panels.

If you're using a single-row Tools panel, you don't see the Apply None button unless you click and hold down the Apply Gradient (or Apply Color) button.

# Adding Layers

*Layers* are like transparent sheets stacked on top of one another. If you add layers to a drawing, you can create the appearance that graphics are stacked on top of one another. The Layers panel allows you to create new layers, delete layers you don't need, or even rearrange layers to change the stacking order. You can even duplicate an InDesign file, and then add or remove layers to create an alternative version of the document.

Here's how to work with layers in InDesign:

**1.** **Open the Layers panel by choosing Window⇨Layers.**

This panel allows you to create, delete, and arrange layers.

**2.** **Draw a shape on the page using a shape tool.**

Create the shape anywhere on the page and make it large enough so that you can easily stack another shape on top of part of it.

**3.** **Click the Create New Layer button, on the bottom of the Layers panel, to create a new layer.**

A new layer is stacked on top of the selected layer and becomes the active layer.

**TIP**

Double-click a layer to give it an appropriate name or, even better, hold down the Alt (Windows) or Option (Mac) key and click the Create New Layer button to open the Layer Options dialog box before the layer is created.

**WARNING**

Make sure that the layer you want to create content on is selected before you start modifying the layer. You can tell which layer is selected because it's always highlighted in the Layers panel. You can easily add content to the incorrect layer if you don't check this panel frequently. (If you inadvertently add an item to the wrong layer, you can always cut and paste items to the correct layer.)

4. **Make sure that a shape tool is still selected, and then create a shape on the new layer by dragging the cursor so that part of the new shape covers the shape you created in Step 2.**

   The new shape is stacked on top of the shape you created in Step 2.

For more information about working with layers, refer to Book 3, Chapter 8.

# Creating QR Codes

You can use InDesign to create and modify QR code graphics. *QR codes* are a form of barcode that can store information such as words, numbers, URLs, or other forms of data. The user scans the QR code using her camera and software on a device, such as a smartphone, and the software makes use of the encoded data; for example, it opens a browser with the encoded URL, identifies a product, tracks a package, and so on. InDesign lets you encode hyperlinks, text, text messages, email messages, or business cards.

InDesign treats QR codes as graphics, so you can scale and modify the colors like other artwork in your documents. You can even copy and paste them into Illustrator!

You add a QR code to an empty frame in InDesign. Follow these steps to add one to your document:

1. **Click and drag the Rectangle Frame tool on the page to create an empty frame.**

2. **With your new frame selected, choose Object⇨Generate QR Code.**

   The Generate QR Code dialog box appears, with the Content tab active.

3. **Select what type of data to encode using the Type menu.**

   Select Web Hyperlink, Plain Text, Text Message, Email, or Business Card. The content area below this menu updates depending on what Type you choose.

**4.** **Enter the data to encode in your QR code.**

The area below the Type menu updates with text boxes to enter your data in. For example, if you chose Email, you enter an address, subject, and message to send. Or if you chose Business Card, you need to fill in Name, Organization, addresses, and so on.

**5.** **Click the Color tab and choose a color swatch.**

This sets the color for your QR code, affecting how it displays on the page. You can modify the color after placing the QR code on the page by changing the Fill and Stroke attributes of the selected frame.

**6.** **Click OK.**

The QR code is added to the selected frame. If you need to edit it further, select the text frame and choose Object⇨Edit QR Code.

Chapter **5**

# Understanding Color

C olor is an important part of design. Advertisements often rely on color to relay brands or effective messages — think of the package delivery company based on brown or a soft drink company known for its red cans and bottles. Color can enhance your message and, when used consistently, helps create a brand identity. When you use color, you want it to be accurate, whether you're printing or viewing the color online. In this chapter, you find out some of the fundamental aspects of working with color and the basic instructions on how to prepare documents for printing.

## Selecting Color with Color Controls

You have several different color modes and options to choose when working in InDesign. In this minibook, you find out how to add color to drawings with the Color panel. In this section, you use the Color panel to choose colors and apply them to elements on your page. You also discover how to save colors as swatches so you can easily reuse them.

You should use swatches whenever possible because they use named colors that can be matched by others more easily. A swatch can have exactly the same appearance as any color you choose that's unnamed, but a swatch establishes a link between the color on the page and the name of a color, such as a Pantone color number. Discover more about these kinds of color in the later section "Using Color Swatches and Libraries."

You can use these color controls for choosing colors for selections in a document:

>> **Stroke color:** Choose colors for strokes and paths in InDesign. A hollow box represents the Stroke color control.

>> **Fill color:** Choose colors for filling shapes. A solid square box represents the Fill color control.

In the Tools panel, you can toggle between the Fill and Stroke color controls by clicking them. Alternatively, you can press X on the keyboard to toggle between selected controls.

>> **Text color:** When you're working with text, a different color control becomes active. The Text color control is visible and displays the selected text color. Text can have both the stroke and fill colored.

To apply colors to selections, you can click the Apply color button below the color controls in the Tools panel. Alternatively, you can select and click a color swatch.

REMEMBER

The default colors in InDesign are a black stroke and no fill color. Restore the default colors at any time by pressing D. This shortcut works while using any tool except the Type tool.

# Understanding Color Models

You can use any of three kinds of color models in InDesign: CMYK (Cyan, Magenta, Yellow, Black), RGB (Red, Green, Blue), and LAB colors (Lightness and *A* and *B* for the *color*-opponent dimensions of the color space). A *color model* is a system used for representing each color as a set of numbers or letters (or both). The best color model to use depends on how you plan to print or display your document:

>> If you're creating a PDF that will be distributed electronically and probably not printed, use the RGB color model. RGB is how colors are displayed on a computer monitor.

>> You must use the CMYK color model if you're working with *process color.* Instead of having inks that match specified colors, you have four ink colors layered to simulate a particular color. Note that the colors on the monitor may differ from the ones that are printed. Sample swatch books and numbers can help you determine which colors you need to use in a document to match colors printed in the end.

>> If you know that the document needs to be printed by professionals who determine what each color is before it's printed, it doesn't matter whether you

use CMYK, RGB, or Pantone colors. In many cases, CMYK colors give you a more accurate representation of what can be printed, because RGB colors are often more vivid and bright on your monitor.

# Using Color Swatches and Libraries

The Swatches panel and swatch libraries help you choose, save, and apply colors in your documents. The colors you use in a document can vary greatly. For example, one publication you make with InDesign may be for a newsletter that has only two colors; another may be a catalog printing with CMYK along with a separate spot color. For each document, you should customize the available swatches so you can work more efficiently.

## The Swatches panel

You can create, apply, and edit colors from the Swatches panel. In addition, you can also create and save solid colors. Choose Window⇨Color⇨Swatches to open or expand the Swatches panel.

To create a new color swatch to use in a document, follow these steps:

1. **Click the panel menu drop-down located in the upper-right corner of the Swatches Panel; choose New Color Swatch.**

   The New Color Swatch dialog box opens.

2. **Leave the Name with Color Value checkbox selected or deselect to name your new color swatch.**

   The colors in the Swatches panel are named by their color values as a default.

   The name you choose is displayed next to the color swatch when it's entered into the panel.

3. **Choose the color type from the Color Type drop-down list.**

   Are you using a spot color, Pantone, for example, or Process, which is used when printing a color with Cyan, Magenta, Yellow, and Black (CMYK)?

4. **Choose the color mode.**

   From the Color Mode drop-down list, select a color mode. For this example, we use CMYK. Many of the other choices you see are prebuilt color libraries for various systems.

**5.** **Create the color by using the color sliders.**

Note that if you start with Black, you have to adjust that slider to the left to see the other colors.

If you choose a spot color, such as Pantone, you are presented with a list of available color swatches instead of the color sliders.

**6.** **Click OK or Add.**

Click Add if you want to continue adding colors to the Swatches panel or click OK if this color is the only one you're adding. The color or colors are added to the Swatches panel. If you clicked Add, click OK when you're done adding color swatches.

You can make changes to the swatch by selecting it in the Swatches panel and then choosing Swatch Options from the panel menu, or by simply double-clicking it in the Swatches panel.

# Swatch libraries

*Swatch libraries,* also known as color libraries, are standardized sets of named colors that help you because they're the most commonly and frequently used sets of color swatches. You can avoid trying to mix your own colors, which can be a difficult or tedious process to get right. For example, InDesign includes a swatch library for Pantone spot colors and a different library for Pantone process colors. These libraries are quite useful if you're working with either color set. If you skipped over it, you may want to review the earlier section "Understanding Color Models," where we explain the difference between spot and process colors.

To choose a swatch from a swatch library, follow these steps:

**1.** **Choose New Color Swatch from the Swatches panel menu.**

The New Color Swatch dialog box opens.

**2.** **Choose the color type you want to work with from the Color Type drop-down list.**

Choose from Process or Spot Color types.

**3.** **Select a color library from the Color Mode drop-down list.**

The drop-down list contains a list of color swatch libraries to choose from, such as Pantone Process Coated or TRUMATCH. After choosing a swatch set, the library opens and appears in the dialog box. For this example, we chose PANTONE+ Solid Coated, which is standard. If you're looking for the standard numbered Pantone colors, this set is the easiest to choose from. The Pantone Solid-Coated library of swatches loads.

4. **Pick a swatch from the library.**

   If you were provided with a Pantone number, type it into the Pantone textbox. Most companies have set Pantone colors that they use in order to keep their color consistent no matter where it is printed or displayed. You can also scroll and click a swatch in the library's list of colors, shown in Figure 5-1.

**FIGURE 5-1:**
Choose a color
from the swatch
library to add it
to the Swatches
panel.

**WARNING**

Your monitor doesn't provide the most accurate representation of a color or show you how a color will print. If color accuracy is critical, you should consider purchasing a color swatch book from Pantone, such as the Pantone Color Bridge Set. For more details about this guide, go to www.pantone.com and search for *Color Bridge*.

5. **Click the Add button.**

   This step adds the swatch to your list of color swatches in the Swatches panel. You can add as many color swatches as you like.

6. **When you finish adding swatches, click the OK button.**

   After you add a new color, the swatch is added to the list of swatches in the swatches panel and is ready to use in your project. Look in the swatches panel to see the newly added colors.

IN THIS CHAPTER

» **Transforming objects with the Transform panel**

» **Transforming objects with the Free Transform tool**

» **Rotating and scaling objects**

» **Shearing and reflecting objects**

» **Adding a clipping path**

» **Aligning and distributing objects in a layout**

Chapter **6**

# Clipping Paths, Alignment, and Object Transformation

I n this chapter, you discover several different ways to manipulate and arrange objects on a page. You find out how to use the Transform panel and other tools in the Tools panel to transform objects on page layouts. You can make the same transformation to an object several different ways in InDesign, so we show you a couple different ways to do the same job.

Aligning and distributing objects and images helps you organize elements logically on a page. In this chapter, you find out how to align objects by using the Align panel. In Chapter 4 of this minibook, we touch on paths. This chapter provides more information about clipping paths. We show you how to create a new path to use as a clipping path for an image in your document.

# Working with Transformations

Chapter 4 of this minibook shows you how to transform graphic objects by skewing them. You can manipulate objects in InDesign in many other ways. You can transform an object by selecting an individual object and choosing the Transform panel, which is available by choosing Window⇨Object & Layout⇨Transform, or by using the Free Transform tool to visually adjust objects.

## Looking at the Transform panel

The Transform panel, shown in Figure 6-1, is extremely useful for changing the way an image or graphic looks and also for changing the scale, rotation, or skew of selected objects. You can choose from a range of values for some of these modifiers or manually set your own by typing them.

Reference point indicator — Panel menu — Rotating angle — Constrain proportions — Scale Y percentage — Shear X angle — Scale X percentage

The Transform panel offers the following information and functionality:

>> **Reference point:** Indicates which handle is the reference for any transformations you make. For example, if you reset the X and Y coordinates, the reference point is set to this position. In Figure 6-1, the reference point is in the top-left corner, as indicated by the solid square.

>> **Position:** Change these values to reset the X and Y coordinate positions of the selected object.

>> **Size:** The W and H text fields are used to change the current dimensions of the object.

>> **Scale:** Enter or choose a percentage from the Scale X Percentage and Scale Y Percentage drop-down lists to scale (resize) the object on either of these axes.

>> **Constraining proportions:** Click the Constrain Proportions button to maintain the current proportions of the object being scaled.

>> **Shearing:** Enter or choose a negative or positive number to modify the shearing angle (skew) of the selected object.

>> **Rotation angle:** Set a negative value to rotate the object clockwise; a positive value rotates the object counterclockwise.

When you're scaling, shearing, or rotating an object in your layout, it transforms based on the reference point in the Transform panel. For example, when you rotate an object, InDesign considers the reference point to be the center point of the rotation.

Click a new reference point square in the Transform panel to change the reference point of the graphic to the equivalent bounding box handle of the selected object.

## Using the Free Transform tool

The multipurpose Free Transform tool lets you transform objects in different ways. Using the Free Transform tool, you can move, rotate, shear, reflect, and scale objects.

The functions of the Free Transform Tool are represented in InDesign by different cursors, as shown in Figure 6-2.

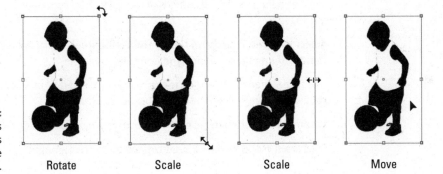

Rotate          Scale          Scale          Move

**FIGURE 6-2:**
Different cursors indicate options for using the Transform tool.

To move an object by using the Free Transform tool, follow these steps:

1. **Use the Selection tool to select an object on the page.**

   You can use an object that's already on the page or create a new shape by using the drawing tools. When the object is selected, you see handles around its edges.

2. **Select the Free Transform tool from the Tools panel.**

   The cursor changes to the Free Transform tool.

3. **Move the cursor over the middle of the selected object.**

   The cursor changes its appearance to indicate that you can drag to move the object. (Refer to Figure 6-2.) If you move the cursor outside the edges of the object, the cursor changes when other tools, such as rotate, scale, and shear, become active.

4. **Drag the object to a different location.**

   The object is moved to a new location on the page.

## Rotating objects

You can rotate an object by using the Free Transform tool, the Rotate tool, or the Transform panel. Use the panel to enter a specific degree that you want the object to rotate. The Free Transform tool lets you visually manipulate the object on the page.

To rotate an image by using the Free Transform tool, follow these steps:

1. **Select an object on the page with the Selection tool.**

   Handles appear around the edges of the object. You can rotate any object on the page.

2. **Select the Free Transform tool in the Tools panel and move it near the handle of an object outside the bounding box.**

   The cursor changes when you move it close to the handle of an object. For rotation, you must keep the cursor just outside the object.

3. **When the cursor changes to the rotate cursor, drag to rotate the object.**

   Drag the cursor until the object is rotated the correct amount.

Alternatively, you can use the Rotate tool to spin an object by following these steps:

1. **With the object selected, select the Rotate tool in the Tools panel by clicking and holding the arrow in the lower corner of the Free Transform tool, then move the cursor near the object.**

   The cursor looks similar to a crosshair.

2. **Click the cursor anywhere on the page near the object.**

The point that the object rotates around is set on the page.

3. **Drag the cursor outside the object.**

The object rotates around the reference point you set on the page. Hold the Shift key if you want to rotate in 45-degree increments.

You can also rotate objects by using the Transform panel. Here's how:

1. **Select an object on the page with the Selection tool.**

The bounding box with handles appears around the selected object.

2. **If the Transform panel isn't open, choose Window⇨Object & Layout⇨Transform.**

The Transform panel appears.

3. **Select a value from the Rotation Angle drop-down list or click the text field and enter a percentage.**

The object rotates to the degree you set in the Transform panel. Negative angles (in degrees) rotate the image clockwise, and positive angles (in degrees) rotate the image counterclockwise.

## Scaling objects

You can scale objects by using the Transform panel (refer to Figure 6-1), the Scale tool, or the Free Transform tool. Use the Transform panel to set exact width and height dimensions that you want to scale the object to, just as you can set exact percentages for rotating.

To scale an object by using the Free Transform tool or the Scale tool, follow these steps:

1. **Select an object on the page.**

A bounding box appears around the object.

2. **Select the Free Transform tool or the Scale tool from the Tools panel.**

3. **Move the cursor directly over a corner handle.**

The cursor changes into a double-ended arrow. (Refer to Figure 6-2.)

4. **Drag outward to increase the size of the object; drag inward to decrease the size of the object.**

If you want to scale the image proportionally, hold down the Shift key while you drag.

**TIP**

5. **Release the mouse button when the object is scaled to the correct size.**

To resize an object using the Transform panel, select the object and enter new values into the W and H text fields in the panel. The object then resizes to those exact dimensions.

## Shearing objects

*Shearing* an object means that you're skewing it horizontally, slanting it to the left or right. A sheared object may appear to have perspective or depth because of this modification. You use the Shear tool to create a shearing effect, as shown in Figure 6-3.

**FIGURE 6-3:**
The original image is on the left, and the sheared image is on the right.

Follow these steps to shear an object:

1. **Select an object on the page.**

The bounding box appears around the object that's selected.

2. **Choose the Shear tool in the Tools panel by clicking and holding the Free Transform tool.**

The cursor changes so that it looks similar to a crosshair. Click the corner of the object that you want to shear from, and a crosshair appears (refer to Figure 6-3).

3. **Click anywhere above or below the object and drag.**

The selected object shears depending on which direction you drag. Press the Shift key while you drag to shear an object in 45-degree increments.

**TIP**

To shear objects with the Free Transform tool, begin dragging a handle and then hold down Ctrl+Alt (Windows) or ⌘+Option (Mac) while dragging.

You can also enter an exact value into the Transform panel to shear an object. Select the object and then enter a positive or negative value in the panel representing the amount of slant you want to apply to the object.

**TIP**

You can apply shear by choosing Object⇨Transform⇨Shear to display the Shear dialog box.

## Reflecting objects

You can reflect objects to create mirror images by using the Transform panel menu. The menu provides several additional options for manipulating objects.

Follow these steps to reflect an object:

**1.** **Select an object on the page and then choose Window⇨Object & Layout⇨Transform to open the Transform panel or open it from the Window menu.**

The object's bounding box and handles appear. The Transform panel shows the current values of the selected object.

**2.** **Click the panel menu in the Transform panel.**

The menu opens, revealing many options available for manipulating the object.

**3.** **Select Flip Horizontal from the Transform panel menu.**

The object on the page flips on its horizontal axis. You can repeat this step with other reflection options in the menu, such as Flip Vertical.

**TIP**

You can also reflect objects with the Free Transform tool by dragging a corner handle past the opposite end of the object. The object reflects on its axis.

# Understanding Clipping Paths

Clipping paths allow you to create a path that crops a part of an image based on the path, such as removing the background area of an image. This shape can be one you create using InDesign, or you can import an image that already has a clipping path. InDesign can also use an existing alpha or mask layer, such as one created using Photoshop, and treat it like a clipping path. Clipping paths are useful when you want to block out areas of an image and have text wrap around the leftover image.

Clipping Paths, Alignment, and Object Transformation

You can create a clipping path directly in InDesign by using a drawing tool, such as the Pen tool. You use the tool to create a shape and then paste an image into this shape on the page. If you expect you'll want to reuse the clipping path and the image in the future, create the path in Photoshop and save it as part of the image instead. See Book 3, dedicated to Photoshop, for more details on how to do this.

Here's a quick way to remove the background of an image using InDesign:

1. **Choose File⇨Place and browse to locate and open an image.**

2. **With the Pen tool, create a path right on top of the image.**

   The path should be created so that it can contain the image.

3. **With the Selection tool, click to select the image and then choose Edit⇨Cut.**

4. **Select the shape you created in Step 1 and choose Edit⇨Paste Into.**

   The image is pasted into the selected shape you drew with the Pen tool.

If an image placed into your InDesign layout already includes a clipping path, you can choose to use it by selecting Show Import Options at the time you place the image into your layout. On the Mac OS, click on the Options button to be able to check the Show Import Options checkbox.

If that image contains multiple paths, you can choose which path to use by selecting Object⇨Clipping Path⇨Options, and then selecting either Alpha Channel or Clipping Path from the Type menu, depending upon what is used in the image.

If an image you import into your layout was photographed against a solid light colored or white background — such as a picture of a product for a catalog that was taken against a white background — you can have InDesign create a clipping path for that image. Here's how:

1. **Find an image that has a solid background and place it into your document. Using the Selection tool, click to select the image.**

2. **Choose Object⇨Clipping Path⇨Options.**

3. **In the Clipping Path dialog box, click the Type drop-down menu and choose Detect Edges. Adjust the threshold slider until the background surrounding the image disappears.**

4. **Click OK.**

   The path is created so that the image is visible and the background has been removed. The image can be placed over any other object, and it will reveal any items behind it.

**TIP**

For a clipping path to reveal objects behind it, the object with the clipping path needs to be at the top-most layer or the top-most object within its layer. You can check this by selecting the object and choosing Object⇨Arrange⇨Bring to Front and also using the layers panel, available by choosing Window⇨Layers.

# Arranging Objects on the Page

This section covers the additional ways you can arrange objects, which gives you more control over the placement of elements in your document.

## Aligning objects

In InDesign CC, you can align visually without the need for any extra tools or panels. If you keep Smart Guides activated (they're on by default), when you use the Selection tool to select and move objects around a page, guides appear automatically. These guides appear when the selected object is aligned with other objects on the page or with the page itself. If viewing these pesky guides starts to bother you, choose Edit⇨Preferences⇨Guides & Pasteboard (Windows) or InDesign⇨Preferences⇨Guides & Pasteboard (Mac) and turn off the four options underneath the Smart Guide Options heading.

You can also align objects on a page by using the Align panel: Choose Window⇨Object & Layout⇨Align. This panel gives you control over the way elements align to one another or to the overall page. The Align panel has many buttons to control selected objects. Mouse over a button to see its tooltip describe how that button aligns elements.

**TIP**

If you're not sure what each button does after reading the associated tooltip, look at the icon on the button. The icon is sometimes helpful in depicting what the Align button does to selected objects.

Here's how to align elements on the page:

1.  **Select several objects on the page with the Selection tool.**

    Hold the Shift key while clicking each object to select several objects.

    Each object is selected when you click it on the page. If you don't have a few objects on a page, quickly create a couple new objects by using the drawing tools.

2. **Choose Window⇨Object & Layout⇨Align.**

   The Align panel opens.

3. **Select the kind of alignment you want to apply to the selected objects.**

   Try clicking the Align Vertical Centers button. Each selected object aligns to the vertical center point on the page.

## Distributing objects

In the previous section, you find out how to align a few objects on a page, but what if the objects you're aligning aren't distributed evenly? Maybe their centers are lined up, but there's a large gap between two of the images and a narrow gap between the other ones. In that case, you need to *distribute* objects and align them. Distribute objects on the page to space them relative to the page or to each other in different ways. Here's how:

1. **Select objects on a page that are neither aligned nor evenly distributed by using the Selection tool while holding the Shift key.**

   The objects are selected when you click each one. All objects you select will be aligned to each other on the page.

2. **If the Align panel isn't open, choose Window⇨Object & Layout⇨Align.**

   The Align panel opens.

3. **Click the Distribute Horizontal Centers button and then click the Align Vertical Centers button directly above it on the Align panel.**

The selected objects are distributed evenly and aligned horizontally on the page.

Don't forget about the cool Multiple Place feature: It lets you distribute and align on the fly! Try this handy option to place several images at one time:

1. **Choose File⇨Place.**

2. **Press Ctrl (Windows) or ⌘ (Mac), select multiple images, and then click the Open button.**

3. **Before clicking to place the images, hold down Ctrl+Shift (Windows) or ⌘+Shift (Mac).**

The cursor appears as a grid, as shown in Figure 6-4.

**FIGURE 6-4:** Place multiple images by holding down Ctrl+Shift (Windows) or ⌘+Shift (Mac) and dragging.

4. **Click and drag to create the rectangle that you want your images aligned to and distributed within.**

The images are aligned and distributed automatically, as shown in Figure 6-5.

**FIGURE 6-5:** Images are aligned and distributed automatically when placed.

IN THIS CHAPTER

» **Checking (preflighting) documents**

» **Packaging documents for delivery**

» **Understanding file formats**

» **Exporting to different file formats**

» **Printing documents**

Chapter **7**

# Exporting to PDF and Printing

n addition to printing, you can also export InDesign documents into several different kinds of file formats. In this chapter, you take a closer look at the preparations for delivering a file to a print vendor, as well as many of the different kinds of files you can create electronically from an InDesign document. Before you print a document, it's good to make sure you have everything you need, so we start by looking at the preflight option.

## Preflight: Preparing Your Documents for Printing

The *Preflight* feature in InDesign helps confirm that everything you need to print your document is ready and available. It also provides information about the document you're printing, such as listing its fonts, print settings, and inks used. Using Preflight can help you determine whether your InDesign document has unlinked images or missing fonts before printing it. Here's how to use the Preflight option:

1. **If you don't have a file to work with, you can access the file named Preflight in the Book04_InDesign folder in the DummiesCCfiles folder located at** https://www.agitraining.com/dummies.

   This page intentionally has missing fonts and images.

2. **With the file still open, choose Window⇨Output⇨Preflight.**

   The Preflight panel opens.

3. **Make sure the On checkbox is selected and the Profile is set to [Basic] (working).**

   These settings provide a basic preflight of the document, confirming that all images and fonts are available for printing.

4. **If any errors are noted in the document, click the page number listed to the right of the error in the preflight window to view the error.**

   Common errors, such as missing fonts and overset text (text that doesn't fit completely into a text frame) are all listed in the Preflight panel, and can generally be corrected easily with a little time. It's much better to fix errors before you print them!

TIP

When the Preflight option is turned on, a small green or red circle appears along the bottom-left corner of the document window. Green indicates that the document is preflighted and no errors are reported, whereas red indicates a possible error. You can simply click the errors drop-down along the bottom-left corner of the Document window to open the Preflight panel and investigate any possible errors.

# Packaging Your Documents

If you need to deliver your documents to a print service provider or to another designer, you'll want to provide everything that provider needs to continue working on the InDesign file. This is where the Package command is helpful. Package gathers copies of all images and fonts used in the document along with a copy of the InDesign document itself into a single folder that you can easily deliver to a print service provider or to a colleague. You can even use this option to archive completed jobs, to make sure that all necessary elements are stored together. Here's how:

1. **Choose File⇨Package.**

   The Package dialog box opens. The Summary screen shows you all current images and fonts in the document, based on an analysis of that document.

2. **Click Fonts in the list on the left side of the dialog box.**

Any fonts in your document are listed on this screen. Select fonts from this list and click the Find Font button to discover where they're located. Click the More Info button to see the path to the font. These fonts are saved directly into the package folder when you finish.

3. **Click Links and Images in the list on the left side of the dialog box.**

The Links and Images screen lists the images within your document. If any images aren't properly linked, your document is incomplete and prints with pictures missing. Find the image, update it, and repair links before packing the file.

4. **When you're finished, click the Package button at the bottom of the dialog box.**

Your document and all its associated files are saved into a folder. You're given the opportunity to name the folder, specify a location on your hard drive, and add instructions for printing.

**TIP**

If you're taking a file to a professional print service provider, you can give the vendor your original InDesign document or you can create a high-quality PDF file suitable for printing. It's a good idea to ask your print service provider about the file type it prefers to receive. By providing an InDesign file, you give the printing service a chance to fine-tune the document before printing, and if you provide a PDF, the document has limited capabilities for editing. Different print vendors prefer to receive different file types.

# Understanding File Formats

The kind of file you decide to create by exporting depends on your needs. The first thing to determine is where you'll use the exported file. For example, you might need to

>> Put an image of your InDesign document, or page, on the web.

>> Send an entire document to someone who doesn't have InDesign, but wants to receive it by email.

>> Import the content into a different program, such as Adobe Animate or Illustrator.

>> Take a particular kind of file somewhere else to print it.

Exporting InDesign documents lets you make them "portable" so that they can be used in different ways — such as on the web or in another program. You can choose from the many file formats InDesign supports, and you can control many settings related to the files you create.

Some of the file formats you can create from InDesign are listed in Table 7-1.

**TABLE 7-1** **File Formats**

| File Format | Description |
| --- | --- |
| JPEG (Joint Photographic Experts Group), PNG (Portable Network Graphics) | Either of these commonly used formats for compressed images is a good choice for creating a picture of an InDesign page to post on a website. This is only a picture and is good for something like a thumbnail image representing a document. Don't use this if you want someone to actually read the InDesign file on the web — for that you'll want to export to PDF. This is simply a picture preview of what a document page looks like. |
| EPS (Encapsulated PostScript) | A self-contained image file that contains high-resolution printing information about all the text and graphics used on a page. This format is commonly used for high-quality printing when you need to have an image of an InDesign page used within another document — such as a picture of a book cover created with InDesign that needs to appear in a promotional catalog — so that you can use an EPS of the book cover in your layout. |
| XML (Extensible Markup Language) | Let's you separate the content from the layout so that all the content on a page can be repurposed and used in different ways — online or in print. Corporations commonly use XML for storing their product data when they have a large amount of information — such as thousands of items in a catalog. |
| PDF (Portable Document Format) | Used to exchange documents with users on different computer systems and operating systems. This format is used extensively for distributing files such as e-books and brochures. You may need to distribute the file to a wide audience or to a service provider for printing. Anyone who has installed Adobe Reader (also known as Acrobat Reader) on a computer can view your document. You can export PDFs designed for printing by selecting PDF (Print). Select PDF (Interactive) if your PDF contains hyperlinks or movies and will be distributed online instead of being printed. |
| Rich or Plain text (text files) | Can include formatting (Rich) or plain text only (Plain). A text file is a simple way to export content. If you need the text from your document to incorporate or send elsewhere, you can export it as Plain (Text Only), Tagged, or Rich Txt. If you need to send a document to someone who doesn't have InDesign, exporting it as text may be a good option. |
| EPUB | Use the e-pub file format to create electronic books that can be read using an electronic book reader, including devices such as the nook or iPad, or using any e-book reader software. With additional conversion, this file can also be read on the Amazon Kindle. |
| HTML | Use the HTML file format to export a document as HTML (HyperText Markup Language), which is the language used by web browsers. Documents exported using this option typically require some HTML editing for formatting and design, which you can do using Adobe Dreamweaver. |
| IDML | Use the InDesign Markup Language option to export InDesign documents in a format that can be read by earlier versions of InDesign. For example, a colleague is using InDesign CS6, but you are using InDesign CC. Export the document using the IDML option so that your colleague can successfully open it in InDesign CS6. If you simply save the file, the older version of InDesign is not able to open the document. |

**REMEMBER**

JPEG, PDF, and EPS files can be exported from InDesign and then imported into other software programs. You can export these images for use in print after they're imported into a different graphics program, or you can use the images on the web. It all depends on how you set up the document for export and the settings you use.

After determining which file format to export your file in, learn how to export the file and the different kinds of settings you can control when doing so. The rest of this chapter shows you how to export different file types from InDesign.

# Exporting Publications

You can export publications from the Export dialog box. After you open it by choosing File⇨Export, you can choose the file format, name, and location. After specifying a name and location and a format to export to, click Save. A new dialog box opens, where you can make settings specific to the file format you picked. We discuss in the following sections some of the most common file formats you're likely to use for export.

## Exporting PDF documents for printing

Create a PDF file of your document if you want to make sure that viewers see exactly what you have created — even if they don't have InDesign. A PDF file also limits the editing capabilities, making it unlikely your document will be changed. If you choose to export a PDF document, you have many options to customize the document you're exporting. You can control the amount of compression in the document, the marks and bleeds it has in InDesign, and its security settings. Here's how to export to PDF:

1. **Choose File⇨Export.**

   The Export dialog box opens.

2. **Choose a location in which to save the file and then enter a new filename.**

   Browse to a location on your hard drive using the Save In drop-down list (if you're using Windows) and name the file in the File Name text field. If you're using a Mac, name the file in the Save As text field and select a location from the Where drop-down list.

3. **Select Adobe PDF (Print) from the Save As Type (Windows) or Format (Mac) drop-down list at the bottom of the Export window.**

## 4. Click Save.

The Export Adobe PDF dialog box appears with the General options screen open, as shown in Figure 7-1.

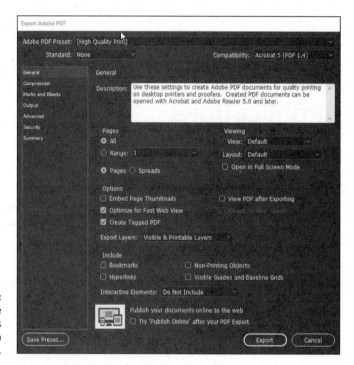

## 5. Choose a preset from the Adobe PDF Preset drop-down list.

These presets are easy to use. If you're familiar with Adobe Acrobat and the Adobe Distiller functions, they're the same. (For more detailed information about what each setting does, see Book 6.)

**TIP**

The presets on the Adobe PDF Preset drop-down list automatically change the individual export settings of a document. For example, you can select Smallest File Size from the list if you're displaying your work online or select High Quality Print if you plan for the PDF to be printed on home printers. Select Press Quality if you intend to have the PDF professionally printed.

## 6. Leave the Standard drop-down list at None.

Leave it at None unless, of course, you know about the PDF/X standards used for sharing advertisements. (For more on PDF/X, see Book 6.)

7. **Select a range of pages to export by typing the start page (and then a hyphen) and the end page in the Range text box.**

   You can also export nonconsecutive pages by separating the page numbers with a comma.

   By default, all pages are exported.

8. **Choose a compatibility setting for the PDF from the Compatibility drop-down list.**

   Compatibility settings determine which kind of reader is required in order to view the document. Setting compatibility to Acrobat 5 (PDF 1.4) ensures that a wide audience can view your PDF files. Some older PDF readers may not be able to interpret certain features in your document if you choose compatibility for a higher version. Setting this value to Acrobat 5 or later ensures that anyone who has installed Adobe Reader or Acrobat in the past ten years will be able to view the PDF file.

9. **Choose whether to embed thumbnails and whether to optimize the document, and then choose which kinds of elements to include in the file by selecting the checkbox to the left of the options in the Include section.**

   Other settings specify the inclusion of bookmarks, links, and other elements in the file. Unless you've added any of these elements, you don't need to worry about selecting these options. You may want to embed thumbnail previews, but Acrobat creates thumbnails automatically when the file is opened, so this can add to the file size unnecessarily.

**TECHNICAL STUFF**

   Click Security in the list on the left of the Export Adobe PDF dialog box to open the Security screen, where you can specify passwords to open the document. You can also choose a password that's required to print or modify the PDF file.

10. **Click the Export button to export the file.**

    The file is saved to the location you specified in Step 2.

## Exporting EPS files

From InDesign, you can export EPS files, which are useful for importing into other programs. EPS files are single-page graphics files, which means that each exported InDesign page is saved as a separate EPS file.

**TIP**

You do not need to export an EPS file to place one InDesign file into another! If you're creating classified pages or any page that contains other InDesign pages, you can save yourself a few steps by simply choosing File➪Place and selecting the InDesign file. InDesign can import InDesign files into a layout, or even PDFs — so the only reason to export to EPS is to create a picture for an older software or database that doesn't work with newer file formats.

Here's how to export EPS files:

**1. Choose File⇨Export.**

The Export dialog box opens.

**2. Select a location on your hard drive to save the EPS files, enter a new filename, and select EPS from the Save As Type (Windows) or Format (Mac) drop-down list; click Save.**

The Export EPS dialog box opens.

**3. Choose a page or range of pages to export.**

Select the All Pages option to export all pages or select the Ranges option and enter a range of pages. If you want spreads to export as one file, select the Spreads radio button.

If you're creating more than one EPS file (for example, exporting more than one page of your InDesign document), the file is saved with the filename, an underscore, and then the page number. For example, page 7 of a cats.indd file would be saved as cats_7.eps in the designated location.

**4. From the Color drop-down list, select a color mode; from the Embed Fonts drop-down list, select how to embed fonts.**

From the Color drop-down list, select Leave Unchanged to retain the color mode you're using for the InDesign document. You can also change the color mode to CMYK (Cyan, Magenta, Yellow, Black), Gray (grayscale), or RGB (Red, Green, Blue). For more information on color modes, flip back to Chapter 5 of this minibook.

From the Embed Fonts drop-down list, select Subset to embed only the characters used in the file. If you select Complete, all fonts in the file are loaded when you print the file. Selecting None means that a reference to where the font is located is written into the file.

**5. Choose whether you want a preview to be generated for the file by choosing from the Preview drop-down list.**

A *preview* (a small thumbnail image) is useful if an EPS file can't be displayed. For example, you're browsing a library of images and you see a small thumbnail image of the EPS file; so whether or not you use the image or open it on your computer, you can see what the file looks like. From the Preview drop-down list, you can select TIFF to generate a preview; select None if you don't want a preview to be created.

**6. Click the Export button to export the files.**

The files are saved to the location you designated in Step 2.

# Exporting JPEG and PNG files

You can export JPEG and PNG files from an InDesign document. These file formats are commonly used in web publishing and are useful if you need to place a picture of an InDesign document or page online. You can export a single image on a selected page, or even entire pages and spreads as a JPEG or PNG. JPEG and PNG files allow you to effectively compress full color or black-and-white images, which is useful if you need a picture of an InDesign page to appear on the web.

To export a JPEG or PNG image, follow these steps:

**1.** Select an object on a page or make sure that no object is selected if you want to export a page or spread.

**2.** Choose File⇨Export.

The Export dialog box opens.

**3.** Type a filename, locate the spot where you want to save the file on your hard drive, and select either JPEG or PNG from the Save As Type (Windows) or Format (Mac) drop-down list; click Save.

The Export JPEG or PNG dialog box opens.

**4.** If you want to export a page, select the Pages radio button and enter the page number in the Range text field; if you want to export the selected object, make sure that the Selection option is selected.

The Selection option is available only if a selection was made in Step 1.

**5.** Choose an image quality and format to export by selecting from the Image Quality and Format Method drop-down lists.

The Image Quality drop-down list controls the amount of compression that's used when you export a JPEG or PNG file. Choose from these options:

- *Maximum:* Creates an image with the largest file size and highest quality

- *High:* Creates an image with a larger file size and high quality

- *Medium:* Creates an image with medium file size and medium quality

- *Low:* Creates a smaller file of lesser quality because it includes less image information

If you select the Baseline format from the Format Method drop-down list, the entire image has to be downloaded before it's displayed in a web browser. Select Progressive to show the image in a progressively complete display as it downloads in a web browser.

The Format Method options do not appear if you are creating a PNG image.

6. **Click the Export button.**

   The file is exported and saved to the location you specified in Step 3.

# Exporting to Flash

Using InDesign CC, you can export an InDesign document as a Flash Professional file (FLA) that can be edited in Flash Animate CC (formerly Flash), or as a Flash Player (SWF) file that can be viewed, but not edited.

**REMEMBER**

Many modern web browsers do not support the SWF file format. This includes the browsers on the Apple iPhone and iPad, and there is limited support in some of the Microsoft browsers. Because the Flash file format is currently on the decline, you should carefully consider whether you want to export to Flash at all. We suggest you review other options for exporting digital documents, which we cover in the next chapter in this minibook. However, because Flash export is still an available option, we cover it here.

To export to the Flash Player (SWF) format, follow these steps:

1. **Choose File⇨Export.**

   The Export dialog box appears.

2. **Choose a location to save the files, enter a new filename, and choose Flash Player (SWF) from the Save As Type (Windows) or Format (Mac) drop-down list.**

**TIP**

   If you need to include video, audio, animation, or complex interactivity, export the file in the Flash Professional (FLA) format because you can then use Animate to modify and edit the file until it meets your exact needs. While the SWF format will quickly create a SWF version of your document that can be viewed online, it doesn't provide you with an option to refine and edit your choices after exporting.

   In the Export SWF dialog box, you can set the output size, specify pages to include, and make various conversion and compression choices.

3. **Choose the size you want for the exported file.**

   If you do not want to change the size of the exported file, select the Scale option and leave the drop-down list at 100%. Otherwise, select the Fit To option to select and option from the drop-down list, or select the Width option and enter your own dimensions in the Width and Height drop-down lists.

4. **Select which page or pages you want to export.**

   Select the All Pages option to export the entire document; select Range to enter a page number if you want to export only a specific page or pages.

5. **Select the Interactivity options you want by choosing whether you want to include all interactive options or only those that affect appearance.**

6. **Select whether you want Page Transitions to export, or select from the list of included transitions such as Dissolve or Wipe.**

7. **Choose whether you want an interactive page curl to appear at the top corner of the document page.**

8. **Click OK to export your InDesign document as a SWF file.**

# Exporting text files

You can extract text from an InDesign document so that it can be edited or used elsewhere. The text formats vary slightly depending on the text in your document.

To export text, follow these steps:

1. **Select the Text tool from the toolbox and select some text within a text frame in your document, or place the cursor within a text frame where you want to export all the text.**

   The cursor must be in a text frame in order to export text.

2. **Choose File⇨Export.**

   The Export dialog box opens.

3. **Enter a filename, select a location to save the file in, and select Text Only from the Save As Type (Windows) or Format (Mac) drop-down list; click Save.**

   The Text Export Options dialog box opens.

4. **Choose a platform and encoding for the export.**

   Select either PC or Macintosh from the Platform drop-down list to set the PC or Mac operating system compatibility. Select an encoding method for the platform you choose from the Encoding drop-down list; you can choose either Default Platform or Unicode.

The universal character-encoding standard *Unicode* is compatible with major operating systems. *Encoding,* which refers to how characters are represented in a digital format, is essentially a set of rules that determines how the character set is represented by associating each character with a particular code sequence.

5. **Click the Export button.**

   The file is exported and saved to the location you specified in Step 3.

# Printing Your Work

You can print your work from an InDesign document in many different ways, with many kinds of printers and processes. You can either use your home or office printer, or you can take your work to a professional printing service. Both printers and printing services vary in the quality of production they can offer you.

The following sections look at the different ways you can set up a document for printing and the kinds of issues you may encounter during this process.

## Understanding bleed

If you want an image or span of color to go to the edge of a page, without any white margins, you *bleed* it off the edge of the document. *Bleeding* extends the print area slightly beyond the edge of the page into the area that will be cut and removed during the printing process. (Professional printers sometimes print your documents on a larger page size than necessary, and then trim off the extra paper.) You can bleed your own work, too. While you're designing, you can turn on crop and bleed marks to show where the page needs to be trimmed to make sure that the image bleeds far enough off the edge of the page area. We cover this topic in the next section.

## Doing it yourself: Printing and proofing at home or the office

Because many InDesign documents are designed to be professionally printed, the available print settings are quite robust. Just because they are robust doesn't make them complicated, though. We demystify the settings for you here:

Choose File⇨Print to open the Print dialog box. Choose the printer you intend to use from the Printer drop-down menu. If you don't have a printer, choose Adobe PDF from the Printer drop-down menu to follow along with the steps below.

Many printing options are available in the list on the left side of the Print dialog box. Clicking an item causes the dialog box to change, displaying the settings you can change for the selected item. Click each of the items below to better understand these common printing options:

>> **General:** Set the number of copies of the document you want to print and the range of pages to print. You can select the Reverse Order checkbox to print from the last to first page. Select an option from the Sequence drop-down list to print only even or odd pages instead of all pages. If you're working with spreads that need to be printed on a single page, select the Spreads radio button.

>> **Setup:** Define the paper size, orientation (portrait or landscape), and scale. You can scale a page so that it's as much as 1,000 percent of its original size or as little as 1 percent. You can (optionally) constrain the scale of the width and height so that the page remains at the same ratio. The Page Position drop-down list is useful when you're using paper that's larger than the document you've created. This option helps you center the document on larger paper.

>> **Marks and Bleed:** Turn on or off many of the printing marks in the document, such as crop, bleed, and registration marks. For example, you may want to show these marks if a bleed extends past the boundaries of the page and you need to show where to crop each page. You see a preview of what the page looks like when printed, and you can select options to print page information (such as filename and date) on each page.

**REMEMBER**

>> **Output:** Choose how to print pages — for example, as a separation or a composite, using which inks (if you're using separations), or with or without trapping. InDesign can separate and print documents as plates (which are used in commercial printing) from settings you specify. Depending on the printer you have selected, you may or may not have separations as an option.

>> **Graphics:** Control how graphics and fonts in the document are printed. The Send Data drop-down list controls bitmap images and specifies how much of the data from these images is sent to the printer. Here are some other options available when printing:

- *All:* Sends all bitmap data. Use this for the highest quality printing, but it may take a long time for your jobs to print if you're using high-resolution images.

- *Optimized Subsampling:* Sends as much image data as the printer can handle. Use this if you are having difficulty with printing high-quality images when using the All option.

- *Proxy:* Prints lower-quality images mostly to preview them.

- *None:* Prints placeholder boxes with an X through them. This option lets you quickly print a proof of a layout to just get a quick understanding of a page design.

>> **Color Management:** Choose how you want color handled when it's output. If you have profiles loaded in your system for your output devices, you can select the profiles here. Color management is more commonly used by commercial print vendors and vendors with critical color needs. It's a complex topic — entire books are available on the subject of color management — and we don't have space to cover it in depth here.

>> **Advanced:** Determine how you want images to be sent to the printer. If you are unfamiliar with Open Prepress Interface (OPI), you can leave this setting at the default. Also known as image-swapping technology, the OPI process allows low-resolution images inserted into InDesign to be swapped with the high-resolution version for output. It's a highly specialized setting used by commercial print vendors — such as catalog print vendors — that work with a large number of images.

Flattening needs to be addressed if you use a drop shadow, feather an object in InDesign, or apply transparency to any objects, even if they were created in Photoshop or Illustrator.

Use the preset Medium Resolution for desktop printers and High Resolution for professional press output.

>> **Summary:** You can't make modifications but you can see a good overview of all your print settings.

TIP

After you finish your settings, click the Save Preset button if you want to save the changes you've made. If you think you may print other documents with these settings repeatedly, using the Save Preset feature can be a great timesaver.

After you click the Save Preset button, the Save Preset dialog box opens, where you can enter a new name to save the settings. The next time you print a document, you can select the saved preset from the Print Preset drop-down list in the Print dialog box.

Click the Print button at the bottom of the Print dialog box when you're ready to print the document.

IN THIS CHAPTER

» **Digital document essentials**

» **Alternate layouts for varying devices**

» **Liquid Layout rules**

» **Exporting to EPUB 2.0 (Reflowable)**

» **Exporting to EPUB 3.0 (Fixed Layout)**

# Chapter **8**

# Creating Digital Documents Using EPUB

nDesign was built more than a decade ago as a tool for creating printed documents not for creating digital documents and electronic books. As of InDesign CS5, however, Adobe added the capability to create digital documents for distribution on tablets, e-readers, and the web. Since then, many new features have been added to InDesign that are focused on creating digital documents.

Because publishing on tablets is still relatively new, the workflows, tools, and features are still in their infancy. In some cases, we find the process a bit clumsy and the tools added to InDesign feel like an afterthought, but, unless you want to learn to code HTML5 and CSS3, the Creative Cloud tools are your best bet for getting your content delivered onto a tablet or e-reading device.

Digital documents can be optimized to appear on a variety of devices, and in different formats. In this chapter, you discovered two such formats:

» **EPUB 2.0 (reflowable):** The standard for electronic books that can be viewed online and offline is EPUB. If your content is text-heavy, the EPUB 2.0 (reflowable) file format is what you should use.

>> **EPUB 3.0 (fixed layout):** If your document is highly stylized and designed, the new EPUB 3.0 (fixed layout) is a better alternative and allows for animation and interactivity.

In this chapter, you discover how to create documents for distribution using both of these EPUB formats.

# Adapting Content for Digital Distribution

Creating a digital document requires more than just selecting an output type and pressing the Export button. To make effective documents, you must design them according to the needs of the device upon which they will be viewed.

To do this, you can design the document's layout for specific devices, such as an iPad vertical or iPad horizontal layout, using alternative layouts. The Liquid Layout feature aids in the creation of these alternative layouts.

# Creating Digital Documents

These days, you should intentionally design your documents for digital distribution. If you must adapt a print document for electronic distribution, you should save a copy of the original InDesign document and work on the copy as a dedicated electronic document.

To convert an existing print document to a digital document layout, follow these steps:

**1.** **Open the existing document and choose File⇨Save As and name the copy of the document. Then click Save.**

Choose a name that relates to your intended distribution. Consider including terms such as EPUB or iPad in the filename so you can distinguish the electronic version from the print version.

**TIP**

If you're creating an EPUB document for a book that primarily uses text and that will be viewed on many readers, after Step 1 you can go directly to Step 5, because you do not need to specify layout details or size details for specific devices. For EPUB documents that require highly formatted layouts, continue with Steps 2 through 4.

2. **Choose File➪Document Setup. In the Document Setup window, choose Mobile from the Intent drop-down menu, and select the desired Page Size and orientation (vertical or horizontal).**

3. **Click OK to close the Document Setup window and then choose File➪Save to save these changes.**

4. **Scroll through the document and make adjustments to the layout based upon the available page size. Use the Selection tool to move objects and use the Pages panel to add pages as needed.**

5. **Choose Window➪Articles to open the Articles panel.** Use the Selection tool to drag items from your layout into the Articles panel, defining the order in which they will be displayed in an EPUB. If you have something that you don't want to include in the digital version of the book, simply don't drag it into the Articles panel. If you have images that are specific to an area of text, make sure that those images are anchored to the text. This ensures that the images appear near the text, as opposed to at the end of the story. Save your document after dragging all elements to be exported to the Articles panel.

# Creating liquid layouts

The Liquid Layout feature, borrowed from the idea of Responsive Design in the web design community, lets you use InDesign as a tool for creating alternate layouts with less manual work.

To use Liquid Layout, follow these steps:

1. **Choose Layout➪Liquid Layout to open the Liquid Layout panel, as shown in Figure 8-1.**

   If you notice a yellow triangle in your liquid layout panel, it means that Layout adjustment is enabled with the document. You must disable this before you continue. Go to Layout➪Margin and Columns and uncheck the Enable Layout Adjustment checkbox.

2. **From the Liquid Layout panel, choose a Liquid Page Rule. You can choose a different rule for each page depending on its content. With the Scale, Re-center, and Guide based options, you can choose to auto-fit your images to their new size. With the Object-based option, you can choose auto-fit as well as object constraints and you can determine how to anchor your images when they move.**

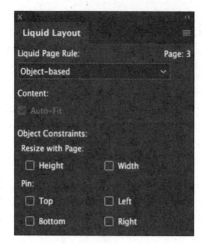

3.  **Test the Liquid Layout by selecting the Page tool from the Tools Panel. Click and drag the page handles and see how the objects on the page are modified.**

    If you selected the Scale option, the page objects should all reduce in size as you reduce the size of the page using the Page tool. The page tool will not change the size of your page; it just previews how it will look.

## Creating alternate layouts

After you have indicated how you want your pages to change using the Liquid Layout rules, you can create separate horizontal and vertical layouts for your document. When you export your document, the document will include information in the Cascading Style Sheets (CSS) that adapts the layout based upon the way it is being viewed.

To create an alternative layout, follow these steps:

1.  **From the Layout menu, choose Layout⇨Create Alternate Layout to create an additional alternative layout to your current layout.**

    For example, if you have a horizontal layout, you may want to also create a vertical version of the layout, or you may need to create a larger or smaller version of your content.

2.  **Name the alternate layout, specify the page attributes, and then click OK, as shown in Figure 8-2.**

FIGURE 8-2:
Create an
alternate
layout.

A new layout of all pages is created with the alternate size or orientation, and the content from the original pages is duplicated and linked onto the new layout.

**3.** **Modify the layout of page elements on the alternate layout as needed.**

Keep in mind, the Liquid Layout feature is not a perfect fit for all designs. You may need to make additional changes to your layout once you have created the alternate layout.

REMEMBER

Notice that any text frames and image frames that were duplicated onto the alternate layout also contain a link symbol in the upper-left corner. This indicates that the text and images on the alternate layout are linked to the original. Changes made to the items in the original layout are reflected on the alternate layout. If an item in the alternate layout is different from the original layout, a yellow triangle appears instead of the link symbol. Double-click the yellow triangle, and the item in the alternate layout is then synchronized with the original layout. Any changes made to an alternate layout will not be reflected in the original layout.

## Other digital document features

There are many interactive features in InDesign that can be added to your digital files. Depending on what your final export version will be, these features will work for you; however, some are not supported in the EPUB 2.0 version.

Use these features to add interactivity to your digital documents:

>> **Animation panel:** Use the Animation panel to apply animation to objects on your page. For example, you can have an object fade in as the page appears, or fade out and disappear. Access this panel by choosing Window⇨Interactive⇨ Animation, and apply animation to individual objects by selecting them and choosing an animation option from the Preset drop-down menu in the Animation panel.

>> **Timing panel:** Use the Timing panel to modify animations you have created using the Animation panel. Access this panel by choosing Window⇨ Interactive⇨Timing. Use the Event drop-down list to specify when an object's animation occurs, and use the Delay option to specify if the animation should wait before it occurs.

>> **Buttons and Forms:** Use this panel to convert text or images to buttons that become interactive when the InDesign document is exported to EPUB 3.0. Access this panel by choosing Window⇨Interactive⇨Buttons and Forms. Buttons can have actions associated with them, so that something occurs when they are clicked. For example, when clicked, a button can play a movie or sound, navigate to a specific page, or play an animation.

# Exporting EPUB

Books displayed using iBooks, Nook devices, Kobo readers, or Sony eReaders all use the EPUB file format. Books displayed on the Kindle begin as EPUB files but undergo an additional conversion process into Amazon's proprietary Kindle format. The bottom line if you want to create electronic books: You need to know about creating EPUB files. When you have either created the digital version of your layout or converted your print document to a digital layout, this is how to create an EPUB file using InDesign:

## Exporting EPUB (Reflowable)

The EPUB – Reflowable version is best for documents that are text-heavy, such as novels and cookbooks. Prior to exporting you should make sure that all of your images are anchored and that the order in which you want your content to flow is dictated in the Articles panel.

**1.** **With an InDesign document open, choose File⇨Export.**

The Export dialog box appears.

2. **From the Save as Type (Windows) or Format (Mac) drop-down list.** Select EPUB (Reflowable) and then find a location on your hard drive or network for the document to be saved. Enter a name for the EPUB file in the File Name portion of the Export dialog box.

3. **Click the Save button.**

   The EPUB – Reflowable Layout Export Options dialog box appears, as shown in Figure 8-3, with the General options available for editing.

**FIGURE 8-3:**
The reflowable
Layout Export
Options.

Here is an overview of essential settings in the General tab when creating an EPUB:

- *Version:* By default, the EPUB 2.0.1 option is selected. This will allow readers on older devices to be able to view your reflowable content.

- *Cover:* If you want InDesign to generate the cover image displayed for the EPUB, choose whether it should use the first page (Rasterize First Page) of the document or choose a specific image file to use instead.

- *Navigation:* Choose Multi Level (TOC Style) if you want InDesign to automatically generate a table of contents that will be used by readers to more easily navigate the EPUB file.

- *Content:* For Order, choose Same as Articles Panel. This flows your content based on how you added your images and stories into the Articles panel.

4. **Additional Options available in the Text and Objects tab, on the left side of the dialog box.**

   You can specify additional options for how your text (bullets and numbering lists) and graphics (fixed or relative size) will be displayed under the Text and Objects tabs.

5. **Click the Conversion Settings tab, on the left side of the dialog box.**

   In the Conversion Settings, specify the resolution that images should be set at when created for the EPUB. If you choose Automatic for the format, InDesign will determine whether to save an image as a JPG, GIF, or PNG.

6. **Make these adjustments as needed, before creating the EPUB:**

   - *EPUB Metadata:* Select the Metadata tab. Document metadata is used by EPUB readers to describe the book title, publisher, ISBN, and other information. You can enter the Publisher here and the ISBN number for your book in the Identifier text box.

   - *CSS Options:* Select the CSS tab. If you have created Cascading Style Sheets (CSS) to control the formatting for your EPUB files, you can add a style sheet, by selecting Add Style Sheet.

**TIP**

Additional document metadata can be entered in the Document Information field. Access this by choosing File➪File Info.

7. **Click the Viewing Apps tab in the EPUB – Reflowable Layout Export Options dialog box.**

   The View EPUB after Exporting option causes the EPUB to open and be displayed in the default EPUB reader after InDesign generates the EPUB file.

**TIP**

There are many free EPUB readers available. iBooks on a Mac and Adobe Digital Editions (available for Windows and MAC) are just two examples. It is a good idea to preview your EPUB file on multiple e-readers to make sure that what you designed looks good across multiple readers and devices.

8. **Click the OK button.**

   The EPUB is generated. If you selected the View EPUB after Exporting checkbox, the EPUB file opens using your default EPUB reader.

**TECHNICAL STUFF**

If the EPUB Options dialog box looks similar to the HTML Export window, it is because EPUBs actually use HTML as their foundation. Electronic book readers are essentially specialized browsers designed to display books formatted using HTML and CSS. All the HTML and CSS content for an EPUB file is contained within the compressed folder named with the EPUB file extension.

# Exporting EPUB (Fixed-Layout)

If your document is heavily designed and has a very graphic layout, or contains any of the interactive elements of InDesign, you will want to use the EPUB (Fixed-Layout) option. The steps to export your document and many of the options are the same as those for the EPUB (Reflowable). However, below you will find information about the General Options for Fixed Layout Export.

1. **With an InDesign document open, choose File⇨Export.**

   The Export dialog box appears.

2. **From the Save as Type (Windows) or Format (Mac) drop-down list.** Select EPUB (Fixed-Layout) and then find a location on your hard drive or network for the document to be saved. Enter a name for the EPUB file in the File Name portion of the Export dialog box.

3. **Click the Save button.**

   The EPUB – Fixed Layout Export Options dialog box appears with the General options available for editing, as shown in Figure 8-4. Here is an overview of essential settings in the General tab when creating an EPUB:

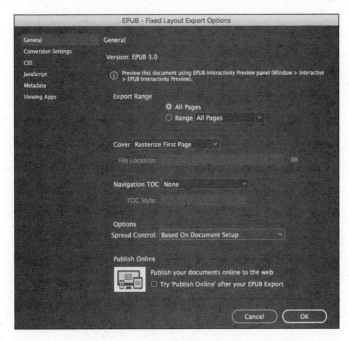

**FIGURE 8-4:**
The Fixed Layout Export Options.

- *Version:* By default, the EPUB 3 option is selected and no other version can be chosen if you want a fixed layout.

- *Navigation:* Choose Multi Level (TOC Style) if you want InDesign to automatically generate a table of contents that will be used by readers to more easily navigate the EPUB file.

  However, if you are exporting a graphic heavy book such as a children's book, you can choose none and the table of contents will be not be re-created in the sidebar of the reader.

- *Options:* For Spread Control, depending on how you created your document, using Facing Pages or not, you can control how these pages are displayed in the reader. If you choose Based on Document Setup, InDesign will output your pages as either single pages or spreads, depending on how you defined your pages in the Document Setup Dialog Box.

4.  **For additional Export Layout Tab options, see the definitions for Export Reflowable.**

5.  **Click OK to save.**

**TECHNICAL STUFF**

Both EPUB file formats are created using HTML and CSS. The HTML and CSS from an EPUB Reflowable is easily changed using a web editor such as Dreamweaver or Sigil. However, if you need to make a change to an EPUB (Fixed Layout) file, it is best if you go back to the original InDesign file, make your changes and reexport your document. The HTML and CSS for fixed layout EPUBs is rather complex and difficult to make changes to.

# 5

# Illustrator CC

# Contents at a Glance

## Chapter **1**

# Discovering Illustrator CC

Adobe Illustrator goes hand in hand with other Adobe products but serves its own unique purpose. Although Illustrator can create multiple-page artwork (with artboards), it isn't meant to create lengthy documents with repeated headers, footers, and page numbers. Those types of files are more appropriate for applications such as InDesign. Typically, you wouldn't create artwork in Illustrator that's made from pixels, such as images edited or created in Photoshop. Illustrator is generally used to create vector logos, illustrations, maps, packages, labels, signage, art for applications, websites, and more. (See the nearby "Vector graphics" sidebar for more information.)

This chapter gets you started with Illustrator and helps you understand when Illustrator is the tool best suited for creating your art.

## Deciding When to Use Illustrator CC

How do you draw a line in the sand and decide to create graphics in Illustrator rather than in Photoshop? The following questions can help you make up your mind:

>> Does the graphic need to be scaled? Will it be used in sizes that you cannot predict at this time?

» Is the artwork technical in nature? Are precise measurements and placement of elements critical?

» Does the artwork require the use of spot colors, using a system such as the Pantone Matching System (PMS)?

» Will the artwork be used frequently in different formats, such as print and onscreen in apps or websites?

» Is the artwork illustrative with many solid colors and occasional gradients and vignettes? (If you have a photograph, or an illustration that contains many variations of tonal values, use Photoshop for your editing.)

If you answered yes to any of these questions, it is probably best to create and edit your artwork in Illustrator.

Keep in mind that by using Illustrator, you gain these benefits:

» **Illustrator can save and export graphics into most file formats.** By choosing to save or export, you can create a file that can be used in most other applications. For instance, Illustrator files can be saved as `.bmp`, `.jpg`, `.pdf`, `.svg`, `.tiff`, and `.png` files, to name a few.

» **Illustrator files are easily integrated into other Adobe applications.** You can save Illustrator files in their native format and open or place them in other Adobe applications such as InDesign, Photoshop, and Adobe XD. You can also save Illustrator artwork as Portable Document Format (`.pdf`) files, which lets anyone using the free Acrobat Reader software open and view the file but maintains editing capabilities when the file is opened later in Illustrator.

» **Illustrator artwork is reusable because the resolution of vector artwork isn't determined until output.** In other words, if you print to a 600-dpi (dots per inch) printer, the artwork is printed at 600 dpi; print to a 2,400-dpi printer, and the artwork prints at 2,400 dpi. Illustrator graphics are quite different from the bitmap images you create or edit in Photoshop, where resolution is determined as soon as you scan, take a picture, or create a new bitmap (created from pixels) document.

» **Illustrator has limitless scalability.** You can create vector artwork in Illustrator and scale it to the size of your thumb or to the size of a barn, and either way, it still looks good. See the nearby sidebar "Vector graphics" for more information.

# VECTOR GRAPHICS

*Vector graphics* are made up of lines and curves defined by mathematical objects called *vectors.* Because the *paths* (the lines and curves) are defined mathematically, you can move, resize, or change the color of vector objects without losing quality in the graphic.

Vector graphics are *resolution-independent:* They can be scaled to any size and printed at any resolution without losing detail. On the other hand, a predetermined number of pixels creates bitmap graphics, so you can't *scale* (resize) them easily — if you scale them smaller, you throw out pixels; if you scale them larger, you end up with a blocky, jagged picture.

The following figure shows the differences between an enlarged vector graphic (left; notice the smooth edges) and an enlarged bitmap graphic (right; note the jagged edges). Many designers create company logos as vectors to avoid problems with scaling: A vector graphic logo maintains its high-quality appearance at any size.

# Creating a New Document

In Illustrator CC, you may see a start screen when you launch Adobe Illustrator, as shown in Figure 1-1.

To create a new document in Illustrator, click the New button on this screen.

*Note:* If you prefer not to see this start screen, you can choose to turn it off by unchecking Show the Start Workspace When No Files Are Open button in Edit⇨Preferences⇨General (Windows) or Illustrator⇨Preferences⇨General (Mac).

**1.** **If you do not see the start screen, choose File⇨New.**

The New Document dialog box appears, as shown in Figure 1-2. You use it to determine the new document's profile, size, measurement unit, color mode, and page orientation as well as the number of artboards (pages) you want in the document.

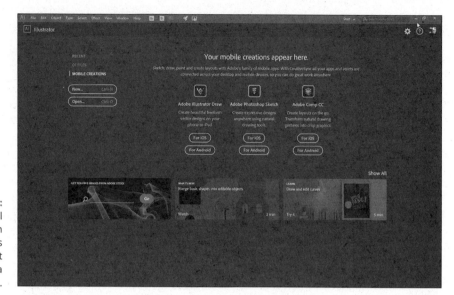

**FIGURE 1-1:**
The initial start screen in Illustrator allows you to see recent files or start a new file.

**FIGURE 1-2:**
The New Document interface offers options for different types of files and templates.

If you are working with the default preferences, you see a rather large New Document window that allows you to choose a new document specific to the artwork you need to create, Mobile, Web, Print, Film & Video, Art & Illustration. Each of these choices comes with preset details that you can edit on the right side of the New Document dialog box. These options also come with templates that you are free to use in order to get a jump-start on your design.

**TIP**

If you would prefer to see the legacy New Document window, you can click on the More Settings button at the bottom of the Preset Details section. You can set your preferences to always see the legacy New Document window by choosing Edit➪Preferences➪General (Windows) or Illustrator➪ Preferences➪General (Mac) and checking the Use legacy "File New" interface option.

In this example, the legacy New Document window is referenced.

2. **Click on More Settings at the bottom of the Preset details section.**

The legacy New Document dialog appears, as shown in Figure 1-3.

**FIGURE 1-3:**
The legacy
New Document
window.

3. **Enter a name for your new file in the Name text field.**

You can determine the name of the file now or later when you save the document. This can be done when you initially save your file as well.

4. **Choose a profile from the New Document Profile drop-down list.**

Selecting the correct profile sets up preferences, such as resolution and colors. If you choose a Print profile, your basic color swatches are built from CMYK colors (Cyan, Magenta, Yellow, and Black), and your settings default to a higher resolution. For the web, your color swatches are built from RGB colors (Red, Green, Blue), and your default resolution is set to a lower amount.

You can choose from the following default profiles: Print, Web, Mobile, Film and Video, Art & Illustration, Devices, and Basic RGB.

Based upon the profile that you select, you will be provided with certain size options. In this example, Print is selected as the profile and Letter is selected as the size.

**5.** **In the Number of Artboards text box, you can enter the number of artboards you want in the document.**

If you want a single-page document, leave this setting at 1. Creating a document with multiple artboards is discussed later in this chapter in the section "Creating multiple artboards."

**6.** **Enter in the Spacing text box the amount of space to leave between artboards.**

You do not have to bother with making changes in this section unless you selected multiple artboards. If you want pages to abut, enter **0** (zero) or enter additional values if you want a little space between each artboard. If you're adding artboards, you can enter in the Columns text box the number of columns of artboards you want arranged in the document.

**7.** **Select from the Size drop-down list or type measurements in the Width and Height text fields to set the size of the document page.**

You can select from several standard sizes in the Size drop-down list or enter your own measurements in the Width and Height text fields. As previously mentioned, these size options are dependent upon your profile selection.

**8.** **Select from the Units drop-down list to select the type of measurement you're most comfortable with.**

Your selection sets all measurement boxes and rulers to the increments you choose: points, picas, inches, millimeters, centimeters, or pixels.

**9.** **Pick the orientation for the artboard.**

The *artboard* is your canvas for creating artwork in Illustrator. You can choose between *Portrait* (the short sides of the artboard on the top and bottom) and *Landscape* (the long sides of the artboard on the top and bottom).

**10.** **Add values in the Bleed text boxes, if necessary.**

A *bleed value* is the amount of image area that extends beyond the artboard. To print from edge to edge, enter a value for the bleed. Keep in mind that most desktop printers need a *grip area,* which is the part of the page that a printer needs to grab on to the paper. It typically forces any image area near the edge of a page to not print. Bleeds are typically used in jobs to be printed on a press.

**11.** **When you're finished making selections, click OK.**

One or more Illustrator artboards appear.

# Try a Template

**TIP**

In the New Document dialog box, click the Templates button to get a precreated artboard that can be used for web banner ads, business cards, and more.

# Opening an Existing Document

It's a good idea to familiarize yourself with the workspace before starting to work in Adobe Illustrator, but to do this you should have a document open. In this section, you jump right in by opening an existing document. Here's how:

1. **Launch Adobe Illustrator CC.**

2. **Choose File⇨Open and select a file in the Open dialog box.**

   For this exercise, you can open one of your own files or one of the sample files located in the DummiesCCfiles folder that you can download from www.agitraining.com/dummies. If you choose to use the samples provided, open the sample file called CrazyFish.ai.

   Keep this file open so that you can follow along with the explanation of the workspace in the next section.

# Taking a Look at the Document Window

To investigate the work area (shown in Figure 1-4) and become truly familiar with Illustrator, have a document open, like the AI_Sample file you were directed to in the preceding section, or create a new document and take a look around. In the Illustrator work area, a total of 227 inches in width and height helps create your artwork (and all artboards). That's helpful, but it also leaves enough space to lose objects! The following list explains the tools you work with as you create artwork in Illustrator:

>> **Imageable area:** If you're planning to print your Illustrator document, choose View⇨Show Print Tiling. A dotted line appears that marks the printing area on the page. Many printers can't print all the way to the edges of the paper, so the imageable area is determined by the printer you set in the Print dialog box. If you don't want to see the print tiling, choose View⇨Hide Print Tiling.

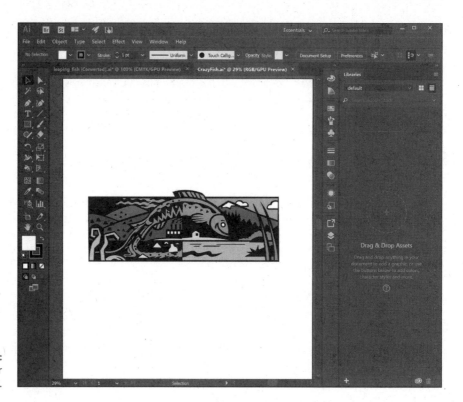

**FIGURE 1-4:**
The Illustrator
work area.

You can move the imageable area around on your page by using the Print
Tiling tool. See the nearby sidebar, "The Print Tiling tool," for more on this tool.

» **Artboard:** This area, bounded by solid lines, represents the entire region that
can contain printable artwork. By default, the artboard is the same size as
the page, but it can be enlarged or reduced. The U.S. default artboard size is
8.5 x 11 inches, but it can be set as large as 227 x 227 inches. If you're using
the default settings for Illustrator, the edge of the artboard is indicated by a
transition from a white to a medium gray canvas.

» **Scratch area:** This area outside the artboards extends to the edge of the
227-inch square window. The scratch area represents a space on which you
can create, edit, and store elements of artwork before moving them onto the
artboard. Objects placed onto the scratch area are visible onscreen, but they
don't print. However, objects in the scratch area appear if the document is
saved and placed as an image in other applications.

**TIP**

If you're having a difficult time seeing your items in the scratch area, choose
Edit➪Preferences➪User Interface (Windows) or Illustrator➪Preferences➪
User Interface (Mac) and select White for the Canvas color.

## THE PRINT TILING TOOL

Use the Print Tiling tool to move the printable area of your page to a different location. For example, if your printer can print only on paper that's 8.5 x 11 inches or smaller but the page size is 11 x 17, you can use the Print Tiling tool (a hidden tool accessed by holding down the mouse button on the Hand tool) to indicate which part of the page you want to print. Follow these steps to use the Print Tiling tool:

1. **When adjusting page boundaries, choose View⇨Fit All in Window so that you can see all your artwork.**

2. **Hold down the mouse button on the Hand tool to select the hidden Print Tiling tool.**

   The pointer becomes a dotted cross when you move it to the active window.

3. **Position the mouse pointer over the artboard and click and drag the page to a new location.**

   While you drag, the Print Tiling tool acts as though you're moving the page from its lower-left corner. Two gray rectangles are displayed. The outer rectangle represents the page size, and the inner rectangle represents the printable area of a page. You can move the page anywhere on the artboard; just remember that any part of a page that extends past the printable area boundary will not print.

# Taking Advantage of Artboards

As you already discovered, the page itself is referred to as the *artboard.* The options available to you when using artboards include the following:

» You can have multiple artboards in one document, creating essentially a multipage document.

» You can name and rearrange artboards by using the Artboard panel.

» You can copy entire artboards, allowing you to quickly create multiple versions for your artwork.

» You can use artboards to define a print area, eliminating the need to use the Print Tiling tool.

# Creating multiple artboards

To create a document with multiple artboards, follow these steps:

1. **Launch Adobe Illustrator CC and choose File⇨New.**

   The New Document dialog box appears, as shown in Figure 1-5 (if you still have the "Legacy" New Window option checked).

2. **Specify the number of artboards to start with by entering a number in the Number of Artboards text box.**

   In our example, we added four artboards.

3. **To specify how to arrange the artboard, click a grid or row arrangement icon to the right of the Number of Artboards text box, as shown in Figure 1-6.**

   Using these grid boxes, you can

   - Specify how many rows and columns to use.
   - Change the direction of the layout from left to right or right to left.

**FIGURE 1-6:**
Choose how
you want the
artboards
arranged.

**4.** **Enter an amount in the Spacing text box to determine the distance between artboards.**

Enter **0** (zero) if you want the artboards to butt against each other, or a higher value if you want some space between them.

**5.** **Click OK to create your new document. (See Figure 1-7.) The document will not have multiple sized artboards or content.**

**FIGURE 1-7:**
A document
created using
four artboards.

# Exploring enhanced artboard features

After you create multiple artboards, choose Window⇨Artboards to see a panel with artboards listed individually, as shown in Figure 1-8.

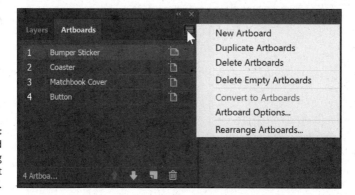

Here are some swell things you can do to artboards from the Artboard panel:

>> **Navigate to a specific artboard.** Just double-click the artboard's number.

>> **Rearrange artboards.** Drag the artboards inside the Artboard panel to reorganize their stacking order.

>> **Delete an artboard.** Drag it to the Trash icon.

>> **Copy an existing artboard.** Drag it to the New Artboard icon.

>> **Create a new artboard.** Click the New Artboard icon.

>> **Edit additional artboard options, such as size and orientation, by selecting Artboard Options from the panel menu.** The Artboard options appear as you see in Figure 1-9. Keep in mind that each artboard can be a different size than others in the same document.

>> **Rename an artboard.** Double-click the Artboard name right in the Artboards panel, type a new name, and then press the Tab or Enter key.

## Printing a document with multiple artboards

Pay close attention before you print a document with multiple artboards, or else you may print needless pages. To control which artboards are printed, follow these steps:

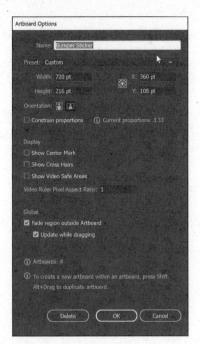

**FIGURE 1-9:**
Edit existing
artboards
by using the
Artboard Options
dialog box.

## 1. Choose File⇨Print.

The Print dialog box appears, as shown in Figure 1-10.

**FIGURE 1-10:**
Printing a
document
with multiple
artboards.

2. **Click the arrows underneath the Preview box in the lower-left corner to preview the artboards.**

3. **After you decide which artboards to print, enter them into the Range text box.**

   To print all artboards, select the All radio button; otherwise, enter a consecutive range such as **1–3** in the Range text box. You can also print nonconsecutive pages by separating them with commas — enter **1, 3, 4** to print only artboards 1, 3, and 4.

4. **Click Print to print the selected artboards.**

**TIP** If you want to define an artboard within an artboard, select the Artboard tool and then hold down the Shift key when dragging out a new artboard.

# Becoming Familiar with the Tools

As you begin using Illustrator, you'll find it helpful to be familiar with its tools. Tools are used to create, select, and manipulate objects in Illustrator. The tools should be visible as a default, but if not, you can access them by choosing Window➪Tools.

Table 1-1 lists the tools that we show you how to use throughout this minibook. Hover the cursor over the tool in the Tools panel to see the name of the tool in a tooltip. In parentheses on the tooltip (and noted in Column 2 of Table 1-1) is the keyboard command you can use to access that tool. When you see a small triangle at the lower-right corner of the tool icon, it contains additional, hidden tools. Select the tool and hold the mouse button to see it.

**TABLE 1-1**   **Illustrator CC Tools**

| Icon | Tool or Keyboard Command | Task | See Minibook Chapter |
|------|--------------------------|------|----------------------|
|  | Selection (V) | Activate objects | 2 |
| | Direct Selection (A) | Activate individual points or paths | 2 |
| | Group Selection (A) | Select grouped items | 2 |

| Icon | Tool or Keyboard Command | Task | See Minibook Chapter |
|------|--------------------------|------|----------------------|
| | Magic Wand (Y) | Select based on similarity | 2 |
| | Lasso (Q) | Select freehand | 2 |
| | Pen (P) | Create paths | 4 |
| | Curvature tool (Shift+~) | Create curves | 4 |
| | Type (T) | Create text | 5 |
| | Line Segment (/) | Draw line segments | 5 |
| | Rectangle tool (M) | Create shape objects | 3 |
| | Paint Brush (B) | Create paths | n/a |
| | Shaper (Shift+N) | Create shapes | n/a |
| | Eraser (Shift+E) | Erase vector paths | 4 |
| | Rotate (R) | Rotate objects | 9 |
| | Scale (S) | Enlarge or reduce objects | 9 |
| | Width tool (Shift+W) | Adjust strokes to variable widths | 9 |

*(continued)*

**TABLE 1-1** *(continued)*

| Icon | Tool or Keyboard Command | Task | See Minibook Chapter |
|---|---|---|---|
| | Free Transform (E) | Transform objects | 9 |
| | Shape Builder (Shift+M) | Combine, edit, and fill shapes | 3 |
| | Perspective Grid (Shift+P) | Provide perspective plane | 11 |
| | Mesh (U) | Create a gradient mesh | 10 |
| | Gradient (G) | Modify gradients | 8 |
| | Eyedropper (I) | Copy and apply attributes | 8 |
| | Blend (W) | Create transitional blends | 10 |
| | Symbol Sprayer (Shift+S) | Spray symbols | 10 |
| | Column Graph (J) | Create graphs | n/a |
| | Artboard tool (Shift+O) | Add or edit artboards | 1 |
| | Slice (Shift+K) | Create HTML slices | n/a |
| | Hand tool | Push document window | 1 |
| | Zoom (Z) | Increase and decrease the onscreen view | 1 |

# Checking Out the Panels

The standardized interface in Adobe Creative Cloud is a useful boost for users because the Illustrator panel system is similar to all other products in the Creative Cloud. This consistency makes working and finding tools and features easier.

When you first open Illustrator, notice that some panels may have been reduced to icons on the right. To select a panel, click the appropriate icon, and the panel appears.

If all you see is an icon, how do you know which icon brings up which panel? Good question. If you're hunting around for the appropriate panels, you can

>> Choose Window⇨*Name of Panel*.

>> Position your mouse on the left side of the icons and, when you see the double-arrow icon, click and drag to the left. The panel names appear.

>> Click the Expand Panels button on the gray bar at the top of the icons, as shown in Figure 1-11. The panels expand so that you can see their contents and names.

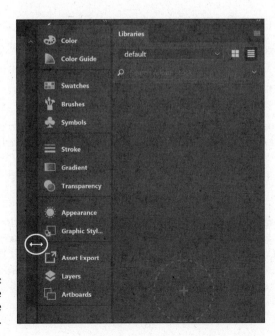

**FIGURE 1-11:**
Expand the panels to see more options.

The panels you see as a default are docked together. To *dock* a panel means to attach the panel in the docking area for organizational purposes.

You can arrange panels to make them more helpful for production. You may choose to have only certain panels visible while working. Here's the lowdown on using Illustrator panels:

>> To see additional options for each panel (because some options are hidden), click the panel menu in the upper-right corner of the panel. (See Figure 1-12.)

**FIGURE 1-12:**
Many panels have additional menu options.

>> To move a panel group, click and drag above the tabbed panel name.

>> To rearrange or separate a panel from its group, drag the panel's tab. Dragging a tab outside the docking area creates a new, separate panel.

>> To move a tab to another panel, drag the tab to that panel.

Look out for those panels — they can take over your screen! Some panels, but not all, can be resized. A panel that you can resize has an active lower-right corner (denoted by three small lines on the PC). To change the size of a panel, drag its lower-right corner (Windows) or drag the size box in the lower-right corner of the panel (Mac).

TIP

As you become more efficient, you may find it helpful to reduce the clutter on your screen by hiding all panels except the ones necessary for your work. You can save your own panel configuration by choosing Window⇨Workspace⇨New Workspace. Choose Window⇨Workspace⇨Essentials to return to the default workspace. You may need to reset the Essentials workspace if it still doesn't look like the default. Choose Window⇨Workspace⇨Reset Essentials.

# Changing Views

When you're working in Illustrator, precision is important, but you also want to see how the artwork looks. Whether for the web or print, Illustrator offers several ways in which to view your artwork:

>> **Preview and Outline views:** By default, Illustrator shows Preview view, where you see colors, stroke widths, images, and patterns as they should appear when printed or completed for onscreen presentation. Sometimes this view can become a nuisance, especially if you're trying to create a corner point by connecting two thick lines. At times like this, or whenever you want the strokes and fills reduced to the underlying structure, choose View➪Outline. You now see the outline of the illustration, shown in Figure 1-13.

**FIGURE 1-13:**
Preview mode (top) and Outline mode (bottom).

>> **Pixel view:** If you don't want to be surprised when your artwork appears in your web browser, use Pixel view. This view, shown in Figure 1-14, maintains the vectors of your artwork but shows how the pixels will appear when the image is viewed onscreen, as though it's on the web.

**FIGURE 1-14:**
See how your artwork translates into pixels in Pixel view.

**TIP**

Pixel view is helpful for previewing the look of text onscreen — some fonts just don't look good as pixels, especially if the text is small. In Pixel view, you can review fonts until you find one that's easily readable as pixels.

» **Overprint view:** For people in print production, the Overprint preview can be a real timesaver. Choose Window⇨Attributes to bring up the Attributes panel, which you can use to set the fill and stroke colors to overprint. This view creates additional colors when printing and aids printers when trapping abutting colors.

*Trapping* is the slight overprint of a lighter color into a darker color to correct for press *misregistration* — that is, when the printed colors don't align exactly. When several colors are printed on one piece, the likelihood of perfect align-ment is slim! Setting a stroke to Overprint on the Window⇨Attributes panel is one solution. With Overprint selected, the stroke is overprinted on the nearby colors. This mixing of color produces an additional color but is less obvious to the viewer than a white space created by misregistration. Select Overprint (View⇨Overprint Preview) to see the result of overprinting in Overprint view, as shown in Figure 1-15. With the Crazy Fish image, the Overprint Stroke is grayed out.

**FIGURE 1-15:**
Overprint view. Image is of the Attributes panel.

# Navigating the Work Area with Zoom Controls

You can navigate the work area efficiently by using the Hand tool and the various zoom controls. You can change the magnification of the artboard in several ways, including using menu items, the Zoom tool, and keyboard commands. Choose the method you feel most comfortable with:

» **Hand tool:** Scroll around the Document window by using the scroll bars or the Hand tool. The Hand tool lets you scroll by dragging. You can imagine that you're pushing a piece of paper around on your desk when you use the Hand tool.

Hold down the spacebar to temporarily access the Hand tool while any tool (except the Type tool) is selected. Holding down the spacebar while the Type tool is selected gives you only spaces!

» **View menu:** Using the View menu, you can easily select the magnification you want by using Zoom In, Zoom Out, Fit in Window (especially useful when you're lost in the scratch area), and Actual Size (provides a 100-percent view of your artwork).

» **Zoom tool:** Using the Zoom tool, you can click the Document window to zoom in; to zoom out, Alt-click (Windows) or Option-click (Mac). Double-click on the Zoom tool to quickly resize the Document window to 100 percent. Control which elements are visible when using the Zoom tool by clicking and dragging over the area you want zoomed into.

» **Keyboard shortcuts:** Even if you normally dislike using keyboard shortcuts, you may change your mind about using them for magnification. They make sense and are easy to use and remember. Table 1-2 lists the most popular keyboard shortcuts to change magnification.

**TIP**

The shortcuts in Table 1-3 require a little coordination to use, but they give you more control in your zoom. While holding down the keys, drag from the upper-left corner to the lower-right corner of the area you want to zoom to. A marquee appears while you're dragging; when you release the mouse button, the selected area zooms to the size of your window. The Zoom Out command doesn't give you much control; it simply zooms back out, much like the commands in Table 1-2.

**TABLE 1-2**  ## Magnification Keyboard Shortcuts

| Command | Windows Shortcut | Mac Shortcut |
| --- | --- | --- |
| Actual Size | Ctrl+1 | ⌘+1 |
| Fit in Window | Ctrl+0 (zero) | ⌘+0 (zero) |
| Zoom In | Ctrl++ (plus) | ⌘++ (plus) |
| Zoom Out | Ctrl+– (minus) | ⌘+– (minus) |
| Hand tool | Spacebar | Spacebar |

**TABLE 1-3**  ## Zoom Keyboard Shortcuts

| Command | Windows Shortcut | Mac Shortcut |
| --- | --- | --- |
| Zoom In to Selected Area | Ctrl+spacebar+drag | ⌘+spacebar+drag |
| Zoom Out | Ctrl+Alt+spacebar | ⌘+Option+spacebar |

# Chapter **2**

# Using the Selection Tools

I f someone has been coaching you in using Adobe Illustrator, you may have heard the old line "You have to select it to affect it," meaning that if you want to apply a change to an object in Illustrator, you must have that object selected or no change will occur. Although making selections may sound simple, it can become tricky when you're working on complicated artwork. This chapter shows you the tools that will help save you editing time when working in Adobe Illustrator.

## Getting to Know the Selection Tools

In the following sections, you take a quick tour of anchor points (integral to the world of selections), the bounding box, and, of course, the selection tools. (Yes, Illustrator has several selection tools.)

TIP

See our website at www.agitraining.com/dummies to find files that you can practice with in this section.

### Anchor points

To understand selections, you must first understand how Illustrator works with *anchor points*, which act like handles and can be individually selected and moved to other locations. You essentially use the anchor points to drag objects or parts of objects around the workspace. After you place anchor points on an object, you can create strokes or paths from the anchor points.

You can select several anchor points at the same time, as shown in Figure 2-1, or only one, as shown in Figure 2-2. Selecting all anchor points in an object lets you move the entire object without changing the anchor points in relationship to one another. You can tell which anchor points are selected and active because they appear as solid boxes.

**FIGURE 2-1:**
Multiple anchor points are selected.

**FIGURE 2-2:**
One anchor point is selected.

## Bounding boxes

As a default, Illustrator shows a bounding box when an object is selected with the Selection tool. This feature can be helpful if you understand its function but confusing if you don't know how to use it.

By dragging the handles, you can use the bounding box for quick transforms, such as scaling and rotating. To rotate, you pass the mouse cursor (without clicking) outside a handle until you see a rotate symbol and then drag.

If the bounding box bothers you, you can turn off the feature by choosing View⇨Hide Bounding Box.

## Selection tools

Illustrator CC offers five main selection tools:

> **Selection:** Selects entire objects or groups. This tool activates all anchor points in an object or group at the same time, allowing you to move an object without changing its shape.

> **Direct Selection:** Selects individual points.

> **Group Selection:** Hidden in the Direct Selection tool in the Tools panel and used to select items within a group. This tool adds grouped items as you click objects in the order in which they were grouped. This selection tool becomes more useful to you as you find out about grouping objects in Illustrator.

> **Magic Wand:** Use the Magic Wand tool to select objects with like values, such as fill and stroke colors, based on a tolerance and stroke weight. Change the options of this tool by double-clicking it.

> **Lasso:** Use the Lasso tool to click and drag around anchor points you want to select.

You can select an object with the Selection tool by using one of three main methods:

> Click the object's path.

> Click an anchor point of the object.

> Drag a marquee around part or all of an object. (In a later section named "Using a marquee to select an object," we discuss using the marquee method.)

# Working with Selections

After you gain an understanding about the basics of selections, you'll probably be eager to try some techniques. In the following sections, you see the basics: Make a selection, work with anchor points and the marquee, make multiple selections, and of course, save your work.

**TECHNICAL STUFF**

*Smart guides*, turned on by default in Illustrator CC, can help you make accurate selections. These guides are visible as you're drawing. They display names such as anchor point and path, and they highlight paths when you're lined up with endpoints or center points. You can come to love these helpful aids, but if you don't want to see them, simply choose View⇨Smart Guides or press the keyboard shortcut Ctrl+U (Windows) or ⌘+U (Mac) to toggle the smart guides off and on.

# Creating a selection

To work with selections, you need to have something on the page in Illustrator. Follow these steps to make a selection:

1. **Create a new page in Adobe Illustrator. (Any size or profile is okay.)**

   Alternatively, you can open an existing illustration; see Chapter 1 of this minibook for instructions. Skip to Step 3 if you're working with an existing illustration.

2. **If you're starting from a new page, create an object to work with.**

   For example, click and hold down the Rectangle tool to select the Star tool. Then click and drag from the upper left to the lower right to create a star shape.

   Exact size doesn't matter, but make it large enough that you can see it. To start over, choose Edit➪Undo or press Ctrl+Z (Windows) or ⌘+Z (Mac).

   As a default, all shapes start with a black stroke and a white fill. (See Figure 2-3.) If yours isn't black and white, press D, which changes the selected object to the default colors.

**TIP**

You can see the width and height of your object while you click and drag. If you don't want those values to display, choose Edit➪Preferences➪Smart Guides (Windows) or Illustrator➪Preferences➪Smart Guides (Mac) and deselect the Measurement Labels check box.

**FIGURE 2-3:**
A shape created by a selection tool.

3. **Using the Selection tool, click the object to make sure it's active.**

   All anchor points are solid, indicating that they're all active. (Refer to Figure 2-3.) You see, as a default, many additional points you can use to transform your selected object.

4. **Click and drag the shape to another location.**

   All anchor points travel together.

5. **When you're finished relocating your selection, use one of these three methods to deactivate your selection:**

- Choose Select⇨Deselect.

- Ctrl-click (Windows) or ⌘-click (Mac) anywhere on the page.

- Use the keyboard shortcut Ctrl+Shift+A (Windows) or ⌘+Shift+A (Mac).

**TIP**

To select an object behind another, use the Select–behind keyboard shortcut. Simply place the cursor over the area where you know that the object (to be selected) is located and press Ctrl-click (Windows) or ⌘-click (Mac OS). (You may have to do this twice to ensure you select the object behind.)

## Selecting an anchor point

When you have a selection to work with (see the numbered list), you can deselect all active anchor points and then make just one anchor point active. Follow these steps:

1. **Choose Select⇨Deselect to make sure the object isn't selected.**

2. **Select the Direct Selection tool (the white arrow) from the Tools panel.**

3. **Click one anchor point.**

   Only one anchor point (the one you clicked) is solid, and the others are hollow, as shown in Figure 2-4.

**FIGURE 2-4:**
Select only one anchor point.

4. **Click and drag that solid anchor point with the Direct Selection tool.**

   Only that solid anchor point moves.

**TIP**

Note that an anchor point enlarges when you cross over it with the Direct Selection tool. This enlargement is a big break for people who typically have to squint to see where the anchor points are positioned.

# Using a marquee to select an object

Sometimes you can more easily surround the object you want to select by dragging the mouse to create a marquee. Follow these steps to select an object by creating a marquee:

1. **Choose the Selection tool.**

2. **Click outside the object and drag over a small part of it, as shown in Figure 2-5.**

   The entire object becomes selected.

**FIGURE 2-5:**
Select an entire object.

You can also select only one anchor point in an object by using the marquee method:

1. **Choose Select⇨Deselect to make sure the object isn't selected, and then choose the Direct Selection tool.**

2. **Click outside a corner of the object and drag over only the anchor point you want to select.**

   Notice that only that anchor point is active, which can be a sight-saver when you're trying to select individual points. (See Figure 2-6.)

**FIGURE 2-6:**
Select individual anchor points.

TIP

You can use this method to cross over just the two top points or side anchor points to activate multiple anchor points as well.

# Selecting multiple objects

If you have multiple items on a page, you can select them by using one of these methods:

>> **Select one object or anchor point, and then hold down the Shift key and click another object or anchor point.** Depending on which selection tool you're using, you select either all anchor points on an object or additional objects (Selection tool) or additional anchor points only (Direct Selection tool).

You can use the Shift key to deactivate an object as well. shift-click a selected object to deselect it.

>> **Choose Select⇨All or press Ctrl+A (Windows) or ⌘+A (Mac).**

>> **Use the marquee selection technique and drag outside and over the objects.** When you use this technique with the Selection tool, all anchor points in the objects are selected; when using the Direct Selection tool, only the points you drag over are selected.

## Saving a selection

Spending way too much time trying to make your selections? Illustrator comes to the rescue with the Save Selection feature. After you have a selection that you may need again, choose Select⇨Save Selection and name the selection. The selection now appears at the bottom of the Select menu. To change the name or delete the saved selection, choose Select⇨Edit Selection. This selection is saved with the document.

# Grouping and Ungrouping

Keep objects together by grouping them. The Group function is handy when you're creating something from multiple objects, such as a logo. Using the Group function, you can ensure that all objects that make up the logo stay together when you move, rotate, scale, or copy it.

## Creating a group

Follow these steps to create a group:

1. **If you aren't already working with an illustration that contains a bunch of objects, create several objects on a new page — anywhere, any size.**

   For example, select the Rectangle tool and click and drag the page several times to create additional rectangles.

2. **Select the first object with the Selection tool and then hold down the Shift key and click a second object.**

3. **Choose Object⇨Group or press Ctrl+G (Windows) or ⌘+G (Mac).**

4. **Choose Select⇨Deselect, and then click one of the objects with the Selection tool.**

   Both objects become selected.

5. **While the first two objects are still selected, Shift-click a third object.**

6. **With all three objects selected, choose Object⇨Group again.**

   Illustrator remembers the grouping order. To prove it, choose Select⇨Deselect to deselect the group and switch to the Group Selection tool. (Hold down the mouse button on the Direct Selection tool to access the Group Selection tool.)

7. **With the Group Selection tool, click the first object; all anchor points become active. Click the first object again; the second object becomes selected. Click the first object again, and the third object becomes selected.**

   The Group Selection tool activates the objects in the order you grouped them. After you group the objects, you can treat them as a single object.

To ungroup objects, choose Object⇨Ungroup or use the keyboard shortcut Ctrl+Shift+G (Windows) or ⌘+Shift+G (Mac). In a situation where you group objects twice (because you added an object to the group, for example), you have to choose Ungroup twice.

## Using Isolation mode

When you use *Isolation mode* in Illustrator, you can easily select and edit objects in a group without disturbing other parts of your artwork. With the Selection Tool, simply double-click a group, and it opens in a separate Isolation mode, where all objects outside the group are dimmed and inactive. Do the work you need to do on the group and exit from Isolation mode by clicking the arrow to the left of Group in the upper-left corner of the window, shown in Figure 2-7.

**FIGURE 2-7:**
In Isolation mode, you can edit group contents without disturbing other artwork.

With an object selected, click the Isolate Selected Object button in the Control panel to quickly access the Isolation mode.

# Manipulating Selected Objects

In the following list, you discover a few other cool things you can do with selected objects:

>> **Move selected objects:** When an object is selected, you can drag it to any location on the page, but what if you only want to nudge it a bit? To nudge an item one pixel at a time, select it with the Selection tool and press the left-, right-, up-, or down-arrow key to reposition the object. Hold down the Shift key as you press an arrow key to move an object by ten pixels at a time.

>> **Constrain movement:** Want to move an object over to the other side of the page without changing its alignment? Constrain something by selecting an object with the Selection tool and dragging the item and then holding down the Shift key before you release the mouse button. By pressing the Shift key mid-drag, you constrain the movement to 45-, 90-, or 180-degree angles!

>> **Clone selected objects:** Use the Selection tool to easily *clone* (duplicate) an item and move it to a new location. To clone an item, simply select it with the Selection tool and then hold down the Alt key (Windows) or Option key (Mac). Look for the cursor to change to two arrows (see Figure 2-8) and then drag the item to another location on the page. Let go of the mouse before you let go of the Alt or Option key. Notice that the original object is left intact and that a copy of the object has been created and moved.

**FIGURE 2-8:**
Drag the double arrow to clone an object.

>> **Constrain the clone:** By Alt-dragging (Windows) or Option-dragging (Mac) an item and then pressing Shift, you can clone the item and keep it aligned with the original.

Don't hold down the Shift key until you're in the process of dragging the item; otherwise, pressing Shift deselects the original object.

**REMEMBER**

After you clone an object to a new location, try this neat trick to create multiple objects the same distance apart from each other by using the Transform Again command: Choose Object⇨Transform⇨Transform Again or press Ctrl+D (Windows) or ⌘+D (Mac) to have another object cloned the exact distance as the first cloned object. (See Figure 2-9.) We discuss transformations in more detail in Chapter 9 of this minibook.

FIGURE 2-9:
Using the
Transform Again
command.

>> **Use the Select menu:** By using the Select menu, you can gain additional selection controls, such as choosing Select⇨Inverse, which allows you to select one object and then turn your selection inside out. Also, choosing the Select⇨Same option lets you select one object and then select additional objects on the page based on similarities in color, fill, stroke, and other special attributes.

Take advantage of the Select Similar button on the Control panel to easily access that feature. Notice that in Figure 2-10 you can hold down the arrow to the right of the Select Similar button to choose which similarities should be considered to make the selection.

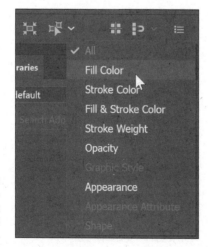

FIGURE 2-10:
Define the simi-
larities you want
your selections
based on.

# Chapter **3**

# Creating Basic Shapes

Basic shapes, such as squares, circles, polygons, and stars, are used in all types of illustrations. With the right know-how and use of the right tools, you can easily create any shape that you want for your artwork. In this chapter, you find out how to use the shape tools to create shapes based on precise measurements, and combine shapes to create custom shapes. You also learn how to edit and resize your shapes.

## The Basic Shape Tools

As a default, the only visible shape tool in the Tools panel is the Rectangle tool. If you click and hold down that tool, you can access hidden tools such as the Rounded Rectangle, Ellipse, Polygon, and Star tools, shown in Figure 3-1. (Although you see the Flare tool, it isn't a basic shape.)

**TIP**

You can tear off this tool set so that you don't have to find the hidden shapes later. Click and hold the Rectangle tool and drag to the arrow on the far-right side, and then release the mouse button. These tools are now on a free-floating toolbar that you can drag to another location.

**FIGURE 3-1:**
Basic shape tools.

## Creating rectangles and ellipses

Rectangles and ellipses are the most fundamental shapes you can create. (See Figure 3-2.) To create a rectangle shape freehand, select the Rectangle tool and simply click and drag on the page where you want the shape to appear. Then drag diagonally toward the opposite side, drag your mouse the distance you want the shape to be in size, and release the mouse button. You can drag up or down. You do the same to create a circle or oval by using the Ellipse tool.

**FIGURE 3-2:**
Click and drag
diagonally to
create a shape.

 After you create the shape, adjust its size and position by using the Selection tool. Reposition the shape by clicking the selected object and dragging. Resize the object by grabbing a handle and adjusting in or out. To adjust two sides together, grab a corner handle. To resize a shape proportionally, Shift-drag a corner handle.

## Using the Rounded Rectangle tool

You can create a rounded rectangle by using one of two methods:

>> Click and drag freehand to create the rounded rectangle shape.

>> Click the artboard once to open the Rounded Rectangle dialog box, where you can enter values to define the shape.

The difference between these two methods is that when you open the Rounded Rectangle dialog box (see Figure 3-3), you can enter a value in the Corner Radius text field, which determines how much rounding is applied to the corners of the shape.

**FIGURE 3-3:**
Customize the
size of a rounded
rectangle.

TIP

Change the rounded corner visually by pressing the up and down keys on your keyboard *while* you're dragging out the Rounded Rectangle shape on the artboard.

The smaller the value, the less rounded the corners; the higher the value, the more rounded the corners. Be careful: You can round a rectangle's corners so much that it becomes an ellipse!

## Using the Polygon tool

You create stars and polygons in much the same way as you create rectangles and ellipses. Select the Polygon tool and click and drag from one corner to another to create the default six-sided polygon shape. You can also select the Polygon tool and click once on the artboard to change the Polygon tool options in the Polygon dialog box.

You can change the polygon shape by entering new values in the Radius and Sides text fields, as shown in Figure 3-4. The radius is determined from the center to the edge of the polygon. The value for the number of sides can range from 3 (making triangles a breeze to create) to 1,000. Whoa — a polygon with 1,000 sides would look like a circle unless it was the size of Texas!

**FIGURE 3-4:**
Creating a
polygon shape.

Creating Basic Shapes

# Using the Star tool

To create a star shape, select the Star tool from the Tools panel. (Remember that it may hide under other shape tools.) If you click the artboard once to open the Star dialog box, you see three text fields in which you can enter values to customize your star shape:

>> **Radius 1:** Distance from the outer points to the center of the star

>> **Radius 2:** Distance from the inner points to the center of the star

>> **Points:** Number of points that comprise the star

The closer together the Radius 1 and Radius 2 values are to each other, the shorter the points on your star. In other words, you can go from a starburst to a seal of approval by entering values that are close in the Radius 1 and Radius 2 text fields, as shown in Figure 3-5.

**FIGURE 3-5:**
Radius 1 and Radius 2 are closer to each other in the star on the bottom.

# Resizing Shapes

You often need a shape to be an exact size (for example, 2 x 3 inches). After you create a shape, the best way to resize it to exact measurements is to use the Transform panel, shown in Figure 3-6. Have the object selected and then choose Window➪Transform to open the Transform panel. Note that on this panel you can enter values to place an object in the X and Y fields as well as enter values in the width (W) and height (H) text fields to determine the exact size of an object.

**FIGURE 3-6:**
Precisely set the
size of a shape.

In many Adobe Illustrator panels, you may see measurement increments consisting of points, picas, millimeters, centimeters, or inches, which can be confusing and maybe even intimidating. But you can control which measurement increments to use.

**TIP**

Show rulers by choosing View➪Rulers➪Show Rulers or press Ctrl+R (Windows) or ⌘+R (Mac). Then right-click (Windows) or Control-click (Mac) the ruler to change the measurement increment to an increment you're more familiar with. Using the contextual menu that appears, you can change the measurement increment directly on the document.

Alternatively, you can simply type the number followed by a measurement extension into the width and height text fields in the Transform panel (refer to Figure 3-6), and the measurement converts properly for you. Table 3-1 lists the extensions you can use.

| TABLE 3-1 | **Measurement Extensions** | |
|---|---|---|
| Extension | Measurement Unit |
| in (or ") | Inch |
| pt | Point |
| mm | Millimeter |
| pp | Pica |

TIP

If you don't want to bother creating a freehand shape and then changing its size, select the Shape tool and click the artboard. The Options dialog box specific to the shape you're creating appears, and you can type values into the Width and Height text fields.

If you accidentally click and drag, you end up with a tiny shape on your page. Don't fret. Simply get rid of the small shape by selecting it and pressing the Delete key, and then you can try again.

# Tips for Creating Shapes

The following simple tips can improve your skills at creating basic shapes in Illustrator:

>> Press and hold the Shift key while dragging with the Rectangle or Ellipse tool to create a perfect square or circle. (See Figure 3-7.) This trick is also helpful when you're using the Polygon and Star tools — holding down the Shift key constrains them so that they're straight.

**FIGURE 3-7:**
Use the Shift key to constrain a shape while you create it.

>> Create a shape from the center out by holding down the Alt (Windows) or Option (Mac) key while dragging. Hold down Alt+Shift (Windows) or Option+Shift (Mac) to pull a constrained shape out from the center.

>> When creating a star or polygon shape by clicking and dragging, if you keep the mouse button down, you can then press the up- or down-arrow key to interactively add or subtract points or sides to your shape.

## Creating advanced shapes

At times, it may be wise to use advanced tools in Illustrator to create unique shapes. The Pathfinder panel is an incredible tool you can use to combine, knock out (eliminate one shape from another), and even create shapes from other intersected shapes.

You use the Pathfinder panel, shown in Figure 3-8, to combine objects into new shapes. To use the Pathfinder panel, choose Window⇨Pathfinder.

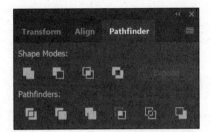

**FIGURE 3-8:**
Combine objects into new shapes.

Across the top row of the Pathfinder panel are the Shape modes, which let you control the interaction between selected shapes. You can choose from the Shape modes listed in Table 3-2.

**TIP**

If you like the result from using Exclude Overlapping Shapes mode, you can also create a similar effect by selecting several shapes and choosing Object⇨ Compound Path⇨Make. This command "punches" the topmost shapes from the bottom shape.

**TABLE 3-2**    **Shape Modes**

| Button | Mode | What You Can Do with It |
|---|---|---|
|  | Unite | Unite selected shapes into one shape. |
|  | Minus Front | Cut out the topmost shape from the underlying shape. |
|  | Intersect Shape Areas | Use the area of the topmost shape to clip the underlying shape as a mask would. |
|  | Exclude Overlapping Shape Areas | Use the area of the shape to invert the underlying shape, turning filled regions into holes and vice versa. |

**TIP**

The shapes remain separate so that you can still adjust them, which is helpful if you like to tweak your artwork (but it drives some people crazy). You can turn the result of using the Shape Mode buttons into one shape either by clicking the Expand button after selecting the Shape mode or by holding down the Alt key (Windows) or Option key (Mac) when clicking a Shape Mode button. Option on a Mac makes separate objects. Expand makes multiple objects from a compound path.

## Using the Pathfinders

*Pathfinders* are the buttons at the bottom of the Pathfinder panel that let you create new shapes from overlapping objects. Table 3-3 summarizes what each Pathfinder does.

**TABLE 3-3**    **The Pathfinders**

| Button | Mode | What You Can Do with It |
|---|---|---|
|  | Divide | Divide all shapes into their own individual shapes. This tool is quite useful when you're trying to create custom shapes. |
|  | Trim | Remove the part of a filled object that's hidden. |
|  | Merge | Remove the part of a filled object that's hidden. Also, remove any strokes and merge any adjoining or overlapping objects filled with the same color. |

| Button | Mode | What You Can Do with It |
|---|---|---|
| | Crop | Delete all parts of the artwork that fall outside the boundary of the topmost object. You can also remove any strokes. If you want strokes to remain when using this feature, select them and choose Object⇨Path⇨Outline Stroke. |
| | Outline | Divide an object into its shape's line segments or edges. This tool is useful for preparing artwork that needs a trap for overprinting objects. |
| | Minus Back | Delete an object that's behind the front-most object. |

## Using the Shape Builder tool

Using the Shape Builder tool, you can intuitively combine, edit, and fill shapes on your artboard. Follow these steps to create your own unique shape using the Shape Builder tool:

1. **Create several overlapping shapes.**

2. **Select the shapes that you want to combine.**

3. **Select the Shape Builder tool and then click and drag across the selected shapes, as shown on the left in Figure 3-9.**

**FIGURE 3-9:**
Create several shapes in order to use the Shape Builder tool.

The selected shapes are combined into one shape, as shown on the right in Figure 3-9.

The Shape Builder tool also enables merging objects, breaking overlapping shapes, subtracting areas, and more.

4. **Create another shape that overlaps your new combined shape.**

Creating Basic Shapes

5. **Using the Selection tool, select both shapes.**

6. **Select the Shape Builder tool again.**

7. **Hold down the Alt (Windows) or Option (Mac) key and click and drag across the newly added shape, as shown in Figure 3-10.**

   It's subtracted from the underlying shape.

**FIGURE 3-10:**
Use the Shape
Builder tool to
subtract from
another shape.

Coloring fills and strokes is easier now, too. When you're finished making your shape, you can use the Live Paint Bucket tool that is hidden in the Shape Builder tool to intuitively fill your shape with color.

# Chapter **4**

# Using the Pen Tool and Placing Images

You've seen illustrations that you know are made from paths, but how do you make your own? In this chapter, we show you how to use the Pen tool to create paths and closed shapes.

**REMEMBER**

Using the Pen tool requires a little more coordination than using other Illustrator tools. Fortunately, Adobe Illustrator includes features to help make using the Pen tool a little easier. After you master the Pen tool, the possibilities for creating illustrations are unlimited. Read this chapter to build your skills using one of most popular tools in the creative industry: the Pen tool's Bézier curve capabilities.

# Pen Tool Fundamentals

 You can use the Pen tool to create all sorts of elements, such as straight lines, curves, and closed shapes, which you can then incorporate into illustrations:

>> **Bézier curve:** Originally developed by Pierre Bézier in the 1970s for CAD/CAM operations, the Bézier curve (shown in Figure 4-1) became the underpinnings of the entire Adobe PostScript drawing model. You can control the depth and size of a *Bézier curve* by using direction lines.

>> **Anchor point:** You can use anchor points to control the shape of a path or an object. Anchor points are created automatically when using shape tools. You can manually create anchor points by clicking from point to point with the Pen tool.

>> **Direction line:** These lines are essentially the handles you use on curved points to adjust the depth and angle of curved paths.

>> **Closed shape:** When a path is created, it becomes a closed shape when the start point joins the endpoint.

>> **Simple path:** A *path* consists of one or more straight or curved segments. Anchor points mark the endpoints of the path segments.

In the next section, we show you how to control the anchor points.

**FIGURE 4-1:**
Bézier curves
are controlled by
direction lines.

# Creating a straight line

A basic function of the Pen tool is to create a simple path. For this next set of steps create a new Illustrator document.

You can create a simple, straight line with the Pen tool by following these steps:

1. **Press D or click the small black-and-white color swatches at the bottom of the Tools panel.**

   You revert to the default colors of a black stroke and a white fill. With black as a stroke, you can see your path clearly.

**TIP**

   The trick of pressing D to change the foreground and background colors to the default of black and white also works in Photoshop and InDesign.

## TURNING OFF THE RUBBER BAND FEATURE

As a default, the Pen tool uses a rubber band feature that hints where your path will go as you reposition your cursor. This feature is distracting to some users. If you prefer to not have that feature enabled, choose Edit⇨Preferences (Windows) or Illustrator⇨Preferences (Mac) and select the Selection and Anchor Display option. Uncheck the Pen option at the bottom of the window, as shown in the figure below.

2. **Click the Fill swatch, at the bottom of the Tools panel, to ensure that the Fill swatch is in front of the Stroke swatch, and then press the forward slash (/) key to change the fill to None.**

3. **Open a new blank page and select the Pen tool.**

   Notice that when you move the mouse over the artboard, the Pen cursor appears with an * beside it, indicating that you're creating the first anchor point of a path.

4. **Click the artboard to create the first anchor point of a line.**

   The * disappears.

   Avoid dragging the mouse or you'll end up creating a curve rather than a straight segment.

5. **Click anywhere else on the document to create the ending anchor point of the line.**

   Illustrator creates a path between the two anchor points. Essentially, the path looks like a line segment with an anchor point at each end. (See Figure 4-2.)

**FIGURE 4-2:**
A path connected by two anchor points.

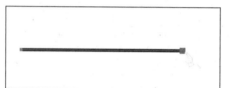

To make a correction to a line you created with the Pen tool (as described in the preceding step list), follow these steps:

1. **Choose Select⇨Deselect to make sure that no objects are selected.**

2. **Select the Direct Selection tool from the Tools panel.**

   Notice the helpful feature that enlarges the anchor point when you pass over it with the Direct Selection tool.

3. **Click an anchor to select one point on the line.**

   Notice that the selected anchor point is solid and the other is hollow. *Solid* indicates that the anchor point you clicked is active, whereas *hollow* is inactive.

4. **Click and drag the anchor point with the Direct Selection tool.**

   The selected anchor point moves, changing the direction of the path while not affecting the other anchor point.

**REMEMBER**

Use the Direct Selection tool (press A to use the keyboard shortcut to select the Direct Selection tool) to make corrections to paths.

Make sure that only the anchor point you want to change is active. If the entire path is selected, all anchor points are solid. If only one anchor point is selected, all but that one point will be hollow.

## Creating a constrained straight line

In this section, we show you how to create a real straight line — one that's on multiples of a 45-degree angle. Illustrator makes it easy; just follow these steps:

1. **Select the Pen tool and click the artboard anywhere to place an anchor point.**

2. **Hold down the Shift key and click another location to place the ending anchor point.**

   Notice that when you're holding down the Shift key, the line snaps to a multiple of 45 degrees.

**REMEMBER**

Release the mouse button before you release the Shift key or else the line pops out of alignment.

## Creating a curve

In this section, you see how to use the Bézier path to create a curved segment. We don't guarantee that you'll love this process — not at first, anyway. But after you know how to use a Bézier path, you'll likely find it useful. To create a Bézier path, follow these steps:

1. **Starting with a blank artboard, select the Pen tool and click the artboard anywhere to place the first anchor point.**

2. **Click someplace else to place the ending anchor point — don't let go of the mouse button — and then drag the cursor until a direction line appears.**

   If you look closely, you see that anchor points are square and that direction lines have circles at the end, as shown in Figure 4-3.

3. **Drag the direction line closer to the anchor point to flatten the curve; drag farther away from the anchor point to increase the curve, as shown in Figure 4-4.**

4. **When you're happy with the curve, release the mouse button.**

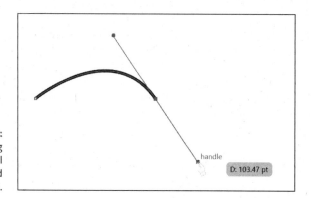

**FIGURE 4-3:**
Click and drag
with the Pen tool
to create a curved
path.

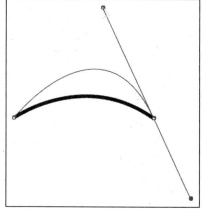

**FIGURE 4-4:**
Adding curve to
the curve.

You've created an *open path*, or a path that doesn't form a closed shape. We show you in the next section how to reconnect to the starting point of the path to make a closed shape.

To alter a curved segment after you create it, follow these steps:

1. **Choose Select⇔Deselect to ensure that no objects are selected.**

2. **Choose the Direct Selection tool and click the last anchor point created.**

   If the direction lines aren't already visible, they appear.

   If you have difficulty selecting the anchor point, drag a marquee around it with the Direct Selection tool.

**TIP**

3. **Click precisely at the end of one of the direction lines; drag the direction line to change the curve.**

# Reconnecting to an existing path

Creating one segment is fine if you want just a line or an arch. But if you want to create a shape, you need to add more anchor points to the original segment. If you want to fill your shape with a color or a gradient, you need to close it, which means that you need to eventually return to the starting anchor point.

To add segments to your path and create a closed shape, follow these steps:

1. **Create a segment (straight or curved).**

   We show you how in the preceding sections of this chapter.

   You can continue from this point, clicking and adding anchor points until you eventually close the shape. For this example, you deselect the path so that you can discover how to continue adding to paths that have already been created. Knowing how to edit existing paths is extremely helpful when you need to make adjustments to artwork.

2. **With the Pen tool selected, move the cursor over an end anchor point on the deselected path.**

3. **Click when you see the Pen icon with a forward slash to connect your next segment.**

   The forward slash indicates that you're connecting to this path.

4. **Click someplace else to create the next anchor point in the path; drag the mouse if you want to create a curved segment.**

5. **Click to place additional anchor points, dragging as needed to curve those segments.**

   Remember that you want to close this shape, so place the anchor points so that you can eventually come back to the first anchor point.

   The shape shown in Figure 4-5 is a result of adding several linked anchor points.

**FIGURE 4-5:**
Adding anchor points to create a shape.

6. **When you return to the first anchor point, move the cursor over it and click when the close icon (a small, hollow circle) appears, as shown in Figure 4-6.**

The shape now has no endpoints.

**FIGURE 4-6:**
Click when the
close path icon
appears.

## Controlling curves

After you feel comfortable creating curves and paths, take control of those curves so that you can create them with a greater degree of precision. The following steps walk you through the manual method for changing the direction of anchor points and reveal a helpful keyboard shortcut to make controlling paths a little more fluid. At the end of this section, we introduce new tools that you may also want to take advantage of to help you get control of the Pen tool.

To control a curve, follow these steps:

1. **Create a new document and then choose View➪Show Grid to show a series of horizontal and vertical rules that act as guides.**

If it helps, use the Zoom tool to zoom in to the document.

2. **With the Pen tool, click an intersection of any of these lines in the middle area of the page to place the initial anchor point and drag upward.**

Let go but don't click when the direction line has extended to the horizontal grid line above it, as shown in Figure 4-7(a).

3. **Click to place the second anchor point on the intersection of the grid directly to the right of your initial point; drag the direction line to the grid line directly below it, as shown in Figure 4-7(b).**

**TIP**

If you have difficulty keeping the direction line straight, hold down the Shift key to constrain it.

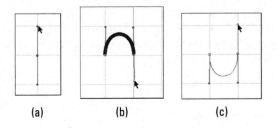

FIGURE 4-7:
Creating a controlled Bézier curve.

(a)    (b)    (c)

4. **Choose Select⇨Deselect to deselect your curve.**

Congratulations! You've created a controlled curve. In these steps, you created an arch that's going up, so you first clicked and dragged up. Likewise, to create a downward arch, you must click and drag down. Using the grid, try to create a downward arch like the one shown in Figure 4-7(c).

## Creating a corner point

To change the direction of a path from being a curve to a corner, you have to create a *corner point*, shown on the right in Figure 4-8. A corner point has no direction lines and allows for a sharp directional change in a path.

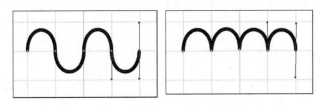

FIGURE 4-8:
Smooth versus corner points.

You can switch from the Pen tool to the Convert Anchor Point tool to change a smooth anchor point into a corner point, but that process is time-consuming. An easier way is to press the Alt (Windows) or Option (Mac) key — the Pen tool temporarily changes into the Convert Anchor Point tool — while clicking the anchor point.

To change a smooth anchor point into a corner point by using the shortcut method, follow these steps:

1. **Create an upward arch.**

We show you how in the preceding section, "Controlling curves." (Refer to Figure 4-7[b]).

2. **Hold down the Alt (Windows) or Option (Mac) key and position the cursor over the last anchor point (the last point that you created with the Pen tool).**

3. When the cursor changes to a caret (that's the Convert Anchor Point tool), click and drag until the direction line is up to the grid line above, as shown on the left in Figure 4-9.

**FIGURE 4-9:**
Converting from smooth to corner.

4. Release the Alt (Windows) or Option (Mac) key and the mouse button, move the cursor to the grid line to the right, and click and drag down.

# The Hidden Pen Tools

Hold down the Pen tool icon in the Tools panel to access additional tools: the Add Anchor Point, Delete Anchor Point, and Convert Anchor Point tools, shown in Table 4-1. In the preceding section, we show you how to create a corner point by using the shortcut method, by pressing the Alt (Windows) or Option (Mac) key to access the Convert Anchor Point tool. You may feel more comfortable switching to that tool when you need to convert a point, but switching tools can be more time-consuming.

**TABLE 4-1**    ## The Hidden Pen Tools

| Icon | Tool |
|------|------|
| | Pen |
| | Add Anchor Point |
| | Delete Anchor Point |
| | Convert Anchor Point |

**TIP**

Even though you can use a hidden tool to delete and add anchor points, Illustrator automatically does this as a default when you're using the Pen tool. When you move the cursor over an anchor point by using the Pen tool, a minus icon appears. To delete that anchor point, simply click. Likewise, when you move the cursor over a part of the path that doesn't contain anchor points, a plus icon appears. Simply click to add an anchor point.

If you prefer to use the tools dedicated to adding and deleting anchor points, choose Edit⇨Preferences⇨General (Windows) or Illustrator⇨Preferences⇨General (Mac); in the Preferences dialog box that appears, select the Disable Auto Add/Delete checkbox. Then, when you want to add or delete an anchor point, select the appropriate tool and click the path.

## Adding tools to help make paths

Some Pen tool modifiers are available in the Control panel in Illustrator CC. You can take advantage of them for many Pen tool uses, but using keyboard shortcuts to switch the Pen tool to its various options is probably still faster. If you're resistant to contorting your fingers while trying to create a path, you should appreciate these tools.

To see the Control panel tools, select the Pen tool and start creating a path. Notice that the Control panel has a series of buttons available, shown in Figure 4-10.

**FIGURE 4-10:**
Control panel tools for easy editing.

## Using the Eraser tool

If you haven't discovered the Eraser tool, you will wonder how you got along without it! Using the Eraser tool, you can quickly remove areas of artwork as easily as you erase pixels in Photoshop by stroking with your mouse over any shape or set of shapes.

New paths are automatically created along the edges of the erasure, even preserving its smoothness, as shown in Figure 4-11.

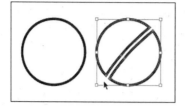

**FIGURE 4-11:**
The Eraser tool deletes sections of a path.

By double-clicking the Eraser tool, you can define the diameter, angle, and roundness of your eraser. (See Figure 4-12.) If you're using a drawing tablet, you can even set Wacom tablet interaction parameters, such as Pressure and Tilt.

**FIGURE 4-12:**
Double-click the Eraser tool to set various tool options.

If you want to erase more than a single selected object, use Isolation mode to segregate grouped objects for editing. Remember that in order to enter this mode, you simply double-click a group of items. You can then use the eraser on all objects in that group at one time without disturbing the rest of your design.

# Tracing Artwork

You can use a template layer to trace an image manually. A *template layer* is a locked, dimmed layer you can use to draw over placed images with the Pen tool, much like you would do with a piece of onion skin paper over the top of an image.

# Creating a template layer

Follow these steps to create a template layer:

1. **Take a scanned image or logo and save it in a format that Illustrator can import from your image-editing program, such as Photoshop.**

   Typically, you save the image as an .eps, a .tif, or a native .psd (Photoshop) file.

2. **Choose File⇨Place to open the Place dialog box.**

3. **In the Place dialog box, locate the saved image; then select the Template checkbox and click Place.**

   On the Mac OS, you must select the Options button in order to be able to check the Template checkbox.

   Note that the Template checkbox is located at the bottom of the dialog box.

   Selecting the Template checkbox tells Illustrator to lock down the scanned image on a layer. Essentially, you can't reposition or edit your image.

   After you click Place, a template layer is automatically created for you, and another layer is waiting for you to create your path. The newly created top layer resembles a piece of tracing paper that has been placed on top of the scanned image.

4. **Re-create the image by tracing over it with the Pen tool.**

5. **When you're done, turn off the visibility of the placed image by clicking the Visibility icon to the left of the template layer.**

   You now have a path you can use in place of the image, which is useful if you're creating an illustration of an image or are digitally re-creating a logo.

For more about layers, check out Chapter 7 of this minibook.

**TIP**

Keep practicing to become more comfortable with clicking and dragging, flowing with the direction line pointing the way you want the path to be created; everything will fall into place.

# Using Image Trace

With the Image Trace feature, you can take raster (bitmap) artwork and automatically trace it to convert it into vector artwork. This means that you can take scans of sketches, illustrations, and even photographs, and convert them into vector artwork that can be edited in Illustrator. The Image Trace feature is not totally new — in previous versions it was known as Live Trace — but with CC it has been greatly improved. Additional options have been added, and you can easily access those options and "test" your trace using the new Image Trace panel. Follow these steps to try out this improved feature:

1. **Choose File⇨Place and place a scan or raster illustration that you want to convert to vector paths.**

   Immediately after placing, you see that the Control panel now has additional buttons available, as shown in Figure 4-13.

**TIP**

Even though you can click Image Trace immediately, you may want to consider selecting Window⇨Image Trace to access the Image Trace panel, which offers you more options and the opportunity to test your selections in advance.

2. **Click the Preset drop-down menu to select a preset most similar to the artwork you want to convert.**

   Many of the presets are defined according to the type of artwork that you are tracing — such as a sketch, technical drawing, or photograph. (See Figure 4-14.) The 3 Colors, 6 Colors, and 16 Colors options are useful when converting a photograph to a vector image.

3. **Expand the Advanced section and note the additional path options available there:**

   - **Paths** determines how accurate a representation of the original art the path trace will be. The higher the percentage, the more accurate the tracing. (See Figure 4-15.) Be careful with this feature — if you set the percentage too high, you can end up with more anchor points than necessary. By default, this setting is at 50%, which should work for most of your artwork.

**FIGURE 4-14:**
Select a preset
that best fits your
placed image.

**FIGURE 4-15:**
The image on
the left has a low
path tolerance
of 0%. The image
on the right
has a high path
tolerance
of 100%.

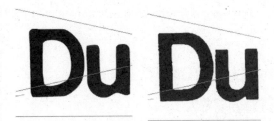

- **Corner** determines how the Image Trace traces corners. A lower percentage produces a more rounded corner; a higher amount a sharper corner. (See Figure 4-16.) Again, the default setting (75%) works for most cases.

- **Noise** determines the minimum details size Image Trace can reproduce. The default of 100 pixels tends to work well. This provides you an area that will be recognized by the Image Trace feature of about 10 x 10 pixels. You might have to play with this setting a bit to see what works best for your image.

## Changing the view

Can't see the results of your trace? Keep in mind that you can change the view. Just select the traced image and click the View drop-down menu in the Control panel. Using this you can turn off and on the view for the original image as well as the tracing results.

Image Trace is a memory-intensive feature, and your computer may take a little more time than normal to preview each preset.

**REMEMBER**

See Chapter 8 of this minibook for more information on painting fills and strokes.

# Other Details You Should Know about Placing Images

In the preceding section, you discover how to place an image as a template. But what if you want to place an image to be used in an illustration file? Simply choose File➪Place.

Click an image once to see its Link checkbox. On the Mac OS, click the Options button in order to see this information. If you keep the checkbox selected, the image is linked to the original file, which is helpful if you plan to reference the file several times in the illustration (it saves file space) or edit the original and have it update the placed image in Illustrator. This option is usually selected by people in the prepress industry who want to have access to the original image file. Just remember to send the image with the Illustrator file if it's to be printed or used someplace other than on your computer.

**TIP**

You can unembed an image by selecting it in the Links panel (Window➪Links) and then choosing Unembed from the panel menu, as shown in Figure 4-17.

If you are worried about keeping all your placed files associated with your Illustrator file, you can now use File➪Package in Illustrator CC. This feature gives you the option to create a folder that contains your linked files, fonts, and a report about your file, as you see in Figure 4-18.

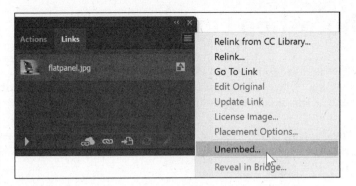

**FIGURE 4-17:**
You can unembed an embedded image by using the Links panel options.

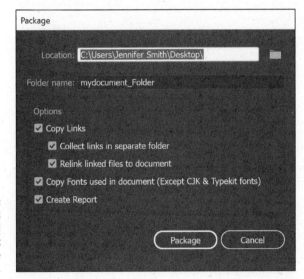

**FIGURE 4-18:**
Collect images and fonts and create a report using the Package feature.

If you deselect the Link checkbox, the image is embedded into the Illustrator file. This option builds the image data into the Illustrator file. With an embedded image you won't need to remember where the original file is stored, but it does make for a larger Illustrator file. Now that you have the ability to choose Unembed from the Links panel menu, you can retrieve the image data and save it for future editing if you need to. In certain instances, such as when you want an image to become a symbol (see Chapter 10 of this minibook), the image will have to be embedded, but most functions work with both linked and unlinked files.

# Using Photoshop Layer Comps

The *Layer Comps* feature in Photoshop lets you set the visibility, appearance, and position of layers. You can take advantage of this useful organizational tool in other Adobe products. Read more about Photoshop in Book 3.

You can place in Illustrator a .psd (Photoshop) image that has saved Layer Comps and choose which layer comp set you want visible.

Chapter **5**

# Using Type in Illustrator

O ne of Illustrator's strongest areas is manipulating text. Whether you're using Illustrator to create logos, business cards, or type to be used on the web, or any number of other screen devices, you have everything you need to create professional-looking text.

In this chapter, you meet the Type tools and discover a few basic (and more advanced) text-editing tricks that you can take advantage of. You then find out about other text tools, such as the Character and Paragraph panels. At the end of this chapter, you get the quick-and-dirty lowdown on the Illustrator text utilities. These utilities can save you loads of time, so don't skip that section.

## Working with Type

You can do all sorts of cool things with type, from the simplest task of creating a single line of text to more complicated creative uses of text, such as placing text along paths and wrapping text around objects.

Click and hold the Type tool to see the hidden type tools, as shown in Figure 5-1. The different tools give you the capability to be creative and also accommodate foreign languages.

**FIGURE 5-1:**
The Type tools.

## Creating text areas

A *text area* is a region that you define. Text, when inserted in this region, is constrained within the shape. To create a text area, click and drag with the Type tool. Lorem Ipsum fills the area.

*Note:* Adobe Illustrator inserts placeholder text for you as a default. If you would prefer that your textbox stay empty, choose Edit➪Preferences➪Type (Windows) or Illustrator➪Preferences➪Type (Mac OS), and then uncheck the Fill New Type Objects With Placeholder Text checkbox.

**TIP**

As you create and finish typing in a text area, you may want to quickly click and drag to create a new text area elsewhere on your artboard. Unfortunately, Illustrator doesn't allow you to do that. You do have two options that will help you to create multiple text boxes quickly on your artboard:

>> Choose Select➪Deselect and then create another area.

>> Hold down the Ctrl (Windows) or ⌘ (Mac) key, and click anywhere on the artboard outside of the active text area. By clicking, you deactivate the current text box so that you can click and drag out a new text area.

## Creating a line of text

To create a simple line of text, select the Type tool and click the artboard. A blinking insertion point appears. You can now start typing. With this method, the line of type goes on forever (even beyond the end of the Scratch area) until you press Enter (Windows) or Return (Mac) to start a new line of text. This excess length is fine if you just need short lines of text for callouts or captions, for example, but it doesn't work well if you're creating a label or anything else that has large amounts of copy.

Many new users click and drag an ever-so-small text area that doesn't allow room for even one letter. If you accidentally do this, switch to the Selection tool, delete the active type area, and then click to create a new text insertion point.

## Flowing text into an area

Select the Type tool and then drag on the artboard to create a text area. The cursor appears in the text area; text you type flows automatically to the next line when it reaches the edge of the text area. You can also switch to the Selection tool and adjust the width and height of the text area with the handles.

Need an exact size for a text area? With the Type tool selected, drag to create a text area of any size. Then choose Window➪Transform to view the Transform panel. Type an exact width measurement in the W text field and an exact height measurement in the H text field.

## Dealing with text overflow

Watch out for excess text! If you create a text area that's too small to hold all the text you want to put into it, a red plus sign appears in the lower-right corner, as shown in Figure 5-2.

> Once upon a time there was a
> cute little boy named Alex. He was
> pleasant and had the most pinch-
> able cheeks you have ever seen. He
> was embarrassed when his Mother
> posted this on Facebook for all of

**FIGURE 5-2:**
The plus icon indicates that text is overflowing.

When Illustrator indicates that you have too much text for the text area, you have three options:

>> Make the text area larger by switching to the Selection tool and dragging the handles.

>> Make the text smaller until you no longer see the overflow indicator.

>> *Thread* this text area (link it to another), which is a topic covered later in this chapter, in the "Threading text into shapes" section.

# Creating columns of text with the Area Type tool

The easiest and most practical way to create rows and columns of text is to use the area type options in Adobe Illustrator. This feature lets you create rows and columns from any text area. You can have only rows, only columns (much like columns of text in a newspaper), or even both.

1. **Select the Type tool and drag on the artboard to create a text area.**

2. **Choose Type⇨Area Type Options.**

   The Area Type Options dialog box appears, as shown in Figure 5-3. At the end of this section, a list explains all options in the Area Type.

Area Type Options

Width: 288 pt          Height: 263 pt

Rows                   Columns

Number: 1              Number: 3

Span: 263 pt           Span: 84 pt

☐ Fixed                ☐ Fixed

Gutter:                Gutter: 18 pt

Offset

Inset Spacing: 0 pt

First Baseline: Ascent      ∨    Min: 0 pt

Options

Text Flow:

☐ Preview        ⟨ OK ⟩    ⟨ Cancel ⟩

**FIGURE 5-3:**
The Area Type Options dialog box lets you create columns of text.

3. **In the Area Type Options dialog box, enter a width and height in the Width and Height text fields.**

   The Width and Height text fields contain the height and width of your entire text area. In Figure 5-3, 288 pt is in the Width text field and 263 pt is in the Height text field.

**4.** **In the Columns area, enter the number of columns you want to create in the Number text field, the span distance in the Span text field, and the gutter space in the Gutter text field.**

The *span* specifies the height of individual rows and the width of individual columns. The *gutter* is the space between columns and is automatically set for you, but you can change it to any value you like.

**5.** **Click OK.**

When you create two or more columns of text from the Area Type Options dialog box, text flows to the next column when you reach the end of the previous column, as shown in Figure 5-4.

**FIGURE 5-4**
One column of text flows into the next.

**TIP**

The following list breaks down the options available in the Area Type Options dialog box (refer to Figure 5-3):

» **Width and Height:** The present width and height of the entire text area.

» **Number:** The number of rows and/or columns that you want the text area to contain.

» **Span:** The height of individual rows and the width of individual columns.

» **Fixed:** Determines what happens to the span of rows and columns if you resize the type area. When this check box is selected, resizing the area can change the number of rows and columns but not their width. Leave this option deselected if you want to resize the entire text area and have the columns automatically resize with it.

>> **Gutter:** The empty space between rows or columns.

>> **Inset Spacing:** The distance from the edges of the text area.

>> **First Baseline:** Where you want the first line of text to appear. The default Ascent option starts your text normally at the top. If you want to put in a fixed size, such as 50 points from the top, select Fixed from the drop-down list and enter 50 pt in the Min text field.

>> **Text Flow:** The direction in which you read the text as it flows to another row or column. You can choose to have the text flow horizontally (across rows) or vertically (down columns).

# Threading text into shapes

Create custom columns of text that are in different shapes and sizes by threading closed shapes together. This technique, of flowing text from one shape to another, works with rectangles, circles, stars, or any other closed shape and can lead to some creative text areas.

Follow these steps to thread text into shapes:

1.  **Create any shape, any size.**

    For this example, we've created a circle.

2.  **Create another shape (it can be any shape) someplace else on the page.**

3.  **With the Selection tool, select one shape and Shift-click the other to make just those two shapes active.**

4.  **Choose Type⇨Threaded Text⇨Create.**

    A threading line appears, as shown in Figure 5-5, indicating the direction of the threaded text.

5.  **Select the Type tool, click the top of the first shape to start the threading, and start typing.**

    Continue typing until the text flows over into the other shape.

If you no longer want the text to be threaded, choose Type⇨Threaded Text⇨Remove Threading, which eliminates all threading from the text shapes. To remove one or more, but not all, shapes from the threading, select the shape you want to remove from the threading and choose Type⇨Threaded Text⇨Release Selection.

**FIGURE 5-5:**
Threaded text
areas flow from
one area to
another.

## Wrapping text

Wrapping text isn't quite the same as wrapping a present — it's easier! A *text wrap* forces text to wrap around a graphic, as shown in Figure 5-6. This feature can add a bit of creativity to any piece.

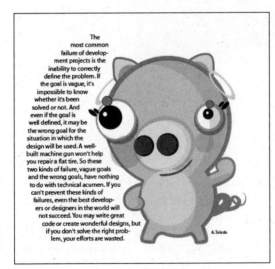

**FIGURE 5-6:**
The graphic is
forcing the text to
wrap around it.

First, create a text area and either enter text or paste text into it. Then place an image that you can wrap the text around. Follow these steps to wrap text around another object or group of objects:

1. **Select the wrap object.**

   This object is the one you want the text to wrap around.

2. **Make sure that the wrap object is on top of the text you want to wrap around it by choosing Object⇨Arrange⇨Bring to Front.**

   If you're working in layers (which we discuss in Chapter 7 of this minibook), make sure that the wrap object is on the top layer.

3. **Choose Object⇨Text Wrap⇨Make.**

   An outline of the wrap area is visible.

4. **Adjust the wrap area by choosing Object⇨Text Wrap⇨Text Wrap Options.**

   The Text Wrap Options dialog box appears, as shown in Figure 5-7.

**FIGURE 5-7:**
Adjust the distance of the text wrap from the object.

You have these options:

- *Offset:* Specifies the amount of space between the text and the wrap object. You can enter a positive or negative value.

- *Invert Wrap:* Wraps the text on the inside of the wrap object instead of around it.

5. **When you finish making selections, click OK.**

If you want to change the text wrap at a later point, select the object and choose Object⇨Text Wrap⇨Text Wrap Options. Make your changes and click OK.

If you want to unwrap text from an object, select the wrap object and choose Object⇨Text Wrap⇨Release.

# Outlining text

Illustrator gives you the opportunity to change text into outlines or artwork. Basically, you change the text into an object, so you can no longer edit that text by typing. The plus side is that it saves you the trouble of sending fonts to everyone who wants to use the file. Turning text into outlines makes it appear as though your text was created with the Pen tool. You want to use this tool when creating logos that will be used frequently by other people or artwork that you may not have control over.

To turn text into an outline, follow these steps:

1. **Type some text on your page.**

    For this example, just type a word (say, your name) and make sure that the font size is at least 36 points. You can change your font size in the Font Size box in the Control panel at the top. You want to have it large enough to see the effect of outlining it.

2. **Switch to the Selection tool and choose Type⇨Create Outlines.**

    You can also use the keyboard command Ctrl+Shift+O (Windows) or ⌘+Shift+O (Mac).

    The text is now grouped together in outline form.

3. **If you're being creative, or just particular, and want to move individual letters, use the Group Select tool or choose Object⇨Ungroup to separate the letters, as shown in Figure 5-8.**

**FIGURE 5-8:**
Letters converted
to outlines.

**WARNING**

When you convert type to outlines, the type loses its *hints,* which are the instructions built in to fonts to adjust their shape so that your system displays or prints them in the best way based on their size. Without hints, letters such as lowercase *e* or *a* might fill in as the letter forms are reduced in size. Make sure that the text is the approximate size it might be used at before creating outlines. Because the text loses the hints, try not to create outlines on text smaller than 10 points.

## Putting text on a path, in a closed shape, or on the path of a shape

Wow — that's some heading, huh? You've probably seen text following a swirly path or inside a shape. Maybe you think that accomplishing such a task is too intimidating to even attempt. In this section, we show you just how easy these tasks are! Some Type tools are dedicated to putting type on a path or a shape (refer to Figure 5-1), but we think you'll find that the key modifiers we show you in the following sections are easier to use.

### Creating text on a path

Follow these steps to put type on a path:

1. **Create a path with the Pen, Line, or Pencil tool.**

   Don't worry if it has a stroke or fill applied.

2. **Select the Type tool and simply cross over the start of the path.**

3. **When an I-bar with a squiggle appears (which indicates that the text will run along the path), click.**

   The stroke and fill of the path immediately change to None.

4. **Start typing, and the text runs on the path.**

5. **Choose Window➪Type➪Paragraph and change the alignment in the Paragraph panel to reposition where the text falls on the path.**

   Alternatively, switch to the Selection tool and drag the first of the three I-bars that appear, as shown in Figure 5-9. This allows you to freely move the text on that path. The path in Figure 5-9 was created with the Pen tool.

**TIP**

Flip the text to the other side of a path by clicking and dragging the middle I-bar under or over the path.

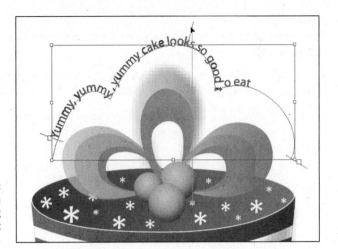

**FIGURE 5-9:**
Use the Selection
tool to drag
the I-bar to adjust
the text.

## Creating text in a closed shape

Putting text inside a shape can add spunk to a layout. This feature allows you to custom-create a closed shape with the shape tools or the Pen tool and flow text into it. Follow these steps to add text inside a shape:

1. **Create a closed shape — a circle or an oval, for example.**

2. **Select the Type tool and cross over the path of the closed shape.**

3. **When you see the I-bar swell or become rounded, click inside the shape.**

4. **Start typing, and the text is contained inside the shape.**

## Text on the path of a closed shape

Perhaps you want text to run around the edge of a shape instead of inside it. Follow these steps to have text created on the path of a closed shape:

1. **Create a closed shape, such as a circle.**

2. **Select the Type tool and cross over the path of the circle.**

3. **Don't click when you see the I-bar swell up; hold down the Alt (Windows) or Option (Mac) key instead.**

   The icon changes into the squiggle I-bar you see when creating text on a path.

4. **When the squiggle line appears, click.**

**5.** **Start typing, and the text flows around the path of the shape, as shown in Figure 5-10.**

To change the origin of the text or move it around, use the alignment options in the Paragraph panel or switch to the Selection tool and drag the I-bar to a new location on the path.

You can drag the middle I-bar in and out of the shape to flip the text so that it appears on the outside or inside of the path.

## Assigning Font Styles

After you have text on your page, you'll often want to change it to be more interesting than the typical 12-point Times font. Formatting text in Illustrator isn't only simple, but you can also do it multiple ways. In the following list, we name and define some basic type components (see Figure 5-11):

**FIGURE 5-11:**
Components
of type.

>> **Font:** A complete set of characters, letters, and symbols of a particular typeface design.

>> **X height:** The height of type, based on the height of the small *x* in that type family.

>> **Kerning:** The space between two letters. Often used for letters in larger type that need to be pulled closer together, such as *W i*. Kern a little to slide the *i* in a little closer to the *W*, maybe even moving into the space occupied by the *W*, as shown in Figure 5-12. Kerning doesn't distort the text; it only increases or decreases the space between two letters.

**FIGURE 5-12:**
Before kerning (left) and after (right).

>> **Leading:** Space between the lines of text.

>> **Tracking:** The space between multiple letters. Designers like to use this technique to spread out words by increasing the space between letters. Adjusting the tracking doesn't distort text; it increases or decreases the space between the letters, as shown in Figure 5-13.

**FIGURE 5-13:**
Tracking set at 0 (top) and 300 (bottom).

AGI TRAINING

A G I  T R A I N I N G

**TIP**

Pretty good tracking and kerning have already been determined in most fonts. You don't need to bother with these settings unless you're tweaking text for a more customized look.

>> **Baseline:** The line that type sits on. The baseline doesn't include *descenders*, type that extends down, like lowercase *y* and *g*. You adjust the baseline for trademark signs or mathematical formulas, as shown in Figure 5-14.

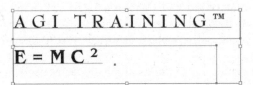

**FIGURE 5-14:**
Adjust the baseline for superscript.

**TIP**

The keyboard shortcuts for type shown in Table 5-1 work with Adobe Illustrator, InDesign, and Photoshop.

**TABLE 5-1**

## Keyboard Shortcuts for Type

| Command | Windows | Mac |
| --- | --- | --- |
| Align left, right, or center | Shift+Ctrl+L, R, or C | Shift+⌘+L, R, or C |
| Justify | Shift+Ctrl+J | Shift+⌘+J |
| Insert soft return | Shift+Enter | Shift+Return |
| Reset horizontal scale to 100 percent | Shift+Ctrl+X | Shift+⌘+X |
| Increase or decrease point size | Shift+Ctrl+> or < | Shift+⌘+> or < |
| Increase or decrease leading | Alt+↑ or ↓ | Option+↑ or ↓ |
| Set leading to the font size | Double-click the leading icon in the Character panel | Double-click the leading icon in the Character panel |
| Reset tracking or kerning to 0 | Alt+Ctrl+Q | Option+⌘+Q |
| Add or remove space (kerning) between two characters | Alt+→ or ← | Option+→ or ← |
| Add or remove space (kerning) between two characters by 5 times the increment value | Alt+Ctrl+→ or ← | Option+⌘+→ or ← |
| Add or remove space (kerning) between selected words; if selected, it changes tracking. Leave cursor in between words. | Alt+← or → | Option+← or → |
| Increase or decrease baseline shift | Alt+Shift+↑ or ↓ | Option+Shift+↑ or ↓ |

# Using the Character Panel

To visualize changes you're making to text and to see characteristics that are already selected, choose Window⇨Type⇨Character or press Ctrl+T (Windows) or ⌘+T (Mac), which opens the Character panel. Click the triangle in the upper-right corner to see a panel menu of additional options. Choose Show Options, and additional type attributes appear, such as baseline shift, underline, and strikethrough.

**TIP**

Pressing Ctrl+T (Windows) or ⌘+T (Mac) is a toggle switch to either show or hide the Character panel. If you don't see the Character panel appear at first, you may have hidden it by pressing the keyboard shortcut. Just try it again.

The following list explains the options in the Character panel (see Figure 5-15):

>> **Font:** Select the font you want to use from this drop-down list.

FIGURE 5-15:
The Character
panel shows
additional
options.

TIP

You can click and drag across the font name in the Character panel or Control panel, and press the up- or down-arrow key to automatically switch to the next font above or below on the font list. Do this while you have text selected to see the text change live!

>> **Set font style:** Select the style (for example, Bold, Italic, or Bold Italic) from this drop-down list. The choices here are limited by the fonts you have loaded. In other words, if you have only Times regular loaded in your system, you don't have the choice to bold or italicize it.

>> **Type size:** Set the size of the type in this combo box. Average readable type is 12-point; headlines can vary from 18 points and up.

>> **Leading:** Select how much space you want between the lines of text in this combo box. Illustrator uses the professional typesetting method of including the type size in the total leading. In other words, if you have 12-point and want it double-spaced, set the leading at 24 points.

>> **Kerning:** To use this combo box, you first need to place the cursor between two letters. Then, to push the letters farther apart from each other, you can click the up arrow or type a value; to decrease the spacing between the letters, type a lower value, even negative numbers, or click the down arrow.

>> **Tracking:** Use the Tracking combo box by selecting multiple letters and increasing or decreasing the space between them all at once by clicking the up or down arrows or by typing a positive or negative value.

>> **Horizontal scale:** Distort selected text by stretching it horizontally. Enter a positive number to increase the size of the letters; enter a negative number to decrease the size.

>> **Vertical scale:** Distort selected text vertically. Enter a positive number to increase the size of the letters; enter a negative number to decrease the size.

Using horizontal or vertical scaling to make text look like condensed type often doesn't give good results. When you distort text, the nice thick and thin characteristics of the typeface also become distorted and can produce weird effects.

>> **Baseline shift:** Use baseline shift for trademark signs and mathematical formulas that require selected characters to be moved above or below the baseline.

>> **Character rotation:** Rotate just the selected text by entering an angle in this text field or by clicking the up or down arrows.

>> **Rotate:** Choose to rotate selected text on any angle.

>> **Underline and strikethrough:** These simple text attributes underline and strikethrough selected text.

>> **Language:** Select a language from this drop-down list. **Note:** The language you specify here is used by Illustrator's spell checker and hyphenation feature. We discuss these features in the later section "Text Utilities: Your Key to Efficiency."

# Using the Control Panel

Use the Control panel to quickly access your Type tools and Type panels. Note in Figure 5-16 that when you have active text, hyperlinked text buttons allow you to quickly access panels, such as the Character and Paragraph panels. You can also use this Control panel as a quick and easy way to select the font, size, alignment, color, and transparency.

**FIGURE 5-16:**
Control panel
type functions.

# Using the Paragraph Panel

Access the Paragraph panel quickly by clicking the Paragraph hyperlink in the Control panel or by choosing Window⇨Type⇨Paragraph. This panel, shown in Figure 5-17, has all the attributes that apply to an entire paragraph (such as alignment and indents, which we discuss in the next two sections, and hyphenation, which we discuss later in this chapter). For example, you can't flush-left one word in a paragraph — when you click the Flush Left button, the entire paragraph flushes left. To see additional options in the Paragraph panel, click the triangle in the upper-right corner of the panel (the panel menu) and choose Show Options.

**FIGURE 5-17:** Use this panel to open typographic controls that apply to paragraphs.

# Alignment

You can choose any of the following alignment methods by clicking the appropriate button on the Paragraph panel:

» **Flush Left:** All text is flush to the left with a ragged edge on the right. This is the most common way to align text.

» **Center:** All text is centered.

» **Flush Right:** All text is flush to the right and ragged on the left.

» **Justify with the Last Line Aligned Left:** Right and left edges are both straight, with the last line left-aligned.

» **Justify with the Last Line Aligned Center:** Right and left edges are both straight, with the last line centered.

» **Justify with the Last Line Aligned Right:** Right and left edges are both straight, with the last line right-aligned.

» **Justify All Lines:** In this *forced justification* method, the last line is stretched the entire column width, no matter how short it is. This alignment is used in many publications, but it can create some awful results.

# Indentation

You can choose from the following methods of indentation:

>> **First Line Indent:** Indents the first line of every paragraph. In other words, every time you press the Enter (Windows) or Return (Mac) key, this spacing is created.

To avoid first-line indents and space after from occurring — if you just want to break a line in a specific place, for example — create a line break or a soft return by pressing Shift+Enter (Windows) or Shift+Return (Mac).

>> **Right Indent:** Indents from the right side of the column of text.

>> **Left Indent:** Indents from the left side of the column of text.

 Use the Eyedropper tool to copy the character, paragraph, fill, and stroke attributes. Select the text you want to change, select the Eyedropper tool, and click the text once with the attributes you want to apply to the selected text.

By default, the Eyedropper affects all attributes of a type selection, including appearance attributes. To customize the attributes affected by these tools, double-click the Eyedropper tool to open the Eyedropper dialog box.

# Text Utilities: Your Key to Efficiency

After you have text in an Illustrator document, you may need to perform various tasks within that text, such as search for a word to replace with another word, check your spelling and grammar, save and create your own styles, or change the case of a block of text. You're in luck because Illustrator provides various text utilities that enable you to easily and efficiently perform all these otherwise tedious tasks. In the following sections, we give you a quick tour of these utilities.

## Find and Replace

Generally, artwork created in Illustrator isn't text heavy, but the fact that Illustrator has a Find and Replace feature can be a huge help. Use the Find and Replace dialog box (choose Edit➪Find and Replace) to search for words that need to be changed, such as changing Smyth to Smith, or to locate items that may be difficult to find otherwise. This feature works much like all other search-and-replace methods.

# Spell checker

Can you believe there was a time when Illustrator didn't have a spell checker? Thankfully, it does now — and its simple design makes it easy to use.

To use the spell checker, choose Edit⇨Check Spelling and then click the Start button in the dialog box that appears. The spell checker works much like the spell checker in Microsoft Word and other popular applications: When a misspelled word is found, you're offered a list of replacements. You can choose to fix that instance, fix all instances, ignore the misspelling, or add the word to the dictionary.

If you click the arrow to the left of Options, you can set other specifications, such as whether you want to look for letter case issues or have the spell checker note repeated words.

*Note:* The spell checker uses whatever language you specify in the Character panel. We discuss this panel in the earlier section "Using the Character Panel."

**TIP**

If you work in a specialized industry that uses loads of custom words, save yourself time by choosing Edit⇨Edit Custom Dictionary and then adding your own words. We recommend that you do so before you're ready to spell check a document so that the spell checker doesn't flag the custom words later (which slows you down).

Don't forget that just because a word is spelled correctly doesn't mean it's the correct word in the context of a sentence. You should still proofread manually your text.

## The Hyphenation feature

Nothing is worse than trying to read severely hyphenated copy. Most designers either use hyphenation as little as possible or avoid it altogether by turning off the Hyphenation feature.

Here are a few things you should know about customizing your hyphenation settings if you decide to use this feature:

>> **Turning the Hyphenation feature on or off:** Activate or deactivate the feature in the Hyphenation dialog box (see Figure 5-18); open this dialog box by choosing Window⇨Type⇨Paragraph, clicking the arrow in the upper-right corner of the Paragraph panel to access the panel menu, and then choosing Hyphenation from the list of options that appears. If you won't use the Hyphenation feature, turn it off by deselecting the Hyphenation checkbox at the top of the Hyphenation dialog box.

**FIGURE 5-18:**
Customizing
hyphenation
settings.

TIP

You can also simply click the Paragraph hyperlink in the Control panel to access the Paragraph panel.

» **Setting specifications in the Hyphenation dialog box:** Set specifications in the dialog box that determine the length of words to hyphenate, the number of hyphens to be used in a single document, whether to hyphenate capitalized words, and how words should be hyphenated. The Before Last setting is useful, for example, if you don't want to have a word, such as *liquidated* hyphenated as *liquidat-ed.* Type **3** in the Before Last text field and Illustrator won't hyphenate words if it leaves only two letters on the next line.

» **Setting the Hyphenation Limit and Hyphenation Zone:** They're not diets or worlds in another dimension — the Hyphenation Limit setting enables you to limit the number of hyphens in a row. For example, type **2** in the Hyphenation Limit text field so that you never see more than two hyphenated words in a row. The Hyphenation Zone text field enables you to set up an area of hyphenation based on a measurement. For example, you can specify **1 inch** to allow for only one hyphenation every inch. You can also use the slider to determine whether you want better spacing or fewer hyphens. This slider works only with the Single-Line Composer (the default).

## The Find Font feature

If you work in production, you'll love the Find Font feature, which enables you to list all fonts in a file that contains text and then search for and replace fonts (including the font's type style) by name. You do so from the Find Font dialog box (see Figure 5-19), opened by choosing Type➪Find Font. Select the font you want to replace from the Fonts in Document list. Next, select a font from the Replace with Font From list. Note that the font must already appear in the document. Click the Change button to replace the font (or click the Change All button to replace all instances of the font) and then click OK. That's it!

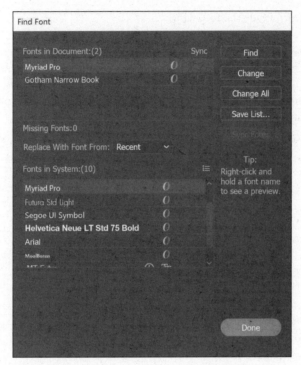

**FIGURE 5-19:**
Use the Find Font dialog box to find and replace typefaces.

This cool feature enables you to replace fonts with fonts from the current working document or from your entire system. Select System from the Replace with Font From drop-down list to choose from all fonts loaded in your system.

## The Change Case feature

Doesn't it drive you crazy when you type an entire paragraph before discovering that you somehow pressed the Caps Lock key? Fix it fast by selecting the text, choosing Type➪Change Case, and then choosing one of these options:

» **Uppercase:** Makes the selected text all uppercase

» **Lowercase:** Makes the selected text all lowercase

>> **Title Case:** Capitalizes the first letter in each word

>> **Sentence Case:** Capitalizes just the first letter in selected sentences

In Illustrator, you use the same type engine used by InDesign for high-quality text control. You're working, as a default, in what's referred to as Single-Line Composer. Select Single or Every Line composer from the Paragraph panel menu.

The options include the following:

>> **Single-Line Composer:** Useful if you prefer to have manual control over how lines break. In fact, this method had been in place in the past. The Single-Line Composer option doesn't take the entire paragraph into consideration when expanding letter space and word spacing, so justified text can sometimes look odd in its entire form. (See Figure 5-20, left.)

>> **Every-Line Composer:** A professional way of setting text; many factors are taken into account as far as spacing is concerned, and spacing is based on the entire paragraph. With this method, you see few spacing issues that create strange effects, such as the ones on the left in Figure 5-20, right.

AGI was founded as a training provider and maintains a presence as a resource for companies and individuals looking to become more productive with electronic publishing software. AGI maintains a strong relationship with electronic publishing software companies including Adobe Systems and Quark as a member of their authorized training provider network. AGI is also a private, licensed school in the Commonwealth of Pennsylvania.

AGI was founded as a training provider and maintains a presence as a resource for companies and individuals looking to become more productive with electronic publishing software. AGI maintains a strong relationship with electronic publishing software companies including Adobe Systems and Quark as a member of their authorized training provider network. AGI is also a private, licensed school in the Commonwealth of Pennsylvania.

**FIGURE 5-20:** Single-Line Composer (left) and Every-Line Composer (right).

## Text styles

A *text style* is a saved set of text attributes, such as font and size. Creating text styles keeps you consistent and saves you time by enabling you to efficiently implement changes in one step rather than have to select the text attributes for each instance of that style of text (say, a heading or caption). So when you're finally happy with the way your headlines appear and how the body copy looks or when your boss asks whether the body copy can be a smidgen smaller (hmm, how much is a smidgen?), you can confidently answer, "Sure!"

If you've created styles, changing a text attribute is simple. What's more, the change is applied at once to all text using that style. Otherwise, you would have to make the attribute change to every occurrence of body text, which could take a long time if your text is spread out.

Illustrator offers two types of text styles:

>> **Character:** Saves attributes for individual selected text. If you want just the word *New* in a line of text to be red, 20-point Arial, you can save it as a character style. Then, when you apply it, the attribute apply to only the selected text (and not to the entire line or paragraph).

>> **Paragraph:** Saves attributes for an entire paragraph. A span of text is considered a paragraph until it reaches a hard return or paragraph break. Note that pressing Shift+Enter (Windows) or Shift+Return (Mac) is considered a soft return, and paragraph styles continue to apply beyond the soft return.

You can create character and paragraph styles in many ways, but we show you the easiest and most direct methods in the following subsections.

## Creating character styles

Create a character style when you want individual sections of text to be treated differently from other text in the paragraph. So rather than repeatedly apply a style manually, you create and implement a character style. To do so, open a document containing text and follow these steps:

1. **Set up text with the text attributes you want included in the character style in the Character panel, and then choose Window⇨Type⇨Character Styles.**

   The Character Styles panel opens.

2. **Select the text from Step 1 and Alt-click (Windows) or Option-click (Mac) the New Style button (the dog-eared page icon) at the bottom of the Character Styles panel.**

3. **In the Character Styles Options dialog box that appears, name your style and click OK.**

   Illustrator records which attributes have been applied already to the selected text and builds a style from them.

4. **Create another text area by choosing Select⇨Deselect and using the Type tool to drag out a new text area.**

   We discuss using the Type tool in the earlier section "Creating text areas."

5. **Change the font and size to dramatically different choices from your saved style and type some text.**

6. **Select some (not all) of the new text and then Alt-click (Windows) or Option-click (Mac) the style name in the Character Styles panel.**

   Alt-click (Windows) or Option-click (Mac) to eliminate any attributes that weren't part of the saved style. The attributes of the saved character style are applied to the selected text.

TIP

When you create a new panel item (any panel) in Adobe Illustrator, InDesign, or Photoshop, we recommend that you get in the habit of Alt-clicking (Windows) or Option-clicking (Mac) the New Style button. This habit allows you to name the item (style, layer, or swatch, for example) while adding it to the panel.

## Creating paragraph styles

Paragraph styles include attributes that are applied to an entire paragraph. What constitutes a paragraph is all text that falls before a hard return (you create a hard return when you press Enter in Windows or Return on the Mac), so this could be one line of text for a headline or ten lines in a body text paragraph.

To create a paragraph style, open a document that contains text or open a new document and add text to it; then follow these steps:

1. **Choose Window⇨Type⇨Paragraph Styles to open the Paragraph Styles panel.**

2. **Find a paragraph of text that has the same text attributes throughout it and put your cursor anywhere in that paragraph.**

   You don't even have to select the whole paragraph!

3. **Alt-click (Windows) or Option-click (Mac) the Create New Style button (the dog-eared icon at the bottom of the Paragraph panel) to create a new paragraph style; give your new style a name.**

   Your new style now appears in the Paragraph Styles panel list of styles.

4. **Create a paragraph of text elsewhere in your document and make its attributes different from the text in Step 2.**

5. **Put your cursor anywhere in the new paragraph and Alt-click (Windows) or Option-click (Mac) your named style in the Paragraph Styles panel.**

   The attributes from the style are applied to the entire paragraph.

TIP

If style doesn't seem to work, make sure that the Character Style is set to Normal Character Style.

## Updating styles

When you use existing text to build styles, reselect the text and assign the style. In other words, if you put the cursor in the original text whose attributes were saved as a style, it doesn't have a style assigned to it in the Styles panel. Assign the style by selecting the text or paragraph and clicking the appropriate style listed in the Styles panel. By doing so, you ensure that any future updates to that style apply to that original text and to all other instances.

Before updating a style, make sure you have nothing selected (Select⇨Deselect). To update a style, simply select its name in either the Character or Paragraph Styles panel. Choose Options from the panel menu, which you access by clicking the arrow in the upper-right corner of the panel. In the resulting dialog box (see Figure 5-21), make changes by clicking the main attribute on the left and then updating the choices on the right. After you do so, all tagged styles are updated.

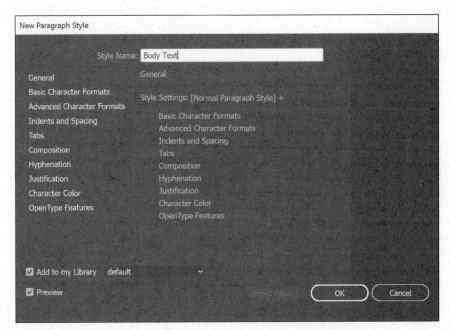

**FIGURE 5-21:**
Updating a paragraph style.

WARNING

Documents created in older versions of Adobe Illustrator (Version 10 or earlier) contain *legacy text*, which is text using the older text engine. When these files are opened, you see a Warning dialog box. If you click the Update button, any text on the document will most likely reflow, causing line breaks, leading, and other types of spacing to change.

Click the OK button to update the file after it's opened to lock down the text. If necessary, you can use the Type tool to click a selected text area to update only the contained text. Another Warning dialog box appears that gives you the opportunity to update selected text, copy the text object, or cancel the text tool selection. This method is the best way to see which changes are occurring so that you can catch any spacing issues right off the bat. See Figure 5-22 for samples of the three options in the Warning dialog box.

FIGURE 5-22:
Original text (left), updated text (center), and text object copied (right).

If you click Copy the Text Object, you can use the underlying locked copy to adjust the new text flow to match the old. Throw away the legacy text layer by clicking and dragging it to the Trash icon in the Layers panel, or click the visibility eye icon to the left of the Legacy Text layer to hide it when you're finished.

**REMEMBER**

IN THIS CHAPTER

» Using rulers

» Using ruler and custom guides

» Working with the Transform panel for placement

» Changing ruler origin

» Rearranging, hiding, and locking objects

» Masking objects

# Chapter **6**

# Organizing Your Illustrations

You can create incredible effects in Illustrator, but if don't organize your artwork, you can make completing your artwork much more difficult. In this chapter, you focus on organizational tricks that will save you time.

## Setting Ruler Increments

Using rulers to help accurately place objects in an illustration is not difficult, but not knowing how to effectively use the rulers in Illustrator can drive you straight over the edge.

To view rulers in Illustrator, choose View➪Rulers➪Show Rulers or press Ctrl+R (Windows) or ⌘+R (Mac). When the rulers appear, their default measurement setting is the point (or whichever measurement increment was last set up in the preferences).

To change the ruler increment to the measurement system you prefer, use one of these methods:

>> Create a new document and select a measurement unit in the New Document dialog box.

>> Right-click (Windows) or Control-click (Mac) the horizontal or vertical ruler and pick a measurement increment from the contextual menu that appears.

>> Choose Edit⇨Preferences⇨Units (Windows) or Illustrator⇨Preferences⇨Units (Mac) to open the Preferences dialog box.

**REMEMBER**

Change the ruler unit only by using the General drop-down list in the Preferences dialog box. If you change the measurement unit on the Stroke and Type tabs, you can end up with 12-*inch* type rather than that dainty 12-*point* type you were expecting.

**REMEMBER**

Setting general preferences changes them in all future documents.

>> Choose File⇨Document Setup to change the measurement unit for only the document you're working on.

# Using Guides

Guides can help you create more accurate illustrations. After a guide is created, you can turn its visibility off or on quickly with the View menu. You can use two kinds of guides in Illustrator:

>> **Ruler guides:** You create these straight-line guides by clicking the ruler and dragging out to the artboard.

>> **Custom guides:** These guides, created from Illustrator objects such as shapes or paths, are helpful for replicating the exact angle of a path, as shown in Figure 6-1.

## Creating a ruler guide

A ruler guide is the easiest guide to create: Click the vertical or horizontal ruler anywhere and drag it to the artboard, as shown in Figure 6-2. By default, the horizontal ruler creates horizontal guides (no kidding), and the vertical ruler creates vertical guides. You can press Alt-drag (Windows) or Option-drag (Mac) to change the orientation of the guide. The vertical ruler then creates a horizontal guide, and the horizontal ruler then creates a vertical guide.

## Creating a custom guide

Create a custom guide by selecting a path or a shape and choosing View➪Guides➪ Make Guides. The selected object turns into a nonprinting guide. Changing a path into a guide isn't a permanent change. Choose View➪Guides➪Release Guides to turn guides back into paths.

# Using the Transform Panel for Placement

Placing shapes and paths precisely where you want them can be difficult even if you have steady hands. Save yourself some aggravation by using the Transform panel to achieve this. Type *x, y* coordinates in the Transform panel to position objects exactly where you want them.

**TIP**

In Adobe Illustrator and InDesign, the Reference Point Indicator icon is on the left side of the Transform panel. Click the handle of the icon to change the point of reference. To measure from the upper-left corner, click the indicator on the handle there. If you want to know the exact center of an object, click the center point in the indicator. The point of reference is the spot on the object that falls at the *x, y* coordinates, which specify the placement of the selected object:

>> ***x* coordinate:** From left to right

>> ***y* coordinate:** From top to bottom

# Changing the Ruler Origin

In Adobe Illustrator, InDesign, and Photoshop, you can change the *ruler origin*, which defines the start of a printing area of an image.

To change the ruler origin, follow these steps:

**1.** **Move the pointer to the upper-left corner of the rulers where the rulers intersect, as shown in Figure 6-3.**

**FIGURE 6-3:**
Changing the ruler's origin.

**2.** **Drag the pointer to the spot where you want the new ruler origin.**

While you drag, a crosshair in the window and in the rulers indicates where the new ruler origin will be placed.

You can restore the original ruler origin by double-clicking the ruler intersection.

TIP

# Thinking about Object Arrangement

Just like the stacks of paper on your desk, new objects in Illustrator are placed on top of existing objects. Change their order by choosing the Object⇨Arrange menu options.

The easiest choices are to bring an object to the front or send it to the back. The results of sending forward or backward can be unnerving if you don't know the exact order in which objects were created. The illustration in Figure 6-4 shows three objects that we plan to rearrange by using four available choices. Figure 6-5 shows the result of each choice.

**FIGURE 6-4:**
Objects in their original positions.

To change the stacking order, select the object (or objects) whose placement you want to change and then choose one of these commands:

» **Object⇨Arrange⇨Bring to Front:** Moves the selected object to the top of the painting order. In Figure 6-5a, the square is brought in front by using the Bring to Front command.

» **Object⇨Arrange⇨Bring Forward:** Moves a selected object in front of the object created just before it or one level closer to the front. In Figure 6-5b, the triangle is moved in front of the square by using the Bring Forward command.

» **Object⇨Arrange⇨Send Backward:** Moves a selected object so that it falls under the object created just before it or one level back. In Figure 6-5c, the triangle is sent backward so that it's just under the circle.

» **Object⇨Arrange⇨Send to Back:** Moves a selected object to the bottom of the painting order. In Figure 6-5d, the triangle is placed on the bottom by using the Send to Back command.

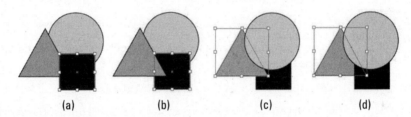

**FIGURE 6-5:**
Rearranging objects.

(a)     (b)     (c)     (d)

# Hiding Objects

Seasoned Illustrator users love the Hide command. Use it when the object you want to select is stuck behind something else or when you need to select one object and another repeatedly activates instead.

A good opportunity to use the Hide command is when you're creating text inside a shape. In Chapter 5 of this minibook, we show you that as soon as you turn a shape into a text area, the fill and stroke attributes turn into None. Follow these steps to hide a shape:

**1.** **Create a shape.**

For this example, we created an ellipse.

2. **Click the Fill color box at the bottom of the Illustrator Tools panel and then choose Window⇨Swatches.**

   The Swatches panel appears.

3. **In the Swatches panel, choose a color for the fill.**

   In this example, yellow is selected. The stroke doesn't matter; this one is set to None.

   Clicking a shape with the Type tool converts the shape to a text area and converts the fill and stroke to None. To have a colored shape remain, you must hide a copy.

4. **After selecting a colored shape, choose Edit⇨Copy; alternatively, you can press Ctrl+C (Windows) or ⌘+C (Mac).**

   This step makes a copy of your shape.

5. **Choose Edit⇨Paste in Back or press Ctrl+B (Windows) or ⌘+B (Mac).**

   This step puts a copy of your shape exactly in back of the original.

6. **Choose Object⇨Hide or press Ctrl+3 (Windows) or ⌘+3 (Mac).**

   The copy of the shape is now hidden; what you see is your original shape.

7. **Switch to the Type tool by selecting it in the Tools panel or pressing T.**

8. **Use the cursor to cross over the edge of the shape and change it to the Area Type tool.**

   You use the Area Type tool to type text in a shape.

9. **When you see the type insertion cursor swell up, as shown in Figure 6-6, click the edge of the shape.**

   The insertion point is now blinking inside the shape, and the fill and stroke attributes of the shape have been changed to None.

**FIGURE 6-6:**
The type insertion cursor on the edge of a shape.

10. **Type some text, as shown in Figure 6-7.**

11. **When you finish entering text, choose Object⇨Show All or press Ctrl+Alt+3 (Windows) or ⌘+Option+3 (Mac).**

    The colored shape reappears with the text in the middle of it, as shown in Figure 6-8.

Alex
is an awesome
kid, he would like to
grow-up and be a
fireman.

Alex
is an **awesome
kid**, he would like to
grow-up and be a
fireman.

Use the Hide command anytime you want to tuck away objects for later use. We promise: Nothing hidden in Illustrator will be lost. Just use the Show All command, and any hidden objects are revealed, exactly where you left them. (Too bad the Show All command can't reveal where you left your car keys!)

# Locking Objects

Being able to lock items is handy when you're building an illustration. The Lock command not only locks down objects you don't want to change, but also drives anyone crazy who tries to edit your files. In fact, we mention locking mainly to help preserve your sanity. Sometimes you need to make simple adjustments to another designer's artwork and can't, unless the objects are first unlocked. Follow these instructions:

>> **To lock an object:** Choose Object➪Lock or press Ctrl+2 (Windows) or ⌘+2 (Mac) to lock an object so that you can't select it, move it, or change its attributes.

>> **To unlock an object:** Choose Object➪Unlock All or press Ctrl+Alt+2 (Windows) or ⌘+Option+2 (Mac). Then you can make changes to it.

You can also lock and hide objects with layers. See Chapter 7 in this minibook for more information about using layers.

# Creating a Clipping Mask

Creating a clipping mask may sound complex, but it's easy and highlights some topics in this chapter, such as arranging objects. Similar to peering through a hole in a piece of paper to the objects underneath it, a *clipping mask* allows a topmost object to define the selected shapes underneath it; with a clipping mask, however, the area around the defining shape is transparent, as shown in Figure 6-9.

You may recall what a film mask looks like — it's black to block out the picture and clear where you want to view an image, as shown in Figure 6-10.

**FIGURE 6-9:**
Some items using the clipping mask feature.

**FIGURE 6-10:**
A conventional film mask.

The clipping mask feature uses the same principle as the conventional film mask. It hides the area outside the mask area. To create a clipping mask, follow these steps:

**1.** **Choose File⇨Place to place an image.**

Masks work with objects created in Illustrator and with objects placed (scanned or otherwise imported) there.

**2.** **Create the item you want to use as a mask by using the Pen tool to create a shape or a closed path.**

For example, in Figure 6-11, the circle is the mask. (The photo underneath it is the placed image from Step 1.) The circle is placed where the mask will be created. The shape's color, fill, and stroke values don't matter because they automatically change to None when you create a mask.

*Note:* When creating a clipping mask, make sure that the object to be used as a mask is a closed shape and is at the top of the stacking order.

**FIGURE 6-11:**
Position the mask shape over the object.

**3.** **Use the Selection tool to select the placed image and the shape.**

Shift-click to add an object to the selection.

**4.** **Choose Object⇨Clipping Mask⇨Make.**

Alternatively, you can use the keyboard shortcut Ctrl+7 (Windows) or ⌘+7 (Mac) to create the clipping mask.

Ta-da! You created the clipping mask. Masked items are grouped, but you can use the Direct Selection tool to move the image or mask individually.

**5.** **To turn off the clipping mask, choose Object⇨Clipping Mask⇨Release.**

**TIP**

You can also use text as a clipping mask: Type a word and ensure that it's positioned over an image or another Illustrator object (or objects). Then select both the text and the object and choose Object⇨Clipping Mask⇨Make.

# Creating a Clipping Path Using the Draw Inside Button

 You can use the Draw Inside button to create a clipping path. The button is at the bottom of the Tools panel. Just follow these steps:

**1. Select your artwork and choose Edit⇨Copy or Cut.**

In Figure 6-12, the artwork to the right has been cut to fit into the star image.

FIGURE 6-12:
Select artwork
and copy or
paste it.

**2. Select the artwork that you want to "paste into" existing artwork and then click the Draw Inside button.**

**3. Choose Edit⇨Paste.**

The artwork is pasted inside the shape, as shown in Figure 6-13.

 After you have pasted your artwork, you can use the Direct Selection tool to reposition it.

TIP

FIGURE 6-13:
Create a clipping
path by using
the Draw Inside
button at the bot-
tom of the Tools
panel.

IN THIS CHAPTER

» **Working with layers**

» **Using layers for a selection**

» **Changing the stacking order of a layer**

» **Moving and cloning objects to another layer**

» **Hiding and locking layers**

Chapter **7**

# Using Layers

This chapter shows you how helpful layers can be when you're producing complex artwork. Layers are similar to clear films stacked on top of your artwork: You can place content (text, shapes, and other objects) on a layer, lift up a layer, remove a layer, hide and show layers, or lock a layer so that you can't edit its content. Taking advantage of the Layers feature can help you:

» Organize the painting (stacking) order of objects.

» Activate objects that would otherwise be difficult to select by using either the Selection or Direct Selection tool.

» Lock items that you don't want to reposition or change.

» Hide items until you need them.

» Repurpose objects for artwork variations. For example, a company's business cards use the same logo and company address, but the name and contact information change for each person. In this case, placing the logo and company address on one layer and the person's name and contact information on another layer lets you easily create a new business card just by changing the person's name and contact details.

# Creating New Layers

When you create a new Illustrator document, you automatically start with a single layer. To understand how layers work, you can create a new file and follow some steps to create new layers and place objects on them:

1. **Choose File⇨New, select Print from the Profile drop-down list, and then click OK.**

2. **If the Layers panel isn't already visible (see Figure 7-1), choose Window⇨Layers.**

**FIGURE 7-1:**
The Layers panel.

3. **Using the Rectangle tool, click and drag anywhere on the artboard to create a rectangle.**

   The size doesn't matter.

4. **Click the Fill button in the Control panel and select any color for the shape from the Color Picker that appears, as shown in Figure 7-2.**

   The Fill button is the swatch with an arrow on the left side of the Control panel.

**FIGURE 7-2:**
Select any color
from the Fill Color
Picker.

This fill color makes the rectangle easier to identify later.

The blue handle color that appears on the active shape matches the blue color bar you see in the Layers panel on the left side of the layer name and the small selection square to the right of the radio button. The small selection square on the right disappears if you choose Select➪Deselect. You use that square to see which layer a selected object is on.

Notice in Figure 7-3 that you've added a shape to this layer, so an arrow appears to the left of the layer name. This arrow indicates that you now have a *sublayer,* which is essentially a layer within a layer. Click the arrow to expand the layer and show any sublayers nested underneath it; sublayers are automatically created when you add objects, which helps when you're making difficult selections.

It helps to name layers with a unique name so that you can identify them while working.

5. **Alt-click (Windows) or Option-click (Mac) the Create New Layer button at the bottom of the Layers panel to create a new layer.**

   The Layer Options dialog box appears (see Figure 7-4), and you can use it to name a layer and change the selection color. You don't have to hold down the Alt or Option key when making a new layer, but if you don't, the Layer Options window does not appear.

6. **Enter the name Circle for the new layer in the Name text box and click OK.**

   In Figure 7-5, we entered **circle** because it's the shape we add in Step 7.

   If you want to stay organized, you can name the original layer **rectangle** by double-clicking Layer 1. Just make sure that you click the circle layer again to make it the active layer.

   A new layer is added to the top of the stack in the Layers panel.

**FIGURE 7-4:**
Creating a new
layer.

**7.** **Make a shape on the new layer and overlap the shape you created in Step 2. (See Figure 7-5.)**

In this example, we created a circle, as shown in Figure 7-5.

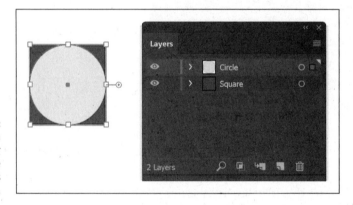

**FIGURE 7-5:**
A circle on
the new layer
overlaps the
rectangle on its
underlying layer.

**8.** **Change the fill color for your new shape.**

Look at the selection handles on the circle that you just created: They change to a different color, indicating that you're on a different layer. The different handle colors are for organizational purposes only and aren't printed.

**9.** **Just to be different this time, choose New Layer from the panel menu.**

The Layer Options dialog box appears.

**10.** **(Optional) In the Layer Options dialog box, change the color of the selection handles by selecting an option from the Color drop-down list.**

You can also hide or lock the contents of the layer.

**11.** Enter the name Star in the Name text field, click OK, and then create a shape on it.

For the example shown in Figure 7-6, we entered **star** into the Name text box and used the Star tool to create a star on the new layer. The Star tool is hidden in the Rectangle shape tool.

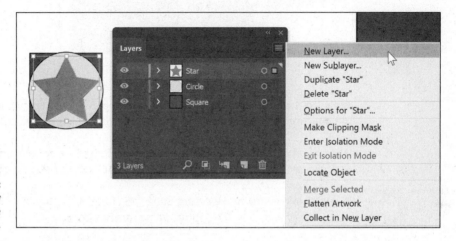

**FIGURE 7-6:**
Create a new layer by using the panel menu.

**12.** Again, change the fill color of your newest shape so that it's different from the other shapes.

**13.** Use the Selection tool to move the new shape so that it overlaps the others slightly.

**TIP**

You can open the Options dialog box for any existing layer by choosing Options for "Layer" (Named Layer) from the panel menu in the Layers panel, or by double-clicking on a layer in the Layers panel.

You've created new layers and now have a file that you can use to practice working with layers.

# Using Layers for Selections

When you have a selected object on a layer, a color selection square appears to the right of the named layer. If you select the radio button directly to the right of the layer's name in the Layers panel, as shown in Figure 7-7, all objects are selected on that layer.

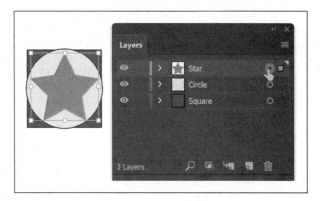

FIGURE 7-7:
Selecting the
entire contents of
a layer.

Sublayers have their own radio buttons. If sublayers are visible, you can use the same technique to select objects that may be buried behind others.

If you need help selecting a specific graphic's layer, select the graphic, and then click the Locate Object button in the lower-left of the Layers panel.

**TIP**

If you think you'll be selecting sublayers frequently, double-click the default name and type a more descriptive name for that layer.

# Changing the Layer Stacking Order

In Chapter 6 of this minibook, we tell you about the Object⇨Arrange feature in Illustrator; with layers, this process becomes slightly more complicated. Each layer has its own *painting order,* the order in which you see the layers. To move a layer (and thereby change the stacking order of the layers), click and drag that layer until you see the black insertion line where you want the layer to be moved.

As you add shapes to a layer, a sublayer is created, and it has its own little stacking order that's separate from other layers. In other words, if you choose to send an object to the back and it's on the top layer, it goes only to the back of that layer and is still in front of any objects on layers beneath it.

**REMEMBER**

Understanding how the stacking order affects the illustration is probably the most confusing part about layers. Just remember that in order for an object to appear behind everything else, it has to be on the bottom layer (and at the bottom of all objects on that bottom layer); for an object to appear in front of everything else, it has to be on the topmost layer.

# Moving and Cloning Objects

To move a selected object from one layer to another, click the small color-selection square (shown in Figure 7-8) to the right of the layer's radio button in the Layers panel, drag the object to the target layer, and release. That's all there is to moving an object from one layer to another.

FIGURE 7-8:
Drag the small square icon to move the selected object to another layer.

You can also *clone* an item, or make a copy of it while you move the copy to another layer. Clone an object by Alt-dragging (Windows) or Option-dragging (Mac) the color selection square to another layer. A plus sign appears while you drag (so you know that you're making a clone of the object). Release when you reach the cloned object's target layer.

TIP

Choose Paste Remembers Layers from the Layers panel to have Illustrator automatically remember which layer you copied an object from. No matter which layer is active, Illustrator always pastes the object back on the original layer it was copied from.

# Hiding Layers

To the left of each layer in the Layers panel is an eye icon — a visibility toggle button. Simply clicking the eye icon hides the layer (the eye disappears, denoting that this layer is hidden). Click the empty square (where the eye icon was) to show the layer again.

Alt-click (Windows) or Option-click (Mac) an eye icon to hide all layers except the one you click; Alt-click (Windows) or Option-click (Mac) the eye icon to show all layers again.

Using Layers

Ctrl-click (Windows) or ⌘-click (Mac) the eye icon to turn just the selected layer into Outline view. In Outline view, all you see are the outlines of the artwork with no stroke widths or fill colors. The rest of your artwork remains in Preview mode, with strokes and fills visible. This tricky technique is helpful when you're looking for stray points or need to close paths. Ctrl-click (Windows) or ⌘-click (Mac) the eye icon again to return the layer to Preview mode.

# Locking Layers

Lock layers by clicking the empty square to the right of the Visibility (eye) icon. A padlock icon appears so that you know the layer is now locked. Locking a layer prevents you from making changes to the objects on that layer. Click the padlock to unlock the layer.

Chapter **8**

# Livening Up Illustrations with Color

This chapter is all about making your illustrations come alive with color. We show you how to create new colors, patterns, and gradients as well as how to edit existing colors and save custom colors. We also explain how to apply and edit color attributes to many objects at the same time.

## Choosing a Document Profile

Whether you are using the default New dialog box or the legacy dialog box, you are offered the option to choose a color profile. In the default dialog, you can choose from Mobile, Web, Print, Film & Video, or Art & Illustration. If you are using the legacy New dialog box, click on More settings, and you can choose a color profile from the Profile drop-down menu, as shown in Figure 8-1. If you must set your preferences every time you create a new file, choose a document profile, as you see in Figure 8-1. This profile determines the default settings from which you create your document. Some of the settings established here are the artboard size, units of measure, color mode, resolution, and more.

**FIGURE 8-1:**
Use the New Document profiles to start with the right colors, resolution, measurement units, artboard size, and more.

Illustrator CC offers several profiles, and they fall into two basic categories: onscreen and print.

The following New Document profiles are used for onscreen display:

>> **Mobile:** This profile ensures a small file size and uses a resolution that is preset for a specific mobile device. You can choose your device from the Size menu.

>> **Web:** This profile provides preset options, such as size and resolution, that are optimized for output to the web.

>> **Print:** This profile provides preset options for size and resoluton defaults that are optimized for print graphics. The colors in the Swatches panel are in CMYK, as well as gradients and patterns.

>> **Film & Video:** This profile provides several preset video- and film-specific crop area sizes. Illustrator also creates only square pixel files so that the sizes are interpreted correctly in video applications.

>> **Art & Illustration:** This profile creates a document in RGB mode with the Raster Effects Resolution set to 72 ppi.

The Print profile is used for print display. By default this profile uses a letter-size artboard, but it provides a variety of other preset print sizes to choose from. A document created with this profile is also set to a default resolution of 300 dpi. Use this profile if you plan to send your file to a commercial printer.

**TIP**

You can change the color mode at any time without losing information by choosing File⇨Document Color Mode.

# Using the Swatches Panel

Accessing color from the Control panel is probably the easiest way to make color choices: You can use the Fill and Stroke drop-down lists to quickly access the Swatches panel, shown in Figure 8-2, and at the same time ensure that the color is applied to either the fill or stroke. How many times have you mixed up colors and assigned the stroke color to the fill or vice versa?

**FIGURE 8-2:**
Use these buttons to quickly access color options.

You can also access the Swatches panel, which you open by choosing Window⇨Swatches. Although limited in choice, its basic colors, patterns, and gradients are ready to go. You can use the buttons at the bottom of the Swatches panel (refer to Figure 8-2) to quickly open color libraries, select kinds of colors to view, access swatch options, create color groups, add new swatches, and delete selected swatches.

You may notice some odd color swatches — for example, the crosshair and the diagonal line.

The crosshair represents the Registration color. Use this swatch only when creating custom crop marks or printer marks. The Registration color looks black, but it's created from 100 percent of all colors. This way, when artwork is separated, the crop mark appears on all color separations.

The diagonal line represents None. Use this option if you want no fill or stroke.

# Applying Color to the Fill and Stroke

Illustrator objects are created from *fills* (the inside) and *strokes* (border or path). Look at the bottom of the Tools panel for the Fill and Stroke color boxes. If you're applying color to the fill, the Fill color box must be forward in the Tools panel. If you're applying color to the stroke, the Stroke color box must be forward.

Table 8-1 lists keyboard shortcuts that can be a tremendous help to you when applying colors to fills and strokes.

**TABLE 8-1**

### Color Keyboard Shortcuts

| Function | Keyboard Shortcut |
| --- | --- |
| Switch the Fill or Stroke color box position | X |
| Inverse the Fill and the Stroke color boxes | Shift+X |
| Default (black stroke, white fill) | D |
| None | / |
| Last color used | < |
| Last gradient used | > |
| Color Picker | Double-click the Fill or Stroke color box |

**TIP**

Try this trick: Drag a color from the Swatches panel to the Fill or Stroke color box at the bottom of the toolbar or the top left of the Swatches panel. This action applies the color to the color box that you dragged to. It doesn't matter which is forward!

To apply a fill color to an existing shape, drag the swatch directly to the shape. Select a swatch, hold down Alt+Shift+Ctrl (Windows) or Option+Shift (Mac), and drag a color to a shape to apply that color to the stroke.

# Changing the Width and Type of a Stroke

Access the Stroke panel by clicking the Stroke hyperlink in the Control panel. In the Stroke panel, shown in Figure 8-3, you can choose to change the Width height by clicking and selecting a preset width from the Width drop-down menu, or you can type in a value. You can also customize the *caps* (the end of a line), *joins* (the endpoints of a path or dash), and the *miter limit* (the length of a point). The Stroke panel also enables you to turn a path into a dashed line

**FIGURE 8-3:**
The Stroke panel
options.

In the Stroke panel options, you can choose to align the stroke on the center (default) of a path, the inside of a path, and the outside of a path. Figure 8-4 shows the results.

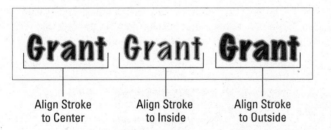

**FIGURE 8-4:**
The Align Stroke
options affect the
placement of the
stroke.

Align Stroke
to Center

Align Stroke
to Inside

Align Stroke
to Outside

This feature is especially helpful when stroking outlined text. Refer to Figure 8-4 to compare text with the traditional centered stroke, as compared with the options for aligning the stroke inside and outside of a path.

**TECHNICAL
STUFF**

You can't adjust the alignment of a stroke on text unless you change the text to outlines first. Select the text with the Selection tool and choose Type➪Create Outlines to enable the Align Stroke options.

You can also customize the following aspects of a stroke from the Stroke panel by clicking the buttons we describe:

- **Cap Options:** The endpoints of a path or dash
  - *Butt Cap:* Makes the ends of stroked lines square
  - *Round Cap:* Makes the ends of stroked lines semicircular
  - *Projecting Cap:* Makes the ends of stroked lines square and extends half the line width beyond the end of the line

- **Join Options:** How corner points appear
  - *Miter Join:* Makes stroked lines with pointed corners
  - *Round Join:* Makes stroked lines with rounded corners
  - *Bevel Join:* Makes stroked lines with squared corners

- **Dashed Lines:** Regularly spaced lines, based on values you set

TIP

To create a dashed line, specify a dash sequence by entering the lengths of dashes and the gaps between them in the Dash Pattern text fields. (See Figure 8-5.) The numbers entered are repeated in sequence so that after you set up the pattern, you don't need to fill in all the text fields. In other words, if you want an evenly spaced dashed stroke, just type the same number in the first and second text fields, and all dashes and spaces will be the same length (say, 12 points). Change that number to **12** in the first text field and **24** in the next to create a larger space between dashes.

**FIGURE 8-5:**
Setting up a
dashed stroke.

TIP

Click the Aligns Dashes button to create improved corners for your dashed object.

>> **Arrowhead:** Arrowheads have been surprisingly difficult for new users to locate and use in previous versions of Illustrator. In CC, you can just open the Stroke dialog box, shown in Figure 8-6, and use simple drop-down lists to set start and end times to your arrowhead as well as the scale.

**FIGURE 8-6:**
Arrowheads are easy to find and use in the Stroke dialog box.

# Using the Color Panel

The Color panel (choose Window➪Color) offers another method for choosing color. You must custom-pick a color using values on the color ramp. You see as a default only the *color ramp* — the large color well spanning the panel. If you don't see all color options, choose Show Options from the Color panel menu. (Click the triangle in the upper-right corner to access the panel menu.)

TIP

If you ever want to create tints of a CMYK color but aren't quite sure how to adjust individual color sliders, just hold down the Shift key while adjusting the color slider of any color. Then watch as all colors move to a relative position at the same time!

As shown in Figure 8-7, the panel menu offers many other choices. Even though you may be in RGB or CMYK color mode, you can still choose to build colors in Grayscale, RGB, HSB (Hue, Saturation, Brightness), CMYK, or web-safe RGB. Choosing Invert or Complement from the panel menu reverses the color of the selected object or changes it to a complementary color, respectively. You can also choose the Fill and Stroke color boxes in the upper-left corner of the Color panel.

**FIGURE 8-7:**
Different color
models are
available in the
Color panel.

You see the infamous cube-and-exclamation-point in the Color panels in most Adobe software. The cube warns you that the color you've selected isn't one of the 216 nondithering, web-safe colors, and the exclamation point warns you that your color isn't within the CMYK print gamut. In other words, if you see the exclamation point in the Color panel, don't expect the cool electric blue you see onscreen to print correctly — it may print as dark purple!

Click the cube or exclamation point symbols when you see them to select the closest color in the web-safe or CMYK color gamut.

TIP

# Saving Colors

Saving your colors not only keeps you consistent, but also makes future edits easier. Any time you build a color, drag it from the Color panel (or the Tools panel) to the Swatches panel to save it as a color swatch for future use. You can also select an object that uses the color and click the New Swatch button at the bottom of the Swatches panel. (Refer to Figure 8-2 to see this button.) To save a color and name it at the same time, Alt-click (Windows) or Shift-click (Mac) the New Swatch icon. The New Swatch dialog box opens, allowing you to name and edit the color, if you want. By double-clicking a swatch in the Swatches panel, you can access the options at any time.

A color in the Swatches panel is available only in the document in which it was created. Read the next section on custom libraries to see how to import swatches from saved documents.

## Building and using custom libraries

When you save a color in the Swatches panel, you're essentially saving it to your own custom library. You import the Swatches panel from one document into another by using the Libraries feature.

Retrieve colors saved in a document's Swatches panel by clicking the Swatch Libraries menu button at the bottom of the Swatches panel and selecting Other Library. You can also access swatch libraries, including those in other documents, by choosing Window➪Swatch Libraries➪Other Library. Locate the saved document and click Open. A panel appears with the document name, as shown in Figure 8-8. You can't edit the colors in this panel, but you can use the colors in this panel by double-clicking a swatch (which adds it to the Swatches panel) or dragging it to the current document's Swatches panel where it can be edited.

**FIGURE 8-8:**
An imported custom swatch library.

**TIP**

You can also click the Swatch Libraries button to access color libraries for Pantone colors, web colors, and some neat creative colors, such as jewel tones and metals.

## Using the Color Guide and color groups

Perhaps you failed at color selection in art class or just don't feel that you pick colors that work well together. Fortunately, you can use the Color Guide to find colors and save them to organized color groups in your Swatches panel. You can create color schemes based on 23 classic color-harmony rules, such as the Complementary, Analogous, Monochromatic, and Triad options, or you can create custom harmony rules.

Sounds complicated, doesn't it? Fortunately, all you have to do is choose a base color and then see which variations you come up with according to rules you choose. Give it a try:

1.  **Choose Window➪Color Guide. Click on the tab and drag the Color Guide panel away from the docking area so that it does not go away when you select another panel.**

    The Color Guide appears, as shown in Figure 8-9.

2.  **Select a color from the Swatches panel. If it isn't visible, choose Window➪Swatches.**

    Immediately, the Color Guide panel kicks in to provide you with colors related to your original swatch.

**FIGURE 8-9:**
The Color Guide
panel identifies
related colors.

Limit the color
groups to colors
in swatch library

Save color group to swatch panel

Edit or Apply colors

3. **Change the harmony rules by clicking the Edit or Apply Colors button at the bottom of the Color Guide panel.**

   The Recolor Artwork dialog box appears.

4. **Change the Harmony Rules by clicking the Harmony Rules arrow to the right of the color bar.**

   A drop-down list appears with many choices for selecting colors, as shown in Figure 8-10.

**FIGURE 8-10:**
Make a selection
from the
Harmony Rule
drop-down list.

5. **Select a color harmony to see your artwork recolored.**

6. **Save your color selection as a color group by clicking the New Color Group icon, located at the top right of the dialog box.**

   If you like, you can rename the color group by double-clicking the group name in the Color Group text field in the Recolor Artwork dialog box.

7. **Click OK.**

The color group is added to the Swatches panel.

TIP

You don't have to use the Recolor Artwork dialog box to save a group of colors. You can Ctrl-click (Windows) or ⌘-click (Mac) to select multiple colors and then click the New Color Group button at the bottom of the Swatches panel.

## Adding Pantone colors

If you're looking for the typical swatches numbered in the Pantone Matching System (PMS), follow these steps:

1. **Click the Swatch Libraries menu button at the bottom of the Swatches panel.**

2. **From the drop-down list, select Color Books and then Pantone Solid Coated or whatever Pantone library you want to access. The Pantone colors appear in a separate panel.**

Colors in the Pantone numbering system are often referred to as PMS 485 or PMS 201 or whatever number the color has been designated. You can locate the numbered swatch by typing the number into the Find text field of the Pantone panel, as shown in Figure 8-11. When that number's corresponding color is highlighted in the panel, click it to add it to your Swatches panel. Many users find it easier to see colored swatches by using List view. Choose Small List View or Large List View from the panel menu.

**FIGURE 8-11:**
Use the Find text box to locate Pantone colors.

# Editing Colors

Edit colors in the Swatches panel by using the Swatch Options dialog box (shown in Figure 8-12), which you access by double-clicking the color or choosing Swatch Options from the Swatches panel menu.

**FIGURE 8-12:**
Edit a color swatch in the Swatch Options dialog box.

Use the Swatch Options dialog box to:

>> **Change color values:** Change the values in a color by using the sliders or typing values in the color text fields. Being able to enter exact color values is especially helpful if you're given a color build to match. Select the Preview checkbox to see results as you make the changes.

>> **Use global colors:** If you plan to use a color frequently, select the Global checkbox. If it's selected and you use the swatch throughout the artwork, you have to change the swatch options only one time, and then all instances of that color are updated.

One important option to note in the Swatch Options dialog box is the Color Type drop-down list. You have two choices: spot color and process color. What's the difference?

>> **Spot color:** A color that isn't broken down into the CMYK values. Spot colors are used for one- or two-color print runs or when precise color matching is important.

Suppose that you're printing 20,000 catalogs and decide to run only two colors: red and black. If you pick spot colors, the catalogs have to be run through the press that contains two ink applications: one for black and one for red. If red were a process color, however, it would be created from a combination of cyan, magenta, yellow, and black inks, and the catalogs would need to be run through a press with four or more ink applications in order to build that color. Plus, if you went to a print service and asked for red, what color would you get — fire engine red, maroon, or a light and delicate pinkish red? But if the red you pick is PMS 485, your printer in Kutztown, Pennsylvania, can then print the same color of red on your brochure as the printer making your business cards in Woburn, Massachusetts.

>> **Process color:** A color that's built from four colors (cyan, magenta, yellow, and black); used for multicolor jobs.

For example, you would use process colors to send an ad to a four-color magazine. Its printers certainly want to use the same inks they're already running, and using a spot color would require another ink application in addition to the cyan, magenta, yellow, and black plates. In this case, you convert to process colors any spot colors created in corporate logos or similar projects.

# Building and Editing Patterns

Using patterns can be as simple or as complicated as you want. If you become familiar with the basic concepts, you can take off in all sorts of creative directions. To build a simple pattern, start by creating the artwork you want to use as a pattern on your artboard — polka dots, smiley faces, wavy lines, or whatever. Then select all components of the pattern and drag them to the Swatches panel. That's it — you made a pattern! Use the pattern by selecting it as the fill or stroke of an object.

**REMEMBER**

You can't use patterns in artwork that will then be saved as a pattern. If you have a pattern in your artwork and try to drag it into the Swatches panel, Illustrator kicks it back out with no error message. On a good note, you can drag text directly into the Swatches panel to become a pattern.

You can update patterns you created or patterns that already reside in the Swatches panel. To edit an existing pattern, follow these steps:

1. **Click the pattern swatch in the Swatches panel and drag it to the artboard.**

2. **Deselect the pattern and use the Direct Selection make changes to the pattern.**

   Keep making changes until you're happy with the result.

3. **To update the pattern with your new edited version, use the Selection tool to select all pattern elements and Alt-drag (Windows) or Option-drag (Mac) the new pattern over the existing pattern swatch in the Swatches panel.**

4. **When a black border appears around the existing pattern, release the mouse button.**

   All instances of the pattern in your illustration are updated.

**TIP**

To add some space between tiles, as shown in Figure 8-13, create a bounding box by drawing a rectangle shape with no fill or stroke (representing the repeat you want to create). Send the rectangle behind the other objects in the pattern and drag all objects, including the bounding box, to the Swatches panel.

**FIGURE 8-13:**
A pattern with
a transparent
bounding box.

Transformations are covered in detail in Chapter 9 of this minibook, but some specific transform features apply to patterns. To scale a pattern, but not the object it's filling, double-click the Scale tool, shown in the margin. In the Scale dialog box that appears, type the value that you want to scale and deselect all options except Transform Patterns, as shown in Figure 8-14. This method works for the Rotate tool as well.

**FIGURE 8-14:**
Choose to scale
or rotate only the
pattern, not the
object.

# Advanced Pattern Editing

In Illustrator CC, you have more control over patterns than ever before. The preceding section tells you how to start your pattern, but what if you want to create the perfect repeat? Or what if you want to align your repeated tile in a different offset — like stacking bricks — instead of just tiling one pattern right next to the other? With Illustrator CC, you can!

These steps show you how to take advantage of the powerful Pattern editor. To do so, first create your pattern art by following the steps outlined in the preceding section. If you don't have a pattern available, you can use one of the default patterns or locate a sample pattern file at www.agitraining.com/dummies. Follow these steps:

1. **After you add the pattern to the Swatches panel, double-click the swatch. The Pattern Options panel appears, and the artboard switches to Pattern Editor Preview mode, as shown in Figure 8-15.**

Save a Copy

**FIGURE 8-15:**
Pattern options allow you to edit pattern art, change the offset, and more.

2. **Click Save a Copy in the upper-left corner of the screen.**

3. **When the New Pattern dialog box appears, type a name to keep a *copy* of your *original* Pattern swatch. Click OK.**

   Keep in mind that the Save a Copy feature allows you to keep a copy of your original pattern swatch, but you'll still be editing your original pattern. (Refer to Figure 8-15.)

   When you click OK, a dialog box appears, indicating that you've just created a copy of your original pattern swatch.

4. **Press OK again.**

5. **Locate the Pattern Options panel and change the name of your pattern, if you want.**

   In this example, we changed the pattern name to `Fish_Brick`, to save a copy before the tile is going to be changed.

6. **Click the Tile Type drop-down menu and select Brick by Row, as shown in Figure 8-16.**

   The artboard displays the change in the pattern repeat.

**FIGURE 8-16:**
Change the Tile
Type using the
Pattern Options
panel.

7. **If you want, change the default Brick Offset by opening that drop-down list and selecting another option.**

**REMEMBER**

8. **You can also edit the size of the repeat by manually entering a size in the Width and Height text boxes, as show in Figure 8-17.**

Keep in mind that you can return to the original size by selecting the Size Tile to Art checkbox below at any time.

**FIGURE 8-17:**
Change the size
of the repeat tile
using the Width
and Height text
boxes.

9. **Change the type of overlap — that is, which item is on top of the stacking order — by using the Overlap section in the Pattern Options panel, as shown in Figure 8-18.**

10. **(Optional) Make further adjustments to the pattern and edit the artwork if needed.**

In the lower section of the Pattern Options panel, you can control the visual look of the pattern preview you're seeing, from the amount of copies that you see, to how dimmed the non-original pattern tiles appear.

You can edit your artwork using the drawing and editing tools, just like you would if you weren't in the Pattern Editor Preview mode. You can see that a pen path is being created in Figure 8-19, and the change is reflected in all the pattern tiles instantaneously.

11. **When you're finished making changes to your pattern, click Done, located to the right of Save a Copy at the top of the editing window.**

**FIGURE 8-18:**
Use the Overlap controls to change which part of the pattern is on the top of the stacking order.

Overlap pattern

**FIGURE 8-19:**
Add and edit artwork right in the pattern editing preview mode.

# Working with Gradients

Create gradients for smooth metallic effects or just to add dimension to illustrations. If you're not sure which swatches are considered gradients, choose Gradient from the Show Swatch Kinds button at the bottom of the Swatches panel. (Refer to Figure 8-2.)

After the Gradient (shown in Figure 8-20) is applied, you can access the Gradient panel for further options by choosing Window⇨Gradient. If the Gradient options aren't visible, choose Show Options from the Gradient panel menu to see more options.

**FIGURE 8-20:**
The Gradient
panel.

On the Gradient panel, use the Type drop-down list to select a *Radial* gradient (one that radiates from the center point) or a *Linear* gradient (one that follows a linear path).

Use the Gradient tool to change the direction and distance of a gradient blend:

1. **Select an object and apply any existing gradient from the Swatches panel to its fill.**

2. **Choose the Gradient tool (press G) and drag in the direction you want the gradient to go.**

   Drag a long path for a smooth, long gradient. Drag a short path for a short, more defined gradient.

**TIP**

Before following the next steps, it would be a good idea to undock your Color panel. Click the Color tab on the Color panel and drag it out to the artboard, essentially separating it from the rest of the panel group.

To create a new gradient, follow these steps:

1. **Click the White/Black Linear Gradient swatch in the Swatches panel, as shown in Figure 8-21, to reach a good base point.**

FIGURE 8-21:
Select the
Linear Gradient
swatch from the
Swatches panel.

**FIGURE 8-21:** Select the Linear Gradient swatch from the Swatches panel.

2. **Notice the Gradient Slider that appears at the bottom of the Gradient panel. On the left and right side of the slider, you see color stops. Click the left color stop on the Gradient Slider to see that this white color stop is set to 100% opacity, as shown in Figure 8-22.**

**FIGURE 8-22:** Click a color stop to activate it.

3. **Click the right black color stop to see that it is also set to 100% opacity.**

   When a color stop is active, the triangle on top turns solid.

4. **If necessary, choose Window⇨Color to access the Color panel. If the ramp on the Color panel is displaying a black-to-white ramp, click the triangle in the upper-right corner to open the panel menu and choose RGB or CMYK colors.**

   This step provides you with additional colors.

5.  Click the color ramp (across the bottom) in the Color panel to pick a random color (or enter values in the text fields to select a specific color) for the active color stop in the Gradient panel.

6.  In the Gradient panel, click the right color stop and change the Opacity to 50%, as shown in Figure 8-23.

FIGURE 8-23:
Change the opacity of the right color stop to 50%.

7.  With the right color stop still selected, click another color in the color ramp in the Colors panel.

To add color stops, click beneath the gradient ramp and then choose a color from the Color panel. You can also drag a swatch from the Swatches panel to add a new color to the gradient. To remove a color stop, drag it off the Gradient panel.

TIP

You can click the gradient ramp to add colors and also to change the opacity of that location of the ramp by entering values in the Opacity text box. This technique is a helpful way to create stripes and other reflective gradients.

## Using the Gradient tool

Take advantage of the Gradient tool to adjust the length and direction of the gradient that you apply to objects. To use the Gradient tool, simply select the object that has the gradient applied to it and then click and drag. A color ramp appears, indicating the length and direction of your gradient, as shown in Figure 8-24.

You can also use the Gradient tool to apply and change colors on the color ramp. To use the Gradient tool, follow these steps:

1.  Apply a gradient to an object.

2.  Select the Gradient tool (or press G) and click and drag to define the length and direction of the gradient.

    Drag a long path for a smooth, long gradient. Drag a short path for a short, more defined gradient.

**FIGURE 8-24:**
Use the Gradient
tool to change
the direction and
length of your
gradient.

3.  **Hover over the gradient ramp (on top of the object), as shown in Figure 8-25.**

    The color ramp appears with the color stops visible.

**FIGURE 8-25:**
Use the Gradient
tool to change
the color stops.

4.  **Double-click the color stop to open the color panel.**

5.  **Select another color and then click outside the Color panel when you're finished editing the gradient ramp.**

## Apply a gradient to a stroke

You can also apply a gradient to a stroke. To apply a gradient to a stroke, follow these steps:

1. **Make sure that you have the stroke of an object selected. You may want to increase the stroke to a larger point size so that you can see the gradient that you will apply a little better.**

   You can do this by bringing forward the stroke at the bottom of the toolbar, or you can click Stroke in the Control panel and then select a gradient from the Swatches menu that appears.

2. **Choose a gradient from the Swatches panel.**

   The gradient is applied.

TIP

   You can't change the direction or distance of a gradient applied to a stroke with the Gradient tool. To make these changes, choose Window➪Gradient and use the angle (for the direction) and the Gradient slider to change the span of the color stops, as you see in Figure 8-26.

**FIGURE 8-26:**
To edit a gradient on a stroke, you must use the Gradient panel.

## Using transparency in gradient meshes

The Gradient Mesh tool helps you to create incredible photo-realistic illustrations using meshes you build on vector objects. If you've already discovered the Gradient Mesh tool, you know how useful this tool is. If you add in the transparency feature, the number of ways you can use it skyrockets.

Follow these simple steps to try the new transparency feature:

1. **Choose a solid color for your fill and no stroke.**

2. **Create a shape.**

   In this example, we created a circle.

3. **Choose Object⇨Create Gradient Mesh and leave the default of 4 Rows and 4 Columns, Appearance, Flat, as shown in Figure 8-27. Click OK.**

A gradient mesh appears in your shape with multiple mesh nodes.

**FIGURE 8-27:** Choose how many rows and columns you want to start your mesh with.

4. **Using the Direct Selection tool, click an individual node.**

5. **Either choose another color to create a blending effect from one color to another or choose Window⇨Transparency and decrease the value of the transparency drop-down list.**

The individual node becomes transparent based on the value you select.

# Copying Color Attributes

Wouldn't it be helpful if you had tools that could record the fill and stroke attributes and apply them to other shapes? You're in luck — the Eyedropper tool can do just that. Copy the fill and stroke of an object and apply it to another object by using the Eyedropper tool:

1. **Create several shapes with different fill and stroke attributes or open an existing file that contains several different objects.**

2. **Select the Eyedropper tool and click a shape that has attributes you want to copy.**

3. **Alt-click (Windows) or Option-click (Mac) another object to apply those attributes.**

Not only is this technique simple, but you can also change which attributes the Eyedropper applies. Do so by double-clicking the Eyedropper tool; in the dialog box that appears, select only the attributes you want to copy.

# Painting Made Easy: The Live Paint Feature

 Don't worry about filling closed shapes or letting fills escape from objects with gaps into unwanted areas. Using the Live Paint feature, you can create the image you want and fill in regions with color. The Live Paint bucket automatically detects regions composed of independent intersecting paths and fills them accordingly. The paint within a given region remains live and flows automatically if any paths are moved.

If you want to give it a try, follow these steps to put together an example to experiment with:

1. **Use the Ellipse tool to create a circle on your page.**

   Make the circle large enough to accommodate two or three inner circles.

2. **Press D (and nothing else).**

   As long as you aren't using the Type tool, you revert to the default colors of a black stroke and a white fill.

3. **Double-click the Scale tool and enter** 75% **in the Uniform Scale text box.**

4. **Press the Copy button and then click OK.**

   You see a smaller circle inside the original.

5. **Press Ctrl+D (Windows) or ⌘+D (Mac) to duplicate the transformation and create another circle inside the last one.**

6. **Choose Select⇨All or press Ctrl+A (Windows) or ⌘+A (Mac) to activate the circles you just created.**

7. **Make sure that the Fill swatch is forward.**

   The Fill swatch is at the bottom of the Tools panel.

8. **Use the Swatches or Color panel and choose any fill color.**

9. **Using the Selection tool, select all the circles. Next, click on the Live Paint Bucket tool, which is hidden under the Shape Builder tool, and click the selection.**

   This turns the selected objects into a Live Paint Group. Now when you move the Live Paint Bucket tool over them again, the different regions become highlighted, indicating they are ready to paint.

   See how the different regions become highlighted?

10. **Click when the region you want to fill is activated.**

    Now try it with other fill colors in different regions, as shown in Figure 8-28.

**FIGURE 8-28:**
Painting objects
with the Live
Paint feature.

A companion feature to the Live Paint Bucket is support for gap detection. With this feature in its arsenal, Illustrator automatically and dynamically detects and closes small to large gaps that may be part of the artwork. You can determine whether you want paint to flow across region gap boundaries by using the Gap Options dialog box, accessible by choosing Object⇨Live Paint⇨Gap Options.

**TECHNICAL
STUFF**

Before you save a file for an older version of Illustrator that uses the Live Paint feature, first select the occurrences of Live Paint and choose Object⇨Expand. When the Expand dialog box appears, leave the options at their defaults and click OK. This setting breaks down the Live Paint objects to individual shapes, which older versions of Illustrator can understand.

# Chapter **9**

# Using the Transform and Distortion Tools

Y ou can apply transformations to objects in Illustrator that include scaling, rotating, skewing, and distorting. In this chapter, you discover how to use the general transform tools as well as some of the interesting liquify and envelope distort features available in Illustrator.

## Working with Transformations

Using just the Selection tool, you can scale and rotate a selected object. Drag the bounding box handles to resize the object, shown in Figure 9-1, or move outside a handle and then, when the cursor changes to a flippy arrow (a curved arrow with arrowheads on both ends), drag to rotate the object.

**TIP**

If you want to scale proportionally, hold down the Shift key while you drag to resize. To rotate an object at 45-degree increments, hold down the Shift key while you're rotating.

**FIGURE 9-1:**
Use the bounding
box to resize
or rotate a
selected object.

When you use the bounding box to rotate a selection, the bounding box rotates with the object, but its handles show the object's original orientation, as shown in Figure 9-2. The orientation can help you keep track of the original placement but can also interfere when you're building additional artwork. To reset the bounding box so that it's straight at the new orientation, choose Object⇨Transform⇨Reset Bounding Box.

**FIGURE 9-2:**
The bounding
box in its original
position and after
it has been reset.

**TECHNICAL STUFF**

When you scale, rotate, or use any other type of transformation in Illustrator, the final location becomes the *zero point*. In other applications, such as InDesign, you can rotate an object by any number of degrees (45 degrees, for example) and later enter **0** for the rotation angle in the Transform panel or in the Rotate dialog box to return the object to its original position. In Illustrator, if you enter **0** for the rotation angle to return a rotated object to its original position, the object doesn't change its position. To return the object to the previous position in Illustrator, you have to enter the negative of the number you originally entered to rotate the object, so you would enter **−45** for the degree of rotation in this example.

# Transforming an object

The Rotate, Reflect, Scale, and Shear tools all use the same basic steps to perform transformations. Read on for those basic steps and then follow some individual examples of the most often used Transform tools. The following sections show five ways to transform an object: one for an arbitrary transformation and four others for exact transformations based on a numeric amount you enter.

## Arbitrary transformation method

Because this transformation method is arbitrary, you're eyeballing the transformation of an object — in other words, you don't have an exact percentage or angle in mind, and you want to freely transform the object until it looks right. Just follow these steps:

1. **Select an object and then choose a Transform tool (Rotate, Reflect, Scale, or Shear).**

2. **Click the artboard once.**

   Be careful where you click because the click determines the point of reference, or *axis point*, for the transformation. In Figure 9-3, the click put the axis point above the right ear. The image is rotated on the axis created at that point.

Point of reference

**FIGURE 9-3:**
The first mouse click creates the axis point.

3. **Drag in one smooth movement.**

   Just drag until you create the transformation you want.

**TIP**

Hold down the Alt (Windows) or Option (Mac) key when dragging to clone a newly transformed item while keeping the original object intact. This trick is especially helpful when you're using the Reflect tool.

## Exact transformation methods

In the methods in this section, you discover how to perform transformations using specific numeric information:

*Exact transformation method 1 — using the tool's dialog box:*

1. **Select an object and then choose the Rotate, Reflect, Scale, or Shear tool.**

2. **Double-click the Transform tool that you selected in the Tools panel.**

   A dialog box specific to your chosen tool appears, as shown in Figure 9-4. In this example, the Rotate tool was selected to open the Rotate dialog box.

**FIGURE 9-4:**
Double-click a Transform tool to open its dialog box.

3. **Type an angle, a scaled amount, or a percentage in the appropriate text field.**

   In Figure 9-4, **45 degrees** is entered.

4. **Select the Preview checkbox to see the effect of the transformation before you click OK; click the Copy button instead of OK to keep the original object intact and transform a copy.**

*Exact transformation method 2 — using the reference point:*

1. **Select an object and then choose the Rotate, Reflect, Scale, or Shear tool.**

2. **Alt-click (Windows) or Option-click (Mac) wherever you want to place the reference point.**

3. **In the Transform tool dialog box that appears, enter values and click OK or click the Copy button to apply the transformation.**

   This method is the best one to use if you need to rotate an object an exact amount on a defined axis.

*Exact transformation method 3 — using the Transform menu:*

1. **Select an object and then choose a transform option from the Object➪Transform menu.**

   The appropriate transform dialog box appears.

2. **Enter some values and click OK or the Copy button.**

*Exact transformation method 4 — using the Transform panel:*

1. **Select an object and choose Window➪Transform to access the Transform panel, shown in Figure 9-5.**

2. **Set your options.**

**FIGURE 9-5:**
Enter values on
the Transform
panel.

Though using the Transform panel is probably the easiest way to change values, it doesn't offer you the capability to specify an exact reference point or other options that apply to the individual Transform tools. Keep in mind that by using the square grid on the left side of the transform panel you can select a point of reference for your object. By using this grid, you can measure from the corners or center point of an object.

## Using the Transform tools

In the following sections, you discover how to use some of the most popular Transform tools to create transformations.

### The Reflect tool

Nothing in life is perfectly symmetrical, right? Maybe not, but objects not created symmetrically in Illustrator can look off-kilter. Using the Reflect tool, you can reflect an object to create an exact mirrored shape of it; just follow these steps:

1. **Open a new document in Illustrator and type some text or create an object.**

   If you want to reflect text, make sure that you use at least 60-point type so that you can easily see it.

2. **Select the Reflect tool (hidden under the Rotate tool) and click the object; if you're using text, click in the middle of the text baseline.**

   This step sets the reference point for the reflection.

3. **Alt+Shift+drag (Windows) or Option+Shift+drag (Mac) and release when the object or text is reflecting itself, as shown in Figure 9-6.**

   This step not only clones the reflected object or text, but also snaps it to 45-degree angles.

**FIGURE 9-6:**
The completed
reflection.

## The Scale tool

Using the Scale tool, you can scale an object proportionally or non-uniformly. Most people like to be scaled non-uniformly — maybe a little taller, a little thinner — but on with the topic. Follow these steps to see the Scale tool in action:

1. **Create a shape and give it no fill and a 5-point black stroke.**

   For this example, we created a circle. See Chapter 3 of this minibook if you need a reminder on how to do it.

2. **Select the shape and double-click the Scale tool.**

   The Scale dialog box appears.

3. **Type a number in the Scale text field (in the Uniform section) and click the Copy button.**

   We entered **125** in the Scale text field to increase the size of the object by 125 percent.

4. **Press Ctrl+D (Windows) or ⌘+D (Mac) to repeat the transformation as many times as you want.**

   Every time you press Ctrl+D (Windows) or ⌘+D (Mac), the shape is copied and sized by the percentage you entered in the Scale text field. This trick, especially handy with circles, creates an instant bull's-eye!

To experiment with the Scale tool, create different shapes in Step 1 and enter different values in Step 3. Remember that if you type **50%** in the Scale text field, the object is made smaller; surpass 100 percent — say, to 150 percent — to make the object larger. Leaving the Scale text field at 100 percent has no effect on the object.

## The Shear tool

The Shear tool lets you shear an object by selecting an axis and dragging to set a shear angle, as shown in Figure 9-7.

**FIGURE 9-7:**
Create
perspective with
the Shear tool.

The axis is always the center of the object unless you use method 1 or 2 from the earlier section "Exact transformation methods." Use the Shear tool in combination with the Rotate tool to give an object perspective.

## The Reshape tool

The Reshape tool lets you select anchor points and sections of paths and adjust them in one direction. You determine that direction by dragging an anchor point with the Reshape tool selected.

The Reshape tool works differently from the other Transform tools. To use it, follow these steps:

1. **Select just the anchor points on the paths that you want to reshape. Deselect any points that you want to remain in place.**

2. **Select the Reshape tool (hidden under the Scale tool) and position the cursor over the anchor point you want to modify; click the anchor point.**

   If you click a path segment, a highlighted anchor point with a square around it is added to the path.

3. **Shift-click more anchor points or path segments to act as selection points.**

   You can highlight an unlimited number of anchor points or path segments.

4. **Drag the highlighted anchor points to adjust the path.**

### The Free Transform tool

 You use the Free Transform tool in much the same way as you use the bounding box. (See the earlier section "Working with Transformations.") This tool is necessary only if you choose View⇨Hide Bounding Box but want free transform capabilities.

# Creating Distortions

You can bend objects — make them wavy, gooey, or spiky — by creating simple to complex distortions with the Liquify tools and the Envelope Distort features.

## The Liquify tools

The Liquify tools can accomplish all sorts of creative or wacky (depending on how you look at it) distortions to your objects.

You can choose from eight Liquify tools. You should experiment with these tools to understand their full capabilities. Here are some tips:

» A variety of Liquify tools are available by holding down the mouse button on the default selection, the Width tool. (Table 9-1 shows the Width tool keyboard shortcuts.) If you use the tools frequently, drag to the arrow at the end of the tools. You can then position the tools anywhere in your work area.

» Double-click any Liquify tool to open a dialog box specific to the selected tool. The Liquify tools are shown in Table 9-2.

» When a Liquify tool is selected, the brush size appears. Adjust the diameter and shape of the Liquify tool by holding down the Alt (Windows) or Option (Mac) key while dragging the brush shape smaller or larger. Press the Shift key to constrain the shape to a circle.

 Using the Width tool, cross over a selected path. When a hollow square appears, click and drag outward (or inward), and the stroke width at that location is adjusted. See Figure 9-8.

If you want a little more accuracy, you can double-click the stroke by using the Width tool and create, modify, or delete the width point by using the Width Point Edit dialog box, shown in Figure 9-9.

**FIGURE 9-8:**
Use the
Width tool.

**FIGURE 9-9:**
Customize the
Width tool in this
dialog box.

**TIP**

To create a discontinuous width point, just create two width points on a stroke with different stroke widths and then drag one width point on to the other width point to create a discontinuous width point for the stroke.

**TABLE 9-1**

## Width Tool Keyboard Shortcuts

| Width Tool Function | Windows | Mac OS |
|---|---|---|
| Create non-uniform widths | Alt-drag | Opt-drag |
| Create a copy of the width point | Alt-drag the width point | Opt-drag the width point |
| Copy and move all the points along the path | Alt+Shift+drag | Opt+Shift+drag |
| Change the position of multiple width points | Shift-drag | Shift-drag |
| Select multiple width points | Shift-click | Shift-click |
| Delete selected width points | Delete | Delete |
| Deselect a width point | Esc | Esc |

Using the Transform
and Distortion Tools

CHAPTER 9  **Using the Transform and Distortion Tools**     **505**

**TABLE 9-2**

## The Liquify Tools

| Icon | Tool Name | What It Does to an Object |
|------|-----------|---------------------------|
| | Width | Increases the stroke width or height when you click and drag a path. |
| | Warp | Molds it with the movement of the cursor. (Pretend that you're pushing through dough with this tool.) |
| | Twirl | Creates swirling distortions within it. |
| | Pucker | Deflates it. |
| | Bloat | Inflates it. |
| | Scallop | Adds curved details to its outline. (Think of a seashell with scalloped edges.) |
| | Crystallize | Adds many spiked details to the outline of an object, such as crystals on a rock. |
| | Wrinkle | Adds wrinklelike details to the outline of an object. |

# Using the Envelope Distort command

Use the Envelope Distort command to arch text and apply other creative distortions to an Illustrator object. To use the Envelope Distort command, you can use a preset warp (the easiest method), a grid, or a top object to determine the amount and type of distortion. In this section, we discuss all three methods.

## Using the preset warps

Experimenting with warp presets is a little more interesting if you have a word or an object selected before trying out the warp options. To warp an object or some text to a preset style, follow these steps:

1. **Select the text or object that you want to distort and then choose Object⇨Envelope Distort⇨Make with Warp.**

   The Warp Options dialog box appears.

2. Select a warp style from the Style drop-down list and then specify any other options you want.

3. Click OK to apply the distortion.

TIP

If you want to experiment with warping but also want to revert to the original at any time, choose Effect⇨Warp. You later change or delete the warp effect by double-clicking it in the Appearance panel or by dragging the effect to the trash can in the Appearance panel. Find out more in Chapters 10 and 11 of this minibook about exciting effects you can apply to objects.

## Reshaping with a mesh grid

You can assign a grid to an object so that you can drag different points and create your own, custom distortion, as shown in Figure 9-10.

FIGURE 9-10:
Custom
distortion using
a mesh grid.

Follow these steps to apply a mesh grid:

1. Using the Selection tool, select the text or object that you want to distort and then choose Object⇨Envelope Distort⇨Make with Mesh.

   The Envelope Mesh dialog box appears.

2. Specify the number of rows and columns you want the mesh to contain and then click OK.

3. Drag any anchor point on the mesh grid with the Direct Selection tool to reshape the object.

TIP

To delete anchor points on the mesh grid, select an anchor point by using the Direct Selection tool and press the Delete key.

You can also use the Mesh tool to edit and delete points when using a mesh grid on objects.

## Reshaping an object with a different object

To form letters into the shape of an oval or to distort selected objects into another object, use this technique:

1. **Create text that you want to distort.**

2. **Create the object you want to use as the *envelope* (the object to be used to define the distortion).**

3. **Choose Object⇨Arrange to ensure that the envelope object is on top, as shown in Figure 9-11.**

**FIGURE 9-11:**
Position the
shape over
the text.

4. **Select the text and Shift-click to select the envelope object.**

5. **Choose Object⇨Envelope Distort⇨Make with Top Object.**

The underlying object is distorted to fit the shape of the top (envelope) object.

TIP

Choose Effect⇨Distort and Transform⇨Free Distort to take advantage of the Free Distort dialog box, shown in Figure 9-12. You can edit or undo effects at any time by clicking or deleting the Free Distort effect from the Appearance menu.

**FIGURE 9-12:**
Distort an
object from the
Free Distort
dialog box.

Chapter **10**

# Working with Transparency and Special Effects Tools

This chapter is full of neat things you can do using some of the more advanced features in Adobe Illustrator. These special effects tools can help you create art that makes an impact: Discover how to make your art look like a painting with the Gradient Mesh tool, create morphlike blends with the Blend tool, become a graffiti artist by trying out the Symbol Sprayer tool, and see what's underneath objects by using transparency.

## The Mesh Tool

If you're creating art in Illustrator that requires solid colors or continuous patterns, you can achieve those results quite easily. But if you're working on an element that requires continuous tones, such as a person's face, you turn to the handy Mesh tool to create smooth tonal variations in your illustration. Choose to blend one color into another and then use the Mesh tool to adjust your blend. You can also apply varying levels of transparency to these mesh points.

The Mesh tool can be as complex or simple as you want. Using the Mesh tool, you can create intense illustrations that look like they were painted with an airbrush or just use the tool to give dimension to an object, as in the illustration shown in Figure 10-1.

**FIGURE 10-1:**
Mesh tool
illustrations can
be complex or
simple.

In this chapter, you discover two ways to create gradient meshes in Illustrator, manually and automatically. By manually selecting where you want mesh points, you gain more freedom. By automatically defining rows and columns, you can be more precise in the placement of your mesh points.

To create a gradient mesh by clicking, follow these steps:

1. **Create any shape by using the shape tools. Make sure the shape has a solid color; any color will do.**

2. **Deselect all objects by choosing Select⇨Deselect.**

3. **Select a fill color that you want to apply as a mesh point to an object.**

   For example, if you want to add a shaded white spot to a red circle, choose white for the fill color.

4. **Select the Mesh tool (the keyboard shortcut is U) and click anywhere in a filled vector object.**

   The object is converted to a mesh object.

5. **Click the object as many times as you want to add more mesh points.**

To create a gradient mesh by setting the number of rows and columns, follow these steps:

1. **Select an object.**

2. **Choose Object⇨Create Gradient Mesh.**

   The Create Gradient Mesh dialog box appears.

3. **Set the number of rows and columns of mesh lines to create on the object by entering numbers in the Rows and Columns text fields.**

4. **Choose the direction of the highlight from the Appearance drop-down list.**

   The direction of the highlight determines which way the gradient flows (see Figure 10-2); you have these choices:

   - *Flat:* Applies the object's original color evenly across the surface, resulting in no highlight

   - *To Center:* Creates a highlight in the center of the object

   - *To Edge:* Creates a highlight on the edges of the object

**FIGURE 10-2:**
Choose a
highlight
direction.

5. **Enter a percentage of white highlight to apply to the mesh object in the Highlight text field.**

6. **Click OK to apply the gradient mesh to the object.**

Working with
Transparency . . .

You can select individual or multiple mesh points and apply varying levels of transparency to them. Follow these steps to apply transparency to a gradient mesh:

1. **Select a shape tool and click and drag to the artboard to add the shape to your document.**

2. **Give the shape a solid fill (any color) and no stroke.**

3. **Choose the Mesh tool and click anywhere in the object.**

   This step adds a mesh point to your object.

4. **Choose Window⇨Transparency and select a percent from the Opacity drop-down list or type in any other value you want in the Opacity text field.**

   As you can see in Figure 10-3, an illustration was sent behind the object to demonstrate transparency in the object.

**FIGURE 10-3:**
The transparency of these mesh points varies.

**TIP**

You can change the color in mesh points by choosing the Direct Selection tool and then either clicking a mesh point and picking a fill color or clicking in the center of a mesh area and choosing a fill. Whether you select the mesh point (see the left side of Figure 10-4) or the area between the mesh points (see the right side of Figure 10-4), it changes the painting result. To add a mesh point without changing to the current fill color, Shift-click anywhere in a filled vector object.

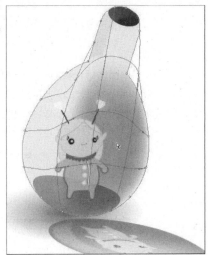

**FIGURE 10-4:**
The mesh point changes the painting result.

# The Blend Tool

 Use the Blend tool (located in the main Illustrator Tools panel) to transform one object to another to create interesting morphed artwork or to create shaded objects. Using the Blend tool, you can give illustrations a rendered look by blending from one color to another or create an even number of shapes from one point to another. Figure 10-5 shows examples of what you can do with this tool.

**FIGURE 10-5:**
Some objects using the Blend tool.

## Creating a blend

Creating a blend isn't difficult, and as you get used to it you can take the process even further, to create incredibly realistic effects. Follow these steps to create a simple blend from one rectangle size to another, creating an algorithmic stripe pattern (a rectangle of one height blended to a rectangle of another height):

1. **Create a rectangle.**

   Size doesn't matter in this example; just be sure that you can see a difference in shapes when you blend. This example uses a rectangle that measures roughly 4 x 1 inches.

2. **Give your shape a fill and assign None to the stroke.**

   You can use other settings, but we recommend keeping it simple if you're new to working with blends.

3. **Using the Selection tool, click the rectangle and Alt-drag (Windows) or Option-drag (Mac) toward the bottom of the artboard to clone your shape; press the Shift key before you release the mouse button to make sure that the cloned shape stays perfectly aligned with the original shape.**

4. **Reduce the cloned shape to about half its original height by using the Transform panel.**

   If the Transform panel isn't visible, choose Window⊃Transform.

   Alternatively, you can hold down the Shift key and drag the lower-middle bounding box handle, shown in Figure 10-6.

**FIGURE 10-6:** Reduce the size of the cloned shape.

5. **In the Swatches panel (choose Window⊃Swatches), change the cloned shape's fill to a different color but keep the stroke set to None.**

   Changing the color just helps you see the blend effect a little better.

6. **Using the Blend tool, click the original shape and then click the cloned shape.**

   As a default action, the Blend tool creates a smooth blend that transitions from one color to another, as shown in Figure 10-7. To change the blend effect, experiment with the Blend Options dialog box.

**FIGURE 10-7:**
Creating a
smooth transition
between
rectangles.

# Setting Blend options

You can change the way a blend appears by using the Blend Options dialog box: Choose Object⇨Blend⇨Blend Options. From the Spacing drop-down list, change the blend to one of these options:

» **Smooth Color:** Blend steps are calculated to provide the optimum number of steps for a smooth transition.

» **Specified Steps:** Determine the number of steps in a blend by typing a number in the text field to the right of the drop-down list.

» **Specified Distance:** Control the distance between steps in the blend by typing a number in the text field to the right of the drop-down list.

You can also choose between two orientation options:

» **Align to Page:** Orients the blend perpendicular to the x-axis of the page.

» **Align to Path:** Orients the blend perpendicular to the path. You probably won't see a difference when changing orientation unless you've edited the blend path.

**TIP**

You can easily access the Blend tool options by selecting a blended object and double-clicking the Blend tool in the Tools panel.

If you're feeling adventurous, try changing a smooth blend (such as the one you create in the preceding step list) into a logarithmic blend. In the Blend Options dialog box, select Specified Steps from the Spacing drop-down list and change the value to **5**. This change creates the blend in 5 steps rather than in the more than 200 steps that may have been necessary to create the smooth blend.

Here are a few more tips to help you become more comfortable using blends. You can

» Blend between an unlimited number of objects, colors, opacities, or gradients.

» Edit blends directly with tools, such as Selection, Rotate, or Scale.

>> Switch to the Direct Selection tool and edit the blend path by dragging anchor points. A straight path is created between blended objects when the blend is first applied.

>> Edit blends that you created by moving, resizing, deleting, or adding objects. After you make editing changes, the artwork is blended again automatically.

# The Symbol Sprayer Tool

The super Symbol Sprayer tool is one you must experiment with in order to understand its full potential. In a nutshell, it works like a can of spray paint that sprays, rather than paints, *symbols* — objects that, in Illustrator, can be either vector- or pixel-based. Each symbol is an *instance*.

## Exploring the symbol tools

Illustrator comes with a library of symbols ready for use in the symbols panel. (If the symbols panel isn't visible, choose Window⟶Symbols.) Use this panel as a storage bin or library to save repeatedly used artwork or to create your own symbols to apply as instances in your artwork, like blades of grass or stars in the sky. You can then use the symbolism tools, described in Table 10-1, to adjust and change the appearance of the symbol instances.

**TABLE 10-1**

### The Symbol Tools

| Icon | Tool Name | What You Can Do with It |
|------|-----------|------------------------|
|      | Symbol Sprayer | Create a set of symbol instances. |
|      | Symbol Shifter | Move symbol instances around; can also change the relative paint order of symbol instances. |
|      | Symbol Scruncher | Pull apart, or put together, symbol instances. |
|      | Symbol Sizer | Increase or decrease the size of symbol instances. |
|      | Symbol Spinner | Orient the symbol instances in a set. Symbol instances located near the cursor spin in the direction you move the cursor. |

| Icon | Tool Name | What You Can Do with It |
|---|---|---|
| | Symbol Stainer | Colorize symbol instances. |
| | Symbol Screener | Increase or decrease the transparency of the symbol instances in a set. |
| | Symbol Styler | Apply or remove a graphic style from a symbol instance. |

**TIP**

Press the Alt (Windows) or Option (Mac) key to reduce the effect of the symbolism tools. In other words, if you're using the Symbol Sizer tool, you click and hold to make the symbol instances larger; hold down the Alt (Windows) or Option (Mac) key to make the symbol instances smaller.

You can also selectively choose the symbols you want to affect with the Symbolism tools by activating them in the Symbols panel. Ctrl-click (Windows) or ⌘-click (Mac) multiple symbols to change them at the same time.

**TECHNICAL STUFF**

Just about anything can be a symbol, including placed objects and objects with patterns and gradients. If you're going to use placed images as symbols, however, choose File⇨Place and deselect the Link checkbox in the Place dialog box.

## Creating and spraying symbols on the artboard

To create a symbol, select the object and drag it to the Symbols panel or click the New Symbol button at the bottom of the Symbols panel. Yes, it's that easy. Then use the Symbol Sprayer tool to apply the symbol instance on the artboard by following these steps:

1. **Select the symbol instance in the Symbols panel.**

   Either create your own symbol or use one of the default symbols supplied in the panel.

2. **Drag with the Symbol Sprayer tool, spraying the symbol on the artboard. (See Figure 10-8.)**

   That's it. You can increase or reduce the area affected by the Symbol Sprayer tool by pressing the bracket keys. Press ] repeatedly to enlarge the application area for the symbol or press [ to make it smaller.

**FIGURE 10-8:**
Using the Symbol
Sprayer tool to
create fish.

Note that you can access all sorts of symbol libraries from the Symbols panel menu. Find 3D, nature, map, flower, and even hair and fur symbol collections by selecting Open Symbol Library.

**TIP**

If you want to store artwork that you frequently need to access, simply drag selected objects to the Symbols panel or Alt-click (Windows) or Option-click (Mac) the New Symbol button to name and store the artwork. Retrieve the artwork later by dragging it from the Symbols panel to the artboard. In fact, you can drag any symbol out to your artboard to change or use it in your own artwork. To release the symbol back into its original art elements, choose Object➪Expand. In the Expand dialog box, click OK to restore the defaults.

# Transparency

Using transparency can add a new level to your illustrations. The transparency feature does exactly what its name implies — changes an object to make it transparent so that what's underneath that object is visible to varying degrees. You can use the Transparency panel for simple applications of transparency to show through to underlying objects or for more complex artwork using *opacity masks,* which can control the visibility of selected objects.

Choosing Window➪Transparency opens the Transparency panel, where you can apply different levels of transparency to objects. To do so, create an arrangement of objects that intersect, select the topmost object, and then change the transparency level of the object in the Transparency panel, by either selecting a percentage from the Opacity drop-down list or entering a value of less than 100 in the Opacity text field.

# Blend modes

A *blending mode* determines how the resulting transparency will look. To achieve different blending effects, choose different blend modes from the Blend Mode drop-down list in the Transparency panel.

**TIP**

Truly, the best way to find out what all these modes do is to create two overlapping shapes and start experimenting. Give the shapes differently colored fills (but note that many blending modes don't work with black-and-white fills). Then select the topmost object and change the opacity to anything other than 0% or 100% and change the blending mode by selecting an option from the Blend Mode drop-down list in the Transparency panel. You see all sorts of neat effects and might even pick a few favorites.

We define each blend mode in the following list, but we'll say it again: The best way to see what each mode does is to apply it — so start experimenting.

>> **Normal:** Creates no interaction with underlying colors.

>> **Darken:** Replaces only the areas that are lighter than the blend color. Areas darker than the blend color don't change.

>> **Multiply:** Creates an effect similar to drawing on the page with magic markers, or like the colored film you see on theater lights.

>> **Color Burn:** Darkens the base color to reflect the blend color. If you're using white, no change occurs.

>> **Lighten:** Replaces only the areas that are darker than the blend color. Areas lighter than the blend color don't change.

>> **Screen:** Multiplies the inverse of the underlying colors. The resulting color is always a lighter color.

>> **Color Dodge:** Brightens the underlying color to reflect the blend color. If you're using black, there's no change.

>> **Overlay:** Multiplies or screens the colors, depending on the base color.

>> **Soft Light:** Darkens or lightens colors, depending on the blend color. The effect is similar to shining a diffused spotlight on the artwork.

>> **Hard Light:** Multiplies or screens colors, depending on the blend color. The effect is similar to shining a harsh spotlight on the artwork.

>> **Difference:** Subtracts either the blend color from the base color or the base color from the blend color, depending on which has the greater brightness value. The effect is similar to a color negative.

» **Exclusion:** Creates an effect similar to, but with less contrast than, Difference mode.

» **Hue:** Applies the *hue* (color) of the blend object to underlying objects but keeps the underlying shading, or luminosity.

» **Saturation:** Applies the saturation of the blend color but uses the luminance and hue of the base color.

» **Color:** Applies the blend object's color to the underlying objects but preserves the gray levels in the artwork; works well for tinting objects or changing their colors.

» **Luminosity:** Creates a resulting color with the hue and saturation of the base color and the luminance of the blend color. This mode is essentially the opposite of Color mode.

## Opacity masks

Just like in Photoshop, you can use masks to make more interesting artwork in Illustrator. You can create an opacity mask from the topmost object in a selection or by drawing a mask on a single object. The mask uses the grayscale of the selected object as its opacity mask. Black areas are transparent; shades of gray are semitransparent, depending on the amount of gray; white areas are opaque. Figure 10-9 shows the effect of using an opacity mask.

**FIGURE 10-9:**
An opacity mask converts the topmost object into a mask that then masks out the underlying objects.

To create an opacity mask, follow these steps:

1. **Open the Transparency panel menu.**

2. **Make sure that the Blend Mode drop-down list is set to Normal.**

3. **Create a shape anywhere on the artboard or open a document that has artwork on it.**

We're using a circle, but the shape doesn't matter. Make sure that the artwork has a fill. A solid color helps you see the effect.

4. **Open the Symbols panel (choose Window⇨Symbols Panel) and drag a symbol to the artboard.**

In this example, we're using the drums symbol.

5. **Using the Selection tool, enlarge your symbol so that it fills the shape.**

See the image on the left in Figure 10-10.

**FIGURE 10-10:**
Creating an
opacity mask.

6. **Select both the symbol and the shape and then click the Make Mask button.**

See the image on the right in Figure 10-10.

The symbol turns into a mask, showing varying levels of the underlying box of the newly created mask, depending on the original color value. Click on the Clip and Invert Mask checkboxes to see how your artwork is affected. To delete an opacity mask, click the Release button.

Click the right thumbnail (which represents the mask) in the Transparency panel, and a black border appears around it, indicating that it's active. You can move the items on the mask or even create items to be added to the mask. The mask works just like the regular artboard, except that anything done on the mask side is used only as an opacity mask. To work on the regular artboard, click the left thumbnail.

Chapter **11**

# Using Filters and Effects

Effects give you the opportunity to make jazzy changes to your Illustrator objects, such as add drop shadows and zigzagged artwork. You can even use Photoshop filters directly in Illustrator. In this chapter, you find out how to apply, save, and edit effects; you also take a quick tour of the Appearance panel (your trusty sidekick when performing these tasks).

## Working with Effects

Adobe Illustrator offers many artistic and creative effects that you can use to add blurs, drop shadows, inner glows, and more. Effects are connected dynamically to the objects they are applied to. You can add, change, and remove effects at any time from the Appearance panel. (Choose Window➪Appearance.)

### Understanding the Appearance panel

Using the Appearance panel you can apply multiple effects to one object and even copy them to other objects. If it isn't visible, choose Window➪Appearance to open the Appearance panel, as shown in Figure 11-1, alongside an object with several effects applied to it.

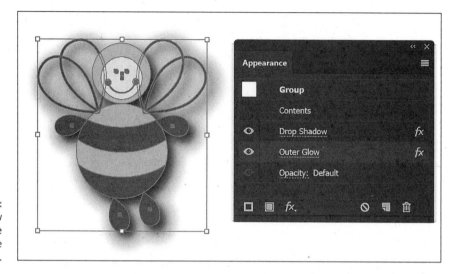

**FIGURE 11-1:**
Discover how
useful the
Appearance
panel can be.

If you have no effects applied, you see as a default only a fill and a stroke listed in the Appearance panel. As you create effects, they're added to this list. You can add more strokes and fills to the list; you find out why that capability is so useful in the following sections.

## Applying an effect

In this section, you see how to apply an effect. You can choose from many effects, and they're all applied in much the same manner. In this example, you create an interesting effect for a border.

Create a new document using any of the default profiles, and then follow these steps to apply an effect:

1. **Make sure that your Appearance panel is visible. Choose Window⇨Appearance and click and drag the panel out of the dock area so that it doesn't collapse while you're working.**

2. **Select the Rectangle tool and click and drag a rectangle out on the artboard.**

   Any size rectangle is fine for this example.

3. **Using Stroke in the Control panel, change the stroke to 3 pt.**

4. **Using Stroke Color in the Control panel, assign any color except the default color of black.**

5. **Notice in the Appearance panel, shown in Figure 11-2, that you can select the Stroke and the Fill. By selecting one or the other, you can apply an effect to just the stroke or the fill. In this example, select Stroke.**

**FIGURE 11-2:**
You can change the stroke and fill attributes right in the Appearance panel.

6. **Choose Effect⇨Distort and Transform⇨Zig Zag.**

Choose the settings that work well to make your straight border appear as a zigzag. In Figure 11-3, we selected Smooth to round out the points of the zigzag effect and changed the Ridges per segment to 15.

**FIGURE 11-3:**
Convert a straight path into a zigzag using the Zig Zag effect.

**REMEMBER**

Effects are linked dynamically to the object they're applied to. They can be scaled, modified, and even deleted with no harm done to the original object.

# Adding a Drop Shadow effect

Creating a drop shadow is a quick and easy way to add dimension and a bit of sophistication to your artwork. The interaction between the object with the drop shadow and the underlying objects can create an interesting look. To add the Drop Shadow effect to an illustration, follow these steps:

1. **Select the object (or objects) to apply the drop shadow to.**

   If you like, you can continue using the rectangle you worked with in the preceding section.

2. **In the Appearance panel, make sure that Stroke is selected.**

3. **Choose Effect⇨Stylize⇨Drop Shadow.**

4. **In the Drop Shadow dialog box that appears, as shown in Figure 11-4, select the Preview checkbox in the lower-left corner.**

   You now see the drop shadow applied as you make changes.

**FIGURE 11-4:**
The Drop Shadow dialog box gives the effect's options and preview.

5. **Choose from the following options in the dialog box:**

   • *Mode:* Select a blending mode from this drop-down list to choose how you want the selected object to interact with the objects underneath it. The default is Multiply, which works well — the effect is similar to coloring with a magic marker.

   • *Opacity:* Enter a value or use the drop-down list to determine how opaque or transparent the drop shadow should be. If it's too strong, choose a lower amount.

- *Offset:* Enter a value to determine how close the shadow is to the object. If you're working with text or small artwork, smaller values (and shorter shadows) look best. Otherwise, the drop shadow may look like one big, indefinable glob.

  The X Offset shifts the shadow from left to right, and the Y Offset shifts it up or down. You can enter negative or positive numbers.

- *Blur:* Use Blur to control how fuzzy the edges of the shadow are. A lower value makes the edge of the shadow more defined.

- *Color and Darkness:* Select the Color radio button to choose a custom color for the drop shadow. Select the Darkness radio button to add more black to the drop shadow. Zero percent is the lowest amount of black, and 100 percent is the highest.

  As a default, the color of the shadow is based on the color of your object, sort of — the Darkness option also has a play in this task. As a default, the shadow is made up of the color in the object if it's solid. Multicolored objects have a gray shadow.

6. **When you're finished, click OK to close the dialog box.**

   Take a look at the Appearance panel, as shown in Figure 11-5, to see that the two Effects that you applied are displayed. Notice that you can turn off and on the visibility of the effect by selecting the Click to Toggle Visibility icon to the left of the effect, and even edit the effect by double-clicking on the effect in the Appearance panel.

**FIGURE 11-5:**
You can toggle the visibility and edit the effects right from the Appearance panel.

7. **Save your combination of effects as a Graphic Style.**

   Choose Window⇨Graphic Styles, and while you have your rectangle selected, choose New Graphic Style from the Panel menu.

8. **Name the Style and press OK.**

9. **Now make another rectangle, any size, and click the thumbnail of graphic style that you just saved in the Graphic Styles panel.**

   All the saved attributes are applied to this new shape.

You find out more about Graphic Styles in the next section.

# Saving Graphic Styles

A *graphic style* is a combination of all settings you choose for a particular filter or effect in the Appearance panel. By saving this information in a graphic style, you store these attributes so that you can quickly and easily apply them to other objects later. If you have already created an object with effects in a previous section, you will have the opportunity to save those effects as a graphic style later in this section.

To apply a saved graphic style, follow these steps:

1. **If the Graphic Styles panel is not visible, choose Window⇨Graphic Styles.**

   The Graphic Styles panel appears. Unless you have added your own style, only some default styles appear in this panel.

2. **Click on the Library icon in the lower left of the Graphic Styles panel and select the Graphic Style library named Vonster Pattern Styles, as shown in Figure 11-6.**

   A second window appears. It's named Vonster Pattern Styles.

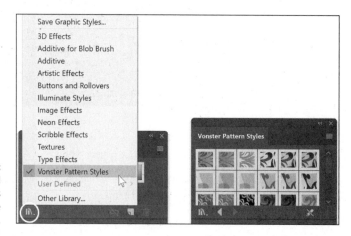

**FIGURE 11-6:** Access additional graphic styles by selecting the Library icon.

3. **Create a new shape, such as a simple rectangle or an ellipse, and click any graphic style in the Vonster Pattern Styles panel to apply it to an active object.**

   Look at the Appearance panel while you click different styles to see that you're applying combinations of attributes, including effects, fills, and strokes. (See Figure 11-7.)

**FIGURE 11-7:** The Graphic Styles panel stores effects and other attributes.

You can store attributes as a graphic style in several ways; we show you two easy methods. If you already applied a combination of attributes to an object, such as the rectangle border that you may have created in the previous section, you can store them by completing one of these tasks:

» With the object selected, Alt-click (Windows) or Option-click (Mac) the New Graphic Style button at the bottom of the Graphic Styles panel. Alt-click (Windows) or Option-click (Mac) allows you to name the style when it's added.

» Drag the selected object directly into the Graphic Styles panel. The panel stores its attributes, but you have to double-click the new style to name it.

After you store a graphic style, simply select the object you want to apply the style to and then click the saved style in the Graphic Styles panel.

You can try this by creating another rectangle and then clicking your saved graphic style in the Graphic Styles panel.

# Creating 3D Artwork

All Illustrator effects are excellent, but the 3D feature is even better because you can not only add dimension by using the 3D effect, but you can also *map artwork* (wrap artwork around a 3D object) and apply lighting to the 3D object. You can then design a label for a jelly jar, for example, and adhere it to the jar to show a client.

Here are the three choices for the 3D effect:

>> **Extrude & Bevel:** Uses the z-axis to extrude an object. For example, a square becomes a cube.

>> **Revolve:** Uses the z-axis and revolves a shape around it. You can use this option to change an arc into a ball.

>> **Rotate:** Rotates a 3D object created using the Extrude & Bevel or Revolve effect or rotates a 2D object in 3D space. You can also adjust the perspective of a 3D or 2D object.

To apply a 3D effect, you need to create an object appropriate for the 3D effect. The Extrude & Bevel feature works well with shapes and text. If you want to edit an object that already has a 3D effect applied to it, double-click the 3D effect in the Appearance panel.

To apply a 3D effect, follow these steps:

1. **Select the object you want to apply the 3D effect to.**

2. **Choose Effect↷3D↷Extrude & Bevel.**

   Options for your chosen 3D effect appear. To see the 3D Extrude & Bevel Options dialog box, see Figure 11-8.

3. **Select the Preview checkbox so that you can see results as you experiment with these settings.**

4. **Click the Preview pane (which shows a cube in Figure 11-8) and drag to rotate the object in space.**

   It makes selecting the proper angle (or *positioning the object in space)* fun to do, or you can choose the angle from the Position drop-down list above the preview.

WARNING

   Never use the Rotate tool to rotate a 3D object, unless you want some funky results; use the Preview pane in the 3D Extrude & Bevel Options dialog box instead.

5. **(Optional) Use the Perspective drop-down list to add perspective to your object.**

6. **In the Extrude & Bevel section of the dialog box, select a depth for your object and a cap.**

   The cap determines whether your shape has a solid cap on it or is hollow, as shown in Figure 11-9.

**FIGURE 11-8:**
The Extrude &
Bevel Options
dialog box.

**FIGURE 11-9:**
Cap on (left), cap
off (right).

**7.** **Select a bevel (edge shape) from the Bevel drop-down list and set the height using the Height drop-down list.**

You have two choices to apply the bevel:

- *Bevel Extent Out:* The bevel is added to the object.

- *Bevel Extent In:* The bevel is subtracted from the object.

**8.** **Select a rendering style from the Surface drop-down list or click the More Options button for in-depth lighting options, such as changing the direction or adding lighting.**

**9.** **Click the Map Art button.**

The Map Art dialog box opens, as shown in Figure 11-10. Use this dialog box to apply artwork to a 3D object.

**10.** **Using the Surface arrow buttons, select the surface you want the artwork applied to and then select a symbol from the Symbol drop-down list.**

The result is shown on the left in Figure 11-10.

**11.** **Click OK to close the dialog box.**

**FIGURE 11-10:**
In the Map Art
dialog box, you
can select a
surface and apply
a symbol to it.

**REMEMBER**

Keep these points in mind when mapping artwork:

>> An object must be a symbol to be used as mapped artwork. You simply need to select and drag to the Symbols panel the artwork you want mapped. By doing so, you make it a selectable item in the Map Art dialog box.

>> The light gray areas in the Preview pane are the visible areas based on the object's present position. Drag and scale the artwork in this pane to place the artwork where you want it.

>> Shaded artwork (enabled by selecting the Shaded Artwork checkbox at the bottom of the Map Art dialog box) looks good but can take a long time to render.

*Note:* All 3D effects are rendered at 72 dpi (dots per inch; low resolution) so as not to slow down the processing speed. You can determine the resolution by either choosing Effect⇨Document Raster Effects Settings or saving or exporting the file. You can also select the object and choose Object⇨Rasterize. After you rasterize the object, you can no longer use it as an Illustrator 3D object, so save the original!

# Adding Multiple Fills and Strokes

Using the panel menu in the Appearance panel, you can add more fills and strokes. You can use this feature to put differently colored fills on top of each other and individually apply effects to each one, creating truly interesting and creative results.

Just for fun, follow along to see what you can do to a single object from the Appearance panel:

**1.** **Create a star shape.**

Neither the size of the shape nor its number of points matters — just make the shape large enough to work with.

**2.** **Use the Swatches panel (choose Window⇨Swatches) to fill the shape with yellow and give it a black stroke.**

**3.** **Choose Window⇨Stroke to use the stroke panel to make the stroke 1 point; alternatively, select 1 from the Stroke drop-down list in the Control panel.**

Notice that the present fill and stroke are listed in the Appearance panel. Even in its simplest form, the Appearance panel helps track basic attributes. You can easily take advantage of the tracking to apply effects to just a fill or a stroke.

**4.** **Click Stroke in the Appearance panel.**

If the Appearance panel isn't visible, choose Window⇨Appearance.

**5.** **Choose Effect⇨Path⇨Offset Path.**

**6.** **In the Offset Path dialog box that appears, enter –10 pt in the Offset text box and select the Preview checkbox, as you see in Figure 11-11.**

Notice that the stroke moves into the fill rather than on the edge.

**7.** **Change the offset to a number that works with your star shape and click OK.**

Depending on the size of your star, you may want to adjust the amount of offset up or down.

Using Filters and Effects

8. **From the panel menu of the Appearance panel, select Add New Fill to add a new fill to the star shape. Click the arrow to the right of the new fill color swatch to open the Swatches panel and change the new fill to a different color, as shown in Figure 11-12.**

   In this next part, you add another fill.

9. **Make sure the new Fill is selected in the Appearance panel (the top one) and choose Effect⇨Distort and Transform⇨Twist.**

10. **In the Twist dialog box that appears, type 45 in the Angle text field and select the Preview checkbox, as you see in Figure 11-13.**

    Notice how only the second fill is twisted.

11. **Click OK to close the Twist dialog box.**

12. **Select the top fill from the Appearance panel again.**

**REMEMBER**

    Always be sure to select the fill or stroke you want before doing anything meant to change just that specific fill or stroke.

13. **In the Transparency panel (choose Window⇨Transparency), select 50% from the Opacity drop-down list or simply type 50% in the Opacity text field.**

    Now you can see your original shape through the new fill.

14. **With the top fill still selected, change the color or choose a pattern in the Swatches panel for a truly different appearance.**

    Continue playing with combinations of fills and strokes for hours if you want. We hope that this process "clicks" and that you can take it further on your own.

**FIGURE 11-13:**
Choose to twist one of the fills.

# Using the Perspective Grid

You can create and edit artwork based on the perspective grid feature, shown in Figure 11-14. The grid is a huge help in creating successful perspective illustrations.

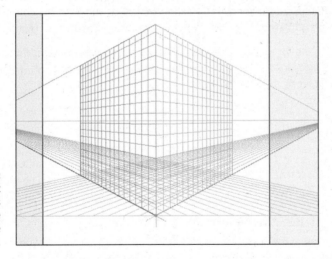

**FIGURE 11-14:**
Build and edit illustrations by using the Perspective Grid tool.

To show or hide the default perspective grid, press Ctrl+Shift+I (Windows) or ⌘+Shift+I (Mac).

To select which perspective plane you wish to work with, you can click on the plane that you wish to draw on in the circle that appears in the upper left, as shown in Figure 11-15.

**FIGURE 11-15:**
Click on a plane
to activate it
before adding a
shape.

 You can use the Perspective Grid tool on the toolbar to fine-tune the grid.

Here are some simple steps to help you start using the perspective grid:

1. **Create a new document and turn on the perspective grid by pressing Ctrl+Shift+I (Windows) or ⌘+Shift+I (Mac).**

2. **Select a shape tool, such as the Ellipse, and click and drag it to create the shape on the perspective grid.**

   Notice that the shape's perspective is controlled by the grid. Remember that you can use the circle in the upper left to change which plane you are drawing to.

3. **Select the Perspective Selection tool.**

   It's the hidden tool in the Perspective Grid tool.

4. **Using the Perspective Selection tool, click and drag the shape to see that it's adjusted in position and location using the perspective grid.**

   Figure 11-16 shows the result of dragging an ellipse with the Perspective Selection tool. You can resize and clone in perspective by Alt- or Option-dragging the selected object.

**FIGURE 11-16:**
Click and drag
to change the
perspective using
the Perspective
Selection tool.

Note that you can also select and drag the grid itself by using the Perspective Selection tool.

**5.** **Choose View⇨Perspective Grid, as shown in Figure 11-17, and then select the type of perspective to apply.**

In this step, you further customize your grid and choose other options to make your illustrations more precise.

IN THIS CHAPTER

» Saving Illustrator files

» Exporting files for use in other applications

» Preparing art for the web

» Flattening your transparency

» Printing in Illustrator

Chapter **12**

# Using Your Illustrator Images

S o you have beautiful artwork but aren't sure how to remove it from your screen. You could have a party and invite all interested clients to stand around your monitor and admire it or share or sell your artwork by posting it on the Internet or printing it.

In this chapter, you discover how to use your illustrations in a variety of work-flows, from using Illustrator files in page layout programs to exporting files for Photoshop (and other programs) and the web. This chapter helps you use your artwork effectively and understand the saving and flattening choices available in Adobe Illustrator.

## Saving and Exporting Illustrator Files

In this section, you discover how general choices differ in the Save As dialog box (choose File➪Save As) and describe their benefits.

When you choose File➪Save or File➪Save As, you save your file in one of these formats: Adobe Illustrator, EPS, PDF, AIT (Illustrator Template), SVG, or SVG Compressed. You read about all these formats throughout this chapter.

If you need a file format not listed in the regular Save As dialog box, choose File⇨Export As to see additional choices. Using the File Export command, you can choose to save your files in any format listed in Table 12-1.

**TABLE 12-1**

## Available File Formats

| File Format | Extension |
|---|---|
| AutoCAD Drawing | .dwg |
| AutoCAD Interchange File | .dxf |
| BMP | .bmp |
| CSS | .css |
| Enhanced Metafile | .emf |
| Flash | .swf |
| JPEG | .jpg |
| Macintosh PICT | .pct |
| Photoshop | .psd |
| PNG | .png |
| Targa | .tga |
| Text Format | .txt |
| TIFF | .tif |
| Windows Metafile | .wmf |

Many formats *rasterize* artwork, so they no longer maintain vector paths and the benefits of being vector. Scalability isn't unlimited, for example. If you think that you may want to edit your image again later, be sure to save a copy of the file and keep the original in the .ai format.

## The native Adobe Illustrator file format

If you're working with the programs in the Creative Cloud, the best way to save a file is as a native Illustrator .ai file. For instance, the .ai format works with Adobe applications such as Adobe InDesign for page layout, Adobe Dreamweaver for web page creation, Adobe Photoshop for photo retouching, and Adobe Acrobat for cross-platform documents.

Understanding when it's best to use the .ai format is important. Saving your illustration as an .ai file ensures that it's editable; it also ensures that any transparency is retained, even if you use the file in another application.

To save and use a file in native Illustrator format, follow these steps:

**1.** **Make an illustration with transparency (50 percent transparent, for example) in Adobe Illustrator and choose File⇨Save As.**

**2.** **Select Adobe Illustrator Document (.ai) from the Save As Type drop-down list, name the file, and click Save.**

**3.** **Leave the Illustrator Native options at their defaults and click OK.**

**TIP**

After you follow the preceding step list to prepare your Illustrator file, you can use the illustration in other Adobe applications:

» **Adobe Acrobat:** Open the Acrobat application and choose File⇨Open. Locate the .ai file. The native Illustrator file opens within the Acrobat application.

» **Adobe InDesign:** Choose File⇨Place. This method supports transparency created in Adobe Illustrator, as shown in Figure 12-1. (However, copying and pasting from Illustrator to InDesign does *not* support transparency.)

**FIGURE 12-1:** InDesign supports transparency, even over text.

» **Adobe Photoshop:** Choose File⇨Place. By placing an Illustrator file into Adobe Photoshop, you automatically create a Photoshop smart object. You can scale, rotate, and even apply effects to the Illustrator file and return to the original illustration at any time. Read more about smart objects in Photoshop in Book 3, Chapter 8.

If you want to take an Illustrator file into Photoshop for further editing, choose File⇨Export and select the Photoshop (.psd) format from the Save As Type drop-down list. Choose a resolution from the Options window. If you used layers, leave the Write Layers option selected.

In Photoshop, choose File➪Open, select the file you just saved in Illustrator in .psd format, and click Open. The file opens in Photoshop with its layers intact.

>> **Adobe Animate:** Use the integration features built in to Adobe Illustrator to cut and paste directly into Adobe Animate. If you choose Edit➪Copy from Adobe Illustrator, you can then switch to Adobe Animate and choose Edit➪Paste. The Paste dialog box appears.

You can also choose File➪Import in Animate for additional import choices. When a native Illustrator file is selected to import to the Stage, the Import to Stage dialog box appears (directly in Animate!) so that you can import only certain layers or sublayers and respond to warning messages about incompatible objects.

>> **Adobe Dreamweaver:** By choosing File➪Save for Web & Devices, you can choose to save your Illustrator document in .gif, .jpg, .png, .svg, .swf, or .wbmp format. You can then insert images in those file formats into Dreamweaver by choosing Insert➪Image in Adobe Dreamweaver.

Click the Image button in the Insert panel in Dreamweaver. When the Select Image Source dialog box appears, navigate to the location where you saved your optimized file. Select it and click OK. If your file is located out of the root folder for the site you're working on, an alert window appears, offering the opportunity to save the file with your other site assets.

## Saving Illustrator files back to previous versions

When saving an .ai or .eps file, you can choose File➪Save As, choose an Illustrator format, and then click OK.

When the Illustrator Options dialog box appears, choose a version from the Version drop-down list. Keep in mind that any features specific to newer versions of Illustrator aren't supported in older file formats, so make sure that you save a copy and keep the original file intact. Adobe helps you understand the risk of saving to older versions by putting a warning sign next to the Version drop-down list and showing you specific issues with the version you selected in the Warnings window.

## The EPS file format

Encapsulated PostScript File (EPS) is the file format that most text editing and page layout applications accept; EPS supports vector data and is completely scalable. Because the Illustrator .eps format is based on PostScript, you can reopen an EPS file and edit it in Illustrator at any time.

To save a file in Illustrator as an EPS, follow these steps:

1. **Choose File⇨Save As and select EPS from the Save As Type drop-down list.**

2. **From the Version drop-down list, select the Illustrator version you're saving to.**

3. **In the EPS Options dialog box that appears (shown in Figure 12-2), select the preview from the Format drop-down list:**

   - *8-Bit Color:* A color preview for either Mac or PC

   - *Black & White:* A low-resolution, black-and-white preview

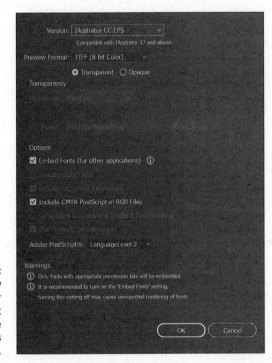

**FIGURE 12-2:**
Select a preview
and other
important
settings in the
EPS Options
dialog box.

4. **Select either the Transparent or Opaque radio button, depending on whether you want the non-image areas in your artwork to be transparent or opaque.**

5. **Specify your transparency settings.**

   These settings are grayed out if you haven't used transparency in the file. (See the "Flattening Transparency" section, later in this chapter, for more about this setting.)

6. **Leave the Embed Fonts (for other applications) checkbox selected to leave fonts you used embedded in the EPS file format.**

7. **In the Options section, leave the Include CMYK PostScript in RGB Files checkbox selected.**

   If you don't know which Adobe PostScript level you want to save to, leave it at the default.

8. **Click OK to save your file in EPS format.**

# The PDF file format

If you want to save your file in a format that supports more than a dozen platforms and requires only Acrobat Reader, available as a free download at www.adobe.com, choose to save your file as a PDF (Portable Document Format) file.

If you can open an Illustrator file in Acrobat, why would you need to save a file as a PDF? For one thing, you can compress a PDF to a smaller size; also, the receiver can double-click the file and then Acrobat or Acrobat Reader launches automatically.

Depending on how you save the PDF, you can allow some level of editability in Adobe Illustrator. To save a file as a PDF, follow these steps:

1. **Choose File⇨Save As, select Illustrator PDF (.pdf) from the Save As Type drop-down list, and then click Save.**

2. **In the Adobe PDF Options dialog box that appears, choose one of these options from the Preset drop-down list:**

   - *Illustrator Default:* Creates a PDF file in which all Illustrator data is preserved. PDF files created using this preset can be reopened in Illustrator with no loss of data.

   - *High Quality Print:* Creates PDF files for desktop printers and proofers.

   - *PDF/X-1a:2001:* The least flexible, but quite powerful, delivery method for PDF content data; requires that the color of all objects be CMYK (Cyan, Magenta, Yellow, Black) or spot colors. Elements in RGB (Red, Green, Blue) or Lab color spaces or tagged with International Color Consortium (ICC) profiles are prohibited. All fonts used in the job must be embedded in the supplied PDF file.

   - *PDF/X-3:2002:* Has slightly more flexibility than the X-1a:2001 method (see preceding bullet) in that color managed workflows are supported elements in Lab and attached ICC source profiles may also be used.

- *PDF/X-4:2008:* Based on PDF 1.4, which includes support for live transparency and has the same color management and ICC color specifications as PDF/X-3. You can open PDF files created for PDF/X-4 compliance in Acrobat 7.0 and Reader 7.0 and later.

- *Press Quality:* Creates a PDF file that can be printed to a high-resolution output device. The file will be large but maintain all information that a commercial printer or service provider needs in order to print files correctly. This option automatically converts the color mode to CMYK, embeds all fonts used in the file, prints at a higher resolution, and uses other settings to preserve the maximum amount of information contained in the original document.

Before creating an Adobe PDF file by using the Press Quality preset, check with your commercial printer to determine the output resolution and other settings.

**TIP**

3. **Click Save PDF to save your file in PDF format.**

If you want to be able to reopen the PDF file and edit it in Illustrator, make sure that you leave the Preserve Illustrator Editing Capabilities checkbox selected in the Adobe PDF Options dialog box.

**REMEMBER**

In the Adobe PDF Options dialog box, to the left of the preset choices, are options you can change to customize your settings. Skim the options to see how to change resolution settings and even add printer's marks. Take a look at Book 6 to find out more about the additional Acrobat PDF options.

Want a press-quality PDF but don't want to convert all your colors to CMYK? Choose the Press setting and then click the Output options. In the Color Conversion drop-down list, select No Conversion.

**TIP**

# Saving Your Artwork for the Web

If you need to save artwork for the web, no feature is better than Save for Web. This dialog box opens a preview pane where you can test different file formats before you save the file.

Before going through the steps to save a graphic for the web, make sure that the artboard is resized to the bounds of the graphic; otherwise, you'll have extra space surrounding your graphic.

**TIP**

To save an Illustrator file that you intend to use in a web page, just follow these steps:

**1. Choose File⇨ Export⇨Save for Web (Legacy).**

The Save for Web dialog box appears, showing your artwork on the Optimized tab. (See Figure 12-3.)

**FIGURE 12-3:**
Use Save for the Web to optimize your images for the web.

**2. Select a tabbed view: Original, Optimized, or 2-Up.**

You see as a default the artwork in Optimized view, which previews the artwork as it will appear based on the settings to the right. The best choice is 2-Up view because it shows your original image versus the optimized version.

**3. Select a setting for your file from the options on the right.**

If you want to make it easy on yourself, select a preset from the Preset drop-down list. Keep these points in mind:

- *Graphics Interchange Format (GIF)* is generally used for artwork with spans of solid color. GIF isn't a lossy format. You can make your artwork smaller by reducing the number of colors in the image — hence the choices, such as GIF 64 No Dither (64 colors). The lower the number of colors, the smaller the file size. You can also increase or decrease the number of colors in the file by changing the preset values in the Color text field or by clicking the arrows to the left of the Color text field.

- *Dithering* tries to make your artwork look like it has more colors by creating a pattern in the colors. It looks like a checkerboard pattern up close and even far away, as shown in Figure 12-4. It also makes a larger file size, so why use it? Many designers don't like the effect and choose the No Dither option.

**FIGURE 12-4:**
The result of dithering.

- *Joint Photographic Experts Group (JPEG)* is used for artwork that has subtle gradations from one shade to another. Photographs are often saved in this format. If you have drop shadows or blends in your artwork, select this format. JPEG is a *lossy* file format — it reduces an image to a lesser quality and can create odd artifacts in your artwork. You have choices, such as High, Medium, and Low, in the Settings drop-down list — choose wisely. You can also use the Quality slider to tweak the compression.

- *PNG-8* is quite similar to the GIF file format. Unless you have a certain reason for saving as PNG-8, stick with the GIF file format.

- *PNG-24* supports the best of two formats (GIF and JPEG). The Portable Network Graphics (PNG) format supports not only those nice gradients from one tonal value to another (such as JPEGs), but also transparency (such as GIFs). With the Transparency box checked, the PNG format allows for incremental transparency; the GIF format, on the other hand, is either fully transparent in areas or not.

**4.** **When you're satisfied with your chosen settings, click Save.**

When saving illustrations for the web, keep these points in mind — they make the whole process much easier for you and anyone who uses your illustrations:

>> **Keep file sizes small.** Don't forget that if you're saving illustrations for a web page, many other elements will also be on that page. Try to conserve on file size to make downloading the page quicker for viewers with dial-up connections. Visitors typically don't wait more than ten seconds for a page to download before giving up and moving to another website.

When you make your choices, keep an eye on the file size and the optimized artwork in the lower-left corner of the preview window. A GIF should be around 10K on average, and a JPEG around 15K. (Though these rules aren't written in stone, *please* don't try to slap a 100K JPEG on a web page.)

You can change the download time by clicking the panel menu in the upper-right corner of the Save for Web & Devices dialog box and choosing Optimize to File Size. Then you can enter a final file size and have Illustrator create your settings in the Save for Web dialog box.

>> **Preview the file before saving it.** If you want to see the artwork in a web browser before saving it, click the Preview button at the bottom-left corner of the Save for Web dialog box. The browser of choice appears with your artwork in the quality level and size in which it will appear. If no browser is selected, click the Select Browser Menu icon (to the right of the Preview button) to choose Other and then browse to locate a browser you want to use for previewing. Close the browser to return to the Save for Web dialog box.

>> **Change the size.** Many misconceptions abound about the size of web artwork. Most people generally view their browser windows in an area measuring approximately 700 x 500 pixels. Depending on the screen resolution, this setting may cover the entire screen on a 14-inch monitor. Even viewers with 21-inch, high-resolution monitors often don't want to have their entire screens covered by a browser window, however, so their areas still measure approximately 700 x 500 pixels. When choosing a size for your artwork, choose one with proportions similar to these. For example, if you want an illustration to occupy about a quarter of the browser window's width, make your image about 175 pixels wide (700 ÷ 4 = 175). If you notice that the height of your image is more than 500 pixels, whittle the height in size as well or else viewers have to scroll to see the whole image (and it will probably take too long to download).

Use the Image Size tab to enter new sizes. As long as the Constrain Proportions checkbox is selected, both the height and width of the image change proportionally. Click the Apply button to change the size, but don't close the Save for Web dialog box.

» **Finish the save.** If you aren't finished with the artwork but want to save your settings, hold down the Alt (Windows) or Option (Mac) key and click the Remember button. (When you aren't holding down the Alt or Option key, the Remember button is the Done button.) When you're finished, click the Save button and save your file in the appropriate location.

# Saving Multiple Assets out of Illustrator

Perhaps you have created artwork for an interactive design such as a mobile application. Using Illustrator's new Assets Export feature, you can easily collect the artwork that you need for development.

To take advantage of this feature, either use the asset.export file available in the DummiesCCFiles folder located at www.agitraining.com/dummies or use your own file. Then follow these steps:

1. **Choose Window➪Assets Export to open the Asset Export panel.**

2. **At this point, simply click and drag artwork from the artboard to the Assets Export panel, as shown in Figure 12-5.**

**FIGURE 12-5:**
Click and drag artwork that you want to export into the Asset Export panel.

3. **Continue adding other artwork to this panel.**

Note at the bottom of the panel that you have a 1X scale selected as a default. Essentially, this means that you are set up to save every one of your assets in the panel at 100 percent. Depending upon the platform your assets will be used on, you may need to supply each piece of artwork in not only 1X (100%) size, but also 2X (200%) and 3X (300%). This can be set up easily in the Asset Export panel.

4. **To add additional saved artwork in other scales, press the + Add Scale button at the bottom of the Asset Export panel. The default 2X and 3X scales are added, but you can choose another size or enter your own custom size by clicking on the arrow indicated in Figure 12-6.**

**FIGURE 12-6:**
Working with the Add Scale button in the Asset Export panel.

5. **Choose a file format for each scale by selecting a file type from the Format drop-down menu.**

6. **Name your exported files by double-clicking on the default name in the Asset Export panel. You can add a suffix in the scale attributes section as well.**

7. **Select the Files you want exported. Press Export when you are ready to export the files that you loaded into the Asset panel. A Pick Location window appears that contains an appropriate folder in which to save your exported files. Either create a new folder, or select a folder and choose Select Folder (Windows) or Choose (Mac).**

Your files have been exported.

 *Note:* If you would like additional options, you can select the Launch the Export for Screens button that is to the left of Export. In this dialog box, you can choose to export only some or all of your artwork or select to export your artboards as individual assets.

# Flattening Transparency

You may find that all those cool effects you added to your illustration don't print correctly. When you print a file that has effects, such as drop shadows, cool gradient blends, and feathering, Illustrator *flattens* them by turning into pixels any transparent areas that overlap other objects and leaving what it can as vectors.

To understand flattening, look at Figure 12-7 to see the difference between the original artwork (on the left) and the flattened artwork (on the right). Notice that in the figure, when the artwork was flattened, some areas turned into pixels. But at what resolution? Flattening helps you determine the quality of art — before receiving an unpleasant surprise at the outcome.

**FIGURE 12-7:** Artwork before and after flattening is applied.

# Flattening a file

If you've taken advantage of transparency or effects using transparency (which we discuss in Chapter 10 of this minibook), follow these steps to produce the highest-quality artwork in your file:

1. **Make sure that the artwork you created is in CMYK mode.**

   You can change the document's color mode by choosing File⇨Document Color Mode.⇨CMYK Color.

2. **Choose Effect⇨Document Raster Effects Settings.**

   The Document Raster Effects Settings dialog box appears, as shown in Figure 12-8. Image should have CMYK as the color mode.

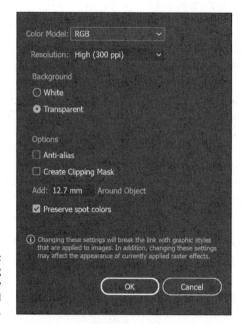

**FIGURE 12-8:** Choosing the quality of rasterized artwork.

3. **Choose the resolution you want to use by selecting an option in the Resolution area.**

   Select the Screen (72 ppi) option for web graphics, Medium (150 ppi) for desktop printers and copiers, and High (300 ppi) for graphics to be printed on a press.

4. **Choose whether you want a white or transparent background.**

   If you select the Transparent option, you create an alpha channel that's retained if the artwork is exported into Photoshop.

**5.** **You can generally leave the items in the Options section deselected:**

- *The Anti-Alias checkbox* applies antialiasing to reduce the appearance of jagged edges in the rasterized image. Deselect this option to maintain the crispness of fine lines and small text.

- *The Create Clipping Mask checkbox* creates a mask that makes the background of the rasterized image appear transparent. You don't need to create a clipping mask if you select the Transparent option for your background.

- *The Add __ Around Object text field* adds the specified number of pixels around the rasterized image.

- *The Preserve Spot Colors checkbox* keeps any spot colors you have defined intact. Leave this selected.

**6.** **Click OK.**

The next step is to set the transparency options in the Document Setup dialog box.

**7.** **Choose File⇨Document Setup.**

From the Transparency section in the middle of the dialog box, click the Preset drop-down list and select the Low, Medium, High, or Custom option. Select the Low option for onscreen viewing, the Medium option for printers and copiers, or the High option for press quality. To control more settings, click the Custom button to the right of the drop-down list.

**8.** **Click OK.**

**TIP**

If you customize settings regularly, choose Edit⇨Transparency Flattener Presets to create and store your own presets.

You can apply the flattening in several ways. Here are three simple methods:

>> **Select the objects that require flattening and choose Object ⇨ Flatten Transparency.** Select a default setting or a custom preset (that you created) from the Preset drop-down list and click OK.

>> **Choose File ⇨ Print and select Advanced from the list of print options on the left.** Select a preset from the Overprint and Transparency Flattener options. If you used the Attributes panel to create overprints (for trapping used in high-end printing), make sure to preserve the overprints.

Overprints aren't preserved in areas that use transparency.

**REMEMBER**

>> **Choose File ⇨ Save As and choose Illustrator EPS.** In the Transparency section of the EPS Options dialog box, choose a flattening setting from the Preset drop-down list. If your transparency options are grayed out, your file has no transparency.

## Using the Flattener Preview panel

If you want to preview your flattening, open the Flattener Preview panel by choosing Window➪Flattener Preview.

The Flattener Preview panel doesn't apply flattening, but it shows you a preview based on your settings. Click the Refresh button and choose Show Options from the panel menu. Test various settings without flattening the file. Experiment with different settings and then save your presets by selecting Save Transparency Flattener Preset from the panel menu. You can access the saved settings in the Preset drop-down list in the Options dialog boxes that appear when you save a file in EPS format or in the Document Setup dialog box.

To update the preview, click the Refresh button after making changes.

TIP

Zoom in on artwork by clicking in the Preview pane. Scroll the artwork in the Preview pane by holding down the spacebar and dragging. Zoom out by Alt-clicking (Windows) or Option-clicking (Mac).

# Printing from Illustrator

Printing from Illustrator gives you lots of capabilities, such as printing composites to separations and adding printer's marks.

To print your illustration, follow these steps:

1. **Choose File➪Print.**

2. **In the Print dialog box that appears, select a printer if one isn't already selected.**

3. **If the PPD isn't selected, select one from the PPD (PostScript Printer Description) drop-down list.**

   A *PPD* is a printer description file. Illustrator needs one in order to determine the specifics of the PostScript printer you're sending your file to. This setting lets Illustrator know whether the printer can print in color, the paper size it can handle, and its resolution, as well as many other important details. If your printer is not a PostScript printer, this area will be grayed out.

**4.** **Choose from other options.**

For example, use the General options section to pick pages to print. In the Media area, select the size of the media you're printing to. In the Options area, choose whether you want layers to print and any options specific to printing layers.

**5.** **Click the Print button to print your illustration.**

That's it. Although printing illustrations can be quite simple, the following list highlights some basic points to keep in mind as you prepare one for printing:

» **Print a composite:** A *composite* is a full-color image, where all inks are applied to the page (and not separated onto individual pages — one apiece for cyan, magenta, yellow, and black). To ensure that your settings are correct, click Output in the print options pane on the left side of the Print dialog box and select Composite from the Mode drop-down list.

» **Print separations:** To separate colors, click Output in the print options pane on the left side of the Print dialog box; from the Mode drop-down list, choose the Separations (Host-Based) option. Select the In-RIP Separations option only if your service provider or printer asks you to. Other options to select from are described in this list:

- The resolution is determined by your PPD, based on the dots per inch (dpi) in the printer description. You may have only one option available in the Printer Resolution drop-down list.

- Select the Convert Spot Colors to Process checkbox to make your file 4-color.

- Click the printer icons to the left of the listed colors to turn off or on the colors you want to print.

» **Printer's marks and bleeds:** Click Marks and Bleeds in the print options pane on the left side of the Print dialog box to turn on all printer's marks, or just select the ones that you want to appear.

Specify a bleed area if you're extending images beyond the trim area of a page. If you don't specify a bleed, the artwork stops at the edge of the page and doesn't leave a trim area for the printer.

**TIP**

After you create a good set of options specific to your needs, click the Save Preset button (which is the disk icon to the right of the Print Preset drop-down list). Name your presets appropriately; when you want to use a particular preset, select it from the Print Preset drop-down list at the top of the Print dialog box for future print jobs.

# Acrobat

# Contents at a Glance

Chapter **1**

# Discovering Essential Acrobat Information

A dobe Acrobat Pro DC provides a variety of tools for sharing and reviewing documents in the Portable Document Format (PDF). Adobe Creative Cloud applications can create PDF files, and you can also use Acrobat to create PDF files from programs that aren't part of the Creative Cloud, such as Microsoft Word. After you create a PDF file, you can use Acrobat to enhance it by adding interactivity, merging it with several related documents into a single PDF, adding comments or annotations, or applying security features that restrict document functions, such as printing, editing, or even opening the PDF file itself.

In this chapter, you find out why you may want to create PDF files and acquaint yourself with the Adobe Acrobat tools and workspace. You see how easy it is to navigate through PDF files with the navigational tools, tabs, and viewing options in Acrobat. In the following chapters of this minibook, you explore how to use Acrobat to create PDF files from documents produced in a variety of programs and discover ways to enhance your PDF files with Acrobat.

# Working with PDF Files

With Adobe Acrobat, you can create, review, and modify PDF files. Because PDF is a common file format, you can use it to share Creative Cloud files for review, approval, or final publication, even with users who don't have access to Creative Cloud programs. When you use a program in the Creative Cloud, such as Illustrator or InDesign, to create a document, others would need the same software to open or edit the original program files. By converting your documents to PDF, they can easily be shared with others who might not have the same software as you. PDF files can be viewed by users on virtually all types of computers, tablets, mobile phones, and operating systems.

PDF provides a common file format for viewing files, regardless of the software program used to create them. Additionally, Acrobat provides extensive tools for reviewing, commenting, and marking files so that you can easily collaborate on a project without modifying the original document, along with tools to make PDF files interactive, merge related documents together, and secure files to restrict viewing or editing.

Because the software to view PDF files is free, you can be assured that those receiving your files don't need to purchase any special software. In fact, the odds are quite good that most users already have some type of free PDF viewing software, such as Adobe Reader, on their smartphone, tablet, or computer.

PDF has become a popular way to share files because it provides a true reproduction of an original document, which can be important for forms, financial documents, brochures, catalogs, and other items sent to a printing vendor. Many businesses also use PDF documents because the electronic documents can be secured, and they accurately represent documents that have been approved for distribution. Even scanned documents can be saved in the PDF format and secured using Acrobat. Graphic artists even use PDF files to send books, such as the one you're reading now, to the printing plant.

Although PDF files provide a high-quality representation of an original file, they're more than just a picture of a document. PDF files retain the high-quality appearance of text while keeping the text searchable. Logos and illustrations created with Adobe Illustrator retain a high-quality appearance when converted to PDF, and intricate details from bitmap images, such as those edited with Adobe Photoshop, can also be maintained. PDF files enable you to distribute a high-fidelity electronic document. When creating a PDF file, you can choose settings that make the file suitable for high-quality printing or make the file smaller and more suitable for posting to a website or sharing as an email attachment. PDF documents can also be used to create enhanced electronic documents and portfolios. Acrobat lets you combine multiple PDF files together into a single portfolio for sharing.

Although Acrobat is part of the Creative Cloud, it's *not* a design tool — rather, it's a tool for distributing documents created in other software programs and enhancing these documents for online distribution. You generally don't use Acrobat to build new documents. Acrobat is a medium for sharing files, not for creating or designing documents. With Acrobat, you can

>> Share documents with users who don't have the same software or fonts that you use.

>> Review and mark PDF files that others send you. With Adobe Acrobat, you can enable a PDF file to be reviewed by users with the free Adobe Reader software.

>> Combine documents created in other programs. You can use Acrobat to merge PDF files together into one document, even files that may have been originally created in different programs.

>> Create a PDF portfolio. You can combine various file formats into a single PDF package and yet retain the files in their original file formats.

>> Edit Adobe PDF files to make minor changes to text or graphics.

>> Apply security to PDF files when you don't want them changed or you want to restrict viewing to certain individuals.

>> Add interactivity to PDF files by enhancing them with sounds, movies, animations, and buttons.

>> Create interactive forms to collect information electronically, avoiding the need for manual data collection.

We cover these capabilities throughout the rest of this minibook.

# Knowing When to Use Adobe PDF Files

So when does it make sense to use Adobe PDF files? Here are some examples:

>> **When you want to review a document quickly and efficiently:** When documents need to be reviewed or approved, Acrobat really shines. The reviewers don't need to have the Creative Cloud software — or whatever you used to create the document. They need only a program to view PDF files, such as the free Adobe Reader or the Apple Preview application. Recipients can then use commenting, markup, and annotation tools to add suggestions and edits to a file. You can even combine comments from multiple reviewers into a single document and manage the review process online or via email.

>> **When you've created a document that you don't want others to edit:** Your recipients may have the same software you used to build the document, but you can keep them from editing the original file by distributing it as a PDF file. Whether you want to secure a spreadsheet from editing or an InDesign document from modification, Acrobat includes security options that allow you to protect your original content.

>> **When you've created a presentation that includes files from different programs:** By converting the documents to PDF, you can combine them into a single file. For example, you can merge PowerPoint, Excel, and InDesign files into a single PDF document. Whether you need to protect your brand and identity by keeping documents from being edited or simply want to ease the process of sharing files, PDF makes it easy to share your ideas.

>> **When you have a sensitive document:** If you have a document containing information that you don't want unauthorized persons viewing or you don't want printed, you can enhance the file with security with the Adobe Acrobat security tools. With the security options, you can require users to enter a password to view the file, or you can limit other features, such as the capability to print or edit the document.

# Introducing the Adobe Acrobat Workspace and Tools

To take advantage of all that Acrobat has to offer, take some time to discover the workspace and tools so you can get around within a PDF file.

When you first launch Acrobat, you may see the Home Screen as shown in Figure 1-1. If you don't see it, click on the Home tab in the upper-left part of the Acrobat window. The Home screen displays a panel on the left with a section named Files that allows you to view recently sent and opened files. There is also a section named Storage. Clicking on any listed storage destinations shows you the recent locations to which you have saved files. The center pane in the Home screen either defaults to show you recently opened files or suggestions for tasks that you can complete using Acrobat.

Click on the Tools tab to see shortcuts to common tools that complete popular tasks in Acrobat, like creating new PDFs from other files, combining multiple PDFs into one file, reorganizing pages in an existing PDF, and more. You can click on the arrow to the right of each shortcut to remove it if you do not use that tool frequently. Type a tool name in the Search window at the top to find a tool that you use more frequently and add it to this shortcut list if you like. (See Figure 1-2.)

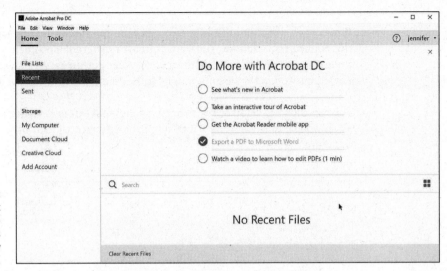

**FIGURE 1-1:**
Use the Acrobat Start screen to open recent files or create new PDF documents.

**FIGURE 1-2:**
You can organize shortcuts for your favorite tools in the Tools window.

To open a document, choose File➪ Open from the menu items at the top of the Acrobat workspace. When a PDF document is open, the menu bar and the toolbar are visible at the top of the work area. The work area displays a document pane in the middle, a navigation pane on the left, and a tools or task pane on the right side.

If you open multiple PDFs you see a tabbed interface that appears at the top of the application window. You can switch to different documents by clicking on the named tabs. A Previous button and a Next button are displayed at the right to navigate through the document tabs if they extend beyond the visible area.

You can click the small arrow to open a panel that offers navigational tools, as well as an option to see any files that might be attached to your open PDF, as shown in Figure 1-3.

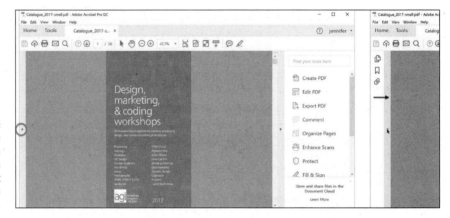

**FIGURE 1-3:**
Click on the small arrow on the left to open a panel that offers navigation options.

When you open a PDF document with Acrobat, you enter the Document view in which you can use the tools in the toolbar to complete tasks as well as the navigation panel on the left to move through a PDF file. For example, a PDF file may contain multiple pages. You can click on the arrow in the panel to the left to open the Page Thumbnail view in Acrobat. You can then click the Page Thumbnails to navigate from page to page, as shown in Figure 1-4.

## Toolbars

The toolbars in Acrobat Pro DC are customizable, so you can display different toolbars or change the location of existing toolbars to meet your needs.

Less than half the toolbars and Quick Tools are visible in the default Acrobat display. You can add more tools to the toolbar well along the top of the Document window by positioning your cursor over an empty spot on the toolbar well and then right-clicking (Windows) or Ctrl-clicking (Mac) to display a list of available tools, as shown in Figure 1-5. For example, to add the Marquee Zoom tool to the toolbar well, right-click (Windows) or Ctrl-click (Mac) and then choose Select & Zoom⇨Marquee Zoom to add this tool to the toolbar well.

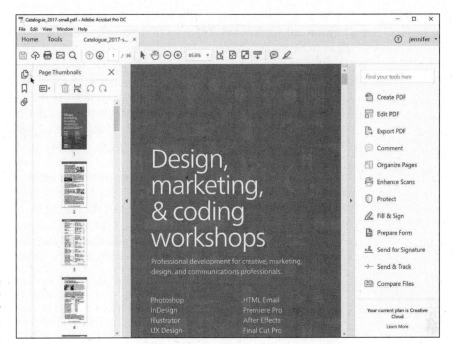

**FIGURE 1-4:**
Use the Page Thumbnail view to navigate from page to page.

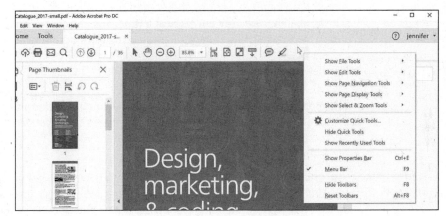

**FIGURE 1-5:**
Customize your toolbar by right-clicking (Windows)/ Ctrl-clicking (Mac) on an empty spot in the toolbar.

Toolbars contain both tools for working on parts of your document and Quick Tools for performing actions which generally impact the entire document.

## Changing page magnification

Sometimes you want to see the entire page of a document; other times, you may only need to read the text or examine a small portion of a page. Acrobat provides several preset viewing options to help you with this, and you can also customize the magnification to zoom in on the page.

If things are a bit too small for you to see clearly, increase the magnification used for viewing pages with the Zoom drop-down list on the toolbar. Preset magnification choices are available in this drop-down list. In the drop-down list, you can also select options to fit the page in the window by choosing the Zoom to Page Level option from the magnification drop-down list. Use the additional choices to fit the width of the page within the Document window or to view the document at its actual size. You can also use the minus (−) and plus (+) symbols to the left of the current magnification level to decrease or increase the zoom level.

In the preceding section, "Toolbars," you discover how to add the Marquee Zoom tool to the toolbar. You can use this tool to identify specific portions of a page that you want to magnify. Select this tool and then click and drag around a portion of the page to increase the magnification. You can also click multiple times on an area with this tool to increase the page magnification, but clicking and dragging a box with the Marquee Zoom tool is generally a much faster way to focus on a portion of a page you want to view.

## Viewing modes

Acrobat provides several viewing modes that control how the document is displayed. For example, you can choose to display the pages of a book or magazine side by side, or view only one page at a time. You can choose which viewing mode is used by choosing View ⇨ Page Display and selecting the viewing option you want.

The viewing modes are

>> **Single Page View:** This mode displays only the current document page onscreen and doesn't show any adjoining pages. When you scroll to the top or bottom of the current page, other pages aren't visible at the same time as the current page.

>> **Enable Scrolling:** With this mode, you can see the current document page, and if you scroll to the top (or bottom) of the current page, the adjoining page is also visible. If you reduce your page viewing magnification, many document pages are visible.

>> **Two-Page View:** Use this mode to see pages as a *spread,* where you can view both the left and right sides of adjoining pages at the same time. When you have documents with pictures or text that spans a pair of pages, use this option to see the pages presented side by side in Acrobat. As with the Single Page mode, other pages that go before or fall after the spread aren't visible — only the one pair of pages is visible onscreen, regardless of the magnification or scrolling.

>> **Two-Page Scrolling:** If you have a document with many pages containing text or pictures on their adjoining pages, you can use this mode to scroll from one pair of visible pages to the next. When the Two-Up Scrolling view is selected, you can see adjoining page spreads. This option is identical to the Two-Page view, but it also shows pages above or below the spread you're presently viewing.

If you have pages where images or text goes across pages, the Two-Page View is useful. When displaying a magazine or catalog, the two-page pairs often display incorrectly. For example, a magazine will display the cover (page 1) and page 2 together, instead of displaying the cover on its own and then pages 2 and 3 together. To correct this, choose View⇨Page Display⇨Show Cover Page in TwoPage View. Additionally, the default option is for Acrobat to display a space between pages that are displayed together in the Two-Up mode. You can replace the space with a dotted line to divide the adjoining pages by choosing View⇨Page Display⇨Show Gaps Between Pages.

## Additional viewing options

Acrobat has some additional options for changing your document display:

>> **Full Screen mode (View⇨Full Screen Mode):** Use the Full Screen mode if you'd like to hide all menus, toolbars, and other parts of the Acrobat interface. This option is useful if you want to focus on the document being displayed, not the program being used to view it. Use this mode, for example, when you've converted a PowerPoint file to a PDF document and want to deliver the presentation with Acrobat. If you're viewing a document in the Full Screen mode, press the Esc key to return to the regular viewing mode.

When using the Full Screen mode, you can select Edit⇨Preferences (Windows) or Acrobat Pro DC⇨Preferences (Mac) and choose Full Screen to define attributes that change the way all files display when using the Full Screen mode. You can set the display to advance automatically from one page to the next at a certain interval, choose from many page transition types, and define the background color.

TIP

You can set a document to automatically open in Full Screen mode. To do so, choose File⇨Properties and then select the Open in Full Screen mode checkbox in the Initial View panel of the Document Properties dialog box.

>> **Read mode (View⇨Read Mode):** The many toolbars and buttons of Acrobat can get in the way of the document you want to review. Use Read mode to temporarily hide all the toolbars and buttons, making it easier to focus on the content of the PDF file.

# Navigation panels

Acrobat offers a variety of panels that are helpful when navigating through PDF documents. The navigation panels appear along the left side of your Document window as small icons. Click an icon to make its panel visible. For example, click the Pages icon to display thumbnail-size representations of each page.

In the Page Thumbnails panel, click a thumbnail page to display that page in the Document window. There are 11 panels: Articles, Attachments, Bookmarks, Content, Destinations, Layers, Model Tree, Order, Page Thumbnails, Signatures, and Tags. You can access any of these by choosing View➪Show/Hide➪Navigation Panes.

Many panels have more advanced uses that are covered in later chapters of this minibook. Here, we provide you with a brief understanding of how you can use the Page Thumbnails panel to more easily navigate through a PDF document. Follow these steps:

1. **Make sure that the Page Thumbnails panel is visible by clicking its panel icon.**

2. **In the Page Thumbnails panel, click any page thumbnail to navigate directly to that page.**

    A border appears around the selected page, and a box within the Page Thumbnails panel indicates what portion of the page is being viewed in the Document window.

    You can click the black square icon in the bottom-right corner of the small box in the Page Thumbnails panel and drag diagonally upward to increase the magnification on the section of the page contained within the box. Alternatively, make the box larger by clicking and dragging down and out to expand the size of the area being viewed. Changing the size of the black box displayed on the page in the Page Thumbnails panel changes the area being viewed as well as the amount it's magnified.

Chapter **2**

# Creating PDF Files

onverting documents to the Portable Document Format (PDF) is a great way to share files when readers don't have the same software as you or when you want to consolidate multiple file types into a single document. Adobe Acrobat lets you create files from all software programs, scanned documents, and even pages from the web. Creating PDF files from other Adobe Creative Cloud programs does not require Acrobat because the ability is already built into the individual program. This includes Photoshop, Illustrator, and InDesign. In this chapter, you find out how to create Adobe PDF files from a variety of programs.

## Creating PDF Files from Microsoft Office

Adobe Acrobat includes tools that make it easy to convert Microsoft Word, Excel, and PowerPoint files to PDF.

**WARNING**

These capabilities are much more robust for the Windows versions of these programs, so Macintosh users may discover that not all these options are available.

When you install Acrobat on your computer, it looks for Microsoft Office programs. If Acrobat locates Word, Excel, PowerPoint, or Outlook, it installs an add-in — the PDF Maker — to these programs that helps convert Microsoft Office documents to PDF in a single click.

You can tell whether the PDF Maker add-in has been installed in your Microsoft Office programs by looking for the Acrobat toolbar or the Acrobat tab, depending upon which version of Microsoft Office you use. In the latest versions of Office the Acrobat tab appears to the right of the View tab.

In earlier versions of Microsoft Office, the toolbar appears at the top of the Document window.

REMEMBER

When you convert documents to PDF, the original file remains unchanged, so you have both the original file and a separate PDF document. The original document and the PDF file aren't linked, so changes to the original source file will not be reflected in the PDF file. The same goes for when you edit the PDF document. The changes will not be reflected in the original document.

## PDF conversion options

PDF Maker is installed within Microsoft Office at the time you install Acrobat. PDF Maker provides a variety of controls over how PDF files are created from Microsoft Office programs, such as Word and Excel. For example, you can have PDF Maker create PDF files from your Microsoft Office documents each time you click the Create PDF button without asking you to confirm the location and name of the file. Acrobat simply saves the file in the same location as the original document. Similarly, you can choose to create PDF files that balance your need for quality and file size.

PDF Maker also provides controls over the type of PDF file you create because some PDF files may need to be of a higher quality for printing and others may need to be smaller to allow for fast electronic distribution. For example, you may want to post a PDF document to a website, where you want to make the file small so that it can be downloaded quickly.

When working in Microsoft Word, Excel, or PowerPoint, you can access the PDF Maker controls by clicking the Acrobat tab and then clicking the Preferences button (Office 2016 or 2016) or by choosing Adobe PDF⇨Change Conversion Settings (in earlier versions of Microsoft Office). In the Acrobat PDF Maker dialog box that appears, you can then choose from a variety of settings that control how the PDF file is created. In this section, we focus on the most useful options for Microsoft Office users.

After you click the Preferences button, the Acrobat PDFMaker dialog box opens. (Note that on the Mac OS, a dialog about Adobe Create PDF Cloud services may open.) In this dialog box, use the Conversion Settings drop-down list to control how the PDF file is generated:

>> **Standard:** Select this option to create PDF files that will be printed on an office laser printer or distributed via email. This setting meets the needs of most users — it provides some compression of graphics, but they remain clear onscreen and look reasonably good when printed. In addition, this setting builds the fonts into the PDF file to maintain an exact representation of the document, regardless of where the file is viewed.

>> **Smallest File Size:** With this setting, you can control the file size of the PDF documents you create. This setting provides significant compression of images and also reduces resolution, which causes graphics within the files to lose some clarity and perhaps appear jagged.

Unlike the Standard option, fonts aren't embedded into the PDF files created with this setting. If the fonts used in the document aren't available on a computer where a PDF created with the Smallest File Size setting is viewed, Acrobat will use a font substitution technology to replicate the size and shape of the fonts used in the document. This feature typically provides a similar appearance to the original document, but it's not always an exact match of the original file.

Because this setting is so lossy, use it only if you need to compress a large file to a small enough size to send as an email attachment. Make certain the recipient has the fonts used in the document installed on his or her computer. Otherwise, Adobe uses font substitution.

>> **High Quality Print and Press Quality:** If you need to provide PDF files to your commercial printer or copy shop, use these settings to create a PDF file that's designed for high-quality print reproduction. Along with including fonts in the PDF file, the graphics aren't significantly compressed, and they maintain a much higher resolution. These files tend to be larger than others created with different settings, but the quality of the PDF file is more important than the file size when you're having it professionally printed. High Quality Print is suitable for a color copier or high-quality laser printer, whereas Press Quality is suitable for a PDF that is sent to a commercial printer.

Several other highly technical options might be useful for you if you have a specialized profession. For example, the PDF/X options are useful if you're submitting advertisements to publications that require the PDF advertisements to adhere to the PDF/X standard.

# PDF conversion options from Microsoft Word and Excel

Although Microsoft Word and Excel are widely used, they aren't always the best choice for distributing documents. Formatting of Microsoft Word documents and Excel spreadsheets changes depending on the fonts available on users' computers, or even the printers with which they print. PDF files, on the other hand, are able to maintain a consistent appearance on various computer types, regardless of fonts installed or printers being used. Microsoft Word and Excel files can be easily edited, and users can also copy and extract information from these files with few limitations. This differs from PDF files that are more difficult to copy from, and offer robust security options.

Converting a Word or Excel file to a PDF file lets you distribute the file to a wide audience, even to people who don't have Word or Excel, without the need to worry about the document format or layout changing. There are two methods for converting Word or Excel documents to PDF. The method you use depends on which version of Microsoft Office you're using:

>> With Microsoft Office, convert your document from inside Microsoft Word or Excel — make sure that the document you want to convert to a PDF file is open and then click the Create PDF button in the Acrobat portion of the main toolbar.

>> With Office 2003 or earlier, choose Adobe PDF⇨Convert to Adobe PDF.

>> With a Mac Office 2016, choose File⇨Save As and select PDF from the File Format drop-down menu.

After you choose to create a PDF file from your Microsoft Office document, you must specify the location of the PDF file that's created and name the file.

**TIP**

In Office 2016, click the Preferences button on the Acrobat tab, or with earlier versions of Office, choose Acrobat⇨Change Conversion Settings. In the Adobe PDF Maker dialog box, deselect the Prompt for PDF Filename option so that PDF files are generated in one step, without inputting the PDF filename. This saves you the step of naming the PDF file each time you create a PDF document.

You can also add more functionality into the PDF documents you create. Click the Preference tab if you're working in Office 2016 or choose Acrobat⇨Change Conversion Settings in earlier versions of Office. In the dialog box that appears, review the following settings:

- **Attach Source File:** Causes the original Office document to become embedded within the PDF file as an attachment. When the PDF file is distributed, the original source file is included within the PDF file.

- **Create Bookmarks:** Adds interactive bookmarks that make navigating the PDF file easy. Bookmarks are added based on Microsoft Word styles, such as text that's styled as Heading 1. The bookmarks appear in the Bookmarks panel when viewing the PDF.

- **Add Links:** Automatically converts Word links, such as web addresses, into PDF links that you can use when viewing the file in Acrobat or Adobe Reader. Within the PDF Maker preferences dialog box, click the Word tab to access additional options that can be built into PDF files created from Word.

## Converting PowerPoint files to PDF

You can convert your PowerPoint presentations to Adobe PDF documents with the PDF Maker add-in that installs with Adobe Acrobat. You can then distribute PDF versions of your PowerPoint presentations, avoiding concerns about your presentation file being edited or concerns that the recipient may not have the same fonts that you used. Distributing the presentation as a PDF ensures the document will look consistent on all computers.

From PowerPoint, click the Acrobat tab on the Ribbon and then click the Create PDF button to save the file as a PDF file. In older versions of Office, you can also choose Acrobat⇨Convert to Adobe PDF from PowerPoint's main menu. If you're working with a new PowerPoint file or one that you've edited, you must save it before PDF Maker will convert the file.

As with Word and Excel, you can select options relating to the conversion of your PowerPoint documents to PDF. To access the preferences, click the Preference button in the Acrobat tab, or if you're using an older version of Office, choose Adobe PDF⇨Change Conversion Settings. Along with the conversion settings that impact the quality of the resulting PDF file, two additional options can enhance your presentation as a PDF:

- **Preserve Slide Transitions:** With this option, you can convert the slide transitions created in PowerPoint into PDF transitions. They will be used when the presentation is in the Adobe Acrobat Full Screen mode option.

- **Convert Multimedia:** Because Adobe PDF files can contain integrated sound and movie files, you can choose this option to have sounds and movies, used in a PowerPoint file, converted into the PDF document.

**TIP**

After you create the PDF, you can use Acrobat as the tool for delivering your presentations that have been created using PowerPoint. After you convert the file to PDF, open it in Acrobat and choose View➪Full Screen Mode. Press Esc to stop viewing a document in the Full Screen mode. You can even distribute the document to users with the free Adobe Reader, then they can use the free Adobe Reader software to view and display the PowerPoint presentation file. To distribute a document so that it always opens in Full Screen mode, open the document, choose File➪Properties, and select the Open in Full Screen Mode checkbox under the Initial View tab.

# Creating PDF Files from Adobe Creative Cloud Applications

You can also convert Photoshop files, Illustrator files, or InDesign documents to the PDF format. In the following sections, we show you how.

## Converting Photoshop and Illustrator files to PDF

Both Adobe Photoshop CC and Adobe Illustrator CC can save documents directly into the Adobe PDF file format. To do so, simply choose File➪Save or File➪Save As. Then, from the File Type drop-down list, choose Adobe PDF (Illustrator) or Photoshop PDF (Photoshop). In these programs, you can create PDF files without Adobe Acrobat or Acrobat Distiller because PDF creation capabilities are integrated into them.

You can use Adobe Reader or Acrobat to view PDF files created from Photoshop or Illustrator. You can also open and edit PDF files using the same program in which they were created — so Photoshop PDF files can be reopened and edited using Photoshop, and the same is true for Illustrator PDF files.

## Converting InDesign documents to PDF

Like Photoshop and Illustrator, the capability to convert InDesign documents to PDF is integrated into the application. With Adobe InDesign, you can choose File➪Export and select either Adobe PDF (Interactive) or Adobe PDF (Print) from the File Type drop-down list. Interactive PDF documents are suitable for sharing online, such as by posting the file to a website, and are designed primarily to incorporate interactive PDF features such as buttons, page transitions, and multimedia elements. If you're creating a PDF document that will be printed, your best option is to select Adobe PDF (Print), even if it will be posted to a website.

If you choose Adobe PDF (Print) when exporting from InDesign, you will find many options for controlling the size and quality of the resulting PDF file. Many of these options are similar to those available in PDF Maker for Microsoft Office.

At the top of the Adobe InDesign Export PDF dialog box, which appears after selecting Save in the Export dialog box, you can choose an option from the Preset drop-down. The choices are many, but the following are the most commonly used settings:

>> **Smallest File Size:** Creates compact Adobe PDF files that are intended for display on the Internet or to be distributed via email. Use this setting to create PDF files that will be viewed primarily onscreen.

>> **High Quality Print:** Creates Adobe PDF files that are intended for desktop printers and digital copiers.

>> **Press Quality:** Use this setting to create PDF files that will be delivered to a commercial printer for high-quality, offset print reproduction.

TIP

When creating PDF files to be used for high-resolution printing, there are specific settings you should use. Select Marks and Bleeds in the list on the left of the Export Adobe PDF dialog box, as shown in Figure 2-1, and specify the amount of space items need to extend off the page, referred to as *bleed*. If you're delivering the file to a printing firm, it can provide you with guidance regarding the required value. A good rule to follow is to use at least 0.125 inch if you have any items in your layout that extend to the edge of your document pages and beyond. Specify the value you want by entering the number in the Bleed and Slug section of the Marks and Bleeds tab. If the amount of bleed needs to be the same on all four sides, type the value in the Top left text box and then click the link chain in the center of all the Bleed text boxes. In Figure 2-1, picas has been selected as the unit of value for the bleed.

# Converting Other Electronic Documents to PDF

As described earlier in this chapter, creating PDF files from Creative Cloud applications and Microsoft Office programs is simple, but you aren't limited to creating PDF files just from these programs. This section explains how you can create PDF files from many other programs.

When you installed the Adobe Creative Cloud on your computer, you also installed a new printer — the *Adobe PDF printer* — which is used to convert electronic documents to PDF files. The Adobe PDF printer captures all the same information that's normally sent to your printer, and, instead of printing on paper, the information is converted into an Adobe PDF file.

To create a PDF file from any program, choose File ↩ Print. In the Print dialog box, select Adobe PDF as the printer and click Print.

To change the type of PDF file that's created, such as a smaller file for web posting or a higher-quality file for delivery to a commercial printer, do this:

>> **Windows:** Click the Setup. . . button in the Print dialog box to open another Print dialog box. Then select the Preferences button to open the Printing Preferences dialog box, as shown in Figure 2-2. Here, you can choose the Adobe PDF Conversion settings you want to use to control the quality and size of the resulting PDF file.

>> **Mac:** To save a file as PDF on a Mac, you can choose File Save As and then choose PDF from the File Format drop-down menu. You can then select the radio box for either electronic distribution or print.

**FIGURE 2-2:**
You can change conversion settings when printing to the Adobe PDF printer.

We discuss the PDF conversion settings earlier in this chapter, in the "PDF conversion options" section.

Using the Print menu to control the quality of PDF files created from non–Adobe programs may appear strange, but it's the easiest way for Adobe to capture all the same information that you'd expect to see when you print your files. This is an easy and standard method for generating PDF files from any program. It's useful to have this method available as an option because it can be used if you're having difficulty with the Export command from an Adobe Creative Cloud application. The Print and Export commands use different processes for creating PDF files, so you can use one option if you have difficulty with the other.

**TECHNICAL STUFF**

Bookmarks, links, page transitions, and multimedia aren't included if a PDF is generated with the Print menu option. You must use the Export or Save As option to have these items included in PDF files.

# Creating PDF Files from Paper Documents and the Web

Adobe Acrobat provides options for converting paper documents and even web pages into PDF format. PDF can be a great way to share documents that you've scanned into your computer, or web pages that may change, or that you want to review when you aren't connected to the Internet.

## Converting paper documents to PDF

To convert paper documents into PDF, you need a scanner to digitize the information. If you expect to scan a large number of pages into PDF, consider purchasing a scanner with an automatic document feeder. These days, some scanners can scan both the front and back of a document at the same time and can even fit easily on your desk so scanning takes very little time. Some printers now even include scanners. If you have a PC and if a scanner is already hooked to the computer on which you use Acrobat, follow these steps to scan in a paper document and then convert it to PDF format:

1. **From the Acrobat main menu, choose File➪Create➪PDF From Scanner.**

   Then choose the type of PDF document you want to create. For pages with text, choose one of the Document options: Black and White Document for line art or text that contains no shades of gray; Grayscale Document for documents that contain varying shades of gray; or Color Document for documents that contain color. For photographs, choose the Color Photograph option.

2. **Make sure that your scanner is turned on, put the document to be scanned into the scanner, and then click the Scan button.**

   If necessary, continue to scan multiple pages into a single document. When you're done scanning, the scanned page appears in Acrobat.

   If you have a PDF open and choose Create PDF from Scanner, a window appears, giving you the opportunity to *append* the file (add to the existing file) or create a new PDF file.

   The scanned document opens in Acrobat.

**TIP**

If the pages need to be rotated, choose View⇨Rotate View and select the option to rotate the view either clockwise or counterclockwise.

3. **Choose File⇨Save to save the finished document as a PDF.**

**TIP**

If the document you scanned contains text, the text will be fully searchable if you use one of the Document preset choices because Acrobat uses Optical Character Recognition (OCR) to convert the image to text. However, if you use one of the Image preset choices, you must manually tell Acrobat to detect the text before it will be searchable. To do this, open a previously scanned file and use the Tools button to access the commands. Choose Tools⇨Content⇨Recognize Text⇨In This File. This command makes previously scanned text searchable.

## Converting web pages to PDFs

By converting online content to Adobe PDF, you can capture content from a website. Because web content can change rapidly, you can capture something that may not remain online for a long period of time. You can convert things, such as news stories or business information, from a website into PDF. Because PDF files can easily be combined together, you can merge a PDF from a website with other PDF files, such as spreadsheets, word-processing documents, and brochures.

If you enable the Acrobat Add-on in Internet Explorer you can click the Convert Web Page to PDF button to create a single page PDF. This step converts the current web page to a PDF.

If you want to convert more than a single web page to a PDF, follow these steps from within Acrobat (not your web browser):

1. **From the Acrobat main menu, choose File⇨Create⇨PDF From Web Page.**

   The Create PDF from Web Page dialog box opens.

2. **In the URL text box, enter the URL for the website you're converting to PDF.**

3. **To capture additional pages that are linked from the main page you're capturing, click the Capture Multiple Levels button and then select one of the following:**

**WARNING**

   ● Select the Stay On Same Path checkbox if you want only pages from the entered URL converted to PDF.

   ● Select the Stay On Same Server checkbox to download only pages that are on the same server as the entered URL.

Be cautious about selecting the Get Entire Site radio button instead of the Get Only radio button. The Get Entire Site option may take an enormous amount of time and not have any relevance to what you need.

**4. Click the Settings button to open the Web Page Conversion Settings dialog box and see accepted file types and change PDF settings (on the General tab).**

**5. On the Page Layout tab of the Web Page Conversion Settings dialog box, make changes to page size, orientation, and margins if the web page requires a wider or longer layout. See Figure 2-3.**

**FIGURE 2-3:**
Changing the
layout of web
pages converted
to PDF.

**6. When you're done making changes in the Web Page Conversion Settings dialog box, click OK.**

**7. In the Create PDF from Web Page dialog box, click the Create button to generate a PDF.**

The Downloading Status window opens, showing the rate of download.

When the download is complete, the selected web page (for the entered URL) appears as a PDF document with *hyperlinks* (links to other pages within the site) intact. When you select links on the converted web page, you can choose to open the linked page in Acrobat or the web browser.

Chapter **3**

# Adding Interactivity to PDF Files

B ecause many PDF documents are viewed online, you should make them easy for readers to navigate. With Acrobat, you can design documents that are easier to navigate than their printed counterparts and that include rich interactive features that simply aren't available with paper documents.

Rather than making readers scroll through a document to find what they want, you can add links within an index or a table of contents, or you can add links to websites and email addresses. Acrobat also includes bookmarks, which are an interactive table of contents. You can even add buttons that link to specific pages within a PDF document or that cause an action to occur when clicked, such as printing the document. We discuss all these features in this chapter.

## Adding Bookmarks to Create Easy PDF Navigation

Users have come to expect documents that involve easy-to-use navigation and ways to quickly find what they need. You can make your PDF documents more user-friendly by adding *bookmarks*, which are the equivalent of a table of contents that's always available, no matter what page the user is viewing in the Document window.

*Bookmarks* provide a listing of contents within a PDF file or links to relevant external content. Bookmarks sit within a panel, and when you click one, you're taken to a specific destination in the PDF document (or possibly to an external file), much like a hyperlink. You can create bookmarks from existing text, or you can use your own text to describe the content, which is useful if the destination of the bookmark is a figure, chart, or graphic.

By default, the Bookmarks icon resides along the left side of the Acrobat Document window in the *navigation panel.* Click the Bookmarks icon to make the panel appear; click the Bookmarks icon a second time to hide it. If the icon isn't visible, choose View⇨Show/Hide⇨Navigation Panes⇨Bookmarks to make it appear.

## Creating bookmarks that link to a page

By navigating to a page, and to a specific view on a page, you can establish the destination of a bookmark link. With a PDF document open, follow these steps:

1.  **If the Bookmark icon isn't visible choose View⇨Show/Hide⇨Navigation Panes⇨Bookmarks.**

    The Bookmarks panel appears on the left of the Document window.

2.  **In the Document window, navigate to the page that you want as the bookmark's destination.**

3.  **Set the magnification of the view that you want viewers to see when they click the bookmark by using the Zoom In and Zoom Out buttons in the toolbar.**

    The zoom level that you're at when you create the bookmark is the view that viewers see when they click the bookmark.

4.  **In the Bookmarks panel, click the New Bookmark icon. (It shows a ribbon with a plus sign.)**

    The new bookmark appears in the Bookmarks panel as Untitled.

5.  **Change the name by typing something more descriptive.**

    If you leave the bookmark as Untitled but want to rename it later, you must right-click the bookmark and then choose Rename, or you can click the Bookmark panel menu in the upper-left corner of the panel and choose Rename Bookmark.

**TIP**

6.  **Test your bookmark by scrolling to another page and viewing it in the Document window; then click your saved bookmark in the Bookmark panel.**

    The Document window shows the exact location and zoom that you selected when you created the bookmark.

Use the Selection tool to highlight text, such as a headline or a caption, that's part of the bookmark destination. Then choose New Bookmark, and the selected text becomes the title of the new bookmark. You can use this shortcut to avoid entering a new name for new bookmark titles. You can also press Ctrl+B (Windows) or ⌘+B (Mac) to quickly create a bookmark, and any selected text becomes the bookmark title.

## Creating bookmarks that link to a website

Although bookmarks are most commonly used to link to content within a PDF file, you can also use bookmarks to create links to other websites or even other documents. To create a link to an external website, follow these steps:

1. **Make sure nothing is selected. Then, choose Options⇨New Bookmark in the Bookmarks panel.**

   The Options menu looks like two circles on top of each other, found in the upper-left corner of the Bookmarks window. On the Mac OS, it is a drop-down menu.

2. **Replace the Untitled bookmark entry that appears in the Bookmarks panel with an appropriate name for the bookmark.**

3. **Choose Options⇨Properties from the Bookmarks panel menu.**

   The Bookmark Properties dialog box appears. With this dialog box, you can change a bookmark so that it links to any web address or even another file. In this example, we use a web address, but the bookmark could be a link to another PDF file, a Photoshop file, or even a Microsoft Excel file. Just remember that this bookmark creates a relative link. The linked file must travel with the PDF document in order for the link to work.

4. **In the Bookmark Properties dialog box, click the Actions tab, select Open a Web Link from the Select Action drop-down list, and then click the Add button.**

   The Edit URL dialog box appears.

5. **Enter the web address to which the users should be taken when they click this bookmark. Then click OK.**

   The bookmarked link is created.

 You can use bookmarks to choose different actions, such as opening another file or even playing a sound or movie.

REMEMBER

# Using bookmarks

Bookmarks are intuitive to use, which makes them an attractive option to add to PDF files. After you click a bookmark, the action associated with it is performed, which typically navigates you to a certain page within the PDF file.

Unfortunately, the Bookmarks panel doesn't open automatically with a document, even when bookmarks are present within a file. To display the Bookmarks panel when a file is opened, follow these steps:

1. **Choose File⇨Properties.**

2. **In the Document Properties dialog box that opens, select the Initial View tab, as shown in Figure 3-1.**

**FIGURE 3-1:**
The Documents
Properties dialog
box in Adobe
Acrobat.

3. **From the Navigation Tab drop-down list, select Bookmarks Panel and Page and then click OK.**

   After you save and reopen the file, the Bookmarks panel displays whenever the document is opened.

# Editing bookmarks

You can change the attributes of bookmarks so that they have a different color, a different text style, or a link to another location. Make these changes by selecting a bookmark and then choosing Options⇨Properties in the Bookmarks panel. (Remember the Options button appears in the upper-left corner of the panel, and it's the icon that looks like a dialog box.) In the Bookmark Properties dialog box that opens, choose the color and font style of the bookmark on the Appearance tab: To change the bookmark's font style, select a style from the Style drop-down list; to change the bookmark's color, click the Color box and choose a color from the Colors panel.

On the Actions tab of the Bookmark Properties dialog box, you can delete existing actions (in the Actions section of the Actions tab) by clicking to select an action and then clicking the Delete button. Also, you can add actions by choosing another action from the Add Action section and then clicking the Add button. You can add more than one action to a bookmark.

# Adding Interactive Links

When viewing a PDF file in Acrobat, you can add links for email addresses, web addresses, and references to other pages. Unlike bookmarks, which are neatly organized in a panel, links are attached to a region of a page, which you identify with the Link tool.

To add an interactive link to your PDF document, follow these steps:

1. **Click on the Tools tab, and from the Tools Center, click on the Edit PDF icon.**

   The Link tool appears in the toolbar above your document.

2. **The Link tool is actually a drop-down menu, which offers options for adding, editing, removing, appending, viewing, or auto-creating links. Choose the Add/Edit Web or Document Link option.**

3. **Using the Link tool, click and drag to select the region where the user will click to activate the link.**

   The Create Link dialog box appears.

4. **In the Link Action section of the Create Link dialog box, choose an action that the link will perform:**

   - *Go to a Page View:* This option is the default, where you'll be able to scroll to the page that is the destination of the link.

- *Open a File:* Alternatively, you can choose to link to another file; you'll be prompted to locate the file.

- *Open a Web Page:* If you choose this option, you're choosing to link to a web address. In the Edit URL text box that appears, enter the complete address of the website to which the link should direct viewers. To create a link to an email address, type **mailto:** followed by an email address. (Note that mailto: is all one word.)

- *Custom Link:* Use this option to choose from other types of links in the Link Properties dialog box.

5. **Set the appearance of the link, such as visible or invisible.**

6. **Click Next and follow the instructions in the next dialog box before clicking OK.**

   The instructions have you navigate to the intended destination of the link, which you should do before clicking OK.

**TIP**

Although the Link tool is relatively simple to use, you may prefer to create links from text using the Selection tool. To do so, click and drag to select the text that will become a link, then right-click (Windows) or Ctrl-click (Mac), and choose Create Link from the contextual menu that appears.

**REMEMBER**

You can also have links transferred automatically from your original Microsoft Office documents when using PDF Maker, or from Adobe InDesign if you use the Hyperlinks panel within InDesign to create the links.

You can edit links by choosing the Link tool and double-clicking the existing link to open the Link Properties dialog box. While editing a link, you can change how it's presented in the Appearance tab. Make a link invisible or add a border to the link, such as a blue border that commonly is used to define hyperlinks. On the Actions tab of the Link Properties dialog box, you can add, edit, or delete actions, just as you can with bookmarks (see the preceding section).

# Adding Buttons to Simplify Your PDF Files

Along with links and bookmarks, buttons provide another way to make your files more useful when they're viewed online. You can create interactive buttons entirely within Acrobat — designing their appearance and adding text to them. Or you can import buttons created in other Adobe Creative Cloud applications, such as Photoshop and Illustrator, and add actions to them within Acrobat. For example, within Acrobat, a button that advances the viewer to the next page in a document will be a simple button with text. However, if you want an arrow icon, you can create it in Photoshop or Illustrator and import the button icon into your PDF page using Acrobat.

**REMEMBER**

You can also create interactive buttons for a PDF document by using InDesign. Buttons created using InDesign carry through to a PDF when you export an interactive PDF document.

You can add buttons directly within Acrobat by using the Add Button tool.

To add a button to your PDF document, follow these steps:

1. **Click on the Tools tab, and from the Tools Center, click on the Rich Media icon. You'll see the Add Button tool appear in the toolbar above your document. Click on it, and the cursor changes to a crosshair, which you can then use to draw the location of the button on your PDF document.** On the Mac OS you will see a box at the crosshair.

2. **Click and drag to specify the location where you want the button to appear in the document.**

3. **Type in an appropriate name for your button in the Field Name dialog box that appears.**

   This is not what will appear on the actual button in your layout.

4. **Click the All Properties button to see the Button Properties dialog box.**

5. **In the General tab, you can enter a name for the button in the Name text box and provide a tooltip in the ToolTip text box. You can also specify whether the button is visible only onscreen or when printing under the Common Properties section.**

   A *tooltip* is the text that appears whenever the mouse cursor is positioned over the button.

6. **In the Appearance tab, establish how your button will look by setting the following options:**

   - *Border Color/Fill Color:* Click the square to the right of the appropriate attribute in the Borders and Colors section of the Appearance tab and then choose a color from the Colors panel.

   - *Line Thickness and Style:* These options don't appear unless you change the border color from None (red diagonal line) to another selection.

   - *Font Size/Font:* Change the size and font of the button text by making a selection from the Font Size and the Font drop-down lists.

   - *Text Color:* Change the color of the text by clicking the color square and choosing a color from the Colors panel.

Adding Interactivity to
PDF Files

7. **In the Options tab, make these selections:**

- *Layout:* Use the Layout drop-down list to specify whether you want to use a *label* (text that you enter in Acrobat that appears on the face of the button) or whether you want an *icon* (an imported button graphic that you may have designed in Photoshop or Illustrator).

- *Behavior:* Select Push from the Behavior drop-down list to create different appearances for a button so that it changes based upon whether the mouse cursor is positioned over the button. The button appearance can also change when clicked.

- *State:* To specify the different appearances (see Behavior, discussed in the preceding paragraph), click the State on the left side of the Options tab, and then choose the Label or Icon status for each state.

- *Label:* If you choose to use a label, enter the text for it in the Label text field.

- *Icon:* If you choose to use an icon, specify the location of the graphic file by clicking the Choose Icon button. You can create button icons in either Photoshop or Illustrator and save them in the PDF format for importing as a button icon.

8. **In the Actions tab, select an action from the Select Action drop-down list and then click the Add button.**

   *Actions* are applied to buttons similar to the way in which they're applied to links and bookmarks:

- To specify when the action occurs, click the Select Trigger drop-down list and choose whether the mouse clicking and being released or being moved over an area causes the action to occur. The default trigger is Mouse Up, which causes the action to occur when the mouse button is depressed and then released. You can choose other actions, such as the mouse cursor merely rolling over the button without the need to click it.

- To choose actions that are a part of the menu commands, such as printing a document, closing a file, or navigating to the next or preceding page, click the Select Action drop-down list, choose Execute a Menu Item, and then click Add to choose the menu command.

9. **After you make all your changes in the Button Properties dialog box, click Close.**

IN THIS CHAPTER

» Manipulating text with the Edit
Text & Images tool

» Modifying graphics and page objects
with the Edit Text & Images tool

» Pulling text and graphics out of PDFs
for use in other documents

# Chapter **4**

# Editing and Extracting Text and Graphics

You may assume that PDF files are mere pictures of your documents and can't be edited, but nothing is further from the truth. Adobe Acrobat includes a variety of tools for editing both text and graphics. You can use these tools as long as the file hasn't been secured to prohibit editing. We introduce you to the tools for modifying PDF documents in this chapter. We discuss security, which allows you to limit access to these tools, in Chapter 6 of this minibook.

## Editing Text

You can access the tools for editing text and graphics by clicking on the Edit PDF icon in the Tools Center. (See Figure 4-1.)

**TIP**

If you do not see the Tools Center, click on the Tools tab at the top left of your Acrobat window.

FIGURE 4-1:
The Tools Center.

TIP

For editing objects, you have three choices in the toolbar at the top (see Figure 4-2):

» **Edit Text & Images tool:** Used to manipulate text and images.

» **Add Text tool:** Used to add new text onto a PDF document page.

» **Add Image tool:** Used to add a new image into a page within a PDF document.

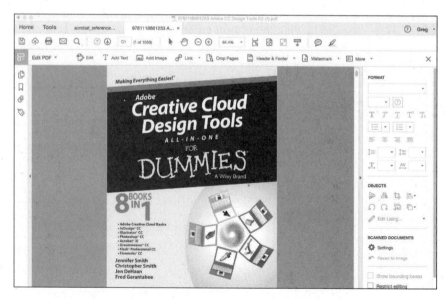

FIGURE 4-2:
The Content
Editing tools.

# Using the Edit Text & Images tool to manipulate text

The Edit Text & Images tool is used for manipulating text. This can include changing actual text characters or the appearance of text. You can change *cat* to *dog*, or you can change black text to blue, or you can even change the Helvetica font to the Times font.

**REMEMBER**

When you change a PDF file, the original source document isn't modified.

You have a few ways to accomplish text edits:

>> Choose the Edit Text & Images tool, click within the text that you want to change to obtain an insertion point, and then start typing the new text.

>> Click with the Edit Text & Images tool in your text and press the Backspace or Delete key to delete text.

>> With the Edit Text & Images tool, drag to highlight text and enter new text to replace the highlighted text.

When changing text — whether you're adding or deleting — Acrobat tries to use the font that was specified in the original document. Sometimes, this font is built into the PDF file, which means that it's *embedded* in the file. Other times, the font may not be available either because it hasn't been embedded or it's been embedded as a *subset* where only some of the characters from the font are included in the PDF file. In these cases, Acrobat may provide the following warning message:

```
Warning! Since the original font is not available, a substituted font for
    editing is used. Any changes to the text of the original font will place a
    new font dependency upon the document.
```

Fortunately, you can change the font if you need to edit the text. However, when you change the font, the text may not retain the same appearance as the original document. In some instances, you may not have the exact same font on your computer as the font used in the PDF document, but you may have a similar font you can use without causing a noticeable change — most people won't notice the difference between Helvetica and Arial or between Times and Times New Roman. Fonts with the same name but from different font designers often look very similar. For example, Adobe Garamond looks similar to ITC Garamond, even though they're two different fonts.

To change the font that's used for a word or a range of words, follow these steps:

1. **With the Edit Text & Images tool, drag over the text you want to select.**

   You may see a Loading System Fonts message followed by another Loading Document Fonts message. Depending on the number of fonts installed on your system, it may take a while for this message to disappear.

   The Tools Pane is activated on the right side of the workspace. If you do not see the Tools pane, you may access it under View➪Show/Hide ➪Tools Pane.

2. **In the Tools pane, choose the typeface you want to use from the Font drop-down list and make any other changes you want. (See Figure 4-3.)**

   In this dialog pane, you can also change the size by selecting or typing a number into the Font Size drop-down list. In addition, you can modify the color by clicking the Fill color swatch.

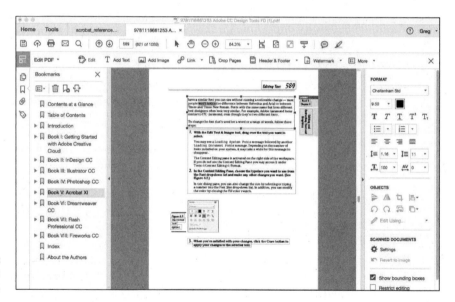

**FIGURE 4-3:**
Text options in
the Tools pane.

## Using the Edit Text & Images tool to edit graphics

You can use the Edit Text & Images tool to access editing software for modifying graphics. For example, you can use the Edit Text & Images tool to select a graphic, bring the graphic into Photoshop, and then save the modified version back into the PDF file. In other words, you can edit the graphics used in PDF documents, even if you don't have access to the original graphic files.

# ADDING TEXT

You can use the Add Text tool to type anywhere on the document. Access the Add Text tool from the toolbar when in Edit Text mode. Then position your cursor where you want to begin typing, click, and start to type, pressing the Enter or Return key whenever you want to add a line. The Tools pane appears after you click on a page. Use the text options in the Tools pane to change the font or size of the text you're adding to the page, and change the type color, style, or alignment.

Likewise, to change the space between the lines, click on the Line Spacing pull-down menu or enter a value. You can move or resize the text block by selecting it with the Add Text tool and either moving or resizing the text box. Your text remains editable. So, if you've made a mistake and want to correct it, or want to add or delete text, you select the Add Text tool again and double-click in the type box.

To edit a photographic file from Acrobat in Photoshop, follow these steps:

1. **Select the image with the Edit Text & Images tool, right-click (Windows) or Control-click (Mac) on a photographic image with the Edit Object tool, and then choose Edit Using⇨Adobe Photoshop from the contextual menu.**

   The image file opens in Adobe Photoshop.

2. **Using Photoshop's tools, make the necessary changes to the graphic and then choose File⇨Save.**

   When you return to the PDF file in Acrobat, the graphic is updated automatically in the PDF document.

**REMEMBER**

If you have the original graphic file, it remains untouched — only the version used within the PDF file is modified. It isn't necessary to have the original graphic file to perform these steps.

You can also use Acrobat to edit vector objects from within PDF files, such as those created with Adobe Illustrator. Just follow these steps:

1. **Select a piece of vector artwork with the Edit Text & Images tool, right-click (Windows) or Control-click (Mac) the vector artwork, and then choose Edit Using⇨Adobe Illustrator from the contextual menu.**

   *Note:* Acrobat displays Edit Using in the contextual menu if it detects an image, and you can then choose whether you want to edit the image using either Photoshop or Illustrator (if you have these tools installed on your computer system).

TIP

If you're editing a complex illustration, be sure to select all its components by holding down the Ctrl (Windows) or ⌘ (Mac) key while clicking them with the Edit Text & Images tool.

After choosing Edit Using⇨Adobe Illustrator, the object opens for editing in Adobe Illustrator.

2. **After you make the necessary changes in Illustrator, choose File⇨Save.**

The graphic is updated in the PDF document.

TIP

If Acrobat doesn't start Photoshop or Illustrator after choosing the Edit with command, you may need to access preferences by choosing Edit⇨Preferences⇨ Content Editing (Windows) or Acrobat⇨Preferences⇨Content Editing (Mac OS) and then specifying which programs should be used for editing images or objects.

TIP

You can also use the Edit Text & Images tool to edit the position of text or graphic objects on a page, which includes the capability to relocate individual lines of text or to change the position of a graphic on a page. After you select an object with the Edit Text & Images tool, you can simply drag it to a new location on the page. Similarly, you can delete objects from a PDF document by selecting them and then pressing the Delete key.

# Exporting Text and Graphics

Although editing text and graphics is helpful, you may need to take text or images from a PDF document and use them in another file. Fortunately, Acrobat also includes tools to make this a breeze. Of course, you should always make certain that you have the permission of the owner of a document before reusing content that isn't your original work.

You can export text, images, or charts from Acrobat by copying and pasting, or by saving as a specific file type. These methods are discussed in detail in the following sections.

## Exporting text with Select, Copy, and Paste

Follow these steps to select, copy, and paste text from a PDF file:

1. **With the Edit Text & Images tool, highlight the text you want to export.**

When you hold this tool over a section of your document, it turns into an I-bar cursor, which you can drag to select the text you want to copy.

**TIP**

Keep in mind that this method only lets you select text within an area. You need to switch to the Selection tool in order to select large areas of text.

If the Cut, Copy, and Paste commands are unavailable after you've selected some text, the author of the document may have set the security settings to disallow copying. If you can't select the text, you may be trying to copy text that's part of an image. If you're trying to select text that's in a single column, a sidebar, or table, press and hold the Ctrl key (Windows) or ⌘ key (Mac) and then click and drag over the area with text to be selected.

**2.** **Right-click (Windows) or Control-click (Mac) the selected text. Then, from the contextual menu, choose Copy to copy the text.**

Being able to extract the text out of a PDF document by selecting and copying it is useful if you don't have access to the original source document, but you need to use the text from a PDF file in another document.

**3.** **Open another text-editing program, such as Adobe InDesign or Microsoft Word.**

You can paste the copied text into a new document or a preexisting file.

**4.** **Insert your cursor in the document at the appropriate spot and choose Edit⇨Paste.**

The text is pasted into the document, ready for you to use.

## Exporting text with Save As Other

Use the File⇨Export To⇨Microsoft Word or File⇨Export To⇨Spreadsheet commands to export all the text in your PDF file. After choosing the location where you want the file saved, click Save to save the Microsoft Word or spreadsheet file.

You can also choose several other formats for exporting your PDF documents:

>> **Rich Text Format:** Use this format to convert the text in a PDF document to an editable RTF file that can be manipulated in common word processing apps such as Microsoft Word.

>> **Encapsulated PostScript and PostScript:** These formats are generally used by commercial printers or IT professionals who need PostScript output.

>> **HTML Web Page:** This is used to attempt to convert the PDF to another file format that can be used for viewing on the web without a PDF plug-in. PDF files do not always convert well to HTML, so be sure to test this option if you want to use it for any important documents.

>> **Graphics:** To save your PDF document as an image, choose File➪Save As and choose from any of the various graphics formats, including JPEG, JPEG2000, PNG, and TIFF, from the Save as Type or File Format drop-down menu. If you choose one of these options, your text will no longer be editable because all the PDF pages will be converted to images, with each page in the PDF becoming a separate image file.

**REMEMBER**

Text that's copied from a PDF file is no longer linked to the original document. Edits made to the extracted text aren't reflected within the PDF file, and it's extremely difficult to have the extracted text reinserted into the PDF document, because the Edit Text & Images tool and Add Text tool are rather limited in their capability to add any significant amount of text onto a page. Think of the extraction process as a one-way trip for the text, which can be extracted but not reinserted.

You can also export portions of text and tables so you can edit them later using a spreadsheet program, such as Microsoft Excel, or a word processing program such as Microsoft Word. Just follow these steps:

1. **Click the Selection Tool tool and click and drag to select the text in the table.**

   Depending upon how the table was created, you may also be able to position your cursor just outside the edge of the table and then draw a box around a table. Remember you can Ctrl-click (Windows) or ⌘-click (Mac) and then drag around a table to select it.

   A border appears around the selected table.

2. **Right-click (Windows) or Control-click (Mac) and choose Export Selection As from the contextual menu.**

   Alternatively, you can save the table directly to a file or copy to the Clipboard to be pasted later: If Acrobat has trouble identifying the text in the table, it may be saved as an image file, which is not editable text.

   - Choose Export Selection As from the contextual menu *to save the text directly to a file.*

   - *To copy the table to the Clipboard so that you can paste it into other documents,* choose Copy with Formatting from the contextual menu.

   After opening Excel or whatever spreadsheet program you have installed on your computer, you can paste the table into the spreadsheet.

   And that's it. You can now use that table in another program.

# Chapter **5**

# Using Commenting and Annotation Tools

O ne of the great features of Acrobat is the capability to mark up PDF documents with virtual sticky notes, mark up text to indicate changes, add annotations, and draw comments. The Acrobat commenting tools don't change the original file, and you can remove the comments at any time. This means that you can disable comments for printing or viewing when you want. In this chapter, you discover these capabilities and we show you how to put them to work for you.

## Creating Comments with the Comment Panel

You can easily add annotations to PDF files, including stamps, text highlights, callouts, and electronic sticky notes by using the Comment panel, which you can access by clicking the Comment button on the Tasks toolbar. This opens the Comment toolbar at the top of the page and the Comment pane on the right of the page.

The Comment toolbar, as shown in Figure 5-1, provides several tools for adding comments to PDF documents. The Comment pane includes a comment list to help manage and review comments. We discuss these tools in the following sections.

## The Add Sticky Note tool

Use the Add Sticky Note tool to add electronic sticky notes to your files. Just click the location where you want the note to appear within a PDF document, and an icon representing the note appears, along with a window where you can enter text. After entering text in the sticky note, close the window so that the document isn't hidden beneath it.

You can change the icon and color used to represent the note by right-clicking (Windows) or Control-clicking (Mac) the note and choosing Properties from the contextual menu. In the Properties dialog box that appears, in the Appearance tab, make the changes to the note icon or color and then click OK to have the changes apply to the note.

## The Text Edit tools

The Text Edit tools are six separate text commenting tools. Use these tools to indicate that selected text should be replaced or to highlight or underline selected text, calling attention to it in the PDF file. You can also add a note to selected text, or indicate that text should be inserted at a specific location, and mark text for deletion.

To use Text Edit tools, follow these steps:

1. **Choose the text edits tool you want to use from Comment toolbar.**

2. **Click and drag the selected tool over the text you want to change, comment on, or highlight.**

   Your selected text edits are displayed on the PDF file.

**TIP**

To use the Insert Text tool, click where you want to insert the type, and then select the Insert Text tool. Then, after Acrobat creates an insertion point, start to type the new text in the pop-up window to add a comment showing the text you want added to the document.

# The Add Stamp tool

You can use stamps to identify documents or to highlight a certain part of a document. Common stamps include Confidential, Draft, Sign Here, and Approved.

The stamps are grouped into sections, and you can access them from the Stamp tool from the Comment toolbar. Some stamps automatically add your default username along with the date and time you applied them to the document; these stamps are available under the Dynamic category in the Stamps menu. The more traditional business stamps, such as Confidential, appear under the Standard Business category. You can access each of the categories by clicking the arrow to the right of the Stamp tool in the Comment toolbar, as shown in Figure 5-2.

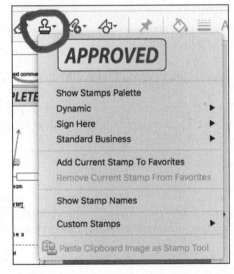

**FIGURE 5-2:** Access the categories of stamps by clicking the Stamp tool in the Comment toolbar.

To apply a stamp to your document, follow these steps:

1.  **Select the Stamp tool by selecting Comments from the taskbar, then clicking the Stamp tool in the Comment toolbar.**

2.  **Click the arrow to the right of the Stamp tool and from the menu, choose either the Dynamic or Standard Business stamp.**

    The first time you use the stamps, you may be asked to input your information so Acrobat can include your identity as the user applying the stamps. If, after you have entered your information, you click the Don't Show Again option when asked to enter your identity, you won't need to do this again.

3.  **Click within your document at the location where you want the stamp to appear.**

# The Highlight Text tool

The Highlight Text tool works similarly to the Text Edits tools. To highlight text, follow these steps:

1. **Select the Highlight Text tool from the Comment toolbar.**

2. **Click and drag over the text that you want highlighted.**

   The text is now highlighted.

# The Attach File tool

With the Attach File tool, you can attach any existing file from your computer or computer network to a PDF document. For example, if you have an Excel spreadsheet that relates to the PDF document, and you want to allow users to work with the data, you could attach the Excel file to the PDF document.

Follow these steps to attach a file to your PDF document:

1. **Select the Add a New Attachment⇨Attach File tool from the Comment toolbar, then place your cursor over the location in the document where you want the attachment icon to be visible.**

2. **Click where you want the attachment noted.**

   The Add Attachment dialog box appears.

3. **In the Add Attachment dialog box, browse to the file that you want to attach and click the Open button (Windows) or Select button (Mac).**

   You can attach text, graphic, or sound files.

4. **The File Attachment Properties window appears.**

5. **In the File Attachment Properties window, select the icon you want to use to represent the file attachment. Then click OK.**

   You can choose from a paperclip, graph, pushpin, or tag. Whatever icon you select appears on your document to denote that another file is attached. When you roll over the icon, a little annotation appears telling you the filename.

**TIP**

   You can use the Record Audio tool to share a verbal comment by using the built-in microphone on your computer or laptop (if you have one) to record a message directly into the PDF. The sound is added as a comment. Follow the preceding Steps 1–5 for adding an attachment, except use the Record Audio tool located below the Attach File tool.

**REMEMBER**

The file(s) that you attach with the Attach File and Record Audio tools becomes embedded within the PDF file, and the size of the file increases. When using attached files, they remain in their original file format, even if the attached file isn't a PDF file. For example, you can attach an Excel spreadsheet to a PDF document, and the recipient will need to use Excel to view or edit the attachment. Attaching a file to a PDF document doesn't convert the attachment to PDF.

## The drawing tools

The Drawing Tools section of the Comment toolbar contains shape tools, line tools, and other drawing tools. Use the drawing tools to add lines, ovals, rectangles, and other shapes to your PDF file to provide feedback and comments on a PDF document. These shapes can call attention to specific portions of a document and make it easy to provide visual feedback on PDF documents you are reviewing. The steps in this section show you how to work with some of the more useful drawing tools.

To use the Cloud Shape tool, follow these steps:

1. **Select the Cloud Shape tool from the Drawing Tools section of the Comment toolbar.**

2. **Click in your document to begin the shape.**

3. **Click again in another position to set the length of the first part of the cloud and then click again to begin shaping your cloud.**

   Click as often as you like to create your shape.

4. **When you're finished with your shape, double-click to close the cloud shape, or click back at the starting point of the cloud.**

**TIP**

Use the Selection tool, found in the page control section of the toolbar to click the shape you created and drag the corner points to resize, if necessary. You can also use the Selection tool after creating a cloud shape to change the color and thickness of the line values. To make these changes, using the Selection tool, right-click (Windows) or Control-click (Mac) the shape and choose Properties from the contextual menu. In the Polygon Properties window that opens, make the desired changes to the appearance. For example, you can use the Style drop-down list in the Properties dialog box to change the appearance of a selected comment. Instead of the cloud edges, you can change them to dotted lines, dashed lines, and so on. When you're finished changing the appearance, click OK.

Using Commenting and Annotation Tools

To use the rectangle- and oval-shaped drawing markup tools, follow these steps:

1. **Select either the Rectangle or Oval Shape tool from the drawing tools in the Comment toolbar.**

2. **Click and drag in your document to draw the shape.**

3. **While the drawing tool you chose is selected, click the shape you created and drag the corner points to resize, if necessary.**

   You can also use the Selection tool if you're having difficulty adjusting the shape or size of a previously created shape.

4. **After creating the shape, right-click (Windows) or Control-click (Mac) the shape and choose Properties from the contextual menu to change the color and thickness of the line values.**

5. **When you're finished, click OK.**

   As with the cloud polygon, you can also use the Style drop-down list in the Properties dialog box to change the appearance of the shape.

## The Add Text Box tool

When creating notes that you want to prominently display on a document, you can use the Add Text Box tool to add text annotations directly onto a PDF document. Text added using the Add Text Box tool is clearly visible on the document without needing to open any dialog boxes or windows.

Follow these steps to add a text box containing comments:

1. **Select the Add Text Box tool from the Comment toolbar. Then click and drag on the PDF document in the location where you want to place the comment.**

   A text field is placed directly on the document.

2. **Add your text comment by typing directly into the text box.**

   A pop-up window appears with font, color, and size information.

3. **To change the appearance of the text box, right-click (Windows) or Control-click (Mac) and choose Properties from the contextual menu to set the color of the text box that contains the note.**

4. **After making your choices to modify the appearance of the text box, click OK.**

TIP

You can select the text box and move it to another position using the Selection tool.

# The Add Text Callout tool

The Add Text Callout tool creates a callout text box that points to a section of your document with an arrow. The callout text box is made up of three parts: the text box, the knee line, and the end point line. You can resize each part individually to customize the callout area of your document.

To use the Callout tool, follow these steps:

1. **Select the Add Text Callout tool from the Drawing Tools section of the Comment toolbar.**

2. **Click where you want the arrowhead point to be located.**

3. **Move the cursor to the location where you want the text box to be positioned and then click again. Begin typing your comment.**

   As with the other drawing markup tools, you can use the Selection tool to relocate the text box or use the anchor points to resize the box.

4. **If you want to change the color of the callout text box, right-click (Windows) or Control-click (Mac) the callout text box (not the text) and choose Properties from the contextual menu.**

   The Callout Properties window opens. You can change the size and color of the box using the Callout Properties window. (If you want to change the color and font characteristics of the text in the callout text box, double-click on the text and a formatting pop-up box will open with font, color, and size information.)

5. **After modifying the appearance of the callout text box, click OK to close the Callout Properties window.**

**TIP**

You can select the callout text box and move it to another position any time you want. You can resize the text box by dragging an anchor point.

# The Draw Freeform tool

With the Draw Freeform tool, you can create freeform lines on your documents. These lines can be useful when you're trying to attract attention to a specific portion of a page. Just follow these steps:

1. **Select the Pencil tool from the Comment toolbar.**

2. **Click and drag to draw on your document.**

3. **You can edit the color and thickness of lines created with the Pencil tool by right-clicking (Windows) or Control-clicking (Mac) the line and choosing Properties from the contextual menu.**

   Alternatively, you can press Ctrl+E (Windows) or ⌘+E (Mac) to access the Properties toolbar.

4. **Make your choices and click OK.**

You can use the Eraser tool to remove portions of lines that had previously been created with the Pencil tool.

# Managing Comments

One of the most powerful features of PDF commenting is the capability to easily manage and share comments and annotations among reviewers. For example, you can determine which comments are displayed at any time, and you can filter the comments by author or by the type of commenting tool used to create the comment. In addition, you can indicate a response to a comment and track the changes that may have been made to a document based upon a comment. Also, you can consolidate comments from multiple reviewers into a single document.

## Viewing comments

Select the Comment panel from the taskbar list to display the list of comments that have been placed in your PDF document. The Comments List shows all the comments in the document, and appears along the right side of the Document window. You can see the author of each comment and any notes entered by reviewers.

If you select a comment, there is a checkbox at the bottom that you can use to indicate that the comment has been reviewed or to indicate that a certain comment needs further attention. Use these checkboxes for your own purposes; their status doesn't export with the document if you send the file to others, so they're for your personal use only.

## Changing a comment's review status

Acrobat makes it easy to indicate whether a comment has been reviewed, accepted, or has additional comments attached to it.

To change the status of a comment, follow these steps:

**1.** **In the Comments List, right-click (Windows) or Control-click (Mac) the comment for which you want to set the status.**

**2.** **Click Set Status and then select Accepted, Cancelled, Completed, or Rejected, depending on what's appropriate to your situation.**

The comment you modified appears in the list, showing the new status you assigned to it.

## Replying to a comment

You can double-click a comment in the Comments List and choose Reply to add a follow-up note to the comment. This way, new comments can be tied to existing comments. If your documents go through multiple rounds of review, adding a reply allows a secondary or final reviewer to expand on the comments from an initial reviewer. This method also allows an author or designer to clearly respond to the suggestions from an editor.

TIP

Using the Selection tool, you can also right-click (Windows) or Control-click (Mac) on a comment located on a document to add a reply. The reply will also be placed in the Comments List.

## Showing and hiding comments

Because the Comments List can become rather large, you can choose to display only some comments in the list. To do so, click the Filter Comments button in the upper-right of the Comment panel. To hide all comments, choose the Hide All Comments option from the Filter Comments menu in the Comments panel. This will hide all comments from the document as well as the list.

To show all the comments within a document, select the Show All Comments option from the Filter Comments menu in the Comments panel. You can then choose to display only certain types of comments, such as the following:

>> Type of comment, such as note, line, or cross out

>> Reviewer, such as Bob or Jane

>> Status, such as accepted or rejected

Use these filtering options to view only those comments that are relevant to your specific review situation.

**TIP**

If you have filtered comments, you can always display all comments again by choosing Show All Comments from the Filter Comments menu in the Comments List.

## Sharing comments

You can share your comments with other reviewers who have access to the same PDF document by following these steps:

1. **Make sure that the Comments panel is visible.**

2. **From the Comments panel, click the Options icon in the upper-right corner of the Comments panel, and choose Export All to Data File.**

   The Export Comments dialog box appears. If you want to share only selected comments, choose the comments from the Comments List and then choose Export Selected to Data File.

3. **Browse to the location where you want the comments to be saved and give the saved file a new name.**

   You now have a file that includes only the comments' information, and not the entire PDF file.

You can share your comments data file with reviewers who have the same PDF file, and they can choose Import Data File from the Options window while viewing the same PDF document. You can use this method to avoid sending entire PDF files to those who already have the document.

## Summarizing comments

You can compile a list of all the comments from a PDF file into a new, separate document. To summarize comments, follow these steps:

1. **From the Comments List of the Comment panel, click the Options icon in the upper-right corner of the Comments List and choose Create Comment Summary.**

   The Create Comment Summary dialog box appears.

2. **Create a listing of the comments with lines connecting them to their locations on the page by selecting the radio button from the top — Document and Comments with Connector Lines on Single Pages.**

   In the Include section, you can choose which comments should be summarized. If you prefer to create a different summary type, such as a list of the comments, select the option you prefer.

3. **Click the Create Comment Summary button.**

This step creates a new PDF document that simply lists all the comments, as shown in Figure 5-3.

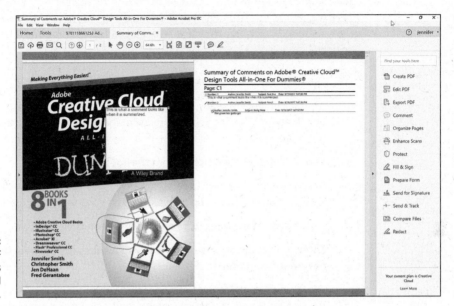

**FIGURE 5-3:**
A new PDF document is created, listing all the comments.

## Enabling commenting in Adobe Reader

Acrobat DC makes it easy to include users of the free Adobe Reader in a review process. To include Adobe Reader users in a review, choose File⇨Save As Other⇨Reader Extended PDF⇨Enable Commenting and Measuring. After saving the file, you can share it with users of the free Adobe Reader, who can then use commenting and markup tools and save their comments into the file. A user of Adobe Acrobat DC must enable commenting in a PDF file before users of Adobe Reader can add comments to a PDF file.

# Reviewing PDF Documents

You can use Acrobat to help manage the PDF review process.

*Email reviews* work with some email software applications, such as Microsoft Outlook, and allow you to send a PDF document to recipients, asking them to add comments and then reply.

# Using email reviews

*Email reviews* are a means of sharing comments in a PDF by attaching them to an email message. By using this feature, you can share comments without needing to upload the file to a server or to sign in to any service. When you use email reviews, comments are added to individual PDF files, and then consolidated back into a single PDF when they are returned to the originator. To initiate an email review:

**1.** **Open the document you wish to share with reviewers.**

If the document is already open, make certain it is saved before proceeding so any comments or edits you have made to the PDF are captured before the document is shared.

**2.** **Choose Send for Comments from the Tools Tab.**

If this is the first time you have initiated an email review, Acrobat will ask you to enter identifying information, then the Getting Started dialog box opens.

**3.** **Confirm the document to be shared and then click Next.**

**4.** **Enter the email addresses of those you want to invite to review the document, and then click Next.**

The Preview Invitation dialog box opens. Confirm the subject and message of the email invitation are appropriate to send.

**5.** **Click the Send Invitation button.**

An invitation to join the document review is sent using your email application. When recipients open the PDF file that you send, they will be asked to click the Send Comments button that appears at the top of the PDF they receive. This information is also contained in the email message sent to the reviewers.

**6.** **When comments on the PDF document are returned to you, open the file you receive and click the Import Data File button in the Options button of the Comment panel to combine the comments you received with any comments you may have entered.**

**TIP**

If you receive comments on a PDF document and Acrobat is unable to locate the original file because it has moved or been renamed, Acrobat will ask you to browse to locate the file at the time you merge comments.

# Chapter **6**

# Securing Your PDF Files

You may think that because you've converted your documents to PDF (Portable Document Format) that they're secure. This isn't quite true because Adobe Acrobat includes tools for changing text and images, as well as extracting them for use in other files. For example, you can use several tools to modify text and graphics (see Chapter 4 of this minibook) or copy a passage of text.

Applying security provides you with control over who can view, edit, or print the PDF documents you create and distribute. You can restrict access to files so that users need a password to view them, or you can restrict certain features of Acrobat, which stops most users from manipulating your files. All Adobe applications recognize and honor security settings applied in Acrobat, but some software ignores Adobe's security settings or can bypass them altogether. For this reason, you should be careful with whom you share your most sensitive PDF documents because even secure PDF files can be accessed by skilled or determined hackers.

In this chapter, we discuss using security protection to limit access to PDF files and show you how to limit what users can do to the contents of your PDF documents.

# Understanding Password Security

By requiring users to enter a password to open and view your PDF files, you limit access to those files so that only certain users can view them. You can also apply security to limit access to certain Acrobat and Adobe Reader features, such as copying text or graphics, editing the file, and printing. Adobe calls this type of security *password security* because it requires a password to either open the document or to change the security that's been applied to the document.

Apply security options to limit the opening or editing of your PDF document, restricting these capabilities to users who have been provided the proper password. If you have your PDF open, you do this by clicking the Protect button in the right-hand toolbar. Then choose Encrypt⇨Encrypt with Password to access the Password Security Settings dialog box.

In the Password Security - Settings dialog box, choose an Acrobat version from the Compatibility drop-down list. The higher the version of Acrobat, the greater the level of security, but the more limited the compatibility.

Remember, not everyone has Acrobat XI. If you intend to share your file with a broad group or if you're uncertain which versions of Acrobat or Adobe Reader your audience is using, you should allow everyone with Acrobat 7 and later to access your file. Your choice here is based on your needs for security and also the version of Acrobat or Adobe Reader that your audience uses. Lower versions of Acrobat provide more compatibility with the widest number of viewers because they support much older versions of the free Adobe Reader. In the following list, we explain the compatibility choices before showing you how to enable security in later sections:

>> **Acrobat 6 and Later or Acrobat 7 and Later:** If the users who receive your PDF files have older versions of the software, you can select Acrobat 6 and Later or Acrobat 7 and Later from the Compatibility drop-down list to ensure that the recipients can view the PDF file you're securing. This option provides compatibility for users who may not have updated their software in many years, and secure the file with 128-bit encryption. These security options will keep the average user from gaining access to your files. However, they won't deter a determined hacker from accessing them and a sophisticated user can circumvent them.

>> **Acrobat X and Later:** When sharing files with users who have access to Adobe Reader or Adobe Acrobat Version X or XI, this option provides expanded security, increasing the security level to 256-bit, which makes the resulting PDF files more difficult for unauthorized users to access.

# Applying Password Security to Your PDF Documents

Selecting the Encrypt with Password option from the Encrypt button in the Protect section of the Tools panel limits access to the PDF file. Only those who know the password can open the file. However, documents are only as secure as the passwords that protect them. To guard against discovery of a password, use passwords that are eight or more characters in length and include at least one number or symbol and vary the case of the characters. Avoid using words in the dictionary and short passwords. For example, the password Minneapolis is less secure than M1nneap0lis, which mixes numbers and letters, and includes an uppercase character along with lowercase characters.

To apply password security to a file, follow these steps:

1. **With a PDF file open, choose Protect⇨Encrypt⇨Encrypt with Password.**

2. **Click Yes when the Applying New Security Settings dialog box appears, verifying that you want to apply security to this PDF.**

   The Password Security – Settings dialog box appears, as shown in Figure 6-1. You can select the Do Not Show This Message Again checkbox if you do not want this message to appear every time you are securing a PDF file using Acrobat.

3. **Select Acrobat 7 and Later from the Compatibility drop-down list.**

   Although Acrobat XI provides more robust security, few people are using version XI of Acrobat, making it difficult to distribute the file with this high level of security.

4. **Select the Require a Password to Open the Document checkbox.**

5. **Enter a password in the Document Open Password text box.**

   Acrobat provides you with guidance about the strength of the password you select, letting you know whether the password can easily be bypassed. You can also add more security settings, which we outline in the next section. Or you can use this setting as the only security to be applied to the document.

   **REMEMBER**

   If password protection is the only security measure you apply to the document, authorized users can access the document by entering a password. Users with the password may also be able to edit or print the document unless you apply additional security measures. We discuss ways to limit the editing and printing of PDF files in the next section.

6. **Click OK.**

7. **Confirm the password and click OK again. Acrobat warns you that Adobe software honors the security settings, but other tools may allow you to bypass the security. Click OK again and the dialog box closes.**

8. **Save, close, and then reopen the PDF file.**

   A password dialog box appears, asking for the password to access the secured file. Every time a user accesses the file, he or she will be required to enter a password.

# Limiting Editing and Printing

In addition to restricting viewing of a PDF file, you can also limit editing and printing, restricting users from making changes to your document. This allows users to view a file but not change it.

To limit editing and printing of your PDF document, follow these steps:

1. **With a PDF file open, click Protect⇨Encrypt⇨Encrypt with Password.**

   The Password Security – Settings dialog box opens.

2. **In the Permissions area, select the checkbox labeled Restrict Editing and Printing of the document.**

   You can now specify a password that will be required for readers to edit the file or change the security settings. (See the preceding section.)

   With this option selected, you can apply a password for access to features, such as printing or editing. This password can be different than the password used to open the document — in fact, you don't even need to use a document open password if you don't want to, but it's a good idea to use both of these passwords for sensitive data. If you apply a document open password without a permissions password, it's easy for an experienced user to bypass the security in the PDF file.

3. **In the Change Permissions Password text box, enter a password.**

   Users who enter this permissions password when opening the document can change the file or the security settings. The permissions password can also be used to open the file, and it provides more privileges than the open password.

4. **Choose whether users can print the document by selecting an option from the Printing Allowed drop-down list.**

   The choices include Low Resolution or High Resolution, or you can prohibit printing by choosing None. The settings you choose here apply to anyone who accesses the document and doesn't know the permissions password.

5. **Select an option from the Changes Allowed drop-down list (see Figure 6-1) to restrict editing.**

   For the most security, choose None.

**FIGURE 6-1:**
Restrict what
users can edit.

Changes Allowed drop-down list

6. **Select the last two checkboxes, if desired:**

   - *Enable Copying of Text, Images, and Other Content:* When deselected, this option restricts copying and pasting of text and graphics from a PDF file into other documents. Selecting this option lets users extract text and images from a file by using the simple Copy and Paste commands.

   - *Enable Text Access for Screen Reader Devices for the Visually Impaired:* When you choose Acrobat 6 or Later from the Compatibility drop-down list at the top of the dialog box, you can also select this checkbox to allow visually impaired users to have the PDF file read aloud to them.

7. **When you're satisfied with the settings, click OK.**

**WARNING**

Choosing more advanced security settings, and choosing the latest version of compatibility, runs the risk of your file not being visible to many users who may not have upgraded to the most recent version of the Adobe Reader or Acrobat. Always understand your audience members and the software versions they're using before distributing files.

# Removing Sensitive Data

Sometimes you may want to make a PDF file accessible, but you may want to remove certain sets of information. For example, you may want to remove a person's name or personal information from a PDF document. You can do this through the process known as *redaction*.

To redact information in your PDF document, follow these steps:

1. **With a PDF file open, choose Tools tab⇨Scroll down to Protect & Standardize⇨Redact⇨Mark for Redaction⇨Text and Images. The using Redaction Tools dialog box appears. Click OK.**

2. **Use the Mark for Redaction tool to highlight all text to be removed from the document. A red box will appear around the highlighted text.**

3. **After marking all text to be removed from the file, choose Apply in the Redact tool bar across the top of Adobe Acrobat.**

   The redacted text is removed from the document.

   WARNING

   Note that this permanently removes all content marked for redaction. This cannot be undone. If you are testing this capability, you should first perform a Save As to create a copy of the document so that you do not permanently remove content from a document unintentionally.

4. **Click Yes to then remove any hidden information in the file, such as the name of the author or the original document name.**

   You can also remove this later by clicking the Remove Hidden Information option under the Redact tools panel.

   TIP

   You can remove specific phrases or words by using the Find Text option found in the Mark for Redaction drop-down of the Redact tools panel.

# 7

# Adobe XD

# Contents at a Glance

# Chapter **1**

# Introducing the Experience Design Workspace

A dobe Experience Design (XD) is a high-fidelity prototyping tool used to demonstrate interactive application and website designs. In this chapter, you find out how to use XD's UX design tools to create visual designs quickly using features such as repeat grid, symbols, layers, and more. Keep in mind that Adobe XD is in beta at time of print. The pace of the beta updates has typically implemented Mac updates ahead of the Windows version of XD. This variation will balance out as the product comes into the final stages, but you might notice that some of the screen captures in this minibook vary from your version of XD.

Adobe Experience Design is included in your Creative Cloud subscription. If you do not have it already installed, launch your Creative Cloud application and install it before trying to follow along with this minibook.

# Understanding the Modern User Interface

Adobe Experience Design has been created from scratch with the user's experience in mind. The UI is clean and simple. After you discover where your primary tools are located, it will be easy for you to use them in your production workflow.

## Creating a new artboard

As with most of the other Adobe applications, you need to define an artboard size before working in Adobe XD. You can choose from artboards that are standard screen sizes, or create a custom-sized artboard. The size of the artboard can be changed at any time.

1. **Choose File⇨New. A start screen appears that introduces you to the XD application and offers you a choice of screen sizes. In Figure 1-1, the iPhone 6/7 is selected.**

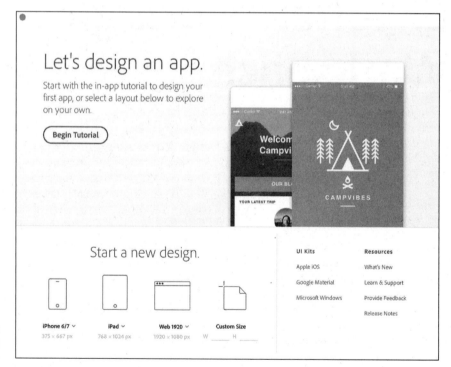

**FIGURE 1-1:**
Selecting the size
of the artboard.

2. **Select your size from the drop-down menu and press the Return or Enter key.**

The artboard appears in the XD workspace.

The workspace includes a work area in the middle, a main menu across the top, an application menu above the work area, a toolbar to the left, and a Property Inspector on the right; see Figure 1-2.

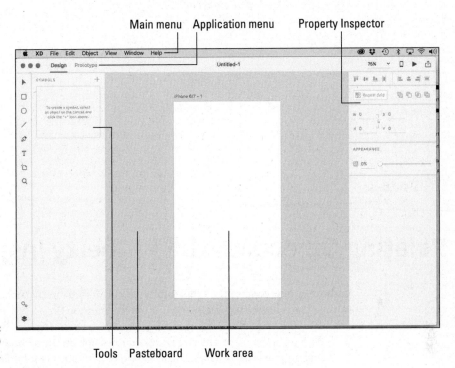

Main menu    Application menu    Property Inspector

FIGURE 1-2:
The XD
workspace.

Tools    Pasteboard    Work area

## Using the tools

In XD, primitive shapes, as well as more advanced drawing tools, are available to you on the toolbar. In addition to that, some other tools, such as the Selection and the artboard tool, might be familiar to you if you use Adobe Illustrator. See all tools in Figure 1-3.

Introducing the Experience
Design Workspace

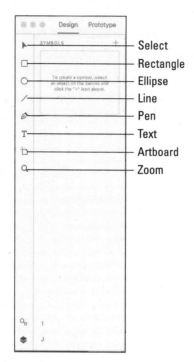

**FIGURE 1-3:**
XD tools.

- Select
- Rectangle
- Ellipse
- Line
- Pen
- Text
- Artboard
- Zoom

# Relating Objects to the Property Inspector

In this section, you use the tools to place some objects on the artboard so that you can see the relationship between your objects and the Property Inspector.

1. **With an artboard of any size open, double-click on the artboard name that appears at the top of the artboard to activate the textbox and change the text to** My first screen.

2. **Choose the Ellipse tool and click and drag an ellipse on the screen.**

TIP

As with your other Adobe applications, you can press the Shift key while dragging to create a perfect circle. You can also press Alt/Option+Shift while dragging to create a circle from a center point.

When the ellipse is complete, properties now appear in the Properties Inspector on the right, as shown in Figure 1-4.

3. **The Ellipse tool is still selected. To avoid unexpectedly creating another circle, click the Select tool.**

Some of the properties, such as the Align options at the top, are not relevant when only one object is selected. (It aligns an object to the artboard if only one is selected.) Others, such as W (width) and H (height) as well as the X, Y coordinates, however, can be helpful.

In the Appearance section, you can change the fill and border (stroke) or deselect either by unchecking the checkbox to the left of the attribute. In this next step, you use the Properties Inspector to change the size, position on the page, and the fill and border color.

1. **With your ellipse selected, click the textbox to the right of W in the Properties panel and type** 100.

2. **Type** 100 **in the textbox to the right of H.**

3. **The X coordinate is the horizontal value; type** 138 **to put your circle close to the center.**

4. **Type** 100 **in the textbox to the right of Y.**

   If you used the standard iPhone 6 artboard, your screen should look similar to the one shown in Figure 1-5.

My first screen

**5.** With the Ellipse still selected, click the box to the left of Fill in the Properties Inspector to open the Color Picker, as shown in Figure 1-6. Choose any color you like. If you want a color that is not displayed, click and drag the Hue slider to the right.

REMEMBER

Color, gradients, and transparency are covered in more detail in Chapter 3 of this minibook.

**6.** Click the box to the left of Border in order to select any stroke color.

**7.** Select the width value to the right of Border and type 10 so that you can see a 10 pt border on your ellipse.

**8.** As a bonus, add a drop shadow using the Properties Inspector. With your ellipse still selected, check Shadow. The values that appear below are the X and Y coordinates and the blur.

**9.** If you have been following along with this exercise, choose File⇨Save now. Name the file My first screen and save to a location that you can easily locate in case you need it. Keep the file open for the next part of this chapter.

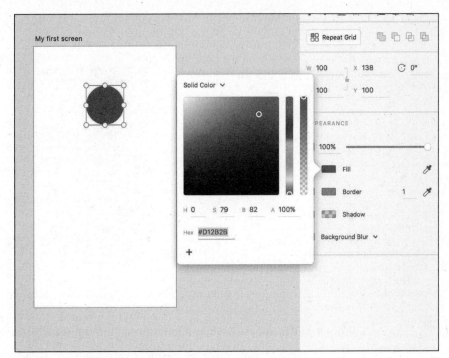

**FIGURE 1-6:**
Choose a color
for your fill from
the color picker.

# A Little Bit about Artboards

You have successfully created an object and changed its properties; now you investigate the artboard options.

Select the artboard tool and click anywhere to create a second, same-sized artboard. While the handles are active, click and drag to change the size. Alternatively, you can change the size, background color, and other attributes using the Properties Inspector. In fact, if you wanted to change the template to an Apple Watch–sized artboard, you could even scroll down in the Properties panel for a complete list of other templates to choose from. In this example, you change the background color and then clone this artboard:

1. **With the new artboard selected, click the box to the left of Fill and select any color of background for your new artboard.**

2. **Check the box to the left of Square in the Properties Inspector in order to display a grid that is only visible to you while working in XD, and change the size to 20 pixels, as shown in Figure 1-7.**

   Now you can clone your original artboard.

**FIGURE 1-7:**
Change the
background
color and add
a grid in the
Properties panel.

3. **If you do not see both artboards, press Ctrl/Command+0 (zero).**

4. **Click the Layers icon at the bottom of the toolbar to see your two artboards. Click the first artboard, which is at the bottom of the list. This selects that artboard.**

TIP

You can Ctrl/Command-click right on the artboard to select it as well.

5. **Right-click (Windows) or Ctrl-click (Mac) and select Duplicate from the contextual menu, as shown in Figure 1-8. Double-click on the artboard name in the Artboard list and rename it** My second screen**.**

**FIGURE 1-8:**
Duplicate and
rename your
screen in the
Artboard panel
that appears
when you click
the Layers icon.

6. Click the Select tool and then select the ellipse on this duplicated artboard. Change the Fill of the circle on this artboard to any other color.

7. In this example, we still have an extra artboard that has not been named. Double-click on the unnamed artboard and name it Home Screen.

8. Click and drag the Home Screen artboard from inside the Artboard panel to the top of the list.

9. Choose File⇨Save and keep this file open for the next section.

Now you add some text to the Home Screen. Just follow these steps:

1. Using the Select tool, click the screen with the background color that you named Home Screen, or select it in the Layers panel.

2. Press Ctrl+3 (Windows) or Command+3 (Mac) to zoom into the selection. You can also use View⇨Zoom to Selection.

3. Select the Text tool from the toolbar and click and drag across the middle area of the screen, as shown in Figure 1-9.

4. Type the word Welcome.

5. Using the Property Inspector, change the text size to 50, choose Center Align, and select White for the fill color. You can see where these properties are located by looking at Figure 1-10.

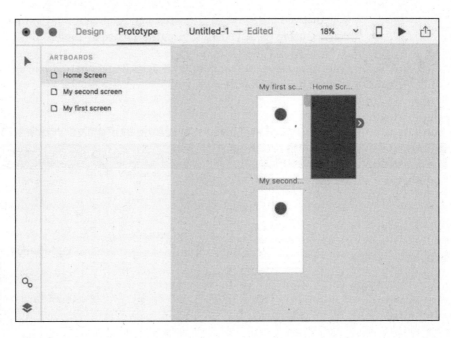

FIGURE 1-9:
Click and drag to create a text area on your Home Screen.

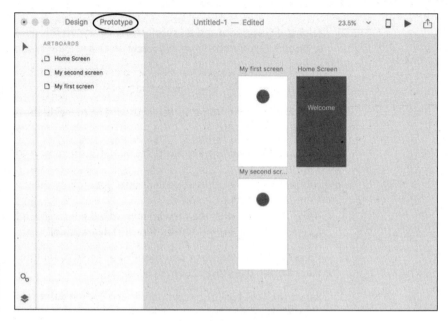

**FIGURE 1-10:**
Turn on the grid
for your artboard
and apply a color.

# Keyboard Shortcuts for Navigating the Workspace

Now that you have several artboards you can practice navigating your workspace.
Practice using the keyboard shortcuts provided in Table 1-1.

**TIP**

On a laptop, you can simply pinch your fingers in and out on your trackpad to
zoom in and out of your artboard.

**TABLE 1-1**    **Keyboard Shortcuts for Navigating the Workspace**

| Function | Windows Shortcut | Mac Shortcut |
| --- | --- | --- |
| Fit all artboards in window | Ctrl+0 | Command+0 |
| Zoom in | Ctrl++ (plus sign)<br>or<br>Alt+mouse wheel | Command++ (plus sign)<br>or<br>Option+mouse wheel |
| Zoom out | Ctrl+– (minus sign) | Command+– (minus sign) |
| Go to 100% | Ctrl+1 | Command+1 |

| Function | Windows Shortcut | Mac Shortcut |
| --- | --- | --- |
| Go to 200% | Ctrl+2 | Command+2 |
| Zoom to selection | Ctrl+3 | Command+3 |
| Full screen | N/A | Ctrl+Command+F |
| Scroll | Spacebar and push with mouse | |
| Horizontal pan | Ctrl+mouse wheel | Shift+mouse wheel |
| Vertical pan | Mouse wheel | Mouse wheel |

# Design View versus Prototype Mode

Now that you are getting a handle on the tools, artboards, and workspace, you can create a simple prototype. You can learn more advanced features about prototyping in the following chapters of this minibook, but think of this as a quick introduction to entering the prototyping mode.

1. **Press Crtl+0 (Windows) or Command+0 (Mac) to make sure that you are viewing all three of your artboards.**

   Notice at the top, in the Application menu, that you have been working in the Design mode of XD. This is where you typically create your artwork. In this next section, you enter the Prototyping mode. The Prototyping mode is where you create the links that add interactivity to your prototype.

2. **Click Prototype in the Application menu, as shown in Figure 1-11.**

## Creating your links

Creating an interactive link is done by creating a wire from one screen to another. You now link your screens together. To do so, just follow these steps:

1. **Click the Home Screen and drag to draw a wire over to the screen called My first Screen.**

2. **When you release, the target for your link is displayed as well as the transition type and duration. Leave these at the defaults.**

3. **Now click the circle in the artboard named** My first screen **and drag a wire from the circle to the third artboard,** My second screen.

4. **Create a full circle by clicking the circle in the artboard named My second screen and dragging a wire back to the Home Screen. Now you are ready to test your interactions.**

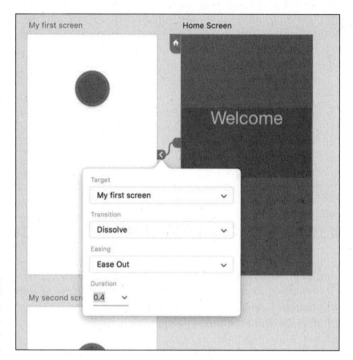

**FIGURE 1-11:**
Click Prototype to
enter the mode
where you can
create links to
other screens.

## Testing your prototype

You can test your prototype by using the Desktop Preview feature:

1. **Select your Home Screen.**

2. **Click the Desktop Preview icon in the upper right of the XD workspace, as shown in Figure 1-12.**

**FIGURE 1-12:**
Preview your
prototype by
clicking the
Desktop Preview
button.

The Desktop Preview button

3. **Click your screens where you designated the links to view your interactions.**

   The Desktop Preview window can stay up while you work and will show live updates, as you work, or you can close it to keep it out of view.

# Chapter **2**

# Working with Artboards

rtboards is a term used in many of Adobe's applications, but in Adobe Experience Design, artboards represent screens for your application or pages in your website. Without screens, you have little interactivity, so it is important that you know how to add, delete, edit the size, and organize these artboards.

## Starting Your Document and Adding an Artboard

Throughout this chapter, lessons take you step-by-step through the process of working with artboards in XD. You can follow along, or you can just read so that you understand the important points you should know about artboards.

When you first launch XD, you see a Start screen that allows you to start with an artboard sized at default sizes. This is helpful, but you can also enter your own size by typing in values underneath the Custom selection, as seen in Figure 2-1.

**FIGURE 2-1:**
In the Start menu,
choose from
preset artboard
sizes or type in
custom values.

In this example, we selected the iPhone 6/7 (375 x 667) from the drop-down menu in the iPhone 6/7 choice, as shown in Figure 2-2.

**FIGURE 2-2:**
You have
additional
artboard
sizes available
with each
selection.

Do this by clicking the arrow to the right of the iPhone 6/7 template selection in the Start menu and selecting the iPhone 6/7 (375 x 667) option.

An artboard appears and you are ready to start working.

# Creating New Artboards

In this example, several artboards with content are created so that you can practice adding, duplicating, and deleting your own artboards.

As a default, artboards are named with the template that you selected followed by a slash and a number in sequential order. In this next step, you type in a custom name:

1.  **Double-click the Artboard name that appears on top of the artboard in the work area and change the name to Home.**

    *Note:* To change the name, you can also select the Layers icon at the bottom of the toolbar and double-click on the artboard name that appears in the Layers panel.

2.  **Using the Text tool, click and drag to create a text area anywhere on the initial art board that appears. Type** This is my home screen — **as shown in Figure 2-3 — so that you can visually identify it while working. You can use the Property Inspector to format it anyway that you want.**

**FIGURE 2-3:** Change the artboard name and add some text to the screen.

# Resizing an Artboard

After you have created an artboard, you can change its size, either by dragging handles surrounding the artboard or by entering values in the Property Inspector.

If your artboard becomes unselected, you can reselect it by choosing the Select tool and then holding down the Ctrl (Windows) or Command (Mac) key and clicking on the artboard.

# Adding a New Artboard

You can easily add artboards as you work in Adobe XD. They are typically the same size throughout an application, but might change properties such as portrait or landscape. Here's how:

1. **Add an artboard of the same size by selecting the Artboard tool and clicking in the pasteboard area of this document.**

2. **Change the orientation for this new artboard by clicking the Landscape icon in the Properties Inspector, as you see in Figure 2-4.**

3. **Double-click the default name above the artboard and change the name to** Home Landscape.

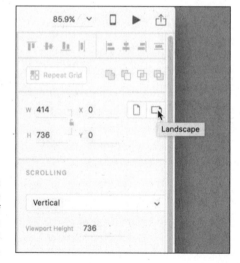

**FIGURE 2-4:**
Change the orientation of your artboard in the Properties panel.

4. **You can also add a screen from other templates using your Property Inspector. To do so, make sure the Artboard tool is still selected and scroll down in the Properties panel until you see a list of available templates. In Figure 2-5, the iPhone 6/7 option was selected, and a new artboard was created to that size.**

5. **Double-click the name of this artboard and change it to** Gallery.

FIGURE 2-5:
Add a new
artboard by
selecting a
template in the
Properties panel.

# Using the Layers Panel

Now that you have several screens, it makes sense to review the Layers panel. The Layers panel is used to select and organize not only your artboards, but also any content on your artboards. Notice in Figure 2-6 that the Layers panel lists the three artboards in this document. They are stacked in the order they were created, the newest artboard appearing at the top of the stack.

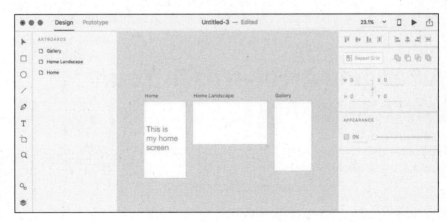

FIGURE 2-6:
Click artboards to
select them in the
Layers panel.

In the following steps, you work with the Layers feature in Adobe XD. Keep in mind that layers in XD work a little differently than they do in programs such as Adobe Photoshop and Illustrator. In addition to changing the stacking order and managing objects, you can also manage your artboards with the XD layer features.

1. **Click on any of the artboards listed in the Layers panel to see that you can activate each artboard.**

2. **Select any artboard; in this example, the Home artboard is selected. You will now move the artboard within the stacking order.**

3. **Click and drag the artboard to the top of the stack. Release when you see a line appear above the other artboards.**

# Duplicating an Artboard

Perhaps you want to work with a version of an existing page. You could copy and paste items from one artboard to another, but it would make more sense to duplicate your artboard and then make revisions.

Duplicate an artboard using one of these methods:

>> Hold down Ctrl+Alt (Windows) or Command+Option (Mac) and then drag to clone an artboard to another location on your pasteboard.

>> Select the artboard in the Layers panel and then right-click (Windows) or Ctrl-click (Mac) and select Duplicate from the contextual menu that appears.

Note that you can also use the contextual menu to copy and paste artboards, as well as delete, rename, and export artboards in an image format.

# Arranging Artboards in Your Pasteboard Area

You can reposition an artboard within the pasteboard area by selecting it with the Select tool and then clicking and dragging. If you would like to select multiple artboards, use any of these methods:

>> Shift+click (while holding down the Ctrl key on a Mac) to add artboards to your selection.

>> Click and drag a marquee around the entire artboard(s) that you want to select, as shown in Figure 2-7.

>> Click and drag through the artboard names in the Layers panel.

>> Shift-click to add artboards to the selection in the Layers panel.

**FIGURE 2-7:**
Click and drag to surround the entire artboard(s) that you want to select.

# Aligning and Distributing Your Artboards

If you find your pasteboard is becoming messy and unorganized, you can align and distribute your artboards using the Properties panel. To do this, follow these steps:

1. Select the artboards that you wish to reposition using Align and Distribute features.

2. Locate the Align and Distribute icons, shown in Figure 2-8, and click any Align option and any Distribute option.

Distribute Vertically

Align Right

Align Center (Horizontally)

Align Left

Distribute Horizontally

Align Bottom

Align Middle (Vertically)

Align Top

**FIGURE 2-8:**
The Align and
Distribute icons.

# Adding Scrolling Capability to an Artboard

There are many times that you want to show items scrolling in your prototype. You can simulate scrolling by changing the size of the artboard while keeping something called the View Point at the original artboard size. If you were following along earlier, you can use any of the artboards you have created, or create a new file with an artboard of any size.

You will first need to create content that extends beyond your screen area. For this, we add some easy shapes:

1. Select the Ellipse tool and click and drag to add a circle to your artboard.

2. Choose the Selection tool. Hold down the Alt (Windows) or Option (Mac) key and drag the circle down to clone it. Repeat this as many times as you need to in order to have content positioned outside the default template size, as shown in Figure 2-9.

**FIGURE 2-9:**
Add content that
extends beyond
the viewing
area so that you
can see how
to implement
scrolling.

3. Now, select the artboard either by clicking on the artboard name or by Ctrl-clicking (Windows) or ⌘-clicking (Mac) on the artboard.

4. Make sure that Scrolling is selected in the Scrolling section of the Properties Inspector. Note the value in the Viewport Height.

5. Click and drag the bottom-middle handle, as shown in Figure 2-10. This extends the artboard, but if you used a default template you should see a dotted guide where the artboard used to end. If you do not see this dotted guide, see the following note.

   *Note:* If you are using a default template, the Viewport Height value will not change when you click and drag to make your artboard longer. If Viewport Height does change, you more than likely created your artboard with custom values. No worries; just type back in the original height into the view box control after you extend your artboard.

6. Now you can test the scrolling by clicking on the Desktop Preview play button in the upper right of your workspace. Note that when the preview appears that you can scroll through your content.

Now that you are familiar with the basics of creating and organizing artboards, you are ready to start putting more content on those screens.

**FIGURE 2-10:**
Extend the
artboard by
clicking and
dragging.

IN THIS CHAPTER

» **Editing shapes**

» **Applying fills**

» **Applying borders**

» **Customizing and saving shapes**

» **Using the Pen tool**

» **Discovering Pen tool tips and tricks**

# Chapter **3**

# Adding Shapes, Paths, and Custom Shapes

You can create your artwork, such as squares, circles, custom shapes, and paths, right in Adobe XD. If you are familiar with Adobe Illustrator, the tools in XD will be relatively easy for you to learn. Keep in mind that you can also create your shapes in Illustrator and copy and paste them right into Adobe XD as well.

## It All Starts with a Shape

In this chapter, you discover how to use the Rectangle, Ellipse, Line, and Pen tools to create custom shapes and paths. These shapes can be used for creating UI such as buttons and menus, as well as custom shapes for creating masks.

### The basic shapes

You can create a shape such as a rectangle or ellipse simply by selecting the tool from the Tools panel and clicking and dragging where you would like to place the shape on your artboard. Simply by clicking and dragging from the upper-left corner to the lower right, you can create a typical rectangle or oval. Try any of these tips to create rectangles that are more controlled in size:

» Shift-drag to make a perfect square of circle.

» Alt (Windows) or Option (Mac) and drag to pull the shape from the center.

» Alt+Shift (Windows) or Option+Shift (Mac) to pull a perfect square or circle from a center point.

## Determining the size

After you have created the square or circle, you can check and change the size by using the Properties panel. In Figure 3-1, you see an active rectangle and its W (Width) and H (Height), as well as its positioning, which is represented in the X and Y coordinates.

**FIGURE 3-1:**
After you
have created a
shape, you can
see and change
properties such
as width, height,
and positioning.

*Note:* The shape tools are sticky, and the tool will remain selected until you switch to another tool such as the Select tool. Keep this in mind because if you try to move your shape, you may just accidently create another shape.

# Creating a Button

For this section, you are directed through the steps to create a simple button with a solid fill and some text. You will have the opportunity to learn more about more advanced fills later in this chapter:

1. **Select the Rectangle tool and click and drag to create a rectangle of any size on an artboard.**

    In this example, we selected the standard iPhone 6 template.

2. **With the rectangle still active, type** 200 **into the Width textbox and** 70 **into the Height textbox. Press Tab after you type each to confirm the value.**

## Applying a solid fill

In this section, you add a solid fill color to your shape:

1. **Make sure your rectangle is still selected. Click the white box to the left of Fill in the Properties panel to open the color picker.**

2. **Scroll through the colors by clicking and dragging on the Hue slider. After you have entered the hue color that you like, click a color in the color panel to apply it to your rectangle.**

    You can save colors that you might use often by clicking the Save Color Swatch plus sign at the bottom of the color picker, shown in Figure 3-2.

**TIP**

    You can apply transparency to your fill by using the slider on the right side of the color picker window.

**TIP**

3. **Uncheck the checkbox to the left of Border to remove the stroke around the rectangle.**

## Rounding your corners

You can leave the corners square or follow either of these next steps to round the corners of the shape:

» You can round corners visually by clicking and dragging the corner widgets inside the corners of the rectangles, as shown in Figure 3-3.

Adding Shapes, Paths, and Custom Shapes

TIP

Hold down the Alt (Windows) or Option (Mac OS) key and drag one corner radius to make it an independent value.

>> You can also enter values for your corner radius entering values in the Corner Radios textboxes in the Properties panel. Notice in Figure 3-4 that you can enter different values for different corners.

## Adding text to your button

Now you add the text to the button:

1. **Select the Type tool from the Tools panel and then click inside your button. A text cursor appears. Don't worry about the exact placement of the textbox because this can be moved later.**

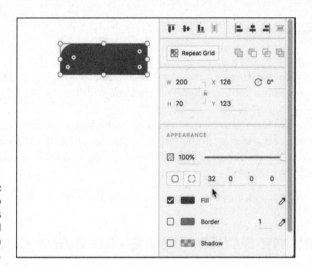

**FIGURE 3-4:**
Enter values into
the Properties
panel to add
varying sizes in
the corner radius.

2. Type the word Submit, **and then select the text by pressing Ctrl+A (Windows) or Command+A (Mac).**

3. **With the word selected, change the properties in the Text area of the Properties panel, as shown in Figure 3-5, to select a font and a type size you like. You can also change the alignment by selecting the Left Align, Center, or Right Align buttons.**

**FIGURE 3-5:**
Select your type
properties using
the Text section
in the Properties
panel.

**TIP**

You can select your current font size in the Font size textbox and press the arrow up or down to increase or decrease the font size.

4. **Click on the Fill box to change the color of your text.**

# Creating a Border

A border, also known as a stroke, can be applied to any of your shapes and paths. When you create a border, you select both the width and color.

1. **If you still have your button selected, make sure the checkbox is on to the left of the Border in the Properties panel; then click the box to the right of the checkbox to open the color picker and select a color that you would like to use for your border.**

2. **To select a width, type a value into the Width textbox.**

## Sampling a color using the eyedropper

Both the Fill and the Border have an eyedropper icon positioned off to the right. You can select the Eyedropper tool in the Properties panel and then click on any color located within your current project. This can be helpful when you have imported images that you want to sample colors from, as shown in Figure 3-6, or if you are trying to match controls that were created in a different application.

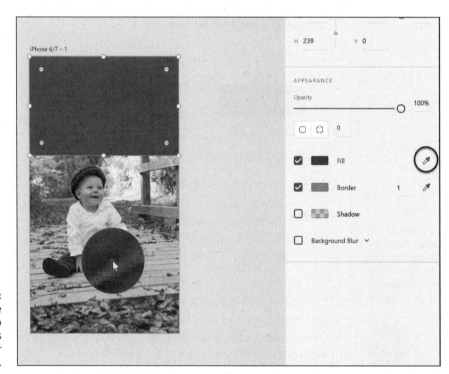

**FIGURE 3-6:**
Use the eyedropper to sample colors from your project.

# Creating a gradient

Adobe XD includes advanced tools that make it simple to create gradients. To create and use a gradient in your project, follow these steps:

1.  **Select a shape. At the time of writing, a gradient can only be applied to a fill.**

2.  **Click the box to the left of Fill in the Properties panel to open the color picker.**

3.  **Click Solid Fill at the top of the picker and select Gradient from the menu that appears, as shown in Figure 3-7. A gradient ramp appears with default colors.**

Adding Shapes, Paths, and Custom Shapes

**FIGURE 3-7:** Select Gradient from the color picker.

4.  **You can either click the gradient ramp at the top of the color picker to add colors, or click directly on the gradient annotator that appears inside the fill of your object, as you see in Figure 3-8.**

5.  **After you click to add a color stop, you can then use the picker to select a color. Continue adding color stops with various colors if you like. Click and drag the color stops to reposition them.**

6.  **Remove any unwanted color stops by selecting one and then pressing the Delete or Backspace key.**

**FIGURE 3-8:**
Click to add color
stops to your
gradient.

7. **Choose a level of transparency by selecting a color stop, and then dragging up or down in the transparency slider on the right side of the color picker.**

# Using the Pen Tool

Using the Pen tool in Adobe XD is very similar to the experience you would have with the Pen tool in other Adobe applications. In this section, you are provided with simple tips in order for you to create your own custom shapes and paths with the Pen tool. See Chapter 4 in Book 5 for Illustrator for more in-depth features that you can take advantage of with the Pen tool in all the Adobe applications.

>> Create a straight path by clicking a start point and then Shift-clicking to create an end point. This creates a path that is either perfectly straight, 45 degrees, or 90 degrees.

>> If you want to stop the Pen tool without closing a shape, in order to create a straight line, for instance, simply press the Esc key.

» When you make a mistake, press Ctrl+Z (Windows) or Command+Z (Mac) in order to undo the step; keep the Pen tool active so you can continue creating your path.

» Create a curved, Bézier path by clicking and dragging, as shown in Figure 3-9.

**FIGURE 3-9:**
Click and drag with the Pen tool to create a custom Bézier path.

» Change the direction of a path by Alt (Windows) or Option (Mac) clicking and dragging on the directional line. (See Figure 3-10.)

**FIGURE 3-10:**
Hold down the Alt or Option key to change the direction of your curved Bézier path.

» Create a closed shape by clicking and connecting from one point to another. Closed shapes can be filled to create UI elements and masks, as shown in Figure 3-11. More about images and masks is covered in Chapter 5 of this minibook.

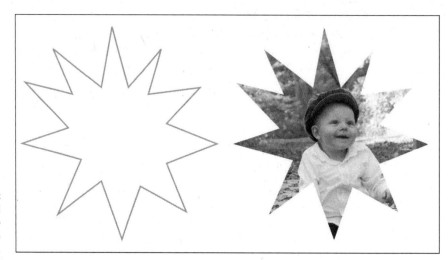

**FIGURE 3-11:**
The Pen tool
can be used to
create custom
shapes in XD.

# Creating Custom Shapes
# with the Path Tools

If your goal is to create a custom shape without using the Pen tool, you can take advantage of the Object⇨Path menu items.

To use this menu, you create two or more shapes that you would like to unite together (Add), subtract one from another (Subtract), save only the intersection of several shapes (Intersect), exclude the overlap of several shapes (Exclude/Overlap), or convert a shape to a path so that you can edit it more freely using the Select tool (Convert to Path).

See Figure 3-12 for examples of examples of these path selections.

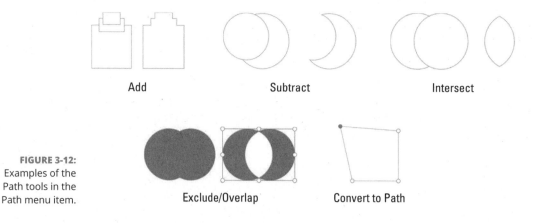

**FIGURE 3-12:**
Examples of the
Path tools in the
Path menu item.

IN THIS CHAPTER

» **Understanding layers**

» **Grouping and ungrouping**

» **Cloning and duplicating objects**

» **Transforming objects**

» **Aligning and distributing**

# Chapter **4**

# Working with Objects

G etting used to an unfamiliar interface can be trying. Something as simple as selecting a single object can cause frustration if you do not have a strong background in or an understanding of the way layers and groups work.

In this chapter, you discover how to organize, select, and group your objects in Adobe XD. You also find out how to scale and rotate your objects, as well as align and distribute them evenly.

## Getting a Leg Up on Layers

If you are an Adobe Illustrator user, you will recognize that layer features in Adobe XD are very similar. Essentially, layers in XD are meant to help you organize your objects. This makes it easier to select, lock, and duplicate your objects. In this section, you find out how layers work.

### Artboards and layers

The best way to explain layers is for you to give it a try yourself. Follow these steps in a document of your own to build confidence in how you use layers in XD:

1. **Create a new file by selecting File⇨New. Use any size template that you wish.**

   In this example, we selected the iPhone 6/7 template.

2. **Click the Layers icon in the lower-left of the window, as shown in Figure 4-1, to see that the artboard, which was created by default, is shown in the panel labeled Artboards. You can also use the keyboard shortcut Ctrl+Y (Windows) or Command+Y (Mac) to toggle the view of this panel on and off.**

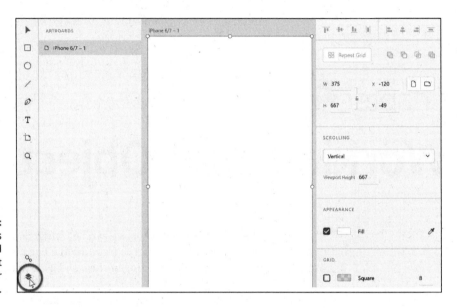

**FIGURE 4-1:**
Click the Layers
icon to reveal
a panel that
displays your
default artboard.

At first, you might be wondering why an artboard is listed in the Layers panel, but don't worry — it will make sense after you start adding objects to this artboard. Note that the artboard has the default name based upon the template you selected and the screen number that is associated with this document. Since this is the first artboard, you see the name iPhone 6/7-1.

3. **Select the Artboard tool from the Tools Panel and click anywhere in the work area to add a second artboard.**

Note that you now have two artboards listed, with the newest artboard appearing at the top of the list and with a –2 following the template name, as shown in Figure 4-2.

**FIGURE 4-2:**
As you add
artboards, they
appear at the top
of the stacking
order.

ARTBOARDS

▢ iPhone 6/7 – 2

○ iPhone 6/7 – 1

4. **Keep the file that you started and experiment with some of the other features available in the Artboards panel.**

# What can you do with your artboards inside the Artboard panel?

Using the Layers panel that appears when you click on the Layers icon, you can rearrange the stacking order, rename, duplicate, delete, and select artboards.

## Rearranging artboards

Click and drag up or down an artboard in the Artboard in the Layers panel in order to move it up or down in the stacking order. If you like working with contextual menus, you can right-click any artboard listed in the Layers panel to see a list of features you can use, including Copy, Paste, Duplicate, Delete, Rename, and Export. Following are other methods you can use to take advantage of these same features.

## Renaming your artboards

You can rename your artboards using one of these methods:

>> Double-click the Artboard name that appears directly above the artboard, and then type a new name.

>> Double-click the Artboard name that appears in the Layers panel, and type a new name, as shown in Figure 4-3.

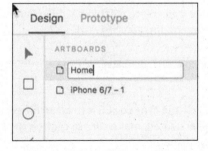

**FIGURE 4-3:** Double-click the artboard name to activate the textbox and change it.

## Copying or duplicating an artboard

To copy your artboard in order to paste it into another document, right-click it and select Copy. Then open a new document or navigate to another open document and choose Edit⇨Paste.

To duplicate an artboard, right-click it and select Duplicate. A new artboard immediately appears at the top of the list and in your work area.

You can also duplicate an artboard by holding down the Alt (Windows) or Option (Mac OS) key and dragging the artboard into the work area.

### Deleting an artboard

Be careful with deleting artboards. It is very easy to do, because you only have to select an artboard in the Layers panel and press the Delete or Backspace key. Fortunately, this step can be undone using Ctrl+Z (Windows) or Command+Z (Mac OS).

### Selecting artboards

Before trying to select artboards, make sure that you have at least three in your project.

» To select an artboard, simply click the artboard name in the Layers panel. You can also click on the artboard name above the artboard to select it.

» To select multiple artboards, click an artboard, and then Shift-click on another. This action selects all artboards in between in the stacking order as well.

» To select artboards that are not contiguous, select an artboard and then hold down the Control+Shift(Windows) or Command+Shift keys and select another.

## Objects you create and layers

In the beginning of this section, you pressed an icon that stated Layers, yet the information that has been covered thus far has been about artboards. In this section, you see how objects that you create on these artboards automatically create layers that you can use for organizing your artwork.

Make sure that you have a document open so that you can follow along with these steps:

1. **Select any shape and click and drag to add it to an artboard. If you do not have your Layers panel activated, make sure to click on the Layers icon in the lower-left side of workspace.**

2. **Notice that when you add an object to an artboard it becomes visible as a layer in the Layers panel as well. In Figure 4-4, a rectangle shape was added to the iPhone 6/7-2 artboard. In fact, you only see the active artboard and any objects on that artboard.**

*Note:* You only see the active artboard and any objects that are on that artboard. If you want to see another artboard, you can either press the back arrow to the left of the Artboard name in the Layers panel or simply select an object on a different artboard in your work area. This either takes you back to the entire list of artboards, or directly to the artboard with the selected object,

After you have placed an object on artboard, you can use the Layers panel to perform many functions, including copying the selected object and pasting an object, as well as duplicating, deleting, renaming, locking, grouping, converting your object to a symbol (covered in Chapter 7 of this minibook), and exporting. You can easily access these options by right-clicking on the object in the Layers panel. If you do not have a right-clicking mouse on your Mac, Ctrl-click to see this same contextual menu, as shown in Figure 4-5.

**TIP**

If you copy an object, you can use the Layers panel to paste only the attributes of the copied object. For instance, if you copied a red circle with a blue border and then selected a square, you could choose Paste Appearance from the Layers panel and have only the circle's properties applied, such as the color and the stroke.

In this section, you have an opportunity to review these functions.

## Renaming objects

To keep your files organized and make associating interactions easier, consider naming your objects with a logical naming structure. Keep your file names in lowercase, or with just an initial capital, with no spacing to keep it uniform with the typical standard for naming files used in development. Most importantly . . . name it something you will recognize if you try to select it from a list.

Example might include *header_nav* or *Submit-button.*

Working with Objects

**FIGURE 4-5:**
You can perform
many functions
with your selected
object in the
Layers panel.

## Selecting objects

As with selecting artboards, you can switch to the Select tool and then click on an object to select it, or you can follow these options for selecting additional objects:

» Using the Select tool, click an object listed in the Layers panel and then Shift+click on any other. Using the Shift key to add to a selection activates any other objects that are in between in the stacking order displayed in the Layers panel.

» Ctrl-click (Windows) or ⌘-click (Mac OS) to select noncontiguous items in the Layers panel.

» Click one object in the artboard and then Shift-click to add additional objects into the selection. When selecting via the artboard, using the Shift key does not select objects in between, as it does in the Layers panel.

» Using the Select tool, click and drag a marquee selection across the items that you want to select, as shown in Figure 4-6. You do not have to fully encompass the object with the marquee . . . just touching it adds it to the selection.

## Grouping and ungrouping objects

Now that you know how to select multiple objects, it seems a logical time to explain grouping. By grouping object, you can keep them together so that selecting them simultaneously is easier. This is especially important if you are building UI made of several parts, such as a button that consists of a shape, icon, and text, as shown in Figure 4-7.

**FIGURE 4-6:**
Click and drag
using the Select
tool to activate
multiple objects.

You can group objects by selecting them in the Layers panel and then right-clicking to select Group. You can also group by selecting the items on the artboard and then pressing Ctrl+G (Windows) or Command+G (Mac).

Notice that when you first group items they appear as Group in the Layers panel. You can rename this group with a more logical name so you can identify the object(s) as you work. Do this by double-clicking the word *Group* in the Layers panel and then typing a new name in the activated textbox.

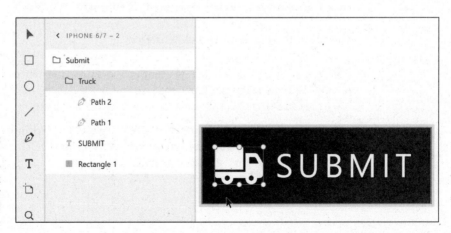

**FIGURE 4-7:**
In this example,
there is a group
named Truck
inside another
group named
Submit.

## Copying and pasting

Use these features if you want to copy something from one artboard to another or from one project to another. Use any of these options to cut and paste:

» Select an object right in the Layers panel and right-click it. In the contextual menu that appears, select Copy, and then right-click it again to select Paste. The object is duplicated in the same location right on the artboard. If you prefer, you can also use the typical keyboard shorts for copy and paste, which are Ctrl+C for copy and Ctrl+V, for paste (Windows), or Command+C and Command+V (Mac).

» As with artboards, you can duplicate an object by right-clicking it in the Layers panel and selecting Duplicate from the contextual menu that appears.

» Right-click a selected object and choose Copy from the contextual menu; then, go to another location in your project, right-click, and select Paste from the contextual menu in order to duplicate the object. When you copy and paste in XD, the object is pasted exactly on top of itself if you stay on the same artboard. Otherwise, it recalls the exact position and uses those same coordinates if you activate another artboard before pasting.

» You can hold down the Alt (Windows) or Option (Mac) key and drag a selected object in order to clone an object right on the artboard.

## Locking an object

In order to keep other objects in position, you may want to lock them as you complete working with them. This is a temporary feature . . . an object can be unlocked at any time.

You can tell when an object is locked because a lock icon appears in the upper-left corner of the object when it is selected, as shown in Figure 4-8.

Use any of these options to lock an object:

» You can lock an object by positioning your mouse to the right of the object's name in the Layers panel and then clicking on the padlock icon that appears. You can also click in that same location to unlock an object.

» You can lock an item by right-clicking (Windows) or Ctrl-clicking (Mac) and selecting Lock from the contextual menu. After an item is locked, you can choose Unlock from the same menu.

**FIGURE 4-8:**
When an object
is locked, a lock
appears in the
upper-left corner.

» In order to lock an item while you are working on the artboard, you can choose Object⇨Lock from the menu items, or press the keyboard shortcut Ctrl+L (Windows) or Command+L (Mac). The keyboard shortcut is a toggle key, meaning that you can select the locked object and press Ctrl/Command+L again to unlock it.

## Hiding an object

You can hide an object to see what is behind it without moving it, or to try various options in your design. To hide an object, follow any of these steps:

The fastest way to hide an object is to click the eye icon that appears when you cross over the area to the right of the named object in the Layers panel. You can see this icon in Figure 4-9.

**FIGURE 4-9:**
Turn on and off
the visibility of an
object by clicking
the Hide eye icon
in the Layers
panel.

Working with Objects

Additional features such as exporting and making a symbol are discussed in Chapters 5 and 7, respectively, of this minibook.

# Transforming Objects

You can scale and rotate your objects quickly and easily right on the artboard, or you can use a more precise method by using the Properties panel.

## Give it a spin

Rotate an object right from the artboard by selecting it with the Select tool and then positioning your cursor outside any of the object's handles. When you see the curved arrows, shown in Figure 4-10, click and drag in the direction you would like to rotate.

**FIGURE 4-10:**
Click and drag outside an object's handle in order to rotate it.

**TIP**

Hold down the Shift key while dragging to jump in increments of 15 degrees.

You can also select an object and then enter a value in the Rotation textbox in the Properties panel, shown in Figure 4-11.

**FIGURE 4-11:**
Enter an exact rotation in the Properties panel.

# Aligning and Distributing

After you start creating many objects, you need to consider the position of those objects and how they relate to each other. In order to lessen noise in your design, you want to keep icons and text aligned and distributed in a clean manner. You can check your alignment in several ways, including using a grid or using guides.

## Turning on your grid

You can turn on a grid that is only visible to you by following these steps:

1. **Select an artboard by clicking the artboard in the Layers panel or clicking the Artboard name above the artboard in your work area.**

2. **Check the checkbox for the Grid in the lower portion of the Properties panel, as shown in Figure 4-12.**

**FIGURE 4-12:** Turn on the Grid feature for your artboard.

3. **If you prefer a different color for your grid, select the square to the right of the grid checkbox and select a color from the color picker. You can also use the Transparency slider to change the level of opacity.**

4. **If you like, change the size of the grid by typing a value in the Grid Size textbox to the right of the checkbox.**

# Be smart about your guides

As a default, XD provides you with guides that turn on as needed. These are called Smart Guides and should be familiar to you if you use other Adobe Products.

To use the smart guides, simply pay attention to the lines and shaded areas that appear as you work. Note in Figure 4-13 that when the one diamond is dragged, a guide appears indicating that it is aligned with the diamond on the left.

**FIGURE 4-13:**
You can use Smart Guides for aligning objects.

## Smart guides can help with distribution as well

Distribution of objects refers to the space between a bounding box created by a first object and a last object. In Figure 4-14, you see uneven distribution of several diamonds on the left, and even distribution of the same objects on the right. In this example, the spacing is evenly distributed horizontally.

**FIGURE 4-14:**
Uneven distribution on the left side and even distribution on the ride side.

When you position objects, you will see shaded areas appear that indicate when the space between the objects is equal. This shading hint also appears when you Alt/Option drag to clone objects, as shown in Figure 4-15.

## Using the Align and Distribute feature

The Align and Distribute feature that is available in the Object menu and in the Properties panel can help you keep items in line and spaced evening.

**FIGURE 4-15:**
Smart guides provide a hint when space is even between objects.

If you select two items, you can take advantage of the Alignment features. If you select three or more objects, you can also use the Distribution features. See Figure 4-16 for a definition of which each icon in the Properties panel represents.

**FIGURE 4-16:**
A visual definition of the Align and Distribute features in the Properties panel.

Align Top
Align Middle (Vertically)
Align Bottom
Distribute (Horizontally)
Align Left
Align Center (Horizontally)
Align Right
Distribute (Vertically)

Keep in mind the trick to determining horizontal versus vertical. The horizon is horizontal. Anything going from left to right on your page should be distributed horizontally. Any objects going from the top to the bottom should be distributed vertically.

Working with Objects

IN THIS CHAPTER

» **Importing raster images**

» **Importing vector graphics**

» **Importing UI elements**

» **Working with Illustrator files**

» **Using custom pen paths for masks**

» **Exporting an object and artboards**

# Chapter 5

# Importing and Exporting from XD

U sing Adobe Experience Design (XD) to build your prototypes is great, but to be able to drop in artwork from Adobe Illustrator, Photoshop, as well as other sources, is even better. Adobe XD has some tools to create UI, but it may lack in some advanced features that you are used to taking advantage of in Adobe Illustrator and Photoshop.

In this chapter, you find out how to import images for your prototype, including vector imagery that you can continue to edit, even if it was created in Adobe Illustrator. You even discover how to mask your images into custom shapes using the masking feature in XD.

You also locate UI kits that provide you with UI specific to styles of controls that are themed for Windows, Apple IOS, and Google Material Design.

## Adding Imagery to Your Prototype

By this point, you have discovered how to create your own UI using some of the tools, such as the Rectangle and Ellipse tools; now you can take your prototype to the next step by adding relevant images. If you do not have images that you can easily access, you can obtain sample images at www.agitraining.com/dummies.

In order to follow some of the examples in this section, you should have an empty artboard ready to go.

There are several methods that you can use in order to bring imagery into your XD prototype:

>> **Browsing your file directory:** You can import the following image formats into XD: JPEG, PNG, GIF using your file directory. To import an image using the file menu, choose File⇨Import and locate an image.

>> **Drag and drop:** You can drag and drop images from your file folders, web pages, and even other applications. Simply click and drag the imagery from the source and release your mouse when your cursor is over the artboard. In Figure 5-1, a group of images was all dragged in at once onto an artboard from a file folder.

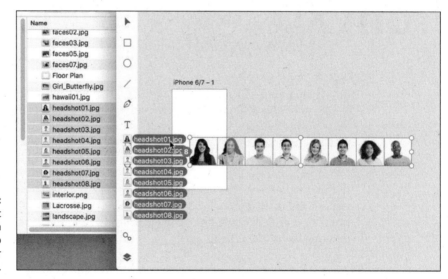

>> **Importing with cut and paste:** You can copy and paste imagery from sources, such as other websites and applications, but transparency is not supported when images are imported in this manner.

# Working with Images in XD

After you have imported your images, you don't have a great deal of editing control, but you can resize and rotate images just like you would any other shape. For a refresher on how to scale and rotate objects, review Chapter 4 of this minibook.

You can also easily round the corners of an imported image using the corner widgets, as shown in Figure 5-2.

**FIGURE 5-2:**
Click and drag a corner widget in order to round the edges of an image.

## Masking your images

By defining a closed shape with a shape tool or pen tool, you can define what becomes a mask. A *mask* offers you the ability to put an image into a custom shape. It also offers you the ability to crop out parts of an image that you do not want to be visible. Follow these steps in order to create a mask:

1. **Import an image on to an artboard.**

2. **Create a shape and size and position it over the image, as shown in Figure 5-3. The placement over the image determines what part of the image will show.**

3. **Using the Select tool, select both the shape and the image. It is important that the shape be on top of the image; if it is not, choose Object⇨ Arrange⇨Bring to Front.**

4. **With both objects selected, choose Object⇨Mask with Shape. The shape now contains the image, as shown in Figure 5-4.**

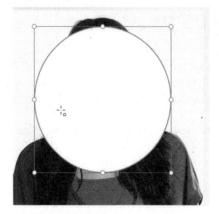

**FIGURE 5-3:**
Position a shape over an image to determine what part of the image you want to show.

**FIGURE 5-4:**
An image masked with a shape.

*Note:* If you would like to edit the positioning of the shape over the image, simply double-click the masked object using the Select tool. When you are finished repositioning your image and shape, click anywhere else on your artboard.

## Taking advantage of masks

In this chapter, the focus is on images, but you can mask any object(s) with a shape. Perhaps you have several items that you want to keep together in a circular shape, or you want to crop a series of repeated images. Both of these tasks can be done by following these steps:

**1.** **After creating your artwork, add a shape on the top, or bring a shape that you wish to mask into to the front using Object⇨Arrange⇨Bring to Front.**

**2.** **Select all the objects that are to be masked in addition to the topmost object, which is the mask, and choose Object⇨Mask with Shape. (See Figure 5-5.)**

FIGURE 5-5:
You can select
multiple objects
and mask them
into one shape.

If you need to edit objects in a mask independently, you can either choose Object⇨Ungroup Mask, or open the Layers panel and double-click on the icon to the left of the object named Mask Group. When you double-click, it allows you to select individual objects.

# Importing Vector Images into XD

In addition to importing images, you can also import vector images from several sources, including the Clipboard, Illustrator, SVG (scalable vector graphic), and Sketch (another popular prototyping tool).

Here are two methods that you can use to import editable vector objects into Adobe XD:

» **Copy and paste:** Select your vector object(s) in applications such as Adobe Illustrator or Sketch and copy them. Return to XD and paste. The vector graphics are placed and retain their editability.

» **Choose File⇨Import:** If you use File⇨Save to save a file from Adobe Illustrator in the SVG format, you can use the import feature in XD to bring in an editable copy of your artwork.

After you have imported your vector artwork into XD, you can continue working with the files and borders using the features available to you in the Properties panel.

# Exporting Your Artwork from XD

Most of this chapter has been about getting artwork into Adobe XD; now you find out how to get your artwork *out* of XD. Follow these steps to export objects out of XD:

1. **Export only selected objects from XD by locating the object(s) on the Layers panel and then right-clicking to select Export from the contextual menu that appears.**

   A Save As dialog box appears with options for saving your file into several different types of web formats.

2. **Enter a name for your artwork in the Save As textbox.**

3. **Navigate to a location where you want to save the exported file.**

4. **Select either the PNG, SVG, or PDF format from the Format drop-down menu.**

5. **If you just want to export one copy, leave the Export For set to Design. The other options, Web, iOS, and Android, offer the capability of saving out multiple fiels at different formats.**

6. **Press Export.**

**TIP**

Export your entire project by using the Save As window. You can choose File⇨Save As and choose from several different file formats that include SnagProj (a popular screen capture software), PNG, JPG, TIFF, GIF, and BMP.

IN THIS CHAPTER

» Reviewing importing onscreen text properties

» Adding and stylizing your text

» Importing text

» Using the Repeat Grid feature

» Importing updated text into your repeated grid

## Chapter **6**

# Adding Text to Your XD Project

Text in Adobe Experience Design (XD) is used for UI elements such as buttons, for navigational elements such as links to other content, and for general content such as descriptions, directions, lists, and more. In this chapter, you find out how to add text to your UI and control the look using the Properties panel. You also discover how to import text from other sources and create a repeated list of items using the Repeat Grid feature. Keep in mind that the Adobe Experience (XD) application is continually changing through its development, so you may see slight changes in UI.

## Adding Text Right in Adobe XD

Adding text is just a matter of selecting the Text tool from the Tools panel and then indicating where you want it placed on your artboard by either clicking or clicking and dragging.

You can see the difference between the methods in Figure 6-1. When you click to create a text insertion point, the text width area is undefined and will run on in a line until you press the Return key. If you want to control the column width, you typically would click and drag to create your text area. The text area can be adjusted using the handles to be larger or smaller.

In Figure 6-1, the text in the top line will go off the artboard unless you create a manual return. The text area in the bottom of the screen allows you to control width and height of the text area with handles.

This is a text insertion point created by clicking on a locationin my artboard. Th

**FIGURE 6-1:** Comparing clicking and clicking and dragging to insert text.

This is a text insertion point created by clicking and dragging on a location in my artboard

# Adjusting Text Properties

When you have text in your project, you can start changing the text properties. These properties include Font Family, Font Size, Font Weight, Alignment, Character Spacing (kerning and tracking), Line Spacing (leading), Fill, Border (stroke), Shadow (drop shadow), and Background Blur. So let's review how those properties are applied.

## About readability and font selections

The selection of a font is of critical importance. You may have many font choices in your system, but only a select few will cut it as a successful choice for onscreen reading. Some characteristics to look for in your font selection include the following:

>> **Serif or non-serif?** In Figure 6-2, you see a font family in the serif style on the top and one in sans serif on the bottom. Serifs have a slight projection that finishes off a stroke of a letter. Sans serif, on the other hand, does not have that slight projection. Sans serif typefaces tend to look more modern and are a popular choice for interactive applications and websites. In the past, it was believed that font families with serifs were easier to read when there was a

large amount of text. Tests performed with eye-tracking devices have proven that there is no major difference in readability between serif or sans-serif, so feel free to pick either style as long as you pay attention to some of the other font characteristics that follow.

**FIGURE 6-2:**
A serif typeface on the top, sans-serif on the bottom.

This is a serif font

This is a sans serif font

>> **Straight, even line widths:** Because your type is going to be created from pixels, it is best not to have lots of variation in the width of your text. In Figure 6-3, you can see the difference, in a pixel preview, between a font choice with variation in the width (top) and a font that is consistent in its width.

**FIGURE 6-3:**
The top font has variation in the thick and thin lines that create the font; the bottom font is consistent and easier to read onscreen.

This font has variations in w

This font is consistent in we

>> **Strong counters:** *Counters* are the holes that you see in letters like "O," "B," and "R." Pay attention to how large those counters are as they can also cause readability issues if they close up when displayed as pixels on a screen. A pixel view of two different font families appears in Figure 6-4; see how the counters look in each in comparison to each other.

**FIGURE 6-4:**
Look for strong open counters in your font family selection.

Minion Pro: abdopqr

Futura: abdopqr

>> **Descenders and cap height:** Short descenders and low cap heights are important for readability on the screen. At the top of Figure 6-5 you see a font family with short descenders and low cap heights; at the bottom, a font with long descenders and high cap heights.

**FIGURE 6-5:**
A font family with short descenders and a low cap height is typically easier to read onscreen.

## short descenders and low cap heights

*long descenders and high cap heights*

## Selecting your font family

Now that you know what makes a better font selection for readability, use the Properties panel to select one. Things to look for when making your selection include the following:

>> **Font family:** After you have entered some type on your screen, you can select it and choose the Font Family drop-down menu in the Text section of the Properties panel. If you know the font you want, simply start typing the font's name into the Font Family textbox, and if it is in your system, it will be found in your list.

**TIP**

Don't forget that you have fonts available to you through Adobe TypeKit. See Book 1, Chapter 3 for specifics of how to use this great extra feature that comes with your subscription to the Adobe Creative Cloud.

>> **Font weight:** After you select a font family, you can choose a weight from the Font Weight drop-down menu. Depending upon the fonts that you have in your system, you will have different font weight choices; see Figure 6-6.

>> **Font size:** You can simply type a font size into the Font Size textbox, but if you are not sure what size works best, you can position your cursor underneath the Font Size textbox and click and drag. Look for the double-headed arrow shown in Figure 6-7 before you drag. Dragging up decreases the size; down increases the size.

>> **Alignment:** You can change your selected text to Align Left, Center, or Right using the Alignment buttons in the Text section of the Properties panel.

>> **Character spacing:** *Character spacing* refers to the space between characters. This is known as *tracking*. In Figure 6-8, you see the result of increasing the spacing between characters.

**FIGURE 6-6:**
Choose a font
family and font
weight.

**FIGURE 6-7:**
Click and drag to
visually change
the font size.

**FIGURE 6-8:**
Characters at
normal spacing,
set at 0 (zero) and
then set at 150.

Note in Figure 6-9 that you can use the same click-and-drag technique that is available in the Font Size textbox in order to visually change the character spacing.

**FIGURE 6-9:**
You can also visually change the size of the character spacing by clicking and dragging.

>> **Line height:** *Line height* is *leading*, the space between the lines of text. This can play an important role in information design, so make sure that you are using this consistently throughout your design. You can also position your cursor below the Line Height textbox and click and drag up or down to decrease and increase your line height.

>> **Color:** Change the Fill color by clicking on the box next to Fill color in the Properties panel. You perform this task the same way you would with any shape. Select the Fill box and select a color from the Color Picker. You can also select transparency for your text from the Transparency slide available on the right of the Color Picker.

>> **Border:** Applying a border puts a stroke around your text. This is not recommended because it may cause readability issues. Use it sparingly and perhaps only for special effects. Figure 6-10 shows an example of a larger typeface that has a thin stroke and a white fill on a darker background. In a situation like this, a border could work, but not with smaller text.

**FIGURE 6-10:**
A small border with a white fill on a dark background.

# Importing Text

Of course, you can type directly into Adobe XD, but sometimes it is easier to import text. This can be completed easily using two different methods:

>> **Cut and paste:** You can copy and paste text into Adobe XD from most other applications, including Adobe applications, as well as Word, Google Docs, text applications, and more.

>> **Drag and drop text:** You can also drag and drop .txt files right from folders into XD. Simply select the .txt file and drag and drop it right onto an artboard in XD. The text appears in a new textbox. In the next section, you see how you to drag a .txt file right on top of a repeated grid and have your text replaced instantly.

# Using the Repeat Grid Feature

Repeat Grid is one of the top timesaving features in Adobe XD. The Repeat Grid feature allows you to create a set of repeated elements with a simple click and drag. When repeated, you can tweak one set of repeated elements and have those changes reflected instantly throughout the rest of the elements. The steps in this section help you experience this great feature.

It is best to follow along with this section if you can. You can find a sample file that has an image and some text in it in the DummiesCCfiles folder at www.agitraining.com/dummies. Open the XD folder and choose the RepeatGrid-Sample file. Then follow these steps:

1. **Open a file that has elements that you want to repeat vertically (down) the page. As previously mentioned, you can create your own or use the RepeatGrid-Sample file that has been provided at our site.**

2. **Select all the items that are to be repeated, and then press the Repeat Grid button in the Properties panel. You could also choose to use the keyboard shortcut, Ctrl+R (Windows) or ⌘+R (Mac).**

   Handles appear on the right and bottom sides of your elements, as shown in Figure 6-11.

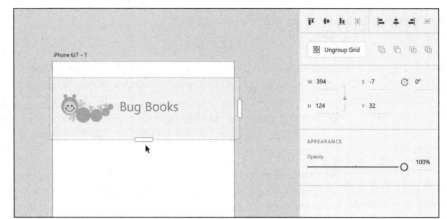

**FIGURE 6-11:**
Select the items
that you would
like to repeat
and then press
the Repeat Grid
button in the
Properties panel.

3. Click and drag down on the bottom handle to see that a repeat is created automatically as you drag, as you see in Figure 6-12. Drag beyond the template to extend the artwork outside the bottom.

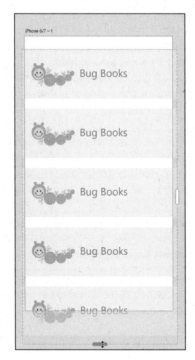

**FIGURE 6-12:**
Repeat selected
items easily using
the Repeat Grid
feature.

4. Go back to your original art and make a simple change. Perhaps change the type size of the title, or scale the image a bit. Notice that as you make changes in this first item the changes are reflected throughout the repeat.

This can be a huge timesaver, but follow along through the next steps to see how you can easily replace the repeated image and text.

## Importing updated images into your repeated grid

After you have repeated items, you may want to demonstrate how your application is going to work with more realistic content. The repeated element does not provide an opportunity to show the various data that your app may be offering. In this next section, you take a folder of images and drop them on top of your repeated grid in order to replace your original image. Just follow these steps:

1. **Locate a folder of images in a format that XD supports, such as JPEG, PNG, or GIF. If you are accessing the DummiesCCfiles folder mentioned earlier, you can find a folder named Insects inside the XD Files folder.**

2. **Position your XD window that contains the artboard with the repeat so that you can see it and also the folder full of images.**

3. **Make sure to select all the images, and then click and drag them onto the Repeated Grid. The images are replaced, as you can see in Figure 6-13.**

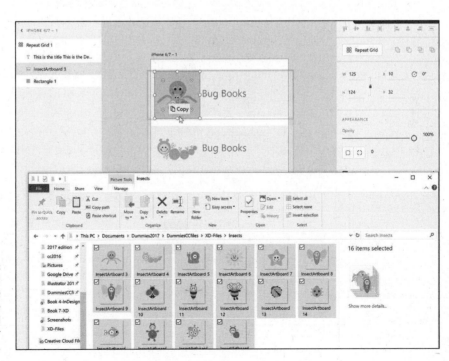

**FIGURE 6-13:**
You can drag and drop multiple images into the repeated grid to replace your image content.

You can drag images from the Bridge application into Adobe XD as well.

## Updating your text in your repeated grid

In this next section, you discover how to update your text in a repeated grid. This is completed in much the same way as with images, but the .txt format is vital to having this process work:

1. **Create text in any application that can save the file in a Plain Text format — that is, with an extension of .txt. The text can be generated from Notepad, Word, downloaded from Google Docs as Plain Text, or exported from many other applications. For this example, you can use the sample text file named Bugtext.txt in the XD-Files folder on our site.**

2. **Position the folder that contains the text file so that you can see the file and the repeated grid.**

3. **As with the process of replacing the repeated image, click and drag the .txt file over your repeated grid text, as shown in Figure 6-14. The text is replaced with text from your file.**

**FIGURE 6-14:**
Click and drag a .txt file over the repeated grid to replace the text.

You can see the example as it appears once the imagery and text have been replaced in Figure 6-15.

iPhone 6/7 – 1

Bug Books

Bug Decals

Bug Toys

Bug Hats

Bug Shoes

**FIGURE 6-15:**
The repeated
grid with new
imagery and text.

4.  **If you extended beyond the viewing area, make sure to click on the artboard name above the artboard to select it.**

5.  **Drag the bottom handle to extend to the length of your repeated grid, as shown in Figure 6-16. This allows the screen to be scrolled in the preview. The dotted line represents the area that previews before the scroll.**

6.  **Click on the Desktop Preview button and scroll to see your repeated grid in action.**

**FIGURE 6-16:**
Click and drag
to extend
the viewing
area of your
repeated grid.

# Chapter 7

# Taking Advantage of Symbols and UI Kits

T his chapter is all about saving time and keeping your artwork consistent. By creating symbols, you can save an object in a form that can be dragged and dropped right unto your artboard and dynamically updated as needed. In this chapter, you also find out how to use UI kits. UI kits are provided so that you can easily locate patterns for popular platforms such as iOS, Android, and Windows.

## Using Symbols

If you find that you are reusing objects in your UI, you should consider converting them to symbols. *Symbols* are linked objects that can be reused across all artboards in a document. Because they are dynamically linked, changes to one reflect across all instances.

In this next set of steps, we use the icon artwork from the DummiesCCfiles folder at www.agitraining.com/dummies. You can use our sample files or one of your own.

To convert an object into a symbol, follow these steps:

1. **Open a document that contains at least one artboard, an icon, and some related text. In this example, shown in Figure 7-1, we open the file from the DummiesCCfiles folder named *delivery-symbol-sample* in Adobe XD.**

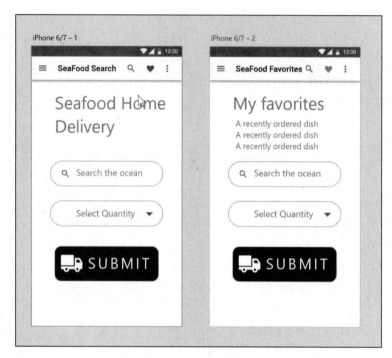

**FIGURE 7-1:**
The *delivery-symbol-sample* file.

2. **Select an object and some text that you want to reuse. In this example, one of the grouped Submit buttons is selected.**

3. **Right-click (Windows) or Ctrl-click (Mac) and select Make Symbol from the contextual menu.**

TIP

If you like keyboard shortcuts, you can select an item and press Ctrl+K (Windows) or ⌘+K (Mac) to convert it into a symbol.

A couple things happen when you convert object(s) into a symbol:

» If you look in the Layers panel, the object that you converted into a symbol now has a symbol icon to the left of the name, as shown in Figure 7-2.

» If you click the Symbols icon in the lower left of the XD workspace, you see your symbol in a thumbnail view, as shown in Figure 7-3.

**FIGURE 7-2:**
In the Layers panel, the symbol has an icon to the left, reflecting that it is a symbol.

ic_favorite_white

appbar

path

Seafood Home Delivery

Submit

**FIGURE 7-3:**
The symbol appears as a thumbnail in the Symbols panel.

SYMBOLS

SUBMIT

# Using your symbol

Perhaps you want to use this symbol in another location. You can do so by following these steps:

1. **If you are using the *delivery-symbol-sample* file, delete the Submit button on artboard iPhone 6/7-2 (use the Delete or Backspace keys to delete). If you are creating your own file, this step is unnecessary.**

2. **Make sure the Symbols panel is open by clicking the Symbols icon in the lower left of the XD workspace.**

3. **Click and drag the newly created symbol from the Symbols panel to the second artboard. Reposition it as necessary.**

   You can also Alt/Option-drag a symbol to clone it to another location.

TIP

# Making edits to your symbol

In this section, you see how edits to one instance of your symbol instantaneously update any other instances. To see how this works, follow these steps:

1. **Click the rectangle in one of your symbol instances.**

2. **In the Properties panel, change the Fill to a different color, perhaps red. Note how that change instantly occurs in both instances of the symbol. This is the case with any property.**

3. **Now double-click the text in either symbol to edit it. Change the word from Submit to** Send. **Notice that this change of text is not reflected in the other instance, as shown in Figure 7-4. This makes a great solution when you want consistency in buttons but don't want the same text in each one.**

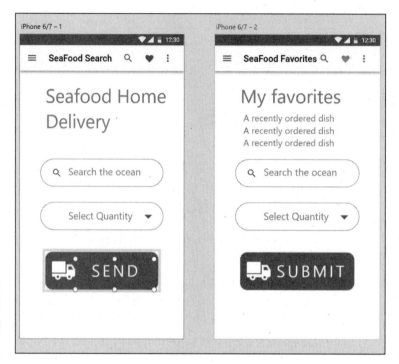

If the text change *is* something that you want reflected in all the symbol instances, right-click and choose Update All Symbols.

## Removing a symbol

If you are no longer interested in keeping your symbol instances linked, you can right-click on the symbol in the Symbols panel and select Remove Symbol from the contextual menu. The objects on the page are not deleted, but they are no longer linked to a symbol and can be edited independently. If you want to remove just one symbol to change it without affecting all instances of the symbol, select the symbol, right-click, and select Ungroup Symbol.

# Taking Advantage of UI Kits

In this section, you are introduced to UI kits. A UI kit is a collection of UI elements that you can copy and paste to use in your designs. At the time of writing there were three default UI kits: Apple iOS, Google Material, and Microsoft Windows. We are sure that resourceful folks will start creating more of these over time.

To open a UI kit, choose File⇨Get UI Kit and select a kit from the menu. This takes you to a website from which you can download the components for each of the available kits. In Figure 7-5, the Google Material UI kit has been selected.

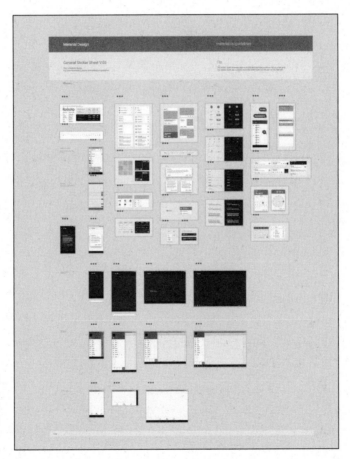

**FIGURE 7-5:**
The Google
Material UI kit
provides patterns
and other
UI elements.

To use these elements, you can either select the items(s) you want from the Layers panel or use your Select tool and then choose Edit➪Copy. If you prefer, you can use the keyboard shortcut Ctrl+C (Windows) or ⌘+C (Mac).

Locate an artboard in a different project in which you would like to use the items and choose Edit➪Paste. The keyboard shortcut is Ctrl+V (Windows) or ⌘+V (Mac).

# Chapter **8**

# Creating Interactivity in Adobe XD

Now that you have some practice creating UI elements in XD, you can start adding interactivity in the form of links from one clickable element to a new screen. This interactivity is created in the Prototype mode in Adobe XD. You can use the links that you make in the Prototype mode to demonstrate your information architecture, navigational functions, or changes to objects when users click on them, like a change in a button or the visibility of a menu.

## Entering Prototype Mode

If you have been working in XD, you might have a file ready to start working on. If not, you can find a file to use for this chapter at www.agitraining.com./dummies. Look for the XD-Files folder inside the DummiesCCfiles folder. In this example, the file named BabyAnimalsApp can be used. To enter Prototype mode, follow these steps:

1. **Open a file that has multiple artboards or open the BabyAnimalsApp that was created for this section. This sample prototype, shown in Figure 8-1, is a simple three-screen project that offers you the opportunity to create links from one screen to another.**

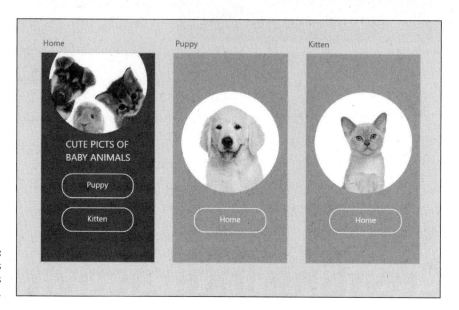

**FIGURE 8-1:**
Use a file that has
multiple screens
to create links.

2. Select Prototype from the top of the Adobe XD workspace, as shown in Figure 8-2. If you see a dialog box explaining what the Prototype mode is, press Got It to move on.

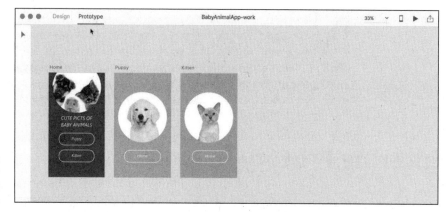

**FIGURE 8-2:**
Create your
interactivity in the
Prototype mode.

3. Click the Puppy button on the Home artboard, and an arrow appears.

4. Click and drag the arrow to the Puppy artboard. A dialog box appears that provides the target artboard name, default transition effect, easing selection, and duration, as shown in Figure 8-3.

**FIGURE 8-3:**
Click and drag
to create links
from an object to
another screen.

Here is an explanation of these options:

- **Target:** The target is the artboard that will be visible when the user clicks the button. The default is the artboard that you dragged to, but you can change the target at any time with this menu.

  *Note:* The None option allows you to undo a link.

- **Transition:** The transition type allows you to decide how one screen transitions, or moves, into another screen. From the drop-down menu, you can choose options that simply dissolve or fade into another screen or slide or push.

  *Note:* The Slide option slides the target screen on top of the current screen. Push pushes the current content out of the way as the new content slides in.

- **Easing:** *Easing* is an animation technique used to provide a more realistic method of accelerating or slowing down an animation. Ease in is when the motion begins slowly before gaining speed. Ease out is when an object in motion slows down before coming to a stop.

- **Duration:** Duration determines the time you want the animation to take to move from one screen to another.

5. **Accept the changes in the dialog box by clicking your work area.**

6. **Test your first animation by clicking the Desktop Preview button (right-facing arrow) in the upper right of your XD workspace.**

7. **If you want more practice, connect the Kitten button to the Kitten artboard and the Home buttons on both the Puppy and Kitten artboards back to home.**

# Previewing Your Artwork

As you tested in the last section, you found out that you could click the Desktop Preview button in order to see your interactivity at work. There is more to this preview than you might expect. It is a live preview, meaning that you can be making changes and still see them in the preview.

TIP

If you want to navigate your screens without links, use your left- and right-arrow keys on your keyboard.

To test this, try moving something on your artboard while viewing that artboard in the desktop preview. Note that the change is made instantaneously. Note that when the cover image was repositioned in Figure 8-4, the preview was updated.

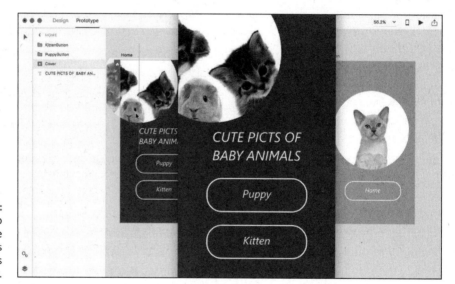

**FIGURE 8-4:**
The desktop preview is live and updates changes immediately.

# Chapter 9

# Sharing Your XD Project

Your prototype exists so that you can test your app or website before you invest lots of money in expensive coding. With XD, you can view your preview on your desktop, as you did in the previous chapter, on a device, with the XD app, or on a share site.

## Viewing Your App/Website on Your Desktop

This section might be a review for those of you who follow the chapters in order, but keep reading. The Desktop Preview doesn't only offer the ability to test and preview your app on your desktop, but it also allows you to create a video of you using your app in the preview mode. This is helpful when you want to show the typical user flow, or when you want to have a demonstration that goes along well with a user story.

You can use your own file or you can use a completed file named BabyAnimalApp-share that is available at www.agitraining.com/dummies in the XD-Files folder inside of the DummiesCCfiles folder. Just follow these steps:

1. **Open a file that has already had interaction applied to it, as discussed in Chapter 8 of this minibook.**

2. **After the file is open, click the Desktop Preview button in the upper right of the work area to see a preview appear. The active artboard is the first to appear in the preview, as shown in Figure 9-1.**

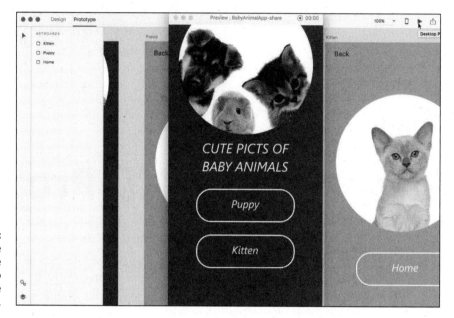

**FIGURE 9-1:**
The active artboard is the first screen to appear in the preview window.

3. **If you are using our sample file, you see that links were created on the two main buttons that you see on the home screen. Click Puppy, you go to the Puppy page; click Back, in the upper left, and you go back to the home screen.**

As you see, the desktop preview allows you to quickly test your links and animations.

# Creating a Movie for Your User Story

In this section, you record your interactions in this prototype in a movie. You can use this movie to demonstrate a user story, post in your portfolio, or share your ideas with others on your team.

To record a video, simply click the timer in the upper-right corner of the work area, as shown in Figure 9-2. The Record button blinks, indicating that your mouse movements and clicks are being recorded. You also see the timer start.

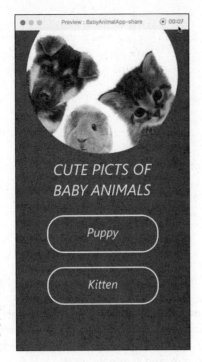

**FIGURE 9-2:**
You can record
your interactions
in a movie using
the Desktop
Preview feature.

It is best to practice your movements prior to recording so that there are no unexpected movements or delays.

When you have finished demonstrating your prototype, click on the timer to stop recording. At this point, you can save your movie.

# Using the Device Preview Feature

Adobe XD allows you to create a clickable prototype right on your phone or other mobile device. To do this, you need to do two things:

>> Download and install the XD mobile app onto your device, iOS or Android. You can find the app at xd.adobe.com/apps or at Google Play or the App Store.

>> Hardwire your device using your USB port and connector on your computer.

After you have completed these steps, click the Preview on Device button that is also in the upper right of your work area, to the right of the Device Preview button, as shown in Figure 9-3.

**Sharing Your XD Project**

**FIGURE 9-3:**
Preview your app right on your device by using the XD app.

# Sharing Your XD File with Others

One of the many benefits of using Adobe XD is the ability to share your prototype with others. By sharing your prototype, you can offer access via a link to your client or remote members of your team. Your prototype is saved to the Creative Cloud where others can open, test, and comment on it.

# Index

# S

# About the Author

Jennifer Smith's expertise bridges the gap between design and development of print, web, and interactive design.

Jennifer's career started when she was one of the first creative directors to push the limits of technology and its integration with design. She has since managed and developed projects for companies such as Adobe, Microsoft, Reebok, Hershey Foods, Hasbro, Nike, and more. Jennifer's expertise lies in interpreting highly technical information and presenting it in a clear and easy-to-understand manner.

In addition to teaching and consulting, Jennifer is also a UX designer who creates educational IOS apps, websites, and apps for Windows devices. She is directly involved in the entire process from brainstorming to research, prototyping, wireframing, testing, and final visual design.

Jennifer has written more than 20 books on technology and design, as well as over 100 publications used for curricula. Her books include: *Digital Classroom: Adobe Illustrator and Photoshop CC*, *The Adobe Creative Cloud For Dummies* (versions CS through CC), *Adobe Creative Suite Web Premium*, *Adobe Illustrator Classroom in a Book*, and more. Jennifer is the co–founder of American Graphics Institute, which has classroom training centers in Boston, New York, and Philadelphia.

**Christopher Smith** is president of the American Graphics Institute. He is the author of more than ten books on web, interactive, and print publishing technology, including many of the Adobe official training guides. Learn more about American Graphics Institute's training programs at www.agitraining.com or follow them on Twitter @agitraining. You can follow Christopher on Twitter @cgsmith.

# Author's Acknowledgments

**Jennifer Smith:** Thank you to the highly professional staff at American Graphics Institute (AGItraining.com). You offered great insight into what people need to know in order to creative projects using Adobe Creative Cloud.

A big thanks to Kelly Walker, who helped make sure content of this book was current and easily understood by readers of all levels.

Thanks to all at John Wiley & Sons, Inc., especially Christopher Morris, who applied just enough pressure to help me meet my deadlines, yet was an absolute pleasure to work with.

Thanks to Amy Fandrei for having faith.

Also, we would like to thank our technical editor, Patti Scully-Lane, for all the extra insight and effort she put into technically reviewing this book.

Grant, Elizabeth, and Edward — thanks for putting up with our long hours in front of the keyboard night after night.

Thanks to all of Kelly and Alex's friends for permission to use their photos.

**Christopher Smith:** Thanks to our team of fellow instructors at American Graphics Institute for their insight and support in the production of this book.

## Publisher's Acknowledgments

**Acquisitions Editor:** Amy Fandrei
**Production Editor:** Siddique Shaik
**Copy Editor:** Christopher Morris
**Technical Editor:** Patti Scully-Lane
**Editorial Assistant:** Owen Kaelble
**Sr. Editorial Assistant:** Cherie Case

**Cover Image:** © CasPhotography/iStockphoto

# Leverage the power

**Dummies** is the global leader in the reference category and one of the most trusted and highly regarded brands in the world. No longer just focused on books, customers now have access to the dummies content they need in the format they want. Together we'll craft a solution that engages your customers, stands out from the competition, and helps you meet your goals.

## Advertising & Sponsorships

Connect with an engaged audience on a powerful multimedia site, and position your message alongside expert how-to content. Dummies.com is a one-stop shop for free, online information and know-how curated by a team of experts.

- Targeted ads
- Video
- Email Marketing

- Microsites
- Sweepstakes sponsorship

**20 MILLION**
PAGE VIEWS
EVERY SINGLE MONTH

**15 MILLION**
UNIQUE
VISITORS PER MONTH

**43%**
OF ALL VISITORS
ACCESS THE SITE
VIA THEIR MOBILE DEVICES

**700,000** NEWSLETTER
SUBSCRIPTIONS
TO THE INBOXES OF
*300,000* UNIQUE INDIVIDUALS
EVERY WEEK

# of dummies

## Custom Publishing

Reach a global audience in any language by creating a solution that will differentiate you from competitors, amplify your message, and encourage customers to make a buying decision.

- Apps
- Books
- eBooks
- Video
- Audio
- Webinars

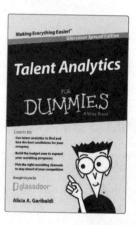

## Brand Licensing & Content

Leverage the strength of the world's most popular reference brand to reach new audiences and channels of distribution.

## For more information, visit dummies.com/biz

# PERSONAL ENRICHMENT

**Staying Sharp**
9781119187790
USA $26.00
CAN $31.99
UK £19.99

**Facebook**
9781119179030
USA $21.99
CAN $25.99
UK £16.99

**Guitar**
9781119293354
USA $24.99
CAN $29.99
UK £17.99

**Investing**
9781119293347
USA $22.99
CAN $27.99
UK £16.99

**Beekeeping**
9781119310068
USA $22.99
CAN $27.99
UK £16.99

**Digital Photography**
9781119235606
USA $24.99
CAN $29.99
UK £17.99

**Meditation**
9781119251163
USA $24.99
CAN $29.99
UK £17.99

**Pregnancy**
9781119235491
USA $26.99
CAN $31.99
UK £19.99

**Samsung Galaxy S7**
9781119279952
USA $24.99
CAN $29.99
UK £17.99

**iPhone**
9781119287133
USA $24.99
CAN $29.99
UK £17.99

**Crocheting**
9781119287117
USA $24.99
CAN $29.99
UK £16.99

**Nutrition**
9781119130246
USA $22.99
CAN $27.99
UK £16.99

# PROFESSIONAL DEVELOPMENT

**Windows 10**
9781119311041
USA $24.99
CAN $29.99
UK £17.99

**AutoCAD**
9781119255796
USA $39.99
CAN $47.99
UK £27.99

**Excel 2016**
9781119293439
USA $26.99
CAN $31.99
UK £19.99

**QuickBooks 2017**
9781119281467
USA $26.99
CAN $31.99
UK £19.99

**macOS Sierra**
9781119280651
USA $29.99
CAN $35.99
UK £21.99

**LinkedIn**
9781119251132
USA $24.99
CAN $29.99
UK £17.99

**Windows 10**
9781119310563
USA $34.00
CAN $41.99
UK £24.99

**SharePoint 2016**
9781119181705
USA $29.99
CAN $35.99
UK £21.99

**Fundamental Analysis**
9781119263593
USA $26.99
CAN $31.99
UK £19.99

**Networking**
9781119257769
USA $29.99
CAN $35.99
UK £21.99

**Office 2016**
9781119293477
USA $26.99
CAN $31.99
UK £19.99

**Office 365**
9781119265313
USA $24.99
CAN $29.99
UK £17.99

**Salesforce.com**
9781119239314
USA $29.99
CAN $35.99
UK £21.99

**Coding**
9781119293323
USA $29.99
CAN $35.99
UK £21.99

**dummies.com**